Always on Sunday

Eleanor Ostman's Best Tested Recipes

Tales of World Travels, Food Celebrities, Family & Minnesota's North Country

*Selected from 30 years
of her column, Tested Recipes,
in the Sunday St. Paul Pioneer Press*

SUNDAY PRESS

All rights reserved undering International and Pan-American
Copyright Conventions. Published in the United States by
SUNDAY PRESS, St. Paul, Minn.

Cover and page design by Kimberleá Weeks.
Printed by Sexton Printing, Inc., St. Paul, Minn.

The publisher acknowledges the St. Paul Pioneer Press for
granting rights to Tested Recipes column material and certain
illustrations, making this publication possible.

ISBN 0-9662614-0-2

Printed and bound in the United States of America

At last . . .

— It took 30 years to write this book —

During the past three decades, when a Tested Recipes reader urged, "You ought to write a cookbook," I'd demure. "Maybe, someday, when I retire ..."

Now that retirement from a 35-year newspaper career is foreseeable and my Sunday sashay into the world of food reached its 30th year, I can procrastinate no longer.

So I've plowed through my "filing system" — boxes and boxes of column clippings — and collected my favorite tales and tastes.

My longtime friend, Betsy Balsley, former food editor for the Los Angeles Times, told me when she'd just emerged from the dark tunnel of cookbook writing in 1982 that she was glad she wasn't in there alone. With a staff of seven, it was a group decision that they should put out a tome of The Times' best recipes. "That way, no one could scream in the throes of deadlines, 'Whose idea was this, anyway?'"

For this project, it's just been me and my computer and those stacks of tattered, yellowed newsprint. The cookbook idea was all mine, one I had intended to accomplish for the 20th, then the 25th anniversary of the Tested Recipes column. Now, for the 30th, the task is done.

When I saw the results of Betsy's project, I told my Sunday readers: We in the Midwest think that the "California Look" is attained through a diet of yogurt and bean sprouts. Forget it. If "The Los Angeles Times California Cookbook" is a true reflection of how Southern Californians eat, they're all chocoholics. Even I, The Town Chocoholic of St. Paul, would be embarrassed to put so many chocolate recipes in one cookbook.

Now that I've sorted through the thousands of recipes I've tested in the last 30 years, seeking my personal favorites and those most frequently requested by readers, it's amazing how many are chocolatey. In fact, I've included a whole chapter of all-chocolate birthday cakes.

Friends in food played a significant role in the column and now in this book. If you didn't meet them the first time around, I'll introduce you to Julia Child, James Beard, Giuliano Bugialli, Marcella Hazan and many more.

Two food cronies even helped name this book. Food writer and restaurant publicist Pat Lindquist and Sue Zelickson, who sends tidbits over the WCCO-AM radio waves, asked me what the title of my book-in-progress would be. It was the night we were helping celebrate Julia Child's 85th birthday, and I mumbled something about "Best Tested Recipes." They said that wouldn't do. Before that conversation was done, they'd focused on the day of the week the column appeared. Playing on the movie title, "Never on Sunday," they came up with "Always on Sunday." Perfect!

Not all of these Sunday recipes have been perfect, which I explained in the August 22, 1976, column:

Even after all these years of being a newspaper reporter, of testing nigh onto a thousand recipes for this column over the past eight years, I remain an optimist.

Recipes are tested with faith in their success. I never try anything thinking it's going to flop. Sometimes, a formula comes along that is improbable but has some potential. Such "show me" recipes are tested with a pinch of skepticism but with at least a cupful of optimism.

However, on that Sunday, I gave readers a recounting of an unmitigated disaster, otherwise known as Whole Wheat Ribbon Bread:

The night we tested, it was a 98-degree record breaker. I dashed home at 5:30. At 6 p.m., our dinner guests were at the door, just in time to keep me company while I finished mixing the bread. I marbled it like a pro and put it in the oven. Not until it came out, not until the rest of the dinner was ready to eat, did I realize that in the flurry of arriving guests, I had forgotten to add onion-mushroom soup mix to the whole-wheat bread batter. So the bread had no flavor.

My friend Mary Lou Gruber, who blends perceptive wit with a keen nose, said it reminded her of gobs of Cream of Wheat and Ralston baked in a loaf. "Maybe covered with milk and sugar for breakfast ..." she said. She's an optimist, too.

Not only was it totally bland, it was about 1 1/2 inches high and generally uncooked in the middle. The only one who seemed to enjoy it was a 4-year-old who carried a hunk around most of the evening to chaw on at whim.

Thinking I must have done something else wrong beside forgetting the soup mix, I made another loaf the next morning and baked it a bit longer. It, too, was the lowliest loaf I have ever seen despite 4 teaspoons of baking powder. A vein of unbaked white "glue" ran through the center. Whole-wheat lumps were sawdusty — but did they have onion flavor! Overpowering!

It's a recipe that had no potential to begin with, but how could we know that before testing?

Later that same October, a reader, who had recently moved to St. Paul, questioned the use of recipes with flaws. My response:

Every week, we print dozens of recipes that we assume are good in other food stories and columns, though you take your chances because we don't test them.

Let's not always be so serious about cooking. Recipes are not sacred. They do occasionally fail, as the letter writer admitted when saying that she tries one new recipe a day "and I know only too well how many bad recipes this world contains."

This column is meant to be entertainment. It is built on the shared realization that we are not all perfect cooks. It is a weekly report of adventures in the kitchen, and how family and friends react to recipes tested.

Pat Lindquist, left, Eleanor and a slightly wooden Julia Child on the night this book was named.

To my knowledge, the column is unique in the country, which may make it unsettling to the letter writer who recently moved here. Other food editors may present themselves as infallible. I do not. I am human. I have failures. I am a journalist, not a home economist. Therein lies all the difference.

How a person reacts to food is about the most personal, subjective thing in the whole world. It would be lovely to print only perfect recipes, but I shudder to think how much testing that would involve. And I do not want to set myself up as an arbiter of taste. If that were the case, you all know darn well I'd run nothing but chocolate recipes because I like them best. As it is, I try to restrain myself.

What I find delicious, others may not. Sometimes, what I don't like, others do. People often tell me that they made a "disaster" recipe after following my suggested modifications, and they liked it.

From a journalist's point of view, it's more fun to write about failures. And readers tell me they wait for me to have a flop just for a good Sunday-morning laugh. Not all recipes turn out on first try, but they can be made better. Moral: We learn through our failures.

So, dear readers, things will go on as they are. If I am willing to put myself and my kitchen antics up to public ridicule, then do me the favor of laughing with me rather than being miffed at me and the newspaper which allows my kind of column.

That tirade drew stacks of supportive mail. The next week, Halloween, 1976:

I am basking in the warmth of your letters about last week's column. Thank you, thank you.

So many of you seem to enjoy, as one person wrote, "The yucks and the yummies." Mary Hoffman of St. Paul wrote, "Half the fun of cooking is in trying recipes for better or for worse." (Sounds like marriage, Mary.) "When you have a flop, look at what it does for the rest of us Kitchen Klutzes." That's me, another Kitchen Klutz.

Gloria Wachtler likes the failures: "I really don't have to try them, you know. After all, we've all done something we can laugh about that's just as silly. I once doubled an old family cookie recipe without doing my math first. It filled my largest mixing bowl and I still had seven cups of oatmeal to add. I finished the recipe with my hands in a punch bowl, and the cookies turned out fine."

Tested Recipes came from everywhere. Cleaning out an old wooden file cabinet I bought when the Pioneer Press was unloading surplus furniture, I found a newspaper lining one of the drawers. It was dated April 19, 1940.

Flipping through that old section, I found the Friday Market Basket pages with food ads: Spare ribs for 9 cents a pound, a 2-pound box of American loaf cheese for 39 cents, and coffee selling 3 pounds for 39 cents. A 1939 Oldsmobile was $735, and "Rebecca" was the latest movie.

And what else did I find on those disintegrating pages? A column called Tested Recipes. There's nothing new in this world — or even at this newspaper. I tried fudge and banana butterscotch pie recipes from that 1940 page for the October 3, 1976 column.

A food writer soon knows who her real friends are — the ones who dare to invite her to dinner. One such friend confided her system. If she's in doubt about the entree, she just extends the cocktail hour and hopes I won't notice.

On January 29, 1978, this appeared under a "It's not my fault department" header: An organization I belong to had neighborhood meetings recently and I called a nearby hostess to ask if I might join the group at her home. On the night of the meeting, she opened the discussion by announcing she had become so rattled at having to cook for this food writer that she had put a half cup of baking powder into her lemon bars. "Hope it wasn't one of my recipes," I interjected. No, she said, it was just her bleary eyes at 6 a.m., baking before leaving for work.

"I had lemon souffle," she said of her airy attempt. Her husband came to her rescue later in the day, baking a batch of perfectly delicious, properly leavened bars that were the hit of the meeting.

I told readers on that Sunday: After 10 years of admitting my cooking misadventures, no one should worry about having me as a guest. I like peanut butter sandwiches just fine.

Nearly a decade into the column, along with a picture of my notorious desk with its teetering stacks of recipes, this appeared as I told about having to move into a new office:

"Wanna match?"

Dozen of my co-workers suggested torching instead of sorting my 10-year accumulation of recipes and releases.

Believe me, there were times when I wanted to strike one of those matches. It would have been one heck of a bonfire. In my new office, I have lots of file space, so I hope never again to reach the state you see in the picture. But I'm not guaranteeing anything — unless the U.S. Mail ceases to function. Stuff just pours in daily.

Recipes, unlike fashion or furnishings information, do not go out of date. That's why it's so hard to throw them away. I feel bad about the thousands I tossed (26 wastebaskets full). But I had to be hard-hearted. More will arrive to take their places.

Actually, I felt like an archaeologist, sifting through layered civilizations. In the 10 years I've been writing about food, massive changes have taken place in how and what we eat, the way we perceive food. Food fads and crises of the past decade were uncovered in those stacks: economical recipes when food prices rose, the trend to unprocessed foods, the gardening explosion. Cycles of popularity were unlayered, from fondue to crepe-making to ethnic foods (Mexico inspired the most). Growing awareness of health and nutrition, cholesterol and diet foods, were evident in those dusty piles. Zillions of Bicentennial recipes, of course, and later, Southern dishes when Jimmy Carter came on the scene. The energy crisis was apparent, too, in no-cook and microwave ideas.

I found foods for all possible holidays, including an April Fool meatloaf that looked like a layer cake. I must have read a hundred recipes for variations on moussaka. Not to mention several thousand for hamburger in various forms.

Too much, too much. It's sad they'll never see print in this paper. But our tastes change, and I might feel guilty today running 10-year-old recipes created before we worried so much about fat or empty calories.

You'll find this hard to believe, but I even threw away chocolate recipes – lots of them. Especially ones that seemed to have split personalities, such as gooey chocolate desserts made with wheat germ. Call sin a sin. Don't try to put a health-food halo on it.

That's what the column — and now this cookbook — is about. Learning from my mistakes, sharing my food experiences, travels, friends, family antics and north country revels.

My mission has been to make food fun, and my approach has been enthusiastic.

The style of this book could be likened to Erma Bombeck meets the Reader's Digest. It's stuffed with vignettes and amusing stories and is meant to be left by the bed or bathtub for moments of miscellaneous reading time. But do try the recipes, too. They're keepers.

Far too many cookbooks published in the past few years have promoted low-fat or high-health cooking. This isn't one of them. What is collected here is the cream from my 30 years of kitchen adventures. Some of the recipes contain cream, and butter and eggs, too, reprinted with no apologies (though I do suggest pasteurized eggs in recipes where they're raw; years ago, raw eggs weren't risky). They're also recipes that reflect moments of time during the last three decades, a barometer of how we've progressed and learned and modernized the way we eat.

Funniest thing, as years went by, as I became more adept and had fewer disasters, I'd hear from readers who thought the Sunday recipes were flawless far too often. They told me they missed my cooking missteps.

An eloquent letter from Francy Reitz of Roseville, nostalgic for the early days of this column "when you and I were young and starting our families," was prompted by a column about son Aric's 18th birthday party. She wrote "with tears in my eyes," saying she again shared another stage in life with me.

"You see, I learned and grew right along with you," her letter said.

"Your life as reported in your column mirrored mine in so many ways. My daughter is just about a year older than Aric. Your stories of his phases of growing up had special significance for me.

"How I used to laugh when you told of your trials and tribulations in the kitchen — just like mine. How my heart ached as your parents grew older and then departed — much like mine. How you cherished your mother's recipes that you were fortunate enough to have written down while she could still give them to you, and how you yearned for those she took with her — just as I did.

"But then those stories were gone. You had sophisticated culinary training and became an expert. If you were caught unprepared in the kitchen, you could improvise without missing a beat.

"Somehow, it isn't the same anymore. But neither is life, is it?"

Amen.

Shrinking product alert: Over 30 years, many cans and packages have been downsized. Where results are dependent on exact amounts, recipes have been revised. With less touchy formulas, use current product sizes or adjust as you wish.

Introduction

Special thanks are due:

To my ever-helpful husband, Ron Aune, quotable son Aric Aune, The Office Hungries and all others who have endured my recipe testings for 30 years.

To the many who contributed recipes, from America's food companies and consortiums to readers to cookbook authors to relatives and friends. Thanks, also, to readers for their ongoing comments, some of them included in the book.

To Pat Lindquist and Sue Zelickson for naming this book.

To my many food colleagues and friends who have shared 30 years of delicious adventures.

To Laura Zahn, Janet Martin and Dian Thomas for divulging their knowledge of self-publishing and encouraging me to follow in their footsteps.

To Pioneer Press management; particularly former publisher Peter Ridder and executive editor Walker Lundy, for granting me the rights to column material and illustrations so this book could be produced.

To the Sexton Printing Company crew who turned my words into a book, especially Paul Heiting, who put the publishing package together, and Kim Weeks, whose design talents shine on the pages you're about to turn.

Eleanor Ostman Aune and Ron Aune celebrate the 30 years of the Tested Recipes column and the completion of this book — and toast the readers of both endeavors.

1968

— Simple beginnings, and, of course, the first recipe is chocolate —

Here's Tested Recipe of the Week

July 21

The column's premise, stated on that first Sunday:

On a homemaker-to-homemaker basis, today we inaugurate a new column that will feature one tested recipe each week. The writer will try each dish, chosen as most appealing (or as Minnesotans say, most "different") from among the dozens of recipes that arrive at the Pioneer Press-Dispatch offices each week. Each will be tested, not from the viewpoint of a scientific experiment, but to see if it tastes as good as it reads. We will include comments on preparation and mention any small disasters so you can learn from them. And as a homemaker, I will let you know how my husband and any guests liked the finished results.

Such a simple idea. Such simple times. The Dow-Jones hovered around 900. The St. Paul Port Authority was building Riverview Industrial Park, and LBJ was looking forward to retirement. The afternoon Dispatch was the stronger St. Paul paper then. Bacon was 59 cents a pound and a 2-pound blade cut pot roast cost a buck.

I was writing to women because men didn't spend much time in the kitchen. And I first mentioned "my husband" who was identified that way for 30 years, thus becoming St. Paul's best known anonymous man.

Since 1968 wasn't a year rife with trends, it was an ideal era for a newly appointed food writer, trained as a journalist, not a home economist, to learn about cooking through the process of trying new recipes. We unraveled French terms and coped with unfamiliar ingredients, such as unflavored yogurt, not a common grocery-store item then.

Disasters — yes, there were disasters, large and small — all dutifully admitted in print. Readers, I soon learned, loved my flubs. I didn't promise to be scientific, and I didn't promise to be perfect. I just promised to keep testing.

Naturally, We Start With Chocolate

July 21

The very first recipe tested — chocolate, of course — was a one-layer version of German chocolate cake:

Try to find a 9-inch baking pan these days! You might get lucky searching garage sales or second-hand shops. If you don't have one, use a deep 8-inch pan or a 7-by-11-incher.

The very first recipe's reported testing results: I'd double the recipe because one 9-inch-square panful didn't last very long. Half the built-in topping stayed in the pan when I right-sided the cake, but it was easy enough to scrape it out and patch the frosting without any telltale signs.

In 1968, I hadn't discovered powdered buttermilk, which works beautifully for baking without having a quart container of residue. Rare in this era of well-equipped kitchens is a recipe that suggests hand beating, but in 1968, that option was common.

CHOCOLATE UPSIDE DOWN CAKE
Makes 9-inch square cake

Topping:
    1/2 cup firmly packed brown sugar
    1/4 cup butter
    2/3 cup pecan halves
    2/3 cup flaked coconut
    1/4 cup evaporated milk

Cake:
    1 package (4 ounces) German's sweet
        chocolate
    1 1/2 cups sifted cake flour
    1 cup granulated sugar
    1/2 teaspoon baking soda
    1/2 teaspoon baking powder
    1/2 teaspoon salt
    1/3 cup butter or margarine
    3/4 cup buttermilk, divided
    1 teaspoon vanilla
    2 eggs

To make topping: In saucepan, combine brown sugar and butter. Melt over low heat. Spread in 9-inch square pan. Sprinkle pecan halves and coconut over sugar mixture. Drizzle with evaporated milk. Set aside.

To make cake: Melt chocolate over low heat. Cool. Sift flour with granulated sugar, soda, baking powder and salt. Stir butter to soften. Add flour mixture, 1/4 cup plus 2 tablespoons buttermilk and vanilla. (Note: If you do not have buttermilk, combine 3/4 cup whole milk and 2 teaspoons vinegar. Let stand for 5 minutes.) Mix until all flour is moistened. Beat for 2 minutes at medium speed of electric mixer or 300 vigorous strokes by hand, scraping bowl occasionally. Add melted chocolate, eggs and remaining buttermilk. Beat for 1 minute with electric mixer or 150 strokes by hand.

To bake cake: Pour batter into prepared cake pan. Bake in 350-degree oven for 45 to 50 minutes, or until cake springs bake when pressed lightly with finger. Cool in pan for 5 minutes. Invert onto serving plate. Serve warm or cooled, topped with prepared whipped topping if desired.

Jiggle It
August 18

Lemon Peach Sponge Pie tasted fine, but I should have listened to my husband about baking it. He happened to be in the kitchen when the timer rang, so I called from upstairs, asking him to take the pie from the oven. After a few seconds, he called me down for a conference.

"It jiggles," he said, shaking the pie slightly. I pressed the sponge top and it felt very firm. I pulled rank as a food editor, and out the pie came.

When I cut it later, it should have been humble pie because the sponge really did need another five minutes of baking. The jiggle my husband detected was a thin under-crust layer of unbaked lemon-egg mixture. Therefore, the longer the pie sat, the soggier it got.

I hope I'm not discouraging any of you women who might like to try this pie that has an unusual, delicate flavor. Just bake it until it doesn't jiggle.

Dabbling With Daube
September 15

Just call me Julia! I really felt like of a French chef as I spent the day making Daube Provencal, which translates basically as beef stew in wine.

When I slow-cooked this beef-wine brew, I didn't know what a daube was, but after trying this recipe, I knew I liked it. This was the first tested recipe that became a repeat favorite at our house. We made it many times in our early married years, usually surrounding the tender, wine-soaked beef with eggy mashed Duchesse potatoes from Julia Child's "French Chef Cookbook."

In 1968, beef cuts could be called anything the butcher declared them to be. Now, this recipe would call for beef top round. Lard and salt pork, though still available, rarely show up in today's fat-phobic recipes.

This recipe came from the Cotes de Provence Wine Information Bureau. Those wine folks probably won't

DAUBE PROVENCAL
Makes 6 servings

3 pounds round of beef, cut into 2-inch cubes
1 teaspoon salt
1/4 teaspoon freshly ground pepper
1 whole allspice
1/4 cup vinegar
1 clove garlic, crushed
4 cups red wine, divided
2 tablespoons lard or butter
12 small white onions
1/4 pound salt pork, diced
3 carrots, cut into 3/4-inch pieces
2 ribs celery, cut into 1/2-inch pieces
1 small bay leaf
Pinch of thyme

To marinate beef: In bowl, combine beef, salt, pepper, allspice, vinegar, garlic and 2 cups wine. Let stand for 2 hours. Turn meat once. Dry meat with paper towel. Strain marinade. Reserve.

To make daube: Heat lard in heatproof casserole. Add onions, salt pork, carrots and celery. Cook until slightly golden. Add meat. Continue cooking until meat is browned. Add bay leaf, thyme, reserved marinade and remaining wine. Bring to a boil. Cover. Bake in 375-degree oven for 5 hours, or until meat is very tender. Serve hot with boiled potatoes.

be too happy to know that I used an inexpensive domestic brand, but the results were delicious. With all the cooking and marinating, beef stew meat would do beautifully, too.

Meatballs, A Party Perennial
December 29

I felt like Typhoid Mary as I mixed these meatballs for a pre-Christmas party. Red Chinese flu with bronchial complications settled in when it was too late to cancel the gathering. I hoped I was past the contagious stage, but if not, apologies to our guests. That affliction totally deadened my sense of taste and smell, so I can't attest to the flavor of this appetizer. However, guests congregated around the chafing dish until every meatball was gone, and every woman there asked for the recipe.

These meatballs became a party perennial at our house for many Christmases thereafter. I'd make 6-pound batches, baking them in the oven because that method is so efficient and spatter-free. Today, these could be made with lean ground beef and with low- or no-fat sour cream and salad dressing (of the mayonnaise persuasion). The meatballs can be made ahead and reheated in the sauce.

Fines herbes had me mystified, I admitted to readers:

Cooking dictionaries define fines herbes two ways, as finely chopped parsley or as a mixture of herbs, such as parsley, chervil, tarragon and even chives. I called the Cereal Institute in Chicago, originators of this recipe. Home economists there were out with the flu, too, and the receptionist couldn't hazard a guess on what was meant by fines herbes.

Not long after that I found bottled fines herbes in a French market, so we were set for future meatball occasions.

APPETIZER OAT-MEATBALLS WITH SOUR CREAM
Makes 6 dozen meatballs and 1 1/4 cups sauce

- 1 1/2 pounds ground beef
- 3/4 cup uncooked rolled oats, quick or regular
- 1 can (2 1/4 ounces) mushrooms stems and pieces, drained and finely chopped
- 1 egg
- 1/2 cup milk
- 1/4 cup finely chopped onion
- 1 1/2 teaspoons salt
- 1/2 teaspoon fines herbes
- 1 cup dairy sour cream
- 1/4 cup salad dressing
- 2 tablespoons chopped chives
- 1/2 teaspoon sugar
- 4 drops hot-pepper sauce

To prepare meatballs: Combine beef, oats, chopped mushrooms, egg, milk, onion, salt and fines herbes. Mix thoroughly. Shape into small balls, using about 1 tablespoon of mixture for each. Place balls 1 inch apart in greased shallow baking pan. Bake in 375-degree oven for 15 to 18 minutes, or until done. (Note: If preferred, meatballs may be pan-fried in small amount of shortening over moderate heat for 10 to 12 minutes, or until done and browned on all sides.)

To prepare sauce: In saucepan, combine sour cream, salad dressing, chives, sugar and hot pepper sauce. Place over low heat. Bring to serving temperature, stirring constantly. Serve with hot meatballs.

A Set of Souffle Dishes

September 29

I told readers that my husband should be writing the column because he tested the recipe:

Wednesday was one of those confused days when our schedules didn't correlate. I had planned to test lobster souffle for an early supper before I had to leave for a meeting. But my husband was planning a fishing trip with business cronies, and he didn't arrive home until a half-hour before I had to depart, too late to start making souffle.

So he offered to test the recipe, and we'd eat when I got home at 10:15 p.m. I didn't arrive until 10:30, when the souffle had descended a bit from its glorious heights, but its taste had not declined.

"It was really fast to make," said my husband. "I just put the egg yolks in one bowl and measured the flour in another, the milk in another, and the lobster, chives and seasonings in another."

Sure enough, on the counter was a line-up of empty bowls, all waiting for me to wash them.

Eleanor types the first Tested Recipes column on a Remington upright.

SUMPTUOUS LOBSTER SOUFFLE

Makes 4 to 6 servings

1 package (9 ounces) frozen rock lobster tails
3 tablespoons butter
3 tablespoons flour
1 cup milk
1 teaspoon chopped chives
1/2 teaspoon salt
1/4 teaspoon pepper
1/8 teaspoon cayenne pepper
4 egg yolks
2 tablespoons sauterne or other white wine
5 egg whites, stiffly beaten

Cook lobster tails as directed on package. Cool in chilled water. Remove and chop lobster meat. (Note: There should be about 1 cup.) Melt butter in saucepan. Blend in flour. Add milk. Cook, stirring constantly, until mixture boils and thickens. Remove from heat. Stir in lobster, chives and seasonings. Beat in 4 egg yolks, 1 at a time. Add wine. (Note: Equal parts of lemon juice and water can substitute for wine.) Fold in beaten egg whites. Pour into 6-cup souffle dish. Heat oven to 400 degrees. Put souffle in oven. Immediately reduce heat to 375 degrees. Bake for 30 to 35 minutes, or until knife inserted in center comes out clean.

Dad, with week-old Aric, burned the soup in his excitement.

1969

— A new baby, a growing adeptness with life's finer foods but not so adept at avoiding typos —

We Welcome Aric
May 11

On April 30, 1969, a future recipe taster entered our lives. Our son, Aric, was born, and the next column I wrote was headlined, Soup Puts New Dad in a Stew:

I'd bought ingredients to test an old-fashioned beef-vegetable soup, but the impending birth sidetracked me to Midway Hospital. Since I was going to be in the hospital for four days, my husband, with new-dad exuberance, offered to test the soup recipe for me. He put the stockpot on to boil, and when the required time was up, he thought he turned the burner off. He then left the house to visit me and to do a little celebrating with friends. By the time he got home, the four quarts of liquid had boiled away and the pot was on the verge of smoking. He'd turned the burner to simmer instead of off, but who can blame a brand-new father for being a little rattled?

We gave the recipe a rerun after Aric and I got home from the hospital.

Tasting is Believing
May 18

Have you ever been both attracted and repelled by something? That's how I reacted when I first saw the recipe for Dill 'n' Cheese Bread. I figured it would probably be terrible, yet I couldn't resist testing it. Pickles and pimento and parmesan cheese don't read like a probable combination.

I guess I'll have to eat my prediction because the bread turned out to be very tasty.

Stewed, Finn-Style
August 3

For the first time, I told readers about my Finnish heritage. Kalamojakka recipes much better than the one described that Sunday appear later in this book:

The copy editor who puts together the Women's section is a fanatical fisherman. For some time, he's been urging me to test a fish recipe. I decided to acquiesce with Finnish Fish Stew.

Although I am of Finnish descent, I can't say I was raised on Finnish fish stew, or kalamojakka, as it is

called by American Finns. My mother used to make it often enough, but I always ate a peanut butter sandwich instead. It's sometimes said that people outgrow their food prejudices, but I'm still a finnicky Finlander as far as that stew stands. I hated it as a kid, and I don't like it any better now.

In correct Finnish, the name is kalakeitto. The Old Country method involves putting the entire cleaned fish — head and all— into the pot. True believers says that the head offers the choicest tidbits of meat. My mother never went that far. "It's those eyes looking up at you that's so gruesome," she says.

One drawback to this recipe is the overpowering fragrance as it cooks. My husband reluctantly agreed to taste it. One spoonful was enough for him. Enough for me, too.

But I knew what to do with that big mess of kalamojakka. I put it in a jar and presented it to the copy editor who was so eager for me to test a fish recipe. He said he loved it, but — funniest thing — he never again asked me to make a fish dish.

Almost, But Not Quite
March 23

Testing Shrimp With Crunch, I attempted to re-create Shrimp de Jonghe, one of my favorite appetizers at our beloved Blue Horse restaurant in St. Paul (my

SHRIMP WITH CRUNCH
Makes 8 appetizer or
4 entree servings

1 pound raw, peeled, cleaned shrimp,
   fresh or frozen
1 egg white, slightly beaten
3/4 cup packaged cornflake crumbs
2 tablespoons butter, melted
1/4 teaspoon salt
1/4 teaspoon dry mustard
1/2 teaspoon Worcestershire sauce
1/8 teaspoon hot-pepper sauce
1/4 cup finely chopped green pepper
Lime-butter sauce:
1/4 cup melted butter
2 tablespoons freshly squeezed lime
   juice

To prepare shrimp: Thaw shrimp. Rinse shrimp. Drain on paper towels. In mixing bowl, stir egg white with shrimp until coated. Mix crumbs, butter, salt, mustard, Worcestershire sauce, hot-pepper sauce and green pepper. Dip shrimp into crumb mixture to coat generously. Arrange in single layer in foil-lined shallow baking pan. Bake in 350-degree oven for 30 minutes.

To make sauce: Combine butter and lime juice. Serve with shrimp.

husband and I courted there). The restaurant's version was more buttery-fried than this oven-baked shrimp appetizer, but the crunch was similar. Garlic, which permeated the Blue Horse shrimp, is totally missing in this mildly flavored version. For today's tastes, add garlic and boost the mustard and Tabasco. As an appetizer, serve a cluster of shrimp on hot toast triangles. Pass the lime-butter sauce in a small pitcher.

Winning the Battle With Wellington
November 30

To see if cheaper meat could do well in Wellington, I tested both beef filet and chuck wrapped under the same blanket of puff pastry, which works wonderfully for the crust. But don't do the dumb thing I did — I completely forget to thaw the pastry rounds. They softened after several minutes in the oven, thank goodness. (That was before any of us owned a microwave, of course.)

The filet portion of the testing was butter-tender, but the chuck had better flavor. Our guests were delighted to be part of the elegant testing. Mixing generations of generals, one said, "No wonder Wellington died a rich and famous man, and Bismarck ended up with a jelly-belly."

Four to six servings from a 3-pound tenderloin? We ate more beef in '69, I guess. Classic French was a white, creamy blend from Wish-Bone, available then, but not now. You could use ranch dressing, or make a vinaigrette dressing and give it body with sour cream or plain yogurt. Back then, sheets of frozen puff pastry weren't being marketed by Pepperidge Farm, but use them now and save yourself the trouble of rolling out individual patty shells.

CLASSIC BEEF WELLINGTON
Makes 4 to 6 servings

3 pounds filet of beef (beef tenderloin)
Salt and pepper to taste
1/2 cup Classic French dressing (use mild-flavored ranch dressing), divided
8 ounces good-quality braunschweiger
1 package (10 ounces) frozen patty shells, thawed, or favorite puff pastry recipe
1 egg, lightly beaten

To roast meat: Season meat with salt and pepper. In roasting pan, place meat on rack. Roast in 375-degree oven for 30 minutes. Baste occasionally with 1/4 cup dressing. Cool to room temperature.

To make classic Wellington: In medium bowl, combine braunschweiger with remaining dressing. Blend until smooth. Spread mixture over top and sides of meat. Increase oven temperature to 450 degrees. Roll out pastry to 12-by-16-inch rectangle. Place pastry over meat, tucking edges underneath. Brush pastry with egg. Bake for 40 minutes, or until pastry is golden brown.

To make economical Beef Wellington: Use 3-pound boneless chuck roast, 2 to 2 1/2 inches thick. Season meat. Roast in 350-degree oven for 2 1/4 hours, or until tender. Baste occasionally with dressing. Cool. Follow directions above to complete Wellington.

Don't Forget the Butter

December 7

Oh, woe! What a wonderful fruitcake, but what a dreadful error. We left out the butter. Phones in the Women's Department started ringing Monday morning, to the point that all of us answered by saying, "Half cup butter." One of my colleagues wearily said, "I never knew so many people started baking before 8 a.m."

It was hard to escape typos in those precomputer days of typewriters and hot type. The next Sunday, I told readers about the missing 1/2 cup butter, thanking everyone for being so good-natured "about our technical hroblem." Typo compounded.

So divine, so full of fruit and nuts that there's hardly any cake to be seen, this is a medium dark cake, but not so dark as to be bitter. All the fruits make it very moist. Supposedly this cake would be better if it aged for a week or two, but half was gone within three days. Caution: Use a sharp knife. There's so much fruit in it that it doesn't always cut perfectly. Maybe if it had been allowed to age a bit ...

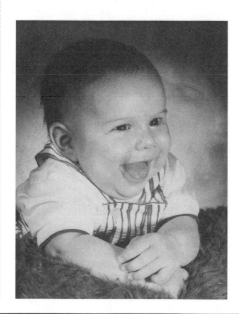

Well-fed Aric at 3 months old.

RAISIN BOURBON FRUITCAKE DELUXE

Makes 9- or 10-inch cake

1 package (15 ounces) dark or golden seedless raisins
1 1/2 cups mixed candied fruits and peels
3/4 cup whole candied cherries
3/4 cup candied pineapple chunks
3/4 cup citron chunks
1 1/2 cups candied orange peel chunks
1 cup pitted dates
1/2 cup bourbon
3/4 cup packed brown sugar
1/2 cup butter
4 eggs
1/4 cup golden or light-flavored molasses
1 cup walnut halves
1/2 cup pecan halves
1 cup sifted flour
3/4 teaspoon salt
1 teaspoon cinnamon
1/4 teaspoon nutmeg
1/4 teaspoon baking powder

In large bowl, combine raisins, candied fruits, peels and dates with bourbon. Cover. Let stand overnight. Beat brown sugar and butter until light and fluffy. Beat eggs until thick. Combine with sugar mixture. Blend in molasses. Sir in fruits and nuts. Resift flour with salt, spices and baking powder into batter. Mix until well blended. Turn into greased 9- or 10-inch tube pan lined with greased brown paper. Bake in 300-degree oven for 3 1/2 hours, or until cake tests done.

1970

— *Seeing in the Seventies with muffins, meatballs and romantic menus* —

As the clock ticked to midnight and the dawn of the 1970s decade, I felt blue. The '60s had been so momentous — a summer in Europe, college graduation, first job, first apartment, getting married, becoming a mom. And my 30th birthday was just months away. The best decade of my life was over.

Ah, the shortsighted vision of the young. The '70s were another wild ride on a roller coaster of activity: founding an international food writers' organization, becoming its president, launching world food travels, all while raising Aric and maintaining a home and a job. And the Tested Recipes column kept chuggin'.

As my Hibbing High schoolmate Bob Dylan had written by then, "The times, they were a'changing." Nutrition was mentioned as "being in the news" in an October column, and we tried some low-cal recipes for the first time after a couple of years of blitheful full-bore cooking.

A reader says . . .

Thanks for all our good cooking together through your column.

— Martha Oviatt, St. Paul

Price Was Sweeter Then
October 4

Food was a bargain. Testing sourdough bread, I wrote that I had paid 85 cents for a loaf of sourdough bread in the San Francisco airport. The next week, a Hastings reader, formerly a San Francisco resident, chastised, "It serves you right to pay that much for sourdough bread if you bought it at the airport. It sells for 40 cents a loaf in San Francisco grocery stores."

One Salad, Many Views
March 15

About Walnut Chicken Condiment Salad:

After our two guests, my husband and I finished the salad, we commented on it as anyone who eats a tested recipe must do. The critique resembled the blind men "seeing" the elephant. One liked it just fine as it was. Another thought the pineapple should be eliminated. I liked the pineapple but not the tomato in that flavor combination. And my husband, whose plate was practically polished, facetiously said he didn't like anything about it.

A Recipe Bombs

April 12

Stuffed Onions are Stomach Bomb was the headline on one of the year's mishaps:

Testing recipes can be likened to the Apollo space program. Have a few successes and a person gets overconfident. Just about the time Apollo 13 spaceship exploded, I had a bomb in my own kitchen.

It's what Homestyle Stuffed Onions do to the digestive tract that's distressing. Immediately after eating two of them, my husband had an after-dinner drink: Alka-Seltzer.

While making the plump onions, I wasn't getting anywhere scooping them out with a curved-tip serrated fruit knife. My husband strolled in, saw me struggling and said, in words to this effect: "Stand aside, woman. Let the master show you how it's done."

Aric takes an early interest in rattling pots and pans.

That was fine with me, but after doing one onion, he quietly strolled out of the kitchen. After that, I found that using a serrated grapefruit spoon works the best.

My husband may have had a bad reaction to the onions, but I'd like to note that our 11-month-old son was very eager to eat the meat filling. He's too young to tell us if he had heartburn, but he didn't seem to be upset. Maybe he has the strongest stomach of us all.

You Mean
She Can Cook?

April 5

My parents were visiting when I tested a Bake-Off ravioli recipe:

My dad, who's suspicious of almost every kind of new food, actually murmured kind words about the ravioli. I never know if he's being charitable, or if his compliments are actually astonishment that his daughter ever learned to cook.

Menu for Romance
May 24

I told my readers everything! Writing about a recipe for braised pork chops:

Back in my single days, whenever I'd have a fellow over for dinner for the first time, I served him my standard menu: French onion soup with melted Swiss cheese floating on top, oven-baked pork chops coated with cracker crumbs, baked potatoes and that green-bean mushroom-soup onion-ring casserole everyone makes. Dessert varied.

Eventually, I served this meal to the man who later became my husband. He was properly dazzled with my cooking ability. He didn't know that I'd had a lot of practice on that particular menu.

American-Made English Muffins
April 26

What is it about English muffins that makes them so appealing? I'm addicted to a brand with a particularly pockmarked texture and a slightly sour taste. When this recipe came along, it was tested in hopes that I could make a homemade version of my favorites. Instead, we munched smooth-textured, slightly sweet muffins. Different, but very good.

The only thing that leaves me in a quandary is what to do with the scraps of dough, crumbs on both sides, left over after the muffins are cut. Lump the dough in a ball and roll it out again with the crumbs interspersed? I don't know. You'll have to make your own decision.

Served hot, these are wonderful with orange marmalade melting into the crevasses.

BITE-SIZED ENGLISH MUFFINS
Makes 4 dozen

2 tablespoons sugar
1 teaspoon salt
1/4 cup butter or margarine, melted
1 cup milk, scalded
1 package dry yeast
1 cup warm water
5 1/2 cups sifted all-purpose flour
2 cups cornflakes, or 1/2 cup packaged cornflake crumbs

To make dough: In saucepan, combine sugar, salt, butter or margarine and scalded milk. Mix well. Cool to lukewarm. In large bowl, soften yeast in warm water. Stir in lukewarm milk mixture. Add 3 cups flour. Beat until smooth. Mix in enough additional flour to make a soft dough. Turn out onto lightly floured board. Knead for 10 minutes, or until smooth and elastic. Place in greased bowl, turning to grease top. Cover. Let rise in warm place for 1 1/4 hours, or until doubled in bulk. Punch down. Divide dough in half.

To cut: If using cornflakes, crush into fine crumbs. On board heavily sprinkled with cornflake crumbs, roll each portion of dough to 1/2-inch thickness. Turn dough once to coat both sides with crumbs. Cut muffins with small, round biscuit cutter, about 1 3/4 inches in diameter. Place rounds carefully on lightly greased baking sheets. Cover. Let rise for 30 minutes.

To bake: Bake in 350-degree oven for 18 minutes, or until nicely browned. Cool. Just before serving, carefully slice muffins in half crosswise with serrated knife. Brush cut surfaces with melted butter or margarine. Broil or grill for 2 minutes, or until toasted.

Meatball Boats for a Sailor
May 10

Writing about a substantial supper:

My husband's brother has been home on leave from the Navy. He's spent two years on a gunboat off the Vietnam coast and is returning for another two years of service. He's been used to the Navy gravy, and he didn't say whether this meatballs-potato combo was better than shipboard food, but his plate was clean at meal's end.

In the 1970s, wines still carried European-style names. Now this recipe might call for chardonnay or white zinfandel. Putting potatoes through a sieve was tedious then, and I wouldn't bother today, either. Your electric mixer should get them smooth enough.

MEATBALL STUFFED POTATOES
Makes 4 servings

Potatoes:
    4 large baking potatoes
    Cooking oil
Savory meatballs:
    3/4 pound ground lean beef
    3/4 cup soft bread crumbs
    1 tablespoon Instant minced onion
    1 teaspoon seasoned salt
    2/3 cup sauterne or rose wine, divided
    1/3 cup ketchup, divided
    1 tablespoon chutney (optional)

Filling:
    1/4 cup sauterne, chablis or other white
      wine
    1/4 cup light cream
    1 teaspoon seasoned salt
    1/4 cup grated parmesan cheese

To bake potatoes: Scrub potatoes. Dry. Lightly rub with oil. Bake in 450-degree oven for 45 to 50 minutes, or until done.

To make meatballs: In large bowl, combine beef, bread crumbs, onion, salt, 1/3 cup wine and 2 tablespoons ketchup. Shape into tiny meatballs. Arrange in shallow pan. Bake in 450-degree oven for 15 minutes, or until done. Combine remaining wine, remaining ketchup and chutney. Stir meatballs into sauce.

To make filling: Remove potatoes from oven. Split lengthwise. Carefully remove potato, leaving 1/4-inch shell so skins will not break. Press potato through sieve so there are no lumps. Beat smooth with wine, cream, seasoned salt and cheese. Spoon a little potato into bottom of each shell. Fill shell with meatballs. Spoon (or press through pastry tube) remaining potatoes to fill shell and surround meatballs. Place potatoes under broiler for a few minutes until lightly browned.

Close Encounters

— *With the Third Grade* —

A hectic travel schedule and guilt about being away from home so much, especially on Aric's ninth birthday, compelled me to promise that he could have any kind of belated birthday party he wanted. He chose to have all his male classmates come for dinner and spend the night. While I was away, he wrote invitations on a tablet that had gotten into our household as a party favor. Each invitation was penned under the logo of the Minneapolis Star, which must have confused a few mothers who know I work for the opposition paper.

My husband promised to help control the bedlam. "We'll tell them no yelling or screaming," he decreed. "Good luck," I laughed.

"I'll let you know if we survived," I promised on May 7, 1978. "If this column does not appear next Sunday, you'll know I'm babbling in an institution somewhere."

The next Sunday, May 14, 1978, I did my babbling in print. Here's the slumber party story recounting that harrowing night:

Close encounters with the third grade ... or how we survived a slumber party.

As we mentioned in last Sunday's Tested Recipes column, our son Aric chose to have his third-grade male classmates over for dinner and a slumber party to celebrate his ninth birthday.

Now that I've caught up on sleep, unpacked the bags under my eyes and regained my composure, I am able to recount, with controlled hysteria, what happened. A sociological study of 9-year-old males, as it were.

At 3 p.m., I arrived at school, loaded the car trunk with sleeping bags and the car with a squad of squirming boys who took great delight in pushing the automatic controls and hanging out the opened windows.

Most had been to our home previously, so en masse they thundered up the stairs to Aric's room. By the time I walked upstairs, they had the record player going, radio earphones on, toys out of the closet and boxing gloves in action. It happened so fast, I felt like I'd been lost in a time warp.

Soon, Aric had them lined up for an afterschool snack. While I poured root beer, he opened a Billy beer bought for his can collection, and passed the brew down the line for all the boys to sip.

Mothers, do not be alarmed. The dozen boys consumed the equivalent of a half can of beer. Aric stashed the rest in the refrigerator for later consumption — but I drank it instead. Fortification for what was yet to come, you know.

Aric opened his gifts, and soon some of them were demolished by boys who would be boys. A couple of kids started to put together a helicopter but abandoned the project. The dog found it on the floor and chewed a few parts.

A horde of boys attracts other hordes of boys. Neighborhood toughs arrived, itching for a rock fight. Usually, Aric avoids them, but with all the third-grade reinforcements ... well, old mom had to break up that battle.

Spaghetti was served on the back deck, sparing my dining-room rug. My neighbor, who earned battle stripes as a Cub Scouts leader, assisted, bless her. Those 10 kids demolished a gallon of spaghetti sauce, two pounds of spaghetti, a pound of carrot sticks and garlic bread, leaving just enough plate scrapings to give the dog garlic breath for the next two days.

Then, it was time to light the candles on the cake. We tried it outside. As the first candle was lit, as if on cue from an unseen conductor, a dozen voices broke into "You Light Up My Life." At the top of their young lungs. I expected police sirens any minute in response to calls from deafened neighbors.

It was windy, so we took the candle-lighting ceremony indoors. With Aric at the head of the table, candles ablaze, my neighbor and I suggested the boys sing "Happy Birthday." Which they did — the third-grade version: "Happy Birthday to you. You live in a zoo. You look like a monkey and smell like one, too." The guest of honor scratched his head and armpits chimpanzee-style.

These are bright kids. It didn't take one boy long to discover that pennies weren't essential to operate the gumball machine. Just unscrew the top. Several paws dipped in before I wrestled it away, visions of a dozen little mouths chewing and spitting out bubble gum dancing through my head.

To wear off some of that incredible 9-year-old energy, we gave them a soccer ball and told them to play. If that didn't work, I thought I'd put them all in the sauna and steam their energy away. Fortunately, there was a two-hour "Incredible Hulk" special on television, so they settled down to watch.

My husband, who had promised to help with this debacle, somehow found numerous errands to do that Friday night, including driving to Wisconsin to transport an aged aunt back to Minneapolis. About 9 p.m., he showed up. The boys' noise was down to a dull roar as they watched TV, snickering at the pantyhose ads, and quietly grinding buttered popcorn into the den carpeting.

I was in a near-catatonic state. In fact, I took it all very calmly. Why, I can't say, except that I knew my screaming would not be heard over their screaming, so why bother?

At one point, they got their second wind and dashed outdoors for a few minutes to ring neighbors' doorbells; they were gone long enough so I could vacuum up the popcorn. Then 10 smelly little bodies rolled out their sleeping bags in the den, the smallest room in our house. It was absolutely wall-to-wall kids.

The rest of the night is a sleepless blur. It was predictable that one boy would get sick and throw up in his sleeping bag at 3 a.m.

They were awake for the first Saturday-morning cartoons while my husband and I fed them pancakes and sausages in two shifts. One good little eater ate a half-dozen sausage patties and three stacks of pancakes.

I'd just cleared the table when they were all back for doughnuts. Nine-year-old boys eat a lot — and often.

Aric and another boy were gone by 8:30 a.m. to the state chess tournament. The rest dribbled away as parents arrived. The last departed at 10:30 a.m., leaving me to remove rubber darts from the ceilings and scrape bubble gum from the den carpeting.

"My mother says you're sure brave to have all the third-grade boys for a slumber party," one of the guests told me before departing. It wasn't bravery as much as it was stupidity.

Aric thought, however, it was the most terrific birthday party he'd ever had. I hope he treasures the memories ... because he's not going to have another one until time dulls my recollections.

The following week, an update on the slumber party:

Dozens of comments from friends, including one from another mother who read the article while muttering, "I could have told her that. I could have told her." Her son also had hosted a slumber party. Trouble with having only child is that the wisdom acquired rearing the first can never be applied to younger siblings.

And from one of the party guests, a complaint: "Why did you put that in the paper? Now my mother isn't going to let me have a slumber party for **my** birthday."

Two years later, on May 11, 1980:

It's a good thing that mothers are forgiving types with short memories. Not that I'll ever forget Aric's first birthday slumber party — "Close Encounters With the Third Grade."

When Aric began campaigning for another birthday sleep-over for his classmates, I figured the boys are two years older now, they won't be so rowdy, it won't be so bad. Dumb, dumb, dumb.

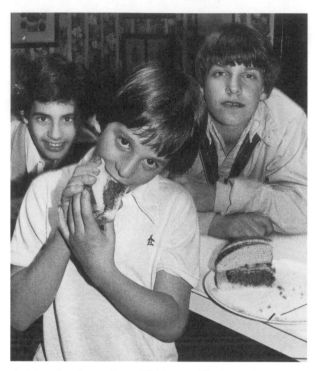

Aric's schoolmate Dean Wolfson wolfs down Giant Cheeseburger; Justin Gardner, left, and John Murphy were other slumber party guests in 1981.

As I was driving several of the kids and their sleeping bags to our house, one of them asked if I was going to write about the slumber party this year. "Only if you drive me nuts. And if you do, this time, I'll name names!"

We found that threats do not work on 11-year-old boys. They can ignore the most dire predictions about being sent home at 1 a.m. when there's a pillow fight to be waged. Each entreaty to stop was only followed by another feathery skirmish.

The grand plan was to take them all to the drive-in movie, a double feature. That would get them out of the house for a few hours and maybe tire them out. Oh, how I underestimate the energy of 11-year-olds.

I envisioned all the kids crammed into the bigger of our cars while my husband and I sat in peaceful bliss in our Subaru. No such luck. At least three, sometimes four kids were in with us most of the night.

Furthermore, they fought over who was going to sit in the comfortable front seat with all the leg room. My husband and I sat knees-to-chin in the back.

Just getting the kids to the movie was near-insurrection. It's darn hard these days to find anything without an R or X rating in those passion pits we call drive-ins. Only one offered less-than-sexy features: "Breaking Away" and "Norma Ray."

The boys ranted: "I've seen them five times." "Baby movies — let's see 'The Jerk.' " "My mother (grandmother, dad, sister) takes me to see R movies all the time."

Not when you're with me you don't. That was the only battle I won all night.

I don't know what concessions my husband offered so the guilty ones would clean up the drips in the drive-in bathroom they "egged." Those eggs were acquired on a supposed scavenger hunt throughout our neighborhood just before we left for the movies. Young minds are so inventive.

And so it went. The only sign that they had put on some age was that their dinner-table conversation was about girls.

Eleven-year-olds are unilaterally ravenous. They went through a mountain of spaghetti, carrot sticks, garlic bread for dinner, which had been preceded by afterschool sustenance of cookies, chips and lemonade.

For once, I got smart and postponed the cake and ice cream until after the movie, when despite popcorn, etc., they were starving and cleaned their plates. It's always galled me to discard homemade cake only half-eaten by kids full from lunch.

I'd agreed to this slumber party at a time when I thought we would have completed all the final touches on a new basement recreation-guest room. Well, it didn't get done, so again, we tried to wedge 11 sleeping bags into our small den, because that's where the TV is.

By morning, most of the boys had migrated to the living room where they burrowed into sleeping bags, dead to the world. I feared that might be too true, that they'd suffocated. But all the mummies lived to slumber party another time. "Not at our house," my husband swears.

It was a bleary bunch eating breakfast pancakes. But they all said they'd had a wonderful time. Kids equate slumber-party success with the level of morning-after exhaustion. Parents wish it were just the opposite.

That wasn't the last slumber party. On May 10, 1981 (funny how a mother's memory dims in just a year), yet another accounting of a slumber party, only this time, we didn't lose any sleep:

You've read in this column about "Close Encounters With the Third Grade." And about fifth-grade pillow fights.

We succumbed to Aric's pleas for one more birthday slumber party, but only after threats about "This is the LAST ONE!" and "Keep the guest list short!"

Either his friends are getting more mature or we're getting accustomed to having grade-school gremlins take over the house. It actually wasn't traumatic this year, mostly because we put them all in the basement to sleep (?) and we couldn't hear the ruckus from our second-floor bedroom, door closed.

If ice-cube fights or assorted 12-year-old mayhem occurred until 3 a.m., don't tell me about it, kids. I slept soundly, knowing that if anyone threw up in a sleeping bag this year, he was old enough to clean it up himself.

The very worst moment was shortly after the mob arrived from school and I'd fed them a snack so they'd survive until dinner. My husband was the first to notice the dark, sticky blob on the stairway ceiling. I feared the worst until we washed away what turned out to be chocolate frosting from chocolate-cherry bars.

For mothers of sixth-grade boys facing a slumber party, I have two pieces of advice:

Take them to a horror movie, double feature if possible. They'll spend all night telling each other gory details and be too scared to run around at midnight ringing the neighbors' doorbells.

Second, stock up on milk and food because they can consume outlandish quantities of both. To the standard slumber-party menu of spaghetti for dinner, pancakes and bacon for breakfast, this year we added an after-movie snack of the biggest hamburger the kids had ever see. That didn't stop them from demolishing it. It's the perfect birthday party main course, but only for older kids. Giant Burger is so thick that it takes at least an 8-year-old's mouth to bite into it.

GIANT CHEESEBURGER
Makes 12 servings

Giant bun:
- 2 3/4 to 3 1/4 cups all-purpose flour, divided
- 1 cup quick or old-fashioned oats, uncooked
- 1/4 cup instant nonfat dry milk
- 2 tablespoons sugar
- 1 package active dry yeast
- 1 teaspoon salt
- 1 cup very warm water (115 to 120 degrees)
- 1/4 cup butter or margarine
- 1 egg, separated
- 1 tablespoon sesame seeds

Giant burger:
- 1 1/2 pounds lean ground beef
- 3/4 cup quick or old-fashioned oats, uncooked
- 3/4 cup ketchup
- 1 egg
- 1 teaspoon salt
- 4 slices American cheese
- Lettuce leaves

To make bun: In large bowl, combine 1 cup flour, oats, milk, sugar, yeast and salt. Mix well. Combine water and butter, stirring until butter is almost melted. Add water mixture and egg yolk to flour mixture. Beat at low speed on electric mixer for 30 seconds, or just until blended. Beat at medium speed for 2 minutes, scraping bowl occasionally. Add 1/4 cup flour. Beat at high speed for 2 minutes, scraping bowl occasionally. Using wooden spoon, stir in enough remaining flour to make a stiff dough. Knead on lightly floured surface for 8 to 10 minutes, or until smooth and elastic. Cover. Let rest for 20 minutes. Shape dough into smooth ball. Flatten into greased 9-inch round cake pan. Brush with slightly beaten egg white. Sprinkle with sesame seeds. Cover loosely with plastic wrap. Refrigerate 2 to 24 hours. (Note: Dough will double in size.)

To bake bun: Uncover dough. Let stand at room temperature for 20 minutes. Bake in 350-degree oven for 40 to 45 minutes, or until golden brown. Cool 10 minutes. Remove from pan. Cool completely on wire rack. Split bun in half to form top and bottom.

To make burger: In medium bowl, combine all burger ingredients, except cheese and lettuce. Mix well. On rack of broiler pan, shape mixture to form a 9-inch diameter patty. Bake in 350-degree oven for 40 to 45 minutes, or until desired doneness. Arrange cheese slices over patty. Continue baking for 1 minute, or until cheese is melted. Arrange lettuce leaves on bottom of giant bun (they will keep it from getting soggy). Place burger on lettuce. Garnish with mustard, ketchup, tomato slices and pickles. Cover with top of bun. Cut into 12 wedges.

Aren't All Birthday Cakes Chocolate?

— *At Our House, They Were* —

When it comes to chocolate, my philosophy is "More is never enough." As my one-time pen pal, cartoonist Sandra Boynton says, "Chocolate is not a privilege. It's a right."

Readers know chocolate has been the flavor of choice for this column over the years and that son Aric inherited the chocolate gene from his mom. Every year, I baked a new version of chocolate birthday cake for him, sharing the recipes with readers. Here are some of our best birthday binges.

First of Many
May 3, 1970

Starting an annual tradition, our son's first chocolate birthday cake:

Aric reached that initial milestone, his first birthday, and in honor of the event, he and several other little ones were taken to St. Paul's Como Park to see the animals and flowers and to have cake and ice cream. His Year One cake would probably win a blue ribbon at the county fair, and the birthday boy ate it with gusto, but it takes time to make, nearly three hours from start to finish.

Aric energetically slices into his fifth birthday cake, chocolate, of course. Jerrold Dial waits for a hunk.

Information attached to the recipe suggested that a blender makes short work of crushing the peppermint candy. Not so. I put mints in the blender, pushed a button, and the machine gave one little growl before dying. Every time I tried, mints got stuck under the chopping blades. My husband, ever the mechanic, came to the rescue, emptied the blender container, started the blades whirling, then dropped in mints a few at a time.

We got pulverized mints, but maybe they were too fine. I told readers to put them in a plastic bag and pound them with a rolling pin or hammer.

Cake to the Third Power
May 7, 1972

Aric graduated from the Terrible Twos, and in honor of his third birthday (and the fact that he hadn't been all that terrible), I baked this cake with a blend of chocolate intensities that makes it so tempting. We reveled in its three lovely layers.

OLD-FASHIONED COCOA-MINT CAKE
Makes 9-inch, 2-layer cake

Cake:
- 2/3 cup vegetable shortening or margarine
- 1 2/3 cups sugar
- 3 eggs
- 2 1/4 cups sifted all-purpose flour
- 2/3 cup cocoa
- 1/4 teaspoon baking powder
- 1 1/4 teaspoons baking soda
- 1 teaspoon salt
- 1 1/3 cups water
- 1/2 cup crushed peppermint candy

Cocoa peppermint frosting:
- 1/3 cup butter or margarine
- 1/2 cup cocoa
- 3 cups sifted powdered sugar
- 1/2 cup scalded milk
- 3/4 teaspoon vanilla
- 1 tablespoon crushed peppermint candy

To make cake: In mixing bowl, cream shortening, sugar and eggs until fluffy. Beat on high speed of mixer for about 5 minutes. Sift together flour, cocoa, baking powder, soda and salt. Reduce speed to medium. Add dry ingredients to creamed mixture alternately with water and peppermint candy. Pour into 2 greased and cocoa-dusted 9-inch cake pans. Bake in 350-degree oven for 35 minutes or until done. Cool. Frost with Cocoa Peppermint Frosting.

To make frosting: In saucepan, melt butter over medium heat. Stir in cocoa. Blend in remaining frosting ingredients. Place pan in bowl of ice water. Beat for 4 to 6 minutes, or until of spreading consistency.

While describing the cake, I groused about sifting powdered sugar, which creates such electricity that the sugar sticks to the bowl and seems to crawl over the edges. The counters are always a mess. Any suggestions?

By the next week, I'd heard from a reader who said I should use a fine-mesh strainer and push the powdered sugar through with a spoon, rather than using a hand-powered sifter. Presto! Messy problem solved.

CHOCOLATE-CHOCOLATE-CHOCOLATE CAKE
Makes 8-inch, 3-layer cake

Cake:
- 3 to 4 teaspoons prepared cocoa mix (or plain cocoa)
- 1/2 cup butter, softened
- 1/2 cup (4 ounces) cream cheese, softened
- 1 1/4 cups sugar
- 2 eggs
- 1 teaspoon vanilla
- 3 cups flour
- 2 teaspoons baking soda
- 1 teaspoon salt
- 2 cups milk
- 4 squares (1 ounce each) unsweetened chocolate, melted
- 1 package (6 ounces) milk-chocolate chips

Creamy chocolate frosting:
- 1 package (6 ounces) milk-chocolate chips
- 1 tablespoon oil
- 1/2 cup (4 ounces) cream cheese, softened
- 1/3 cup butter, softened
- 4 cups sifted powdered sugar
- 1 teaspoon vanilla
- 1 pasteurized egg
- Milk, if needed

To make cake: Grease 3 (8-inch) round cake pans. Dust with cocoa. Set aside. In mixing bowl, cream butter, cream cheese and sugar for 5 minutes, or until light and fluffy. Beat in eggs, 1 at a time. Blend in vanilla. Stir together flour, soda and salt. Thoroughly blend flour mixture into creamed mixture alternately with milk, beginning and ending with flour. Thoroughly blend melted chocolate into batter. Spread half of batter into prepared pans. Sprinkle chips evenly over batter in pans. Pour remaining batter over them. Spread evenly.

To bake cake: Bake in 350-degree oven for 20 to 25 minutes, or until cake tester comes out clean. (Note: Cake tester may hit a chip and come out sticky; if so, clean tester and try again.) Cool for 10 minutes. Remove from pans. Cool thoroughly before frosting with Creamy Chocolate Frosting.

To make frosting: Melt chocolate pieces with oil. Beat together cream cheese and butter until fluffy. Gradually blend in sugar and vanilla. Blend in melted chocolate. Beat in egg. Add milk, 1 drop at a time, if needed, to make frosting of spreading consistency.

Chocolate to the Max
May 5, 1974

Aric, turning 5, ordered a chocolate cake, and he got more of a jolt than this recipe suggests, because this cake was swathed with fudge frosting and light-chocolate decorations. It's a solid cake, which I liked, but his little friends found it to be more than they could finish. Of course, they'd already been into the

HERSHEY BAR CAKE
Makes 10-inch tube cake

**7 to 8 ounces milk-chocolate bars
1 small can (5 1/2 ounces) or 1/2 cup
   chocolate-flavored syrup
1 cup butter or margarine
2 cups sugar
4 eggs
1/2 teaspoon baking soda
1 cup buttermilk
2 1/2 cups sifted cake flour
1 teaspoon vanilla**

In mixing bowl, melt milk-chocolate bars in syrup over hot (not boiling) water. Cream butter or margarine and sugar until light and fluffy. Add eggs, 1 at a time, creaming well after each addition. Mix baking soda with buttermilk. Add to creamed mixture alternately with sifted cake flour. Blend in chocolate mixture and vanilla. Pour into greased and floured 10-inch tube pan. Bake in 350-degree oven for 1 hour and 20 minutes. Cool in pan for 10 minutes. Turn out onto rack. Cool completely. Sprinkle with powdered sugar.

Cracker Jacks in their goodie bags, part of the general party pandemonium.

Lonnee's Cake to Long For
May 2, 1976

Elise Lonnee, who knows I'm crazy about chocolate cake, gave me her family's favorite recipe. She and her husband, Jack, work like fiends in their Four Inns restaurant across the street from the newspaper office (since this column was written, it moved to a bank skyway location in downtown St. Paul, but we still go there regularly).

Their place is always crowded, so much so that recently the cashier wondered if rumors were afloat that the Four Inns was having a sale. No rumors, just fact that the food is good, reasonable and speedy. Yet Jack and Elise always have time to visit with their customers.

Lonnee's cake received the ultimate acclaim in our household. It was designated **the birthday cake** for Aric's seventh party. Its deep reddish color and rich chocolate flavor took me back to my own childhood and the weekly treat of chocolate cake we had at the YWCA camp where I spent part of each summer. Its texture is marvelous, too. Vinegar must play a part.

When I made it, the fudge frosting got sugary. But what do kids know?

Several weeks later, a friend who tried the recipe was worried that her frosting was too runny, so she put it in the refrigerator to thicken. By the time it reached the right consistency, she had taken so many yummy samples to check its progress that she only had enough left to frost half the cake.

We gave Elise the last word: She says the frosting should be thin. She makes it while the cake bakes, and then pours it over the cooled layer so that when it sets, it forms a smooth-as-glass topping. That, of course, means one must keep hands off the cake for a while. For us chocolate freaks, that's torture.

If you happen to be in downtown St. Paul on any Monday, this cake is always baked for Four Inns customers. Jack said he got the recipe from his mother, a renowned cook who lived in Little Falls, Minn.

ELISE AND JACK LONNEE'S ALABAMA CHOCOLATE CAKE

Makes 9-by-13-inch cake

Cake:
- 1/2 cup butter or margarine
- 1 1/2 cups sugar
- 2 eggs, beaten
- 2 cups flour
- 1 teaspoon soda
- 1 cup cold water
- 2 squares unsweetened chocolate, melted
- 1 teaspoon vanilla
- 2 tablespoons vinegar

Fudge frosting:
- 2 squares unsweetened chocolate
- 1 1/2 cups granulated sugar
- 7 tablespoons milk
- 2 tablespoons shortening
- 2 tablespoons butter
- 1 tablespoon white corn syrup

To make the cake: In mixing bowl, cream butter and sugar. Add beaten eggs. Add flour and soda alternately with cold water. Add chocolate and vanilla. Beat on high speed for 2 minutes. Fold in vinegar. Pour batter into greased 9-by-13-inch pan. Bake in 350-degree oven for 30 minutes, or until done. Frost with fudge frosting.

To make frosting: In saucepan, combine all frosting ingredients. Bring to a full boil. Boil for 1 minute. Remove from heat. Cool. Beat until creamy.

Satan, Not Satin
May 6, 1979

Devilishly good and not much more work than a box mix, this cake has a texture that tells the world it's homemade. Box mixes have satin texture; this is more like handsome, homespun linen.

When Aric turned 10, we weren't up to having another slumber party, especially since our house was still in chaos. In midwinter, a water pipe in the attic broke, causing water to cascade through three floors like Niagara Falls, taking ceilings and wallpaper with it. We took the kids roller skating instead, and the rink provided treats.

I could have escaped baking a birthday cake altogether but for the ever-hungry column. Aric's first choice was Poppin' Fresh Pie. Chocolate, of course.

Devilish 10-year-olds Aric, foreground, and friend Dean Wolfson douse candles on Burnt Sugar-Iced Devil's Food Cake.

Besides, after all these years of baking elaborate birthday cakes for kids' parties and then having to throw away most of the slices, I've decided children are too excited at birthday parties to eat cake.

An informal survey reveals that kids, nevertheless, adore birthday parties. (And mothers wish, during those few chaotic hours each year, that they'd remained childless.)

BURNT SUGAR-ICED DEVIL'S FOOD CAKE
Makes 12 servings

Cake:
- 1 cup milk
- 1 tablespoon vinegar
- 2 cups unsifted all-purpose flour
- 1/2 cup unsweetened cocoa
- 2 teaspoons baking soda
- 1/2 teaspoon salt
- 1 cup shortening
- 2 cups sugar
- 2 eggs
- 1/2 cup hot water
- 1 1/2 teaspoons vanilla

Burnt sugar frosting:
- 3/4 cup granulated sugar
- 3/4 cup boiling water
- 3/4 cup (1 1/2 sticks) butter
- 2 pasteurized egg yolks
- 6 cups powdered sugar

To make cake: Combine milk and vinegar. Set aside to sour. Combine flour, cocoa, baking soda and salt. Set aside. In mixing bowl, cream shortening and sugar. Add eggs. Beat until well blended. Alternately add dry ingredients and soured milk to creamed mixture. Beat in hot water and vanilla until well blended.

To bake cake: Pour batter into 3 greased and floured 8-inch cake pans. Bake in 350-degree oven for 40 to 45 minutes, or until cake tester inserted in center comes out clean. Cool for 10 minutes. Remove from pans. Cool completely. Fill and frost with Burnt Sugar Frosting. Garnish with orange slices, if desired.

To make frosting: Pour sugar into large heavy skillet. Heat slowly, stirring until sugar melts and starts to turn a dark golden color. Very gradually add water, stirring constantly. Continue cooking until sugar is completely dissolved. Boil for 2 minutes. Cool completely. Beat butter until smooth. Add egg yolks. Blend thoroughly. Add sugar syrup, reserving 2 tablespoons. Beat in powdered sugar. Fill and frost cake layers. Drizzle cake with remaining syrup.

Mom Bakes Her Own Cake

May 29, 1983

A hectic work and entertaining schedule precluded an at-home party for Aric's end-of-April 14th birthday; a pizza-and-games parlor celebration was more to teen tastes, anyway. However, my birthday, May 14, comes exactly two weeks after his, and that year, this chocolate extravaganza celebrated my 43rd. "Now, this is CAKE! Rich, chewy, remindful of European tortes," I wrote, describing my treat.

WALNUT FUDGE CAKE

Makes 9-inch layer cake

Cake:
- 1 cup walnuts
- 4 squares (1 ounce each) unsweetened chocolate
- 2 cups sifted cake flour
- 2 cups granulated sugar
- 1 teaspoon baking soda
- 1 teaspoon salt
- 1 tablespoon instant-coffee granules
- 1/2 cup butter or margarine, softened
- 1 cup buttermilk
- 1/4 cup water
- 3 eggs

Walnut fudge frosting:
- 2 cups granulated sugar
- 1/4 cup light corn syrup
- 1/2 cup milk
- 1/2 cup margarine or shortening
- 2 squares (1 ounce each) unsweetened chocolate, cut up
- 1/4 teaspoon salt
- 1 teaspoon vanilla
- 1/2 cup chopped walnuts

To make cake: Chop walnuts fine. Set aside. Melt chocolate. Into mixing bowl, resift cake flour, sugar, soda, salt and instant coffee. Add butter, buttermilk, water and chocolate. Beat on low speed for 2 minutes. Add eggs. Beat for 2 minutes. Stir in walnuts.

To bake cake: Turn into 2 greased and floured 9-inch layer cake pans. Bake in 350-degree oven for 25 to 30 minutes, or until cake tests done. Let cake stand in pans for 5 minutes. Turn out on wire racks.

Cool completely. Frost with Walnut Fudge Frosting. Decorate with additional walnut halves.

To make frosting: In deep saucepan, combine sugar, syrup, milk, margarine, chocolate and salt. Stir together over low heat until chocolate and margarine melt. Stirring, bring to a full, rolling boil. Boil for 1 1/2 minutes. Remove from heat. Cool for 10 minutes. Beat mixture until lukewarm. Stir in vanilla and walnuts. Beat smooth. Add a few extra drops of milk, if needed for desired spreading consistency.

One Last Birthday Bash

May 10, 1987

It was like returning to the past when we prepared an 18th birthday dinner party for Aric and his buddies.

"Eighteen! I can remember when Aric was born," my co-workers have exclaimed. So can I, but I won't belabor those details.

I also recall vividly those primary-school birthday/slumber parties when the kids were little interested in slumber.

During junior and senior high, Aric was too grown up for birthday parties, but when he turned 18 on April 30, and he realized that the old gang of his would soon be breaking up, going away to college, he said OK to a revival of the birthday dinner.

Spaghetti, garlic bread and salad, of course — they're traditional. But no chocolate layer cake this time. His favorite is now a cinnamon-chocolate-chip bundt creation that is our household standby whenever I need a cake fast. I first tried the recipe during the 10 years I wrote the Household Forum and Housewives Exchange at the Pioneer Press.

That cake for Aric's birthday was especially good. The original called for sour cream, but I usually use plain yogurt. However, my husband brought home vanilla yogurt, thinking it was the same as plain. It added flavor depth to the cake, so I think I'll make that "mistake" again.

Young men at birthday parties are the same as little kids at birthday parties, though I noticed one moment of sophistication. These teen-age hunks gathered around our dining table were shoveling in spaghetti and garlic bread as if they hadn't eaten in days. I went back to the kitchen to fill the bowls, and when I returned, the dining-room lights had been doused and candles were flickering, creating about as much "atmosphere" as an all-male party could muster. (Or maybe they cut the lights so they couldn't see raw broccoli tossed into the salad.)

I brought in cake, ice cream and chocolate sauce, and they dove right in, making their own desserts. One mixed a chocolate milkshake in his glass.

After dinner, while they decided where to go, discussing which dance would have the best girl-pickings, they roughhoused and guffawed. They were third-graders again, only taller.

And I felt a momentary stab of nostalgia. This would be the last birthday party of the school-kid ilk. Our empty nest will never again have chocolate frosting on the ceiling.

CINNAMON-CHOCOLATE-CHIP BUNDT CAKE

Makes 1 bundt cake

- 1 package yellow cake mix (2-layer size, no pudding added)
- 4 large eggs
- 1/2 cup oil
- 1 package (4-serving size) vanilla instant pudding mix
- 1 cup (8 ounces) plain or vanilla yogurt
- 1/2 cup sugar
- 1 heaping tablespoon cinnamon
- 2 heaping tablespoons cocoa
- 1/2 cup chocolate chips

To make cake: In large mixing bowl, combine cake mix, eggs, oil, pudding mix and yogurt. Beat at medium speed until blended. Beat for 4 minutes on high, or until batter is velvety. In small bowl, combine sugar, cinnamon, cocoa and chocolate chips. In well-greased bundt pan, sprinkle about a third of chocolate-chip mixture. Spoon about half of batter into pan. Repeat layers, ending with remaining chocolate-chip mixture.

To bake cake: Bake in 350-degree oven for 1 hour. Cool in pan briefly. Invert onto serving plate. Cool completely.

1971

— Hello, Office Hungries, healthy bread and garden goods and the first carrot cake —

I was into pressure cooking — not the harried working-woman kind, though that was often the case, but the mechanical type prepared in the pressure cooker my parents gave me for Christmas.

The term "Office Hungries" first appeared, an endearment for my always-willing, all-too-candid co-workers who tasted anything I hauled to work and let me have — often between the eyes — their opinion.

It was also the year that carrot cake first showed up in the column. "I've got to taste this," said one of the office crew when I brought in a tested effort. "I can't believe that carrots can make a cake." How odd that sounds now, when carrot cake is almost everyone's favorite. At the time, I wrote, "With four carrots in it, the cake has a nutrition edge that most sweets don't. In this era of concern over nutrients, this is one time a mother can say, 'Let them eat cake.' "

Food prices I occasionally mentioned are startling to read today. Testing a recipe for skewered veal, I wrote on April 25 that I felt I was getting a bargain. "I was surprised at the economical tariff for veal, only $1.25 for 1 1/2 pounds."

In another column on June 13, I cooked a dinner for clients of my husband rather than entertain them in a restaurant. We served sherried consomme, pan-roasted shrimp, steak Diane, asparagus and liqueur-marinated cherries over ice cream. "I'm not saying this is a budget menu. The ingredients cost between $10 and $12, depending on whether you happen to have sherry one hand."

Those were the days.

Honored Guest Gets It
February 28

Cooking was continual learning process. Recounting a recipe for Chocolate Cream Squares, which was the feature of a baby shower column:

My one disaster taught me a lesson. While adding egg yolks to the cake batter, a bit of shell fell in, and before I could stop the rotating mixer, it was immersed. I had neither the time nor any more unsweetened chocolate to make another batch, so I fished around and found a piece of shell. Unfortunately, another piece remained, and who got it in her cake square but the guest of honor (fashion writer Georgann Koelln, who was expecting her son, Craig, now an engineer and all grown up). Lesson learned: Stop the mixer when adding eggs.

Legalized Addiction
October 17

Among the all-time most requested Tested Recipes was this Poppycock look-alike rich with popcorn, nuts and caramel. A large tin of Poppycock sold for $2.25, which I termed a high-priced snack by 1971 standards. The homemade facsimile was so addictive that I made batches two nights in a row (because my husband found the can of mixed nuts and left only peanuts for the first testing):

OVEN CARAMEL POPCORN
Makes about 8 cups

2 cups brown sugar
2 sticks butter or margarine
1/2 cup corn syrup
6 quarts popped corn (sift out unpopped
   kernels)
1 teaspoon salt
1 teaspoon baking soda
1 teaspoon butter flavoring
Nutmeats, such a peanuts, pecans,
   walnuts and cashews

In large saucepan, boil brown sugar, butter, corn syrup and salt for 5 minutes. Remove from heat. Add baking soda and butter flavor. Stir well over popped corn and nutmeats. Spread on cookie sheets or 2 9-by-13-inch pans. Bake in 200-degree oven for 1 hour, stirring at 15-minute intervals. Remove from oven. Cool in pan, but only briefly or it will solidify. Store in covered container to keep crisp.

A row of blisters marching up my right index finger reminds me to remind you to use a very long spoon or padded gloves when stirring the boiling caramel with the corn and nuts.

Minnesota zealously protected its dairy industry by banning butter substitutes. Yellow-colored margarine wasn't allowed in the state when I was a kid. People used to smuggle it in from Illinois.

I hadn't heard that previously contraband artificial butter flavoring had been made legal by the Minnesota Legislature, and I was surprised to find it in the grocery store when shopping for this recipe. When I asked the man stocking shelves about its legality, he mumbled something about it "being legal soon but, in the meantime, we're stocking it." Buying it, I felt like a black marketeer.

Bonaparte's Delight
May 16

My reputation as the Town Chocoholic was growing, as more and more chocolate recipes appeared in the column. I wasn't the only one in our household:

At 6 a.m., our 2-year-old raided the refrigerator, finding the one remaining Napoleon I'd made but had been too sick with the flu to try. He appeared at our bedside, frosted Napoleon in hand, saying, "See that chocolate on there?" No wonder I made him chocolate birthday cakes every year.

About the Napoleons, I commented: I won't say these are so easy that they can be done with one hand inside your vest. The puff pastry was to be pricked with a fork, a step that I'd inadvertently missed in my flu fog, to keep it from rising overly high, as mine did. My Napoleons looked more like curvaceous Josephines!

Grandma's Garden Grows Big Boys

August 29

Aric didn't eat only chocolate. Writing about a vegetable-rich casserole, I sympathized with gardeners:

All those tiny little seeds purchased last spring have turned into bushels and bushels of homegrown produce, and you don't know what to do with it all. Right? Our refrigerator is rotund with the bounty of my mother's garden — she's a seedaholic, too. This year, her excuse was that she had to plant lots of vegetables for her grandson's good health. He's eating tomatoes and broccoli and beans as fast as he can. But a half acre of garden is too much for a 2-year-old.

Too Rich for Me

November 7

Writing about Cranberry Bonbons:

Have you ever noticed when you serve someone a goodie and she doesn't think it's all that good, but she doesn't want to hurt your feelings, her comment is, "My goodness, it's rich!" That way she can gracefully decline eating it all.

A Weepy Task

January 3

Testing an onion-rich potato casserole for a dinner party:

I turned over the job of dicing vegetables and mincing onion to the teen-age neighbor girl who was helping us that night. "I'll let you do this so my mascara won't run," I told her. So she chopped onions and cried, and **her** mascara ran.

OK, Who Ate the Last Piece?

February 7

In anticipation of George Washington's birthday, which was observed a week early in 1971 because of the new-that-year Monday holiday for Presidents Day, I tried this extravagant and colorful version of baked Alaska built with cherry-vanilla ice cream and a cocoa-enriched meringue. It sat atop what was the first nearly flourless cake I'd ever made, harbinger of a future trend.

In those days, we weren't worried about the health hazards of meringues, a salmonella concern that escalated years later, so that by the early 1990s, other judges and I at a national pie contest were forced to eliminate meringue pies from prize contention. Now, you can again make meringue without qualms by using pasteurized whole eggs.

A mystery remains about this dessert:

We had three guests for dinner, and after second helpings, the equivalent of two servings remained. I packed them into a little Corningware dish and put it on the frigid back porch in a paper bag with a couple of other frozen items.

When I went to get it the next day for a repeat dessert, dish and all had disappeared — but the other items in the bag remained. I don't know if it was man or beast who swiped the Cocoa Cherry Alaska. My husband swears he's not the culprit, and I believe him, because if he had been, the dish would have been left in the sink for me to wash.

COCOA CHERRY ALASKA
Makes 8 to 12 servings

1 quart softened cherry-vanilla ice
    cream
Cocoa cake layer:
  1 teaspoon cocoa for dusting pan
  3 egg yolks, at room temperature
  2/3 cup sugar
  1 1/2 teaspoons vanilla
  1/4 cup sifted cake flour
  1/2 cup cocoa
  3 egg whites, at room temperature
  1/8 teaspoon cream of tartar
  1 tablespoon sugar
  1/3 cup butter, melted and cooled

Meringue:
  5 pasteurized egg whites, at room
    temperature
  3/4 teaspoon cream of tartar
  2/3 cup sugar
  1/3 cup cocoa
Garnish:
  Stemmed maraschino cherries (optional)

To mold ice cream: Firmly pack softened ice cream into 1-quart mixing bowl lined with aluminum foil. Cover with plastic wrap. Freeze completely, at least 2 hours or overnight.

To make cake: Butter 8-inch round cake pan. Dust with 1 teaspoon cocoa. Beat egg yolks and 2/3 cup sugar until lemon colored. Add vanilla. Sift together cake flour and 1/2 cup cocoa. Beat egg whites with cream of tartar until foamy. Continue beating while gradually adding 1 tablespoon sugar. Beat until stiff peaks form. Into yolk-sugar mixture, alternately fold sifted dry ingredients and beaten egg whites. Fold in cooled butter. Pour into prepared pan. Bake in 350-degree oven for 20 to 25 minutes. (Note: Do not overbake.) Cool.

To construct dessert: Place cake layer on 9- or 10-inch board, small cookie sheet or ovenproof plate. Unmold ice cream. Place on cake layer. Return to freezer while preparing meringue.

To make the meringue: In large mixing bowl, whip egg whites and cream of tartar at high speed until frothy. Gradually add sugar. Beat until soft peaks form. Slowly add cocoa, beating at high speed until all cocoa is dissolved. Remove from mixer. Using rubber scraper, carefully fold mixture until it is uniform in color.

To bake: Remove cake and ice cream from freezer. Spread meringue evenly over top and sides of ice cream and around cake layer completely down to plate. (Note: Take care to cover all air holes so meringue insulates ice cream.) Bake in 450-degree oven for 5 minutes, or until lightly toasted. Remove from oven. Serve immediately, or cover and freeze until needed. Garnish with stemmed cherries.

Burgeoning Health Bread

June 27

Health food was taking hold. While writing about a grain-rich bread, I railed:

The health-food movement costs too much. People wishing to improve their health by eating organically grown and nonprocessed foods are burdened by prices twice that of ordinary foods.

Times change. Today, quality and selection are vastly improved, and "organic" now has positive connotations.

Fading from cost commentary to humor in that column, I wrote about Raisin Health Bread:

Making the bread can be quite hilarious. The recipe for these no-knead loaves suggests it takes 2 1/2 hours for the dough to rise. I must have had overactive yeast because within an hour, the dough doubled. I punched it down and divided bundles of the sticky stuff among three bread pans. Within 15 minutes, dough was drooping over the edges. I kept folding it back in, but it kept spilling over like floodwaters on a dike.

I put the bread in the oven and sat crosslegged on the floor to watch the action through the glass door. A cookie sheet was at my side, ready to be tossed into the oven in case the bread cascaded out of the pans. The loaves rose visibly and rapidly in the heat, but not enough to overflow. After 10 minutes, the vigil was no longer necessary.

A reader says . . .

Many of the recipes that have been in your column are in my file, used over and over again, enjoyed each and every time.

— Betty Barrett, St. Paul

RAISIN HEALTH BREAD

Makes 3 loaves

1 cup natural raisins
1 cup golden raisins
4 cups warm water
3 packages yeast
4 cups warm water
3 eggs, beaten
1/3 cup plus 1 tablespoon shortening, melted
3/4 cup honey
1 tablespoon salt
3/4 cup nonfat dry milk
1/2 cup wheat germ
1 1/2 cups cracked wheat
3/4 cup sunflower seeds (unsalted)
7 cups whole-wheat flour
1 egg white
1 tablespoon water

Plump raisins in warm water. Set aside. In very large bowl, dissolve yeast in 4 cups warm water. Add eggs, shortening and honey. Stir until thoroughly blended. Add salt, nonfat dry milk, wheat germ, cracked wheat, sunflower seeds and plumped raisins, mixing well after each addition. Work in whole-wheat flour. Mix until completely blended. Cover. Let rise for 2 1/2 hours, or until double in bulk. Punch down dough. Place in 3 greased 1-pound loaf pans. Combine egg white and water. Brush on tops of loaves. Let rise until doubled. Bake in 375-degree oven for 45 to 50 minutes, or until bread tests done.

1972

*— Turning off the stove, but turning up
the heat with chilies and hot dish —*

Pull the Plug
April 30

We endured our first kitchen remodeling in 1972. My dad, a cabinetmaker, installed dark walnut Formica-faced cabinets. Countertops and appliances were harvest gold, and flooring was a brown and gold Spanish-style vinyl — all so stylish in the early 1970s. We lived with that somber kitchen until 1989, when much more cheerful white cabinets were in vogue.

I tried to keep testing recipes during the 1972 remodeling chaos, but plans to bake some bars were stymied when I heard the flooring man say, "Now, let's disconnect the stove."

Chilly About Chilies
February 27

My, how tender our palates were in 1972, viewed from current times, when we crave jalapenos, Thai chilies and Szechuan stir-fries. On that February Sunday, a small dose of chili powder in a tater-topped beef casserole made us wary:

I told my husband about the 2 teaspoons of chili powder. When Chili Beef emerged from the oven, he stood stoveside and cautiously tasted a cheese potato from the topping, announcing, "I'm afraid of this. I'm really afraid of this." His tender tummy, you know.

At our house that night was one of my husband's co-workers who was on his way home, where his wife had supper waiting. When the hot dish came out of the oven, he said bravely, "I'm not afraid to taste it." He did and proclaimed it to be very good. And it was. Chili made itself apparent without being overpowering. The three of us polished the casserole clean.

Hot About Hot Dish
March 19

On the subject of hot dish, Mrs. D.A. Wickland of St. Paul had a definite opinion:

"You discussed 'hot dish' and called it a Middle America term. I'm from Ohio originally — a middle America state — and 'hot dish' is definitely not part of my vocabulary. I have lived in seven mid-continent states — North Dakota, Oklahoma, Nebraska and

Minnesota among them — and your 'hot dish' terminology is used in only two of them.

"Since 'hot dish' is attached to such a variety of foods — from baked beans to scalloped potatoes to chili to spaghetti to you name it — I find it a totally worthless descriptive. 'Hot dish' can be equated with 'deal,' the catch-all term of a few years ago. It's as meaningless. I make all sorts of casseroles, but I've never put an empty dish in the oven and heated it — my understanding of a 'hot dish.' "

Best "Guests"
July 9

It drives my husband crazy that I'm never specific when I invite people over. Writing about a casual weekend get-together:

"Come about 2:30 or 3 p.m." I told the guests, thinking most would show up about 3:30. One friend, determined for once to be on time, arrived at 2:30 while I was madly vacuuming. At moments like these, true character and strength of friendship are tested.

My friend and her husband — we were meeting him for the first time — pitched in. He kept the kids busy. She took over the vacuum cleaner, then swept the back deck while I tackled the kitchen mess. As

other guests arrived, I put them to work helping with the food and setting the table.

You know, if I were invited to my house for dinner, I'd think twice.

The Shrimp Swims Alone
December 17

Marinated shrimp will be among the snacks served at a holiday gathering today, and I recommend it for your parties as well. At least, I think I do.

How could I be writing about a recipe before I made it? Elementary, dear readers. I'm much too frugal to blow two pounds of shrimp for pre-party tasting. So I made the marinade and marinated one shrimp. That's right — one! It took a lot of fishing to locate that lonely crustacean in the big bowl of sauce. And the opinion that the soaked shrimp is good is mine alone.

A reader says . . .

I want your column, even before the crossword puzzle. It's rather like getting a letter from home!

— Corrine McNamara, Hastings, Minn.

A Sizzling Party Idea
November 12

Fondue pots were the hot gift item in 1972, and we all blithely entertained around a pot of boiling oil, which could cause third-degree burns if it spilled. Writing about a fondue party at which this recipe was a centerpiece, I mentioned a friend, who "fondues" frequently, had told me that adding a lump of butter to the boiling oil keeps it from sputtering when meat is cooked.

Somewhere in the 1980s, fondue pots started showing up in garage sales as that food fashion faded. But by the mid-1990s, fondue was back. That's what comes of writing a food column for so many years. One attains what the Chinese call "the long view."

BEEF `N BEER FONDUE
Makes 4 servings

Beef:
    1 1/2 pounds beef tenderloin, cut in
        3/4-inch cubes
    Peanut oil
Marinade:
    1 cup beer
    1 teaspoon minced onion
    1/2 teaspoon salt
    1 1/2 teaspoons vinegar
    1/4 teaspoon lemon juice
    1 clove garlic, mashed
    1/4 teaspoon oregano
    1/4 teaspoon thyme

Beer-'radish sauce:
    1 package (8 ounces) cream cheese,
        softened
    2 1/2 tablespoons prepared horseradish
    2 tablespoons beer
Beer-onion sauce:
    2 tablespoons dry onion soup mix
    1/2 cup beer
    1 tablespoon prepared mustard
    1 cup sour cream

To marinate meat: Combine all marinade ingredients. Pour over cubed beef. Cover. Refrigerate. Marinate meat for 2 to 3 hours.

To make beer-'radish sauce: Whip cream cheese, horseradish and beer until fluffy. Refrigerate until ready to serve. (Makes 1 1/4 cups.)

To make beer-onion sauce: Combine onion soup mix and beer. Let stand for 5 minutes. Add mustard and sour cream. Heat thoroughly in small saucepan. (Makes 1 1/4 cups.)

To "fondue": Pour approximately 2 inches peanut oil into fondue pot. Heat on top of stove. When oil is hot, transfer pot — carefully — to fondue burner. Drain marinade from beef. Discard marinade. Spear meat with fondue forks. Cook in hot oil. Dip into sauces.

Have Some Chocolates, Please!

November 5

Getting a head start on the holidays, testing chocolate cherry cookies, I recalled:

My grandmother, bless her memory, gave me a box of chocolate-covered cherries every Christmas, from the time I was a kid until I got married. They were loaded with sticky-sweet syrup, and I detested them.

I'd thank Grandma profusely, and she never knew that I gave the candy away to others who were less picky. In fact, she was so sure I was crazy about chocolate cherries that she told other relatives, and some Christmases, I'd get three or four boxes.

Apple Pie for a New Generation of Moms

October 8

This isn't apple pie like mother used to make, but I'll bet mom asks for the recipe. This is apple pie for the new bride who doesn't own a rolling pin. This is apple pie for just about anybody because it tastes great, although more like apple crisp than pie.

Topping amounts here are what I suggested to readers because the original recipe made so much, you'd need an engineer to pile up streusel without creating landslides.

My Little Doughboy

December 3

Aric, sous chef in training:

When our 3-year-old wakes up mornings, his first words are, "Let's make cookies." He hauls a little step

WHOLE-WHEAT APPLE PIE

Makes 6 to 8 servings

Crust:
- 1 1/4 cups whole-wheat flour
- 2 teaspoons sugar
- 1 teaspoon salt
- 1/2 cup cooking oil
- 2 tablespoons milk

Filling:
- 2/3 cup sugar
- 2 tablespoons whole-wheat flour
- 1 teaspoon cinnamon
- 3 to 4 cups (4 medium) cooking apples, thinly sliced
- 1/2 cup dairy sour cream

Topping:
- 1/2 cup whole-wheat flour
- 1/3 cup firmly packed brown sugar
- 1/2 teaspoon cinnamon
- 1/4 cup butter or margarine, softened

To make crust: Combine flour, sugar, salt, oil and milk. Mix well. Pat in ungreased 9-inch pie pan.

To make filling: Combine sugar, flour, cinnamon, apples and sour cream. Spoon into unbaked crust.

To make topping: Combine flour, brown sugar, cinnamon and butter. Sprinkle over apples. Bake in 350-degree oven for 40 to 45 minutes, or until topping is golden brown.

stool to counterside and insists on being chief cook in charge of cracking eggs and spilling flour.

Standing on his little step stool so his tummy was at counter height, Aric got so floury and doughy while helping me make pumpkin doughnuts that he looked like a gingerbread man.

During holiday baking, Aric got very proprietary about the bowl of chocolate frosting being slathered on a chocolate yule log, and let me know that the cake decorating was interfering with his frosting eating. "Gol, Mom, you're using too much," he scolded.

Bubble Trouble With Pralines

March 12

This recipe for Creamy Pralines is a souvenir of Houston, where those of us attending the Pillsbury Bake-Off had lunch prepared by students at the University of Houston's home-economics department. Pralines were dessert. Theirs were a honey-blond hue. Mine, using the same recipe, were definitely brunette.

Because so many people were eager for a sample, I doubled the batch. Two teaspoons of soda make a mighty frothy mixture, which nearly bubbled over twice. The third time, it did. I yelled for my husband, who came running to help me transfer the mixture to a much larger kettle. Even so, it returned to the brink of overflowing several times. Start with a good-sized pot, especially for a double batch, and stir those bubbles down.

I couldn't decide whether to use vanilla or maple extract, so I added equal parts of each.

The pralines seemed to get better with age. If the batch had lasted beyond three days, who knows how good they might have become.

CREAMY PRALINES
Makes about 2 dozen

2 cups sugar
1 teaspoon soda
1/4 teaspoon salt
1 cup buttermilk
2 tablespoons butter or margarine
2 cups pecans
1 teaspoon vanilla or maple extract

In large saucepan, combine sugar, soda, salt and buttermilk. Quickly bring to a boil, stirring constantly, until candy thermometer reaches 210 degrees. Add butter and pecans. Cook over medium heat, stirring constantly, until mixture reaches 230 degrees. Remove from heat. Add flavoring. When bubbling stops, beat until candy loses its gloss. Drop by spoonfuls onto wax paper.

Pizza Gets Gourmet Glamour

October 15

Gourmet pizza as we know it today was yet to be discovered in 1972. Wolfgang Puck hadn't yet arrived on the food scene to introduce us to duck-sausage decorations, and the stuff of pizza parlors was pretty prosaic. This was the first pizza I'd tested for the column:

As I was raving about how wonderful Gourmet Pizza was, my more temperate husband reminded me it was 8 p.m., it had taken 90 minutes to construct the pizzas, and we were so hungry that our judgments were colored. I stood behind my appraisal, criticizing only the saltiness of the flaky, cheese-flavored crust (the recipe below has been adjusted to reduce saltiness, as was suggested on that October Sunday).

We were such penny-pinchers then. I told readers to conserve funds by purchasing mozzarella cheese in

brick form and grating it themselves. We saved 44 cents by doing the extra work.

As far as my mate was concerned, his best praise for this pizza is that it didn't make him reach for Rolaids.

GOURMET PIZZA
Makes 2 (12-inch) pizzas

Crust:
- 2 2/3 cups all-purpose flour
- 1/3 cup grated parmesan cheese
- 2 teaspoons baking powder
- 1/2 teaspoon salt
- 1/4 cup (1/2 stick) butter
- 1/4 cup lard
- 3/4 cup milk
- Parmesan cheese to dust pan

Filling:
- 2 pounds mild Italian sausage
- 1 can (8 ounces) tomato sauce

- 1 teaspoon oregano
- 1 teaspoon sweet basil, crumbled
- 1 clove garlic, minced

Toppings:
- 4 cups (16 ounces) grated mozzarella cheese, divided
- 4 medium tomatoes, thinly sliced
- 16 green pepper strips
- 1/2 pound small fresh mushrooms, thickly sliced
- 2 tablespoons melted butter
- 2 tablespoons grated parmesan cheese

To prepare crust: In large mixing bowl combine flour, parmesan cheese, baking powder and salt. Cut in butter and lard until mixture resembles coarse meal. Gradually add milk. Mix at low speed of electric mixer until mixture leaves side of bowl. Gather dough together. Press into ball. Knead dough in bowl 10 times, or until smooth. Divide in half. On lightly floured surface, roll each half into 13-inch circle. Transfer to 2 (12-inch) pizza pans, buttered and dusted with additional parmesan cheese. Partially bake in 425-degree oven for 9 minutes. Remove to wire racks to cool.

To prepare filling: In skillet, break sausage into bits. Brown lightly, stirring occasionally. Divide cooked sausage into 4 portions. Mix together tomato sauce, oregano, basil and garlic.

To assemble pizzas: Evenly distribute one-quarter of sausage over each crust. Sprinkle each with 1 cup mozzarella cheese. Cover with layer of tomato slices. Top with another portion of sausage. Pour half of tomato sauce mixture over sausage. Arrange pepper strips in spoke fashion to divide each pizza into 8 wedges. Arrange mushroom slices around outside edge. Brush with melted butter. Sprinkle on each pizza 1 cup mozzarella and 1 tablespoon parmesan cheese.

To bake: Bake in 425-degree oven for 20 to 25 minutes. Serve hot.

Variation: In place of sausage, substitute 4 medium onions, thinly sliced and sauteed in butter until transparent. If you like anchovies, use 4 ounces of the salty fish to replace the green pepper strips.

1973

— Energy shortages, energy savers, and we were the first on our block to invite microwave cookery into our home —

It's a Plastic World
March 25

Modern technology has its pitfalls for those who don't keep pace. We know an older gent who was taking a nap when Teflon was invented. While doing his wife the kindness of cleaning up the kitchen, he scrubbed and scrubbed her new griddle. He later berated her for burning the pan so badly that he could get only one corner cleaned down to the metal before he got tired. Destroyed: One new-fangled nonstick utensil.

Not long ago, a lady in a quandary called me. She had roasted some beef in a plastic bag just as the ads suggested, but when she took it out of the oven, the bag had disappeared. Where had it gone? Was the meat poisoned?

After we'd determined that she'd used a food-storage bag, not an oven-tempered bag for roasting meat, a call to the state poison-control office revealed she probably wouldn't die eating the plasticized meat. But, the poison expert suggested, if part of it tasted funny, she should cut that meat away. Lesson: Alligator bags (the kind she'd used) aren't tough enough for the oven.

Where's the Beef?
April 8

Meat prices leapt to costly levels. We were introduced to soy substitutes in such products as Juicy Burger II, a combination of soy protein and hamburger. We used it in Parmesan Beef Balls and thought it performed admirably while saving 40 cents per pound.

Ground turkey was becoming popular as a lowered-fat meat, generally selling for 69 cents a pound, until it became too popular, and prices went up while availability went down.

Do as Julia Says
May 20

Writing about a layered meatloaf:

Readers, I haven't had a cake fall out of the pan or other major disaster for quite a while, but I will always remember this as the meatloaf that fell in the sink. After it baked for 45 minutes, excess juices were to be drained. So there I was, draining juices into the sink, holding the meatloaf in the pan with a spatula, when a whole section let go.

Remembering Julia Child's philosophy that if no one is in the kitchen to see the roast fall on the floor, just pick it up, wipe it off and put it back on the platter, I shoveled the meatloaf from my clean sink back into the pan. Husband, if you are reading this, I apologize. But you're still alive, aren't you?

The next week, I noted a letter from Mrs. Peter J. Lindner who lived on St. Paul's Wheelock Parkway. She wrote that the meatloaf wouldn't have tumbled into the sink if a baster had been used to suck up the fat or liquid. Now, why didn't I think of that?

Filling Space
November 18

In a column that included a quite dreadful pumpkin soup recipe:

Some of you have asked why we run Tested Recipes that flunk the taste test. My usual answer is that I pledged, when this column was inaugurated, to run all recipes we try, A-plus or F-minus. Also, you've told me that the disasters make the most entertaining reading.

Sometimes, other factors are involved. Today's Family Life section is 22 pages and editor Mary Ann Grossmann (who could actually stomach the soup I brought to the office) said, "Run the recipe. I need all the copy I can get."

Those were the glory days of voluminous newspaper space, when two or three photos illustrated every Tested Recipes column.

Santa Brings a Big Gift
December 23

Santa Baby has visited my kitchen already, leaving a dandy new microwave oven for me to play with. Santa (also known as my husband) is experimenting with it daily, too. With the energy crunch on, we're saving electricity. My husband likes to put water in a cup in the microwave, and have hot instant-coffee water in a couple of minutes. It's convenient to heat it in the cup, but that little bit of water could be heated nearly as fast on our gas range.

Anything requiring longer cooking dramatically intensifies energy savings. To demonstrate the oven to a friend, we baked a potato in 3 minutes, and made brownies in 5 minutes. It would take longer than that to preheat a regular oven.

Two-Chicken Soup
February 25

Chicken soup has been in the news lately as an antidote to the common cold. Does that mean that chicken soup is so effective, or that other cold remedies are powerless?

That conundrum led a column featuring this substantial soup. The recipe called for a 5-pound chicken, which even then was hard to find. To get one of that weight we had to buy a roasting chicken at 79 cents a pound. What pudgy poultry it was! It was just plain old-fashioned fat — globby fat. Even the bones were yellow. Fryers or stewing chickens are a lot cheaper, and two 3-pounders would give ample meat for this protein-loaded soup.

Today's cooks don't demand such a high ratio of meat to vegetables. A single 3-pound chicken would be more than ample. Our salt tolerance is also lower these days, so you may wish to use reduced-sodium bouillon cubes.

SAVORY OLD-FASHIONED CHICKEN SOUP

Makes 8 generous servings

1 1/2 quarts water
1 teaspoon salt
1/4 teaspoon ground black pepper
1/4 teaspoon thyme leaves (or more to taste)
2 bay leaves
2 garlic cloves, split
A few celery leaves
1 chicken, 3 to 5 pounds
6 chicken bouillon cubes
4 cups shredded and chopped cabbage
4 medium carrots, cut into 1/2-inch slices
4 medium onions, quartered
1 cup frozen peas, thawed

In large kettle, combine water, salt, pepper, thyme, bay leaves, garlic and celery leaves. Rinse chicken under cold water. Place in kettle. Bring to a boil. Reduce heat. Simmer, covered, for 1 1/2 hours, or until chicken is tender. Remove chicken. Cut meat into bite-size pieces. Discard skin and bones. Strain broth. Let stand for 5 minutes. Skim fat from broth. Return broth to kettle. Add bouillon cubes. Heat, stirring, until dissolved. Add cabbage, carrots and onions. Simmer for 20 minutes, or until vegetables are tender. Add chicken pieces and peas. Simmer 5 minutes, or until peas are cooked. Serve in tureen. Offer lots of crackers.

Gone in a Flash

January 14

You may think the shortest recorded interval of time is that instant between the traffic light turning green and the guy behind you laying on his horn. Not

MARMALADE BUNS

Makes 10 rolls

3 cups sifted all-purpose flour
4 teaspoons baking powder
1/2 teaspoon salt
1/2 cup butter or margarine
1 cup milk
1 cup orange marmalade
1/2 cup chopped raisins
1/2 cup finely chopped nuts

To make buns: Into large bowl, sift together flour, baking powder and salt. Using pastry blender or 2 knives, cut in butter until mixture is in fine, even crumbs. Add milk. Stir only until ingredients are moistened. Turn dough onto lightly floured board. Knead 10 or 12 times, or until smooth ball is formed.

To bake buns: Roll dough on floured surface to 10-by-16-inch oblong. In small bowl, mix orange marmalade, raisins and nuts. Spread evenly over dough. Roll up as for jellyroll, starting at 16-inch side. Cut roll into 10 slices. Place slices, cut side down, in heavily buttered 9-inch round cake pan. Bake in 400-degree oven for 35 to 40 minutes, or until done and lightly browned. Serve warm.

so. It's the time it takes for the office crew to demolish a pan of Marmalade Buns.

These quick sweet rolls were described as a stir-and-roll mixture tasting much like biscuit dough. You might get similar results with Bisquick.

A Burning Issue
July 15

"I read somewhere," said my husband, returning from inspecting the grilling spareribs, "that the secret of great barbecue is to char the outside of the meat and then saturate the crust with sauce."

"Does that mean," I asked suspiciously, "that the ribs are already charred?"

Of course, they were, but these ribs were great once past the most charcoal-hued portions. Horseradish and Tabasco give them character. I said at the time that the ribs could also be broiled or baked. Now, I might mention that parboiling the ribs shortens time on the grill, creating less chance for them to match the charcoal over which they're cooked.

A reader says . . .

I love your column and want you to know you are responsible for many of my successes in the kitchen. I was chicken to try new recipes until I started reading your column. Testing Results are such a big help. Because of them, I've avoided some of the pitfalls that seem to occur when I try other recipes.

— Belinda Dalton, New Richmond, Wis.

BEER-BARBECUED SPARERIBS
Makes 6 to 8 servings

6 pounds spareribs (3 racks)
Sauce:
    2 cups ketchup
    4 tablespoons horseradish
    2 teaspoons steak sauce
    1/2 teaspoon garlic powder
    1 teaspoon whole celery seed
    1/2 teaspoon sage
    1 teaspoon Tabasco sauce
    2 small onions, finely chopped
    1 teaspoon salt
    2 tablespoons soy sauce
    1 cup beer
    2/3 cup dark brown sugar
    Juice of 2 lemons

To grill ribs: Have butcher crack ribs to facilitate carving after they're cooked. Grill ribs on rack 6 inches above gray-hot coals. Brush with sauce every few minutes. Turn frequently until done.

To make sauce: In saucepan, combine all remaining ingredients. Bring to a boil. Simmer over medium-low heat, uncovered, for 5 minutes, stirring constantly. Makes 4 cups sauce. Use 2 cups sauce for basting ribs. Reserve remaining 2 cups in saucepan to reheat when spareribs are finished barbecuing.

To serve: Place barbecued ribs on large serving platter. Pour remaining 2 cups sauce over them.

1974

— A new critic, critical shortages, metric, monster cookies and bowlful of cherries —

Critiquing the Cook
April 14

"Is she a good cook?" is the inevitable question to families of food writers. (These days, the questioner might phrase that, "Is he a good cook?" since more and more men are established in what was mostly a woman's domain when I started this job.)

My food-editor friend, Janice Okun of the Buffalo (N.Y.) News, says her husband always gives the same answer to that query: "We eat out a lot."

My husband hasn't standardized his response, but he always says nice things, bless him. Do I get the same loyalty from the newest member of our family, my 16-year-old stepson, Scott, who's been with us since last summer? When he tells friends he's boarding at a food writer's table, he gets the standard question. He allows that I can cook OK, "but she has to try such weird things."

Augmenting Aric's standard "yuck" about recipes he didn't like, we're getting "gross" or "puke" from Scott. His assessments are brutal. When I gave him meant-for-breakfast Sausage Drop Cookies, he said with typical teen-age tact, "This looks like something you found in the back yard." Though I usually beg tasters for their opinions, Scott was told to "eat it and

keep your comments to yourself" after he kept up a steady tirade about Eggs Mornay Supreme during one testing dinner. He covered his eyes, maintaining it didn't taste too bad if he didn't have to look at it. Oh, the grief he gives me!

But there are occasional compensations to joining a food writer's household, he admits, "especially on the nights she's testing two kinds of strawberry shortcake. Far out!"

How Sweet It Isn't
September 1

Sugar prices rose 400 percent in 1974. When food prices were forecasted by Senator George McGovern to rise 30 percent, it was enough to rattle our pots and pans. By May, a national canned-goods allotment was in effect until the new sugar crop came in, and store shelves were emptying by early summer.

While the Tested Recipes column appeared inside the Family Life section, that summer I wrote a 10-part series for the section's cover on "Winning the Food Game," trying to find economies for readers. One segment, for which we requested rationing recipes from World War II, drew hundreds of reader responses.

For several weeks, just after we learned that retail sugar prices would soon be at $4 for 10 pounds — big money back then — we tested recipes using half the designated amounts of sugar. Results were totally acceptable.

Readers responded after they, too, trimmed sugar in recipes. The most amusing letter was printed on October 13, from a lady who wished to be known only as Nan:

"After I read several weeks ago about cutting sugar in recipes, I tried it with apple squares. This being one of my family's favorites, I was understandably nervous. I used tart apples and would have normally added 1 1/2 cups sugar. I cut it to 2/3 cup and held my breath waiting for screams of outrage. Nobody even noticed! I had to tell our resident mouth, friend husband, what I had done. Now to say this man is frugal is to say the Mississippi is a creek. He smiled for the first time since John F. Kennedy was elected!"

Stretching It Too Thin
August 11

"Is this one of those meat-stretcher recipes?" my husband asked when served an Italian spinach bake that serves six with a half-pound of ground beef. "I'd rather see less 'stretch' and more meat" was his assessment as he muttered something about our not being in a depression yet.

We might have thought prices were high then, but while assembling this book, I noted, printed on the back of that August 11 column, a consumer column comparing meat prices in June 1973, before they started to jump; January 1974, when they were peaking, and June 1974, as they began to drop. At their height, chopped beef chuck (now called lean ground beef) was $1.17 a pound; round steak was $1.94; pork loin was $1.09; and chicken was 63 cents a pound. Large eggs rose to 96 cents a dozen. Now, that's something we'd cackle about even today.

Yogurt Rebellions
October 13

This little marital interchange makes me laugh now that husband eats yogurt daily. But in 1974, I related this conversation:

Husband: What's in this pie?

Me: Cranberries and yogurt.

He: Yogurt! Then, I don't like it.

Me: You ate Pear Yogurt muffins yesterday.

He: Did they have yogurt in them? If I'd known that, I wouldn't have liked them, either."

> **Zucchini bread was becoming the rage, and we ran a recipe enriched with wheat germ on November's first Sunday: In one neighborhood, we hear that the roving kaffee klatsch is held at a different home every morning, and the treat is always zucchini bread.**

Hot and Cold on Souffles
January 6

When chocolate souffle made a January appearance:

I tried to compare it with other chocolate souffles I've tasted, but after a good deal of memory dredging, I couldn't recall ever having one before. No wonder. It's one of those critical desserts that waits for no one. Serve it immediately, or watch it deflate into a brown lump.

About that time, dessert souffles began popping up in restaurants, notably at the Sofitel in Bloomington, south of Minneapolis, the first French hotel built in America. Diners ordered souffle before salad was served, so it could be timed to arrive at the table an instant before all the air whooshed out.

A couple of weeks after experimenting with hot chocolate souffle, I tried a cold Brandy Alexander souffle during a particularly nerve-wracking dinner. Our guests were the owner and chef of St. Paul's best restaurant. The dessert named after a drink was a diet version with the flavor but not the expected creamy richness. It was light and frothy and generally acceptable, although one of our guests thought it tasted like Coke foam.

Measuring Interest in Metric
April 7

Metric measurements started appearing in recipes I received in 1974, as this country contemplated joining the rest of the world, using grams and liters. I (wrongly) predicted:

Metric terms are a foreign language to most of us now, but within the decade we'll be dealing with them daily. Food experts say that recipes will be written in rounded figures, 100 grams of sugar instead of 104, for instance. Thank goodness. I just hope they don't make us turn in our familiar measuring spoons and cups when the changeover comes.

We're nearing the millennium, and metric hasn't come to American cooking yet. Good thing we kept those measuring utensils.

The Secret's in the Pan
December 22

While we were on vacation, I'd missed the furor and phone calls caused by a cranberry bread recipe that ran during my absence. Readers reported many disasters. One sent me a soggy-looking slice to prove her point. Since it had molded by the time I got back to open my mail, I didn't dare taste it.

It turned out the recipe was correct, though it called for less leavening than other quick loaves. I dashed home to make another batch, carefully measuring the soda. The loaf raised enough, although it was by no means towering, but neither was my first batch. It definitely wasn't soggy. Perhaps the difference was that I used a glass loaf pan at 350 degrees, which would intensify the baking, I told readers just before Christmas.

The column continued to be a learning experience.

Monster Cookies for Cookie Monster
October 5

Aric, our resident Cookie Monster, is matriculating in kindergarten this year, and he complains daily that the bitty cookie he gets for snack is gone long before his milk carton is emptied. His teacher won't let him bring an extra cookie just for himself, so he's been campaigning that we should bake a batch for the entire class.

These days, homemade treats aren't allowed in most schools, but back then, we made a double batch, and they were all gobbled by his classmates. This recipe was a harbinger of the supersize cookies that soon would be sold by Mrs. Fields and her cronies. I said at the time that these monsters would become a standard in our house, even replacing classic chocolate-chippers. Aric had a reason: "These cookies have protein in them," he said righteously, reaching for another.

WHEAT-GERM SAUCER COOKIES
Makes 10 (4-inch) cookies

1/2 cup butter, softened
1/2 cup brown sugar, packed
1/2 cup granulated sugar
1 egg
3/4 teaspoon vanilla
3/4 cup regular wheat germ
3/4 cup flour
1 teaspoon baking powder
1/2 teaspoon salt
1/4 cup flaked coconut
1/4 cup quick oats, uncooked
1/2 cup semisweet chocolate pieces

Beat butter with sugars until blended. Beat in egg and vanilla. Mix wheat germ with flour, baking powder and salt. Fold in coconut, oats and chocolate chips. Stir into butter mixture. Place dough by 1/4-cupfuls onto greased baking sheet, about 6 inches apart. Bake in 375-degree oven for 15 to 17 minutes or until golden brown and centers are firm. Cool for 2 to 3 minutes on baking sheet. Transfer to rack. To keep cookies crisp, store in loosely covered container.

Frosting on Cake of Woes
December 29

The end of '74 was a downer. We took a vacation right before Christmas, which meant all the preparations were compressed into a few days. And our house was burglarized while we were away, so there was all that heartache and paperwork to deal with, too. "Cheer up," my husband ordered during one of my low points.

Well, you all know what cheers me up in the food department. Together now, shout it out: Chocolate Cake! For that Sunday, I tried a chocolate cream cake with frosting just in the middle:

This cake reminds me of a grade-school revelation. I'll never forget the day a friend ate a piece of cake that had the frosting in the middle. To avoid losing half the frosting on the wax paper, her mom sliced the piece of sheet cake in half and turned the frosting inward. I really thought that was an inspiration, considering all the times I'd licked wax paper to get every smidgen of frosting.

Life's a Bowl of Cherries
July 4

This dessert topping appeared PC — pre-computer — though we may have graduated to electric typewriters by then:

Looking at my stained fingers on the typewriter keys as I write this is a reminder of the tedious job of quartering and pitting cherries for this sauce, which can be spooned lavishly over ice cream, layered in a parfait, or used to flavor a soda. Once the cherries are chopped, the job is knocked. Cooking the sauce takes less than five minutes.

After the recipe appeared, Doris Philipson of St. Paul wrote to suggest that a touch of almond extract enhanced the sauce even more. Instead of ice cream, she spoons the sauce over squares of almond-flavored white cake, topped with whipped cream dosed with 1/2 teaspoon almond extract and 1 teaspoon sugar.

"Place a fresh cherry, stem intact, on top of the cream. It's lovely to look at and oh, so yummy," Philipson suggested to Tested Recipes readers.

SWEET-CHERRY ICE-CREAM SAUCE
Makes 2 cups

2 cups pitted and quartered fresh sweet cherries
1/2 cup sugar
1/4 cup water
1/4 cup light corn syrup
2 tablespoons cornstarch
2 tablespoons water
1 tablespoon lemon juice

In saucepan, combine cherries, sugar, 1/4 cup water and corn syrup. Blend cornstarch with 2 tablespoons water. Add to cherry mixture. Cook over low heat, stirring constantly, until thickened. Stir in lemon juice.

We Cluck, Aric Yucks
June 9

"As good as any I've had in a restaurant," said my husband about these low-calorie patties. He was in charge of frying the Oriental griddle cakes and found he needed more shortening. Also, some of the foo yungs split when flipped.

Aric, with typical 5-year-old distaste for anything new, said "Yu-u-u-ck" and refused to eat Eggs Foo Yung. That was OK with us, but he got the usual ultimatum about not getting anything else. Thus coerced, he managed to down one small serving. Later, little diplomat that he can be, he said, "Mom, let's have those Chinese pancakes again sometime." Such music to my ears! Such a moral victory! Such a crafty kid, making brownie points against the day he'll have to taste something he really hates.

EGGS FOO YUNG
Makes 4 servings

Patties:
4 eggs
1 tablespoon milk
1/2 teaspoon salt
1/2 small onion, halved
1 can water chestnuts, drained
1 can bean sprouts, drained
1 can broken shrimp pieces, drained
1 tablespoon butter or margarine
Sauce:
3/4 cup water
1 tablespoon cornstarch
2 tablespoons soy sauce
1 tablespoon sugar
1 tablespoon cider vinegar

To make patties: Place all patty ingredients, except shrimp and butter, in blender container. Cover. Process at high speed until blended. Stir in shrimp. Melt butter in frying pan or on griddle. Using 1/4 cup measure per patty, pour batter onto preheated surface. When browned, turn. Brown other side. Place patties on warm serving platter.

To make sauce: Combine all sauce ingredients in saucepan. Heat until clear and slightly thickened.

Note: Leftover pork, chicken or beef cubes can be used instead of shrimp.

1975

*— More fiber and beans, fewer canning lids,
turkey on the trail, parched pie —*

A Good Scrubbing

January 12

We faced up to the need for fiber in '75. I was writing about it elsewhere in the paper, and bringing the message to Sunday Tested Recipes readers as well. When Bran Brown Bread and Bran English muffins were what we awoke to in early January, I said, "Innards, have I got some recipes for you!" Made with sawdust-like unprocessed bran flakes, one of those healthful foods we were learning about, that raw ingredient "came through baking as sturdy and bulky as it was in the bag. I can see those flakes scrub-a-dub-dubbing their way through my GI tract."

> **Meat and sugar shortages were no longer cramping our cooking style, but in the summer of '75, shelves emptied of lids and rings as the nation took to home canning as a money-saver.**

Bag This Pie

February 23

Apple pie baked in a bag was tested, because I thought bagging would brown the crust and contain the drips, a la turkey baked in a bag (popular then, but no longer recommended):

For pie, this method is a turkey. I stuffed the pie into a large brown grocery bag and coaxed that into the small upper oven on my range. When my husband arrived home a short time later, his first words were, "What's burning?" It was the bag, of course, getting crinkly and charred at 425 degrees. He reminded me that paper burns at 451 degrees. It never did actually burst into flames, but fly ash flew around the oven. And the drips soaked through the bag and poured into the oven, then onto the stovetop when I took the pie and the remains of the bag out of the oven after an hour's baking. The crust was gorgeous, but I'm sure if it had baked another 15 minutes as the recipe suggests, it, like the bag, would have been charcoal.

So what's the purpose of the bag unless you like ashes with your pie? It doesn't reduce baking time nor can you save energy by cooking at lower heat. It was an intriguing idea, but it proves you can't improve good old apple pie.

Meet Orville and Euell
March 9

"Yes, friends, there is an Orville Redenbacher," I told readers after he had visited me at the newspaper office. "Orville's a tall, skinny gent who looks as if he never succumbed to a bowl of buttered popcorn in his life."

Though it wasn't written for a Tested Recipes column, I think it was about 1975 that another tall fellow, naturalist and wild-foods scrounger Euell Gibbons came to see me. Rather than just interview him in the office, we went across the Mississippi River from downtown St. Paul, wading through knee-deep snow, as I asked him to do a little winter foraging. We found dried wild grapes and remnants of summer's wild asparagus, not enough for a meal, but enough to prove his theory.

My Husband, My Cook
November 16

My husband was my co-cook, always ready with great ideas, such as adding a slug of vodka to cheese fondue or cheese sauce to smooth it out should it become grainy. In 1975, he took French cooking lessons and was proudly producing tiny apple tarts and spinach-crusted tortes. "I take solace that, despite his new-found training, he underbaked the tart shells. We are two of a kind in the kitchen, after all," I reported.

By November, he was doing more than his share: Hallelujah! I now have a live-in cook. With bedroom privileges. Before you think I'm sinning with the hired help, here's the scoop: My husband has a new business that permits him to get home earlier than I do. Several days last week, he fixed dinner. I was greeted, after an extra-long day at the office, with candles and chilled wine glasses on the table. That's the ultimate liberation for a working woman.

But I was a bit amused (after years of waiting for him to get home in time for dinner) at being berated for being late. "The broccoli's cheese sauce is watery because it was in the oven too long waiting for you," he chided. Oh, how the shoe pinches on the other foot. But I didn't let him see my wry grin. No way am I going to discourage this new arrangement.

His best contribution of 1975 was kebabs made by soaking beef, peppers and onion in Southern Comfort before grilling. We liked them so much that we made that same "Comfort food" for a dinner party, but soaked the ingredients for 48 hours. At the dinner table, my husband decided to flame the high-proof kebabs for extra drama. It was dramatic all right — the fire wouldn't go out.

A Blessed Mess
March 16

By this time, readers knew that I told all. About cooking in my robe and slippers, about all the goofs, about coping with crazy cooking situations. One predawn March morning I was mixing Irish soda bread and realized I didn't have any yeast:

While I was rooting around in the flour drawer, searching for yeast, the buttermilk-margarine mixture started to boil, had to be discarded, and a second panful heated. No matter how slowly you heat it (I learned the second time), buttermilk will separate into nearly clear liquid topped with floating curds. Do not be alarmed.

Meanwhile, way in the back of the drawer under a box of cake flour, I found one beat-up packet of yeast dated January 1974. What the heck — it was better than getting dressed and trying to find a grocery store open at that hour.

This should dispel any notions you may have that we test recipes in an immaculate kitchen from 9 to 5, me in a starched white uniform a la the Betty Crocker home economists. My kitchen is classified by a needlepointed motto which reads "Bless This Mess."

Beans:
Bring in the Troops
January 19

"Anyone in the mood for a bean feed? Come on over — I've got a potful that could feed the Swedish army, if there is one." Two pounds of dry beans cook into a mighty batch, filling my biggest Dutch oven. Ersatz Swedish brown beans, I called them, because they were made with pinto beans, "which is probably making all you good Swedish cooks gnash your teeth." The recipe called for pinto beans on the theory that brown beans are hard to find. It took getting on my hands and knees in the grocery-store aisle to find pinto beans at the back of the bottom shelf, so they're not easily available, either. (Now, it's easy to find most varieties of dry beans.)

Being Finnish, with no brown beans in my heritage, I can't say if pinto beans compare with the real thing. My husband, the family bean connoisseur (if you call a person who eats them cold out of a can a connoisseur) thought these tasted like doctored-up canned beans. But as the recipe says, they improve with reheating.

SWEDISH SWEET-AND-SOUR "BROWN" BEANS
Feeds a crowd

Beans:
- 2 pounds (4 2/3 cups) pinto beans
- 12 cups water
- 1/2 teaspoon baking soda
- 4 teaspoons salt
- 4 tablespoons cooking oil, butter or bacon drippings

Broth:
- 3 slices bacon, cut in 1-inch pieces
- 1/4 cup diced onion
- 1 medium clove garlic, sliced

- 1/4 teaspoon coarse-grind black pepper
- 1/4 teaspoon dry mustard
- 1/4 cup light molasses
- 1 cup ketchup
- 1 to 3 shakes Tabasco sauce
- 1 teaspoon Worcestershire sauce
- 1 1/2 cups light brown sugar
- 1/2 cup cider vinegar
- 3 tablespoons cornstarch mixed with 1/4 cup cold water

To soak beans: In large kettle, bring water to a boil. Add washed beans. Boil for 2 minutes only. Remove from heat. Add soda to cut down cooking time. Cover. Let stand for 1 hour. (Note: Or soak beans with soda in cold water overnight.)

To cook beans: Put kettle of beans with soaking water on high heat. Add salt and oil, butter or bacon drippings to keep down foam. Bring to a boil. Reduce heat to simmer. Cover tightly. Cook for 2 hours, or just until tender.

To flavor and bake beans: Mix together all broth ingredients. Add to cooked, drained beans. Stir carefully with wooden spoon to avoid breaking beans. Cover. Cook slowly over low heat for 1 hour. Or bake, covered tightly, in 325-degree oven for 1 1/2 hours. Serve hot. (Note: Flavor improves with standing and reheating.)

A Pot Roast to Adopt
February 23

People in the East have some pretty funny ideas about Minnesota — that it's still frontier country peopled by Indians in teepees, lumberjacks and dirt farmers living in sod huts. Kind of like Little House on the Prairie 1975.

When a recipe named Minnesota Chuck Roast came to me from a New York food firm, I saw the same down-on-the-farm thinking applied. Does anyone know of a Minnesotan who makes pot roast with apple juice and turnips? This we had to try.

Well, friends, if no one ever made this in Minnesota before, maybe we should add it to our food tradition. The meat was so tender and flavorful in the apple-vinegar juice (like sauerbraten; let's credit Minnesotans of German extraction) that we had to lift it out of the pan in chunks.

Looking at this recipe again with '90s eyes, how strange to see ingredients include MSG. That flavor enhancer has become a culinary stranger. Replace a portion of it with garlic powder, if you wish.

Some recipes are temperamental and shouldn't be tampered with, especially if the dish is destined for company. Chocolate Rainbow Dessert is the tamperee; I was the tamperer. Although the finished dish was delish, probably a bit more for my meddling, it looked more like a mudslide after a cloudburst than a rainbow. — October 5

MINNESOTA CHUCK ROAST
Makes 6 servings

3-pound beef chuck roast
1 1/2 teaspoons monosodium glutamate (optional)
1 1/2 teaspoons salt, divided
1/4 teaspoon pepper
3 tablespoons vegetable oil
3 carrots, pared and cut in half
2 onions, sliced
2 cups apple juice
2 cups water
1/4 cup red-wine vinegar
1 bay leaf
1/4 teaspoon dried leaf basil
1/2 large turnip or 1 medium yellow turnip, pared and cut in large cubes
3 potatoes, pared and cut in half
2 apples, pared and cut in large slices

Sprinkle roast on both sides with MSG, 1 teaspoon salt and pepper. Heat oil in Dutch oven. Brown roast on both sides. Add carrots, onions, apple juice, water, vinegar, bay leaf and basil. Cover. Simmer for 2 hours. Add turnip, potatoes and apples. Cover. Simmer for 30 minutes. Remove turnip and potatoes from Dutch oven. Place in mixer bowl. Add 1/2 cup liquid from pan and remaining 1/2 teaspoon salt. Beat at medium speed until light and fluffy. Remove bay leaf. Serve sliced meat with mashed vegetables, remaining pan vegetables, apple slices and liquid (thickened with flour or cornstarch, if desired).

Turkey on the Rocks

July 6

Cooking conditions weren't exactly hygienic, but northwoods seasonings — a few pine needles, ashes, smudges and smoke from the campfire — made our Canoe Country tested turkey delicious. Even discounting that we had ravenous outdoor appetites and were amazed to be eating a turkey dinner miles from the nearest kitchen conveniences, on a scale of 1 to 10, Grilled Half Turkey rated an 11.

We hauled a solidly frozen cooler full of groceries on a Boundary Waters canoe adventure with four friends, and we ate in high style for four days. The turkey was still slightly frozen in the center when we started cooking. My husband appointed himself chief fire-tender and coals-watcher. For two hours before the

Chief fire-tender and turkey-turner grills a foil-protected turkey for a Canoe Country feast.

GRILLED HALF TURKEY

Makes 6 servings

1 turkey half, about 5 to 6 pounds
1 tablespoon freshly grated orange peel
1/2 cup freshly squeezed orange juice
1/4 cup olive or vegetable oil
1 teaspoon dried rosemary, crushed
1 teaspoon salt
1/4 teaspoon pepper

Wrap turkey in 2 sheets of heavy-duty foil. Tightly seal 3 sides. Combine remaining ingredients. Pour over turkey through open end of foil. Seal foil. Place turkey on grill about 6 inches above medium coals. Cook for 3 to 3 1/2 hours, turning every hour. Open foil. Let turkey stand for 10 to 15 minutes before carving.

turkey hit the grill, he burned wood from a dead cedar tree. Fresh oranges supplied the juice and peel, minced with a hunting knife for lack of a grater. One teaspoon dried rosemary toted from home in a plastic sandwich bag was adequately crushed in the pack sack.

Once on the grill, the turkey required scant attention, leaving us little to do except read and admire the scenery. After three hours, was that turkey done! Cedar coals fanned by a gentle lake breeze supplied more heat than a backyard charcoal fire.

Thanksgiving dinner on the rocks is what we had — eating on a rock ledge, thankful that the weather was good and the bugs weren't bad. For lack of cranberry sauce, we mixed orange marmalade with blackberry jam — terrific! For lack of plain flour, orange-flavored turkey drippings were thickened with biscuit mix. Instant mashed potatoes plus corn and beans flavored with leftover country vegetable soup (the first course) were washed down with plastic cupfuls of chablis. Who says you can't eat well in the woods?

FIRST PLACE

Jury Duty

— *Judging America's Food Contests* —

I've helped distribute nigh unto a million bucks judging recipe contests, a ful**filling** task, a huge responsibility and sometimes a very funny experience.

Waiting for entries to arrive during the 1977 National Pineapple Cooking Classic in Honolulu, my food-editor friends and I got to telling hilarious tales about our previous judging experiences.

Betsy Balsley, then food editor for the Los Angeles Times, topped us all. She once awarded first prize in a cherry-pie contest to an apple pie. "All the cherry pies were so bad," she explained.

Her most breathless judging occurred while rating entries in a homemade ice-cream contest during her years as food editor for the Honolulu Advertiser. "Competitors were as fierce as the competition," she recalled. "After we judges had tasted everything, we ran halfway up Black Point hill, yelled out the name of the winner, and raced to our cars in the parking lot." Losers were in hot pursuit.

A reader says . . .

Thanks for cooking up a storm and helping the rest of us attempt to do the same.

— Cindy Leines, Wayzata, Minn.

Betsy Balsley knows how to cut and run when judging food contests.

Chicken Jokes

August 2, 1981

My dad, who was a bit hard of hearing, had been told I was going to judge the 1981 National Chicken Cooking Contest. Shortly thereafter, he told a friend that I was going to judge a Chicken Plucking Contest — and what did I know about plucking chickens?

I was to have judged that contest — cooking, not plucking — the year before, but I couldn't leave my dying mother. So I asked food-writer friend Janice Okun of the Buffalo (N.Y.) News to go in my stead. I later told readers that, according to Janice, the best cackle during the competition was a "pregnant" whole baked chicken. It arrived in the judging room on a platter, flat on its back, legs skyward, a whole apple stuffed in its tummy. The judging team dubbed it "gynecologist's delight."

Bake-Off Bars Brouhaha

March 3, 1974

Judging sometimes was agonizing, such as the time I tasted nearly 100 apple pies at a Lake City, Minn., harvest festival. At other contests, judging was controversial. Originality of winning recipes was usually the issue. Consider this Pillsbury Bake-Off brouhaha concerning charges that 1974's $25,000-winning Chocolate Cherry Bar recipe was possibly plagiarized:

The day after the winning recipe ran in my column, I received a letter from Mrs. Morris W. Nelson of Willmar, Minn., who wrote that the bars were not original. She had the recipe and sent it for publication to Minnesota's Kandiyohi County Electric Co-Op newsletter last August.

Nelson was aware that one Bake-Off entrant had been disqualified shortly before the event when it was discovered that her recipe was an exact duplicate of one in the 17th Bake-Off (that Michigan woman got the recipe from a friend and didn't know its origin). "I feel if one should be disqualified, all should be treated the same," our Willmar correspondent insisted.

As a Bake-Off judge, I am very concerned about these charges. In fact, the Chocolate Cherry Bars recipe, with only four ingredients and an equally easy frosting, seemed so simple and logical that I specifically queried Pillsbury personnel if they were

CHOCOLATE CHERRY BARS

Makes 24 bars

Bars:
- 1 package pudding-included devil's food cake mix
- 1 can (21 ounces) cherry pie filling
- 1 teaspoon almond extract
- 2 eggs, beaten

Frosting:
- 1 cup sugar
- 5 tablespoons butter or margarine
- 1/3 cup milk
- 1 package (6 ounces) semisweet chocolate chips

To make bars: Beat cake mix, cherry pie filling, almond extract and eggs together by hand until well blended (try not to pulverize cherries). Pour batter into greased and floured 9-by-13-inch cake pan or 10-by-15-inch jellyroll pan. Bake in 350-degree oven for 25 to 30 minutes for 9-by-13 pan, or 20 to 30 minutes for jellyroll pan.

To make frosting: Boil sugar, butter and milk for 1 minute. Stir in chocolate chips. Pour over bars.

certain it was a unique recipe. Their reply: They had researched cookbooks and found nothing like it. Their search, of course, could not extend to such publications as the Kandiyohi Co-Op Kilowatt.

That newsletter is not distributed in Porter, Minn., home of the $25,000 winner, Mrs. Emil Jerzak. My personal feeling after interviewing Jerzak is that the inspiration was her own, polished by experimentation with a number of ingredient combinations. Although her recipe and Nelson's bear striking similarities (and certain differences in the type of cake mix used and the frosting proportions), I believe that such a simple recipe could be dreamed up by a number of people and probably has been. It was Jerzak's good fortune to enter her version in the Bake-Off.

While the controversy raged, I heard from another reader whose cousin had a similar recipe. She thought Pillsbury should give Cousin half the prize money, whether she'd entered or not. I talked to Pillsbury, and they have no intention of revoking any portion of Jerzak's prize money.

This issue again raises the question whether there is any such thing as an original recipe. I know how often women discuss cooking. Ideas travel. The combination of chocolate and cherries is centuries old. At least now, Chocolate Cherry Bars have gained celebrity status.

As the years have gone by, Chocolate Cherry Bars, to which our judging team had awarded top money at that Phoenix Bake-Off, became the recipe I've made most often among all the ones winning Pillsbury prizes. Years later, I judged a chocolate contest in St. Paul, and two people entered Chocolate Cherry Bars. Thankfully, neither contestant (one of them a state official) claimed it as an original recipe.

Over time, the recipe has been adapted to cake mix changes, allowing use of pudding-added product for even moister results. P.S.: Someone told me that adding cherry-flavored liqueur to the frosting makes it even better.

The only judge who didn't have to loosen her belt during the 1969 Bake-Off judging was Eleanor, third from left, seven-months pregnant.

Judges Tumble for Pineapple Split
April 17, 1977

When Super Pineapple Split arrived in the judging room at the National Pineapple Cooking Classic during my second Honolulu stint (tough duty) jurying that single-flavor contest:

I just sat myself down by the dish and spooned it in, keeping up a chorus of mmmm's. Though I campaigned mightily for that dessert, there was a "split" decision in favor of a variation of Blitz Torte, which took the $25,000 first purse (and later proved not to be original).

Mabel Haugen of Beloit, Wis., creator of the Split, won everyone's heart at the prize ceremony when she announced she would spend her $2,500 runner-up money to buy a custom-made electric wheelchair for her arthritic husband. When handed her check, she grinned, "These aren't tears, they're pineapple juice."

I'll tell you, there wasn't a dry eye at the judges' table. It's all so abstract and clinical when we're dissecting recipes and criticizing flavors in the judging room. But when we finally see the reactions of the winners, it gets very emotional.

One of the Office Hungries declared the Split the best recipe I'd ever tested. I predicted it would be the Dessert of the Year, telling readers they'd be tasting it at every wedding shower, bridge luncheon and family reunion.

My only argument with the recipe was that the smooth, rich chocolate sauce should be made first so it can thoroughly cool before the first vanilla wafer is

SUPER PINEAPPLE SPLIT
Makes 12 or more servings

1 package (12 ounces) vanilla wafers
1 cup softened butter or margarine, divided
1 can (20 ounces) crushed pineapple
1 package (8 ounces) cream cheese, softened
2 cups sifted powdered sugar
1/2 cup semisweet real chocolate chips
1 1/2 cups undiluted evaporated milk

2 large or 3 small bananas
2 tablespoons orange or lemon juice
1 pint frozen nondairy whipped topping, thawed
1/2 cup coarsely chopped pecans
1 jar (3 ounces) maraschino cherries, drained

To make crust and filling: Crush vanilla wafers. Mix well with 1/2 cup softened butter. Press over bottom of 9-by-13-inch baking pan. Drain pineapple well. Combine 1/4 cup butter with cream cheese. Blend well. Mix in two-thirds of pineapple (about 1 cup). Spread over wafer crust.

To make sauce: In saucepan, combine remaining 1/4 cup butter, powdered sugar, chocolate chips and evaporated milk. Cook, stirring constantly, until thick and smooth. Cool completely.

To finish: Slice bananas 1/2 inch thick. Drizzle with orange or lemon juice. Drain well. Arrange banana slices over pineapple cream-cheese layer. Top with chocolate sauce. Spread whipped topping over all. Sprinkle with remaining pineapple, pecans and cherries. Chill thoroughly before serving.

crushed. Here's why: If the sauce is at all warm, the whipped topping just slides around and refuses to spread evenly. And it tends to melt into little beige puddles.

Another bit of advice: Don't bother sifting the powdered sugar unless you have to clean the kitchen, anyway.

A Devilish Problem
May 22, 1977

A sister-in-food-judging once told me, "Recipes are like sin. It's hard to do something original." A month after judging the Hawaiian Pineapple Contest, I expounded on the problem of recipe originality, wondering, "Is there such a thing?":

I'll tell you, I'm getting paranoid on the topic. Three out of four of the big national cooking competitions I've judged have had controversial winners. At my first Bake-Off, the grand-prize winner was a sweet roll with baked-in marshmallow filling. After the $25,000 check was presented, it was discovered that a similar concept was in a Betty Crocker cookbook, which made the folks at Pillsbury very uncomfortable.

At my next Bake-Off, we absolutely fell in love with those simple but superb Chocolate Cherry Bars, still one of my favorite caloric indiscretions. No sooner was it named winner than letters began arriving from people who said a similar recipe had appeared in a church cookbook on the West Coast and in a rural electric co-op newsletter in Minnesota.

Well, here we are again in a similar pickle with the $25,000 winner at the Pineapple Cooking Classic. Pineapple Meringue Cake, as our judging panel suspected, is a traditional favorite. Variations, even exact duplicates, have appeared in numerous cookbooks under a spate of names, including Lindy's Cake to honor historic Lindbergh's flight to Paris.

You recall that I had been rooting for Super Pineapple Split to be the top winner. Even that runner-up has first cousins. Last week, I received an unsigned

recipe called Banana Split Sundae — much the same as printed in my account of the contest, except it uses vanilla ice cream in place of cream cheese and the dessert is frozen.

Obviously, there's little truly new in food circles. We usually see variations of classic recipes, though occasionally, a person truly does dream up a shortcut or new twist meriting prize money. Organizations that sponsor contests spend considerable time and money researching finalists' recipes, but obviously, they can't read every church cookbook, every co-op newsletter.

Rarely is a entrant truly devious. Pineapple Meringue Cake had been in the winner's family for a quarter-century, its origins hazy. The entrant got it from her mother and assumed dear old Mom had invented it. Such simple ideas as Chocolate Cherry Bars or the marshmallow rolls could occur to anyone.

Blatant recipe thievery by those who have designs on big contest money always gets found out.

When food editors met in Atlanta last October, a local cooking school director shared a recipe for Grits

PINEAPPLE CHEESE SPREAD
Makes 1 cheese ball

- **1 package (8 ounces) cream cheese, chilled**
- **1/2 cup finely chopped green pepper**
- **1/4 cup finely chopped onion**
- **1/2 can (8-ounce size) crushed pineapple, drained**
- **1/4 to 1/2 cup chopped nuts**

Combine cream cheese, green pepper, onion and pineapple. Form into a ball. Pat chopped nuts onto ball. Serve with crackers. (Note: Best eaten the day it's made before the onion flavor takes over.)

Roulade she had invented. Helen Moore, food editor for the Charlotte (N.C.) Observer, ran the recipe in her column. Some months later, she received word that a Charlotte man was top winner in the Seagram's V.O. recipe competition, whose rules said recipes must be "original and unique, one-of-a-kind creations." Boy, are they dreamers.

Helen Moore scanned the Grits Roulade recipe and realized it was the same one she had printed, even to her parenthetical additions to the directions. At first, the man denied, but later admitted, he had plagiarized.

So beware. Any recipe awarded huge sums of money is going to get a heap of publicity, and it will be carefully scrutinized by others kicking themselves for not entering the contest.

In all the jillions of cookbooks and recipes printed these days, there's bound to be a look-alike to any contest winner. If it's identical, indignant screams will echo throughout the food world.

Nutritionally Safe Snacking
March 22, 1981

National Bake-Offs and cookoffs were a great honor to judge, but I was also pleased, and far more often tapped, to judge local events. Pineapple Cheese Spread, entered by nurse Sue Brotherton in St. Paul's United Hospital nutritious snack contest, is one that intrigued me. To cut the fat, it can be made with Neufchatel or other fat-shaved cream cheeses.

Nostalgic Fudge Sauce
May 1, 1983

At another St. Paul event, the first Chocolate Connection to raise funds for Actors Theatre, I was joined in judging children's chocolate cookery by

IVEY'S FUDGE SAUCE
Makes about 1 1/2 cups

2 squares unsweetened chocolate
1/4 cup butter
3/4 cup sugar
1/4 cup cocoa
1/2 cup cream

In top of double boiler, melt chocolate and butter. Add sugar, cocoa and cream. Stir until smooth. Cook over low heat for about 20 minutes, stirring occasionally. Pour over ice cream.

dedicated theater volunteer Norma Lorshbough of St. Paul and longtime friend Wizzie Fiorito, who at that time co-owned Simply Chocolate, a St. Paul company dealing in high-quality baking chocolates.

When Ivey's Fudge Sauce came to the judging table, it jogged Norma's memory. She recalled Ivey's Chocolate Shop being on Nicollet Avenue, near Bjorkman's fur store, in downtown Minneapolis in the 1940s. "It was a favorite of shoppers looking for a light lunch and a heavy dessert. Ivey's Fudge Sauce was the lure for chocolate-sundae lovers," Norma told us as we spooned into the entry.

When I tried the recipe, sent to the contest by 8-year-old Vanessa Smith of Minneapolis (who must have gotten the recipe from her grandma), it seemed to be done in 10 minutes. Cooking the suggested 20 minutes didn't make it any better.

(P.S. While this book was in its final editing phases, I learned that WCCO-AM food reporter Sue Zelickson was seeking a recipe for Ivey's Fudge Sauce, which she fondly remembers from her childhood. "It's in my book," I told her, requesting that she make the sauce and tell me if it's authentic. She did. It is.)

Another Minnesota Triumph
February 21, 1988

When winners of the 33rd Pillsbury Bake-Off Plus were announced in San Diego, I realized that Minnesotans had taken the grand prize all three times I've judged that contest. Honest, the fix isn't in; we judges never know the entrants' names or home states. It's pure coincidence — and also proves Minnesota is enriched with good cooks.

Proof: Since the first time I judged in 1969, three other Minnesotans have been grand-prize winners in years when I was just a reporter-observer at the contest.

Proof: This year, I was campaigning for another recipe to take first place. Indeed, during the early voting for the $40,000 grand prize, my favorite had the edge. But some very persuasive judges were committed to a chocolate praline cake. After an hour of discussion, we were deadlocked.

As chief judge, it was up to me to solve that impasse, so I swung my vote to the cake. Only after all eight of us had signed the official judging certificate did I learn that the winner was from Minnesota.

I Ate the Who-o-ole Thing
May 15, 1988

"Something different" ingredients intrigue judges. Or so students and staff at the University of Wisconsin-Stout School of Home Economics assumed when choosing finalists in the Country Cooking Cook-Off sponsored by Super Valu stores for customers from 32 states.

Maybe I'm the kind of judge that those recipe sorters had in mind. I thought the "something different" idea of adding Rice Krispies to carrot cake a wonderful idea. They add crunch and lift the cake's texture above its usual leaden weight. I absolutely loved the dessert and did what is unheard of in contest judging — ate an entire piece. (I was sorry later, when more entries tested my capacity, but it sure was irresistible at the moment.)

Finalist Marlene Erb said that during the years she served this cake at her Lena, Ill., tearoom, she refused to divulge the recipe. I can understand why her customers wanted it. It is now my standard for carrot-cake excellence. Had it been up to me alone, this cake would have won some money. It didn't. But I still consider it a prize dessert.

Why is it called Alaska Carrot Cake? I don't know. Perhaps because of its golden hue. Erb spread frosting only between the layers and on top, adding a ring of grated orange peel as final decor. You may want to skimp on the orange extract in the frosting.

Heavenly Chili
October 23, 1988

If you doubt that prayers are answered, the invocation at the first-ever Men's Chili Cook-Off and Country Supper at Roseville Lutheran Church might be convincing.

Senior Minister George Weinman, wearing his cowboy best, led the crowd of 200 in thanks before they all dived into chili and cornbread. The pastor couldn't resist one small commercial. "Oh, Lord," he prayed, "give the judges the good discernment to choose my chili."

Our discernment wasn't quite as good as he had wished, but the Preacher's Original "It's Even Hotter Somewhere Else" Chili won second prize. On my score sheet, where the chilies were identified only by number, I scored the pastor's entry highest. Maybe a heavenly messenger whispered louder in my ear.

ALASKA CARROT CAKE
Makes 12 to 15 servings

Cake:
- 2 cups granulated sugar
- 3/4 cup vegetable oil
- 3 eggs
- 2 cups all-purpose flour
- 2 teaspoons baking soda
- 2 teaspoons ground cinnamon
- 1/2 teaspoon salt
- 3/4 cup buttermilk
- 2 teaspoons vanilla
- 2 cups grated carrots

- 1/2 cup drained crushed pineapple
- 2 cups shredded coconut
- 1 cup Rice Krispies
- 1 cup chopped walnuts

Orange cream-cheese frosting:
- 4 ounces cream cheese
- 6 tablespoons margarine
- 4 cups powdered sugar
- 2 teaspoons orange extract
- 2 tablespoons milk

To make cake: In large mixing bowl, cream sugar and oil. Add eggs, 1 at a time, beating well. Combine flour, soda, cinnamon and salt. Add alternately with buttermilk. Mix until smooth. Add vanilla. Fold in carrots, pineapple, coconut, cereal and nuts.

To bake cake: Pour into 3 greased and floured 8- or 9-inch round cake pans. Bake in 350-degree oven for 55 to 60 minutes, or until done. Cool in pans.

To make frosting: Put cream cheese and margarine in mixing bowl. Set out at room temperature until softened. Add powdered sugar, orange extract and milk. Using electric mixer, blend until smooth. Spread between cake layers, on top, and, if desired, around cake.

We were asked to rate entries on a scale of zero to three, the highest being a chili we would be happy to eat for the rest of our lives. Lutherans don't get technical on judging criteria.

I've never eaten chili so fast in my life! Twenty-two bowls whizzed past, and it was our job to make sure we didn't miss any in our frantic tasting. Our judging team's conversation went like this:

"Who's got Number 12?"

"Send down the Coke."

"Does anyone need crackers?"

Katie Metzger, a high-school student sitting next to me, judging her first food contest, held her tummy and vowed never to eat again. She didn't even try a piece of homemade apple pie afterward. We chili contests veterans were happy to stuff it in.

While we judged numbered entries, contestants were asked what they'd named their batches. My favorite was Steve Burwell's Anchovyless Chili. "If you don't like anchovies, you'll like my chili," he explained.

Preacher Weinman told the crowd how he decided the number of Hershey Kisses added to his chili: "First, I tried seven. That's a good Biblical number, one for each day of Creation. But it needed more, so I made it 10, one for each of the Commandments."

PREACHER'S ORIGINAL "IT'S EVEN HOTTER SOMEWHERE ELSE" CHILI
Makes 6 to 8 servings

- 1 pound lean ground beef
- 1 onion, chopped
- 1/2 fresh garlic clove, minced
- 1 can (15 ounces) whole tomatoes
- 2 cans kidney beans
- 1 can (15 ounces) tomato sauce
- 1 1/2 cups water
- 2 to 3 dashes Tabasco sauce
- 3 to 4 tablespoons chili powder
- 1/4 teaspoon cayenne
- 2 tablespoons chopped mild green chili pepper
- 1 small red chili pepper, chopped
- 1 teaspoon cumin
- 1 teaspoon sweet basil
- 1 teaspoon salt
- 1/2 teaspoon pepper
- 1 tablespoon red-wine vinegar
- 1/2 tablespoon molasses
- 1 dash Worcestershire sauce
- 10 Hershey's Kisses

Brown beef with onion and garlic. In large pot, combine all remaining ingredients, except Kisses. Stir well. Add meat mixture. Bring to a boil. Reduce heat. Simmer for 2 to 3 hours, stirring occasionally. Add Kisses about 15 minutes before serving. Stir well.

Jet-lagged Judging
March 24, 1991

How to expand a dress size in a single week: Judge back-to-back contests in New Orleans and Napa Valley, dining out in those eating meccas since we're there, anyway.

At the American Pie Celebration in New Orleans, the top winner was a cherry pie, but the one I liked best — proven by the fact that I went back for more nibbles even after tasting a tableful of pies — was a rhubarb-apple-pineapple concoction.

We got into a rhubarb over the rhubarb. Some loved it; some hated it. "It's a Yankee pie," sneered one of the Southern judges. After considerable campaigning on my part, the rhubarb mixture was named most creative, earning some money for Louise Davis of Dallas, Texas.

Sound implausible? Try it when your backyard rhubarb sprouts. The interplay of flavors will hook you into craving more nibbles, too.

Judging a hundred entries in Lake City, Minnesota brought on a three-year apple-pie aversion.

RHUBARB, APPLE AND PINEAPPLE PIE
Makes 9 1/2-inch deep-dish pie

Crust:
- 2 cups flour
- 1 teaspoon salt
- 1/2 teaspoon baking powder
- 2/3 cup shortening
- 4 to 5 tablespoons ice water

Filling:
- 1 cup sugar
- 3 tablespoons flour
- 1/8 teaspoon salt
- 1 cup peeled, chopped Macintosh apples
- 1 teaspoon lemon
- 2 cups fresh or frozen unsweetened rhubarb
- 1/2 cup drained canned crushed pineapple
- 1/4 cup honey
- 1 tablespoon butter or margarine

To make crust: In medium mixing bowl, combine flour, salt and baking powder. Using pastry blender or 2 knives, cut in shortening until mixture forms pea-sized chunks. Sprinkle with ice water, 1 tablespoon at a time. Using fork, toss lightly until dough forms a ball. Press between hands to form 2 5- to 6-inch "pancakes." Wrap in plastic wrap. Refrigerate while preparing filling.

To make filling: In small mixing bowl, combine sugar, flour and salt. Place apple slices in large bowl. Sprinkle with lemon juice. Add rhubarb, pineapple and sugar mixture. Toss to mix.

To roll crust: Lightly flour rolling surface and rolling pin. Roll dough for bottom crust into a circle. Trim 1 inch larger than upside-down 9 1/2-inch deep-dish pie plate. Loosen dough carefully. Fold into quarters. Place in pie plate. Unfold. Press into pie plate. Leave overhang on crust. Roll top crust in same manner. (Note: If you want a lattice crust, cut top round into 10 1/2-inch-wide strips.)

To bake pie: Spoon filling into unbaked pie shell. Drizzle with honey. Dot with butter. Moisten pastry overhang with water. Top with crust. Crimp or flute edge. (Note: If making lattice crust, arrange strips over pie, weaving as you go. Crimp or flute edge.) Place pie in 450-degree oven. Immediately reduce heat to 350 degrees. Bake for 60 to 75 minutes, or until filling in center is bubbly and crust is golden brown. Cool to room temperature before serving.

Chicken Every Wednesday
May 30, 1993

Let me tell you why our team of three who did the original judging of Chili Citrus Chicken believed so strongly that it should win. It was the very first dish that came to our table during the National Chicken Cooking Contest in Richmond, Va., proving that it was fast and easy to make. It was attractive, with spice-colored chicken fillets clustered on glossy ruby-hued sauce, adorned with sprigs of green cilantro, lemon slices and tiny red peppers halved to expose strands of minuscule seeds.

But even if we hadn't been watching the clock or if we'd had our eyes closed, taste alone was enough to win maximum points. Wow! I could detect layers of flavor — the heat of chili and cayenne, the sweetness of jalapeno jelly, the sharpness of citrus. Another judge said, "It's a dish I'd make on Wednesday night after work — and make it often." You can't get a better endorsement than that from a busy food writer.

But it didn't win first place. Leading through all the earlier judging rounds, at the last minute, it fell to second, defeated by a more complicated Caribbean-style drumstick recipe. "We wuz robbed!" seven of 15 judges, including me, shouted when the final numbers were tallied. So I asked readers to decide which they liked better, this one or the Caribbean dark horse ... make that dark meat ... winner.

Two weeks later, the results: Your opinions were unanimous. Everyone who called raved about Chili Citrus Chicken, wishing, like me, that it had beat the drumsticks.

CHILI CITRUS CHICKEN
Makes 4 servings

1 1/2 teaspoons chili powder
1/2 teaspoon ground cumin
1/2 teaspoon garlic salt
1/4 teaspoon cayenne pepper
4 broiler-fryer chicken-breast halves, skinned and boned
1 tablespoon vegetable oil
1/4 cup fresh lemon juice
1/4 cup fresh lime juice
3 tablespoons jalapeno-pepper jelly
Garnish:
Cilantro sprigs
Tiny red chili peppers
Lemon slices

To cook chicken: In small dish, combine chili powder, cumin, garlic salt and cayenne pepper. Rub mixture on each chicken-breast half. In skillet, heat oil to medium temperature. Add chicken. Cook, turning, for about 12 minutes, or until chicken is brown and fork can be inserted into chicken with ease. Remove to heated platter. Keep warm.

To make sauce: In skillet, combine lemon juice, lime juice and jalapeno-pepper jelly. Bring to a boil. Cook, stirring constantly, for about 1 minute, or until mixture thickens. Spoon sauce over chicken on platter or individual plates. Garnish with cilantro sprigs, chili peppers and lemon slices.

Judges Give Away the Gold
September 5, 1993

Gilding the lily doesn't always make it shine any brighter. While we judges sampled recipes created by Twin Cities chefs for a party benefiting Courage Center, a suburban Minneapolis facility assisting the physically handicapped, 300 paying guests were gorging on the same desserts in a nearby party room. We'd unanimously judged Marble Tart the winner, but, later, we noticed that the party crowd was treated to a more glittering version.

Azur restaurant pastry chef Chris Gruidl had gilded her Marble Tart for the public, using powdered gold, which, if you're curious, you can buy at Maid of Scandinavia. I liked this chocolate creation — sans gold — so much because it's similar to a beloved chocolate attraction at the St. Paul Grill in the St. Paul Hotel.

Judging Without Tasting
February 13, 1994

Like the old saying, "Water, water everywhere, and not a drop to drink," I was confronted with pork chops, pork chops, 15 kinds of pork chops, and not a bite to eat.

I was invited to observe the judging of the Give Us Your Best Chop, America contest, organized by the National Pork Producers Council and staged in suburban Minneapolis. I sat on the sidelines, salivating.

Actually, it was fun to be the mouse in the corner instead of in my usual role as arbiter of taste. But I did get rather hungry watching the seven hired mouths eat.

Sue Zelickson, food reporter for WCCO-AM Radio and one of the judges, finally noticed I was taking only notes, not nibbles. She offered to give me

MARBLE TART
Makes 12 servings

Pecan crust:
- 2 cups finely chopped pecans
- 1/2 cup sugar
- 1/8 teaspoon cinnamon
- 1/4 cup butter, softened

Caramel:
- 1/4 cup butter
- 1/4 cup sugar
- 4 1/2 teaspoons milk

Filling:
- 1 cup light sour cream
- 1/2 cup milk
- 12 squares (1 ounce each) bittersweet or semisweet real chocolate, melted

To make crust: In large bowl, combine pecans, sugar and cinnamon. Stir in butter until well mixed. Firmly press mixture on bottom and up sides of 10-inch tart pan with removable bottom. Bake in 350-degree oven for 12 to 14 minutes, or until golden. Cool.

To make caramel: In 2-quart saucepan, melt butter. Stir in sugar until dissolved. Cook over medium heat, slowly stirring in milk, until mixture is smooth. Set aside.

To make filling: In 1-quart saucepan, stir together sour cream and milk. Cook over medium heat, stirring constantly, for 2 to 3 minutes, or until heated through. Using wire whisk, slowly stir in melted chocolate until smooth. Pour into completely cooled crust.

To finish pie: Drizzle caramel mixture over chocolate filling. Slowly pull tip of knife through mixture to create marbled effect. Cover. Refrigerate for at least 2 hours.

a taste of anything especially good that came to the table — but it was a long, hungry spell before she deemed anything worthy of sharing.

It was well past my normal lunch time when Robin Kline, director of consumer affairs for the pork council, offered to cook me the chop concoction I most wanted to taste. "Make some Ty's Sweet Chops," I suggested, and, at the point of near starvation, I loved it enough to give it the grand prize, had my vote counted.

When I left the judging room, I thought Ty's were tied for third place. They ended up out of the money

because the judges would have preferred the chops to be quickly pan-browned before they bake in their sweet-savory sauce. You could easily add that step.

Fairest of Fair Food
September 4, 1994

I sat in one of the oddest booths at the Minnesota State Fair. It was among the rare places on the Fairgrounds where food was being given away free. But, at first, there were few takers. Some contestants who had brought their casseroles and salads to enter in the Gold'n Plump chicken cooking contest stayed to watch us eat on a shaded platform adjacent to the Education Building, but most folks strolling by didn't have a clue to what was going on.

One of the judges, Jake Calhoun, high-energy DJ for K102 Radio, tried to make it an event. "Hey, dude, want some food?" he called to a passer-by, inviting him up on stage for a taste of what was on the judging table at that moment. Calhoun's ongoing invitations proved so effective that we had to cut them short after impromptu tasters used up all the available bowls and forks, forcing us judges to eat off napkins.

Forget about Minnesota Nice in that crowd! No one who jumped up on the stage for free eats said "thank you."

Calhoun noticed Lake Wobegon's own Garrison Keillor strolling along the sidewalk and tried to get his attention. Remember when Keillor accused St. Paulites of walking past his former Portland Avenue home, rubbernecking without actually looking at the house? He, too, turned his face away as he passed our booth. Sorry, professional shy guy, you missed a sensational Southwest version of a Caesar salad created by Lisa Schnirring of Roseville. It was our unanimous vote for first place.

TY'S SWEET CHOPS
Makes 6 servings

6 bone-in pork chops, cut 3/4 inch thick
1/2 cup rum or orange juice
1/3 cup sliced green onions
1/4 cup snipped dates
1/4 cup steak sauce
1/4 cup molasses
1 tablespoon chopped parsley
1 teaspoon minced garlic
1/2 teaspoon lemon pepper
1/8 teaspoon onion powder
1/4 teaspoon salt
Hot, cooked rice pilaf or couscous

In bowl, combine rum, green onions, dates, steak sauce, molasses, parsley, garlic, lemon pepper, onion powder and salt. Pour into 9-by-13-inch baking dish. Arrange pork chops on top of mixture. Bake, uncovered, in 350-degree oven for 25 to 30 minutes, or until chops are faintly pink in center. Serve chops and sauce with rice pilaf or couscous.

The Last Word on Contest Judging

One final tale from the judging room:

Longtime Pioneer Press columnist Don Boxmeyer and I were tapped to try recipes when the newspaper's accounting department staged its inaugural Occasional Bake-On contest, otherwise known as a good excuse for a feed.

Don confessed his food-contest experience was limited. "I once judged dill pickles at the South St. Paul Booya contest. Actually, I refereed booya there, too, and I have a taste for oxtail, but I don't see any on this table," he said, surveying the baked goods we were about to sample.

Boxmeyer says he's a bad judge "because I don't dislike anything. I'm like St. Paul's Supermayor Charlie McCarty, who once looked at a menu and said, 'Nothing disagrees with me. Bring me everything in order.' "

After 30 years of judging food contests, I'd say that's the best qualification of all.

SANTA FE CHICKEN SALAD
Makes 4 servings

4 tablespoons olive oil, divided

6 large flour tortillas, cut into bite-sized rectangles

2 teaspoons chili powder, divided

1 teaspoon cumin, divided

1 1/2 pounds boneless chicken breast, cut into bite-sized strips

8 cups romaine lettuce, tightly packed

1 small red bell pepper, seeded, cut into thin slices

1 small green bell pepper, seeded, cut into thin slices

1/2 small purple onion, cut into very thin slices

1 cup pepper cheese, cut into cubes

1/2 cup ranch dressing

1/4 cup salsa

1/4 cup toasted almonds (optional)

To heat tortillas: In nonstick frying pan, heat 2 tablespoons olive oil over low-medium heat. Add tortilla strips. Toss to coat. Sprinkle with 1 teaspoon chili powder and 1/2 teaspoon cumin. Cook, stirring every few minutes until crisp, for 30 to 40 minutes. Remove strips from heat. Set aside.

To cook chicken: Meanwhile, in nonstick frying pan, heat 2 tablespoons olive oil over medium-high heat. Saute chicken with 1 teaspoon chili powder and 1/2 teaspoon cumin for 8 to 10 minutes, or until done. Place chicken in clean bowl. Refrigerate until salad is ready to assemble.

To assemble salad: In large salad bowl, combine lettuce, red and green peppers, onion and cheese. Mix ranch dressing and salsa. Add to vegetables. Toss to coat. Add chicken and crisp tortilla strips. Toss to coat. Garnish with toasted almonds. Serve immediately.

1976

*— In America's 200th year, we greet Testing Results,
Cuisinarts and slow cookers —*

Busy Bicentennial Year
March 14

The Bicentennial year challenged food writers to define American food, no easy task since our fare is such a ragout of countless immigrant ethnic influences and regional food products, interpreted and revised through 200-plus years of ingenuity. That was a watershed year for American food as we focused on it and tried to understand it better. It was also the time when American chefs began to take hold of what's best in this country instead of looking to France.

We wrote about the historical, the regional that year. Chefs pulled us into America's next century by creating a whole new cuisine that, as the Bicentennial year dawned, none of us could have imagined.

But before all that happened, food writers were deluged with "American" recipes, some of them quite awful. I tried a fair number on behalf of readers, willing to eat such extravagances as Bicentennial Cherry Chocolate Cake "now that sugar is cheaper and the economic reason to cut back on it in recipes has disappeared."

The July Fourth Tested Recipe was All-American Pizza, an abomination topped with slices of American cheese and rounds cut from a pound of wieners.

I'm amazed, two decades later, to read what common ingredients now were stumbling blocks then. Sweet Italian sausage was one I couldn't find in 1976. A friendly Italian butcher suggested that I use half regular spicy Italian sausage and half plain ground pork to tone it down. Finding fresh watercress in January 1976 was hopeless "because local supplies are buried in snow." Now, thanks to Twin Cities herb queen Bonnie Dehn and other year-round growers, fresh herbs are available in the depths of winter.

For me, 1976 was a year of travels, which I began sharing with readers, from the recipes we found in New Zealand and Australia, to French dishes collected while taking cooking lessons with the legendary Simone Beck in France (she was Julia Child's co-author on "Mastering the Art of French Cooking"). After returning from Simca's in mid-March, the column revealed, "My suitcase bulged with six bottles of wine, one of French brandy, assorted cooking utensils, knives, molds and a 2-pound tin of powdered vanilla that seemed essential at the time I bought it in France — but now I wonder?"

I still have that 2-pound tin — unopened — 20 years later.

It was also the year that I became president of the Newspaper Food Editors and Writers Association, an international professional organization that I had instigated, then helped found in 1972. Food writers needed a voice, their own meetings and the strength of shared goals and information as we moved away from depending on food companies for information and moved toward doing more original food reporting. That organization, now known as the Association of Food Journalists so it can embrace food writers other than those just working for newspapers, thrives today, and founding it is one of my proudest achievements.

Hello, Testing Results
June 20

We were a decade into the column when Testing Results were finally added to each recipe. Before then, I'd made suggestions and given opinions in the body of the column. St. Paul reader Carole Peterson's letter suggested that readers who just clipped the recipes and not the entire column would be in big trouble. In the previous Sunday, she noted I'd said the cheesecake needed to bake longer, and that fewer marshmallows should be used in the ice cream dessert. "If you've already suffered through these mistakes for us, why not add these notations to the recipe? Is there some rule that you can't change the instructions or ingredients? We need all the help we can get with the cost of food and the limited time we can spend on cooking," she implored. I have always printed the recipes exactly as they were when tested, but Peterson brought up a good issue. I let readers decide.

LaVonne McCombie of Hudson, Wis., spoke for the majority: "Although I faithfully read every word of your comments," she wrote, "then clip the recipe if it sounds like one I may want to try, it may be weeks or months before I actually get around to trying the recipe. Even though I think I'm going to remember what the comments on a particular recipe were, of course, I never can. I think it would be nice to have them at the bottom of the recipe, especially if the suggestion is to use more or less of an ingredient, a good substitute for an expensive or hard-to-find item, or a change in the cooking time."

So, I agreed to list any suggested changes "or just assure you that in our opinion, the recipe is A-OK," I promised readers, starting Testing Results July 18. By adding that extra paragraph, "we can have the best of both worlds," concurred Mary Louise Klas of St. Paul.

No More Bloody Knuckles
August 8

"Processor ends knuckle woes," headed the column when I introduced readers to my brand-new Cuisinart, then an almost-unknown cooking convenience, now found in nearly every kitchen:

The importer of that French-made machine promises it will change our lives in the kitchen, and he's absolutely right. I'm a true believer after having that machine for just over a week. What it does is fascinate the man of the household so much that he's in the kitchen puttering and chopping and grinding like crazy. We had the machine for at least five days before I got near it. Now, that's what I call making my culinary life easier. This is one little secret we women can keep to ourselves, OK?

I told readers we made corned-beef hash in about eight seconds, "and it wasn't even seasoned with knuckle scrapings."

I'd been hankering for one of these machines, partly because of what they do, and partly because they're such a status symbol in the food world. Well, maybe they were once. Recently, when interviewing a New York chef, I was carrying on about my Cuisinart. He let it be known that he bought one "when they were expensive."

"What do you mean?" I countered. "They just went up to $225 from $190." Then came his put-down. He succumbed in the days when they were just introduced in this country, when only the likes of James Beard, Craig Claiborne and Julia Child owned them, and the asking price was $300.

It's nice to know that equipment really does get cheaper through mass production.

Aric, My Assistant
January 11

Aric, now able to read recipes, often insisted on being part of the testing process. But the tasting process? This is where he got stubborn:

When I was testing a vegetable-flecked casserole, he greeted the news about macaroni and cheese with delight because he loves it. But when he saw me adding tomatoes and green peppers, he rebelled. He got a box of Kraft dinner from the cupboard and threatened to make his own. "Just try one bite. You'll probably like this," I commanded. He dug his heels into the kitchen linoleum and declared, "No matter what, I'll say yuck." He did, too. No critic is more unflinching than a 6-year-old.

"I think this one's going to hatch," announced Aric as he cracked eggs, guest-testing Bunny Pound Cake just before Easter (reported in the April 11 column). Aric likes to cook, but only if he has complete control of the project. "I'm in charge here," he says to anyone who tries to help.

Why is it little boys like chopping things so much? It takes true grit on a mother's part to give a kid a knife and a carrot to chop without envisioning blood and gore. Little boys also tend not to scrape batter or frosting bowls too clean — more for them to lick. Mothers have to be stern or cakes will be mighty flat.

"Are you going to put my name in the paper?" wondered Aric, tapped as official tester (for the July 11 column). I assured him I would. "Then, why don't you put my picture in the paper, too?" asked my media-wise second-grader. Sorry kid, my editor has to draw the line somewhere.

Given the task of making Wheat-Germ Fudge Nut Squares as a summer vacation distraction, he rolled graham cracker crumbs, melted butter and stirred the sugar-egg-butter mixture. Then his interest waned. "I need a break," he complained. "You have to stir until it starts to thicken," I told him.

The Lemonade Kid of Lincoln Avenue tries his hand at commerce as well as in the kitchen.

"Mom," he insisted, "I need a break. I need something to drink. I've been standing over a hot stove." He'll make a good housewife someday.

On September 19, this addendum appeared:
Erma Bombeck, I feel for you. You're always writing about your kids' single, all-purpose word, "gross." Aric has come up with a variation, which he applies to nearly everything: "grossome." He started using it during this summer, so it can't be the latest word making the rounds at school. I assume that in his second-grade mind, he is compounding "gross" and "gruesome." And he uses it with such inflection, Erma.

The Jury is Out
April 25

As if work and family and cooking and traveling weren't enough on my plate that year, I also was nabbed for jury duty. My husband took pity on me and cooked a special dinner on the night our jury went into deliberations and I didn't get home until 10 p.m.:

My sweet husband, unaware that I'd be sitting in the courthouse all night, invested $17 in a crown roast of lamb, and as a special treat, cooked a spectacular dinner: fresh asparagus, tomatoes filled with tiny peas, avocado salad and chilled white wine. He and Aric ate by candlelight while I was closeted with the jury. The county did feed us — as long as we kept it under $5 — so I had an uninspired plate of chow mein instead of a lamb dinner. There is no justice — at least for this juror.

TOMATOES STUFFED WITH GUACAMOLE
Makes 6 servings

6 ripe medium tomatoes
3 ripe large avocados, peeled and
   seeded
2 tablespoons chopped onion
1 tomato, peeled, seeded and chopped
1 tablespoon lemon juice
Salt
Tabasco, to taste
Lettuce leaves

Make 3 crosswise cuts into tops of tomatoes, cutting almost to but not through bottom. Spread sections apart to form cup. Mash avocados. Mix with onion, chopped tomatoes and lemon juice. Add salt and hot-pepper sauce to taste. Mix well. Stuff tomatoes with avocado mixture. Arrange on crisp lettuce.

The Dawn of the Fresh Vegetable Age
May 9

"Tomatoes Stuffed With Guacamole are about the prettiest vegetable ever to grace a plate," I wrote back when most of our vegetable choices came out of a can or a frozen box, whether dining at home or in a restaurant. The recipe hinges on having absolutely ripe avocados, so plan ahead or substitute, which I did when avocados at the store were rock hard. I used a frozen avocado puree, then flavored it as the recipe suggests.

Cutting Corners
June 6

The eternal issue of buttermilk resurfaced:

Just the other day, a reader called, and we commiserated about recipes that call for a cup of buttermilk, leaving us nonbuttermilk swillers with that mostly full carton taking up refrigerator space.

By 1976, dry buttermilk powder was available, which I often used. I had to laugh when the problem came up again in the spring of 1997. I said in print that I wished buttermilk was packed in 1-cup cartons, just enough for one recipe. Readers told me it is, indeed, available. A few days later, digging through Tested Recipes columns while writing this book, I came across the same wish for 1-cup cartons, voiced in a 1970 column. Maybe I gave dairy companies the idea way back when.

I baked two of these cakes and shared them with a Junior League committee meeting, the bachelors next door, the office crew and my own family.

"My husband tends to cut corners when sampling," I revealed about his coffeecake tastes. "That way, it doesn't seem like I'm taking a whole piece," he reasons. The octagon-shaped remainder was taken to

LEMON SPICE COFFEECAKE
Makes 8 servings

Batter:
- 1/3 cup butter
- 3/4 cup sugar
- 1 egg
- 1 1/2 cups sifted flour
- 1 1/2 teaspoons baking powder
- 1/2 teaspoon soda
- 1/2 teaspoon salt
- 1/4 teaspoon nutmeg
- 1/4 teaspoon cinnamon
- 1/2 cup buttermilk
- 1/2 cup seedless raisins
- 1 teaspoon grated lemon rind
- 1/4 cup chopped walnuts

Crumb topping:
- 2 tablespoons butter, melted
- 1/3 cup packed brown sugar
- 2 tablespoons flour
- 1/4 teaspoon nutmeg
- 1/4 teaspoon cinnamon
- Dash of salt
- 1/4 cup chopped walnuts
- 1 teaspoon grated lemon rind

To make batter: Beat butter and sugar together until creamy and fluffy. Beat in egg. Sift together dry ingredients. Add dry ingredients alternately with buttermilk, mixing well. Fold in raisins, lemon rind and nuts. Spread half of batter in greased 9-inch square baking pan.

To make topping: Mix topping ingredients until blended. Sprinkle half of topping over batter. Spread with remaining batter. Sprinkle with remaining topping.

To bake: Bake in 350-degree oven for 40 to 45 minutes. Serve warm.

the office. If I hadn't, there would be comments from the Office Hungries when the recipe hit print: "What coffeecake? We didn't see any coffeecake? You know how much we like coffeecake!"

SLOW-COOKED BEEF BARBECUE
Makes 5 generous servings
(recipe can be doubled)

- 1 1/2 pounds boneless chuck steak, 1 1/2 inches thick
- 2 tablespoons salad oil
- 1/2 onion
- 1 clove garlic
- 1/3 cup ketchup
- 2 tablespoons unsulphured molasses
- 1 tablespoon vinegar
- 1 tablespoon Worcestershire sauce
- 1 teaspoon seasoned salt
- 3 to 4 drops hot-pepper sauce
- 1/2 teaspoon chili powder
- 1/2 teaspoon dry mustard
- 1 teaspoon cornstarch

Cut meat across grain into slices 1/4 inch wide and about 2 inches long. In large skillet, heat oil. Brown meat on all sides. Transfer meat to slow-cooker. In blender or food processor, place all remaining ingredients. Blend until onion is finely minced. (Note: If neither appliance is available, chop onion, mince garlic and combine with remaining ingredients.) Pour barbecue sauce over meat. Cover. Cook on low heat for 5 to 6 hours. (Note: If slow-cooker is less than a third full, place a circle of aluminum foil over surface of meat.) If possible, stir barbecue once about halfway through cooking time.

Supper Slows Down
September 19

In a year when food processors made kitchen tasks faster, slow-cookers were becoming popular, too. We tried this "so nice to come home to" barbecue:

The slow-cooker beef simmered itself done while I was at work, though I did make one dash home to stir it. What I should have done was bring the slow-cooker to the office and drive my co-workers mad with desire from the aromas of barbecuing beef. Seven against one, they probably would have overpowered me and appropriated the potful. Then, what would my family have eaten for dinner? Better to run home and stir the sauce.

The allure of this recipe is its simplicity, its tenderness and its slightly sweet flavor. My husband, expecting barbecue that would send smoke curling from his ears, thought the sauce was sissified, but I liked its sweet nature. You could boost the Tabasco, chili powder and dry mustard if you like heat.

Strawberries Rare as Truffles
October 17

We're so accustomed to finding strawberries in produce departments year-round now, but when testing this recipe in 1976, finding fresh strawberries was a many-store excursion. "If all else fails, use frozen whole berries," I counseled.

The beauty of this strawberry version of Cherries Jubilee is that it is achieved so quickly. Watch where you do it, though. It should be made in all its flaming glory in front of awe-struck guests. But when we tested it for the first time for a dinner of food professionals, we made it in the privacy of the kitchen ... and almost set the hostess's curtains on fire when the brandy flamed.

To the same party, we brought a shrimp appetizer flavored with truffles. Finding the rare fungus was also a challenge. At one store, the manager kept them under lock and key. It was the teeniest can I've ever seen, but he wouldn't sell it to me because the lid bulged. "Not many people ask for these, you know," he said, marveling that he'd had another request for them "just the other week."

Truffles, I explained to readers, are those little black warty bits of fungus that pigs sniff in France. Considering the price of truffles, French swine must have a heckuva union.

STRAWBERRIES JUBILEE
Makes 6 servings

2 pints fresh strawberries
3 tablespoons butter
1/4 cup sugar
2 tablespoons water
3 thin strips lemon peel
1 tablespoon orange-flavored liqueur
   (such as Grand Marnier)
2 tablespoons brandy
1 quart vanilla ice cream

Wash berries. Drain on toweling. Set aside. In chafing dish, heat butter until bubbly. Add sugar, water, lemon peel and liqueur. Stir over high heat for 2 to 3 minutes, or until sugar dissolves and mixture is syrupy. Warm brandy. Ignite and pour over syrup. When flames die, stir in 1 scoop of ice cream until melted. Add berries. Poach for 1 minute, continually spooning sauce over berries. Spoon remaining ice cream into dessert dishes. Top with berries and sauce. Serve at once.

1977

— *Drinks (pleasant and otherwise),*
the dressing of our dreams,
dreaded microwaves and beloved chocolate —

Hostess With the Leastest Time

January 2

I had a good laugh reading a recent issue of a food magazine. Spread over a half-dozen pages were day-by-day details related by a woman who found herself with **only** a week to plan and prepare a dinner party for 12 guests.

One day, she conferred with her butcher; on another, she polished silver and wrote place cards. By week's end, she managed to serve an elegant though not especially complicated meal. As far as I could determine, she had no 9-to-5 commitments to distract from her menu-planning.

My laughter was especially hysterical because I'd just invited friends to a pre-Christmas dinner party that was to feature Leg of Lamb en Croute. I took an entire afternoon off work to clean house, set the table, roll puff pastry, cook the lamb, make soup and creamed onions for the adults, and a separate menu for the children, whose task was trimming the Christmas tree. Seems to me there was at least one dash to the store during those six hours (not six days) of party preparation.

Everything got done — except, shucks, never did write any place cards. Wonder if that magazine would like to print a diary of my dinner party? It's more typical of the way most of us entertain.

A Snowball's Chance in Hot Oil

January 30

Slogging through testing, some recipes were fine, others frustrating, but fried ice cream was nothing short of a monumental disaster:

"Say, I have this idea for the St. Paul Winter Carnival," was the way PR master Joe Ferris brought fried ice cream to my attention. He's been buddies with Don the Beachcomber for decades, and is writing a book about the restaurateur. Don the B. told Joe about the way he deep-fries frozen ice-cream snowballs in batter or dough and serves them with flaming liqueur. Don didn't share the recipe — he's probably saving it for his own book.

Ferris also heard from his sister in New Jersey about a similar recipe, again nothing specific. She suggested a batter of equal parts flour and beer, that the ice cream be rolled into balls and refrozen solidly, and that one should be prepared to clean the stove after frying.

So with Joe's encouragement and the Winter Carnival imminent, I went home to try frying ice-cream snowballs. Freezing them solid was no problem in our sub-zero weather. I just put them on the back porch.

So I made the beer batter and heated cooking oil to 375 degrees.

So I rolled a frozen orb in batter and dropped it into the oil. It spattered. It sputtered. The batter slid away immediately, and naked ice cream was left to the mercy of bubbling oil.

So I strained away all that mess and spooned an extra-heavy coating of batter on my next attempt. Same result. My husband arrived home and told me what I should be doing: "Roll the ice cream in batter and refreeze it. Then roll it in batter again before frying. That way, the second batter will have something to stick to."

So I did that, and again had an oil-drenched ice-cream ball, denuded of dough. By that time, I was running out of ice cream and patience.

I'd noticed on a billboard that Amalgamated Underground (a restaurant west of Minneapolis, no longer in business) serves fried ice cream. When I called to ask the manager how they contrive to keep their ice cream batter-bound, he said, "That's a tight secret." He did admit they don't use batter.

So I give up for the time being. If anyone knows the secret, please tell me. Reflecting on my failures, it seems logical that the ice-cream balls should be rolled in cookie crumbs so the dough will have something to grab. In the meantime, you'll have to eat your fried ice cream at the Amalgamated. I'll eat mine — unfried — at home. Pass the chocolate sauce.

That wasn't the end of it. For the May 1 column, Toni Koller of St. Paul sent me a fried ice-cream recipe she'd found in an old issue of Ebony magazine, adapted from the dessert served at the Strand Hotel in Stockholm.

Ebony's food editor discovered it there, then spent several months developing a facsimile. I can see why — it's tricky, tricky, tricky. His concept is like fried baked Alaska, meringue insulating ice cream wrapped inside a crepe. When I tried it, the ice cream did stay somewhat solid, but I fried the balls for only about 20 seconds before the outer layers were mahogany. If I'd oil-boiled them for 2 minutes as the recipe suggested, crust and ice cream would have been cremated.

A restaurant friend tells me that at the State Fair, they freeze ice cream in dry ice, then dip it in batter, and it won't melt in hot oil.

Maybe ... Oh, forget it!

I've decided to let sleeping dogs snooze. The original fried ice-cream idea was a real mongrel, and this second-generation technique has no pedigree, either.

Food's Pitfalls Trip Us Up
February 6

It's not much fun being a food writer these days: Doing research for a story on how overeating, especially fats, may be cancer-linked. Reading reports that food colors and growth hormones are suspect. Hearing daily from special-interest groups promoting diets higher in bran, lower in protein, deeper into natural foods, more vigilant about vitamins. And then everyone seems to be on a diet. Gets very depressing.

That moan and groan appeared in conjunction with two Valentine's Day recipes. For one containing cherry pie filling, I had to call Jeno's in Duluth to find out if its Wilderness cherry pie goo contained Red No. 4. The company, I learned, had been experimenting with alternative colors for two years "because we know the consumer will not accept a brown cherry pie. They'd probably add their own food coloring at home — more than we'd put in," a Jeno's official said.

4675: The Year of the Serpent

February 13

Another product that we consider commonplace today was hard to find in 1977 — ginger root, discussed in a Chinese New Year recipe column that year:

If you can find fresh ginger, use it — but substituting powdered ginger will not bring the Curse of the Serpent upon your house.

For the Chinese recipe testing, my husband bought himself an absolutely lethal-looking Chinese cleaver. So far, we haven't had any fingertips in our stir-fry, but I've decided not to pick any fights in the kitchen.

Time — and Food — Goes By

February 20

Flipping through a stack of Tested Recipes clippings the other day brought the startling realization of how fast the years are passing. Could it really be three years since we brought that recipe to the lake supper? Or four since we had that dinner party? How depressing to have one's life measured by weekly efforts at chocolate mousse and tuna hot dish.

Come Home, Marco Polo

March 6

Anyone else out there a Marco Polo junkie?

For all of you who haven't the slightest idea what Marco Polo is, or are convinced it is a "who," be advised that it is a creamy, tantalizing, tart salad dressing that lured us Family Life types at least

weekly to the St. Paul Hilton for lunch. We didn't care what salad was underneath as long as mysterious MP was slathered lavishly over the top. Our officeful of Marco Polo addicts had to have a regular hit or deal with the MP DTs.

Every visiting home economist, anyone with discerning taste buds, was enlisted, over lunch, to analyze the dressing.

We knew it included capers, and bits of parsley and carrot were visible. A good dose of vinegar and mustard. Oil, of course. But we never could duplicate it.

Poor Frank Klare, food and beverage czar at the Hilton. I nagged him endlessly for the recipe. "If you tell me, I won't tell anyone else," I vowed. "It's made in Chicago in huge vats, and I don't have the recipe," beleaguered Klare would wail as he hid under his desk. So I wrote to Chicago and begged for the recipe. No dice. I even wrote to Gourmet magazine. No luck.

As the St. Paul Hilton went, so went Marco Polo. The new Radisson owners made valiant efforts with substitutes, but none had that sharp bite we loved. Not everyone was crazy about it; my husband thought MP was awful. One loved it or was very happy to leave it.

In the midst of our mourning for delightful but departed Marco, a bottle of the vinegary ambrosia arrived at the office. No message was attached, but it did have a Radisson Corp. return address.

To celebrate our windfall, office retiree Betty Roney (a confirmed MP addict) came in from Stillwater; co-workers Carole Nelson and Georgann Koelln and I met her at the Hilt...pardon me, Radisson, for salad. We smuggled in the dressing and had a feast, just like the good old days.

For that column, I tested a salad dressing recipe that measured up in every way, except in comparison to Marco Polo. The next week, I told readers that a message was tucked in my typewriter, signed "From an employee of the Old Hilton." It chided, "You forgot the curry power, the most important ingredient."

Of course, that's it. How could we be so dense not to connect Marco Polo, explorer of the East, and a spice blend of the East in his namesake salad dressing?

Color provided no clue, however. The dressing was white, and we associate curry powder with bright yellow. Turmeric is what makes it yellow, so a colorless curry powder is quite possible, a person versed in Indian cooking tells me.

Despite that advice, I've never found — or invented — a recipe that duplicates the flavor, and it's been so long since I savored it that I don't know if, today, I can exactly recall Marco Polo's true character.

Real Cooks Still Make Quiche

June 26

Imagine my chagrin. A couple of years ago, when I was helping plan, for the Junior League, a midnight supper party menu that included quiche, a friend mentioned that in New York, quiche was "dead." No one served it anymore. It had been overdone and was blacklisted as a fashionable food.

Maybe we St. Paulites aren't that fashion conscious when it comes to our eats, because the 200 at the party gobbled mini-quiches without complaint. Maybe, like so much fashion gossip, the rumor of the egg pie's demise was greatly exaggerated.

Another dish that seems to have its fashionable moments, though not so much lately, is ratatouille. A few years back, everyone seemed to be serving it during summer-vegetable season.

I learned long ago that old recipes never die. They just get recycled. (The column's recipes that Sunday were an a la king quiche and ratatouille casserole strengthened with wheat germ.)

Definitely "in" during 1977, as mentioned in the July 24 column, was frozen yogurt:

Any observer of the food scene these days knows that frozen yogurt is one of the biggest phenoms to hit the market in recent memory. At the National Restaurant Show in Chicago in May, we noted a dozen-plus companies selling yogurt mix or dispensing machines.

Protein Diets Do Us In

August 14 and 21

A reader wrote asking for the "recipe" for liquid protein mentioned last Sunday. Well, madame, first you take a thousand beef hides ...

The week before, there was no Tested Recipes, because, I told readers: I'm not eating. I'm drinking. Predigested liquid protein. It's the Last Chance Diet in which nothing (oh, agony) is ingested, except for cough-syrup-like protein solution. Everyone's either talking about it or trying it.

After I wrote a lengthy piece about the diet for last Monday's Pioneer Press, many have given me meaningful looks and asked, "Have **you** tried it?" "No," I admitted. "High time," they were thinking.

The following week: Never has anything in this column provoked such volumes of mail (as people wrote for copies of my story, and told me about their favorite diets). One lady warned me that my hair would fall out.

Last week, I promised to tell you how I survived the Last Chance Diet. Here I am, 10 pounds lighter after swigging predigested liquid protein. I would have lost more, but I cheated.

You may be assuming I am going to endorse the starvation concept of dieting. Who would argue with success?

I will.

You see, there are two types of people. Some, like my husband (who shed 35 pounds by swigging), feel just fine on the liquid. There are even those extremists who say they feel so good on a protein fast that they leap from bed in the morning to wash walls or climb mountains.

There are others, like me, who after two or three days, don't have enough energy to climb on the scale (even if it's gratifying to see diminishing numbers on the dial).

It appears that my engines run best when fueled with carbohydrates. (Note: This was before anyone heard of carbo-loading.) Not just fudge, mind you. But fruits and vegetables and cereals balanced with proteins. One of the first symptoms I notice when going on a low-carbohydrate kick is that the corners of my mouth become dry and sore. It's not that I salivate too much thinking about food. Something's amiss in my intake.

What drives a person to food is the liquid protein itself. A cherry soda it's not. Gaggiest of the lot are the natural-flavored ones. I stood over the kitchen sink and retched after tasting it au natural. Pity my poor husband. When he first went on the diet, he stocked up on three quarts of the plain stuff and had to drink it all. That's diet dedication.

Chilling the liquid isn't a great idea. It may temper the flavor a bit but the texture becomes thick and difficult to swallow. Like drinking rubber cement.

After giving liquid protein a try on behalf of my readers and waistline, I was soon back to testing recipes. The next week, I was at the State Fair watching judges evaluate baked goods.

"Here she is, back for chocolate cake," chorused the judges. I protested that I was just waiting for a photographer. But what could I do? A judge appeared brandishing a big knife that she used to slice into

Milky Way chocolate cake. "You eat that," she commanded. I obey anyone who's got me at knife point.

That was my first big dose of chocolate in a couple of weeks, and just like an old soak, I fell right off the wagon and went home to test Chocolate Pistachio Cake.

Hitting the Spot
December 25

Liquid protein never crossed my lips or slimmed my hips again. On Christmas Day, the column opened with this observation:

An astute merchandiser at the Drake Hotel in Chicago, where food editors were meeting, displayed a sweater embroidered with French culinary terms. I bought one, as did most of my colleagues. At first wearing, I noticed that emblazoned across my round tummy is "Glace au Chocolat." How appropriate. It's chocolate ice cream that helped pad my rounded shape.

Your Fingers Won't Fry
November 13

More and more homes were equipped with microwaves, yet the saturation was only about 10 percent, and some people worried about using them.

"Let me ask a dumb question," said a member of a women's group that I was addressing. She was worried about a television ad in which the woman who owned a microwave oven with a turntable was serenely smug as four other women, who bought different brands, had to keep opening their ovens to turn food so it would cook evenly.

"I don't own a microwave," she said, "but aren't all those women cooking their hands when they put them in the oven?"

She wasn't alone in her confusion. Most, like the questioner, are concerned about microwave-oven safety for two reasons: They don't know how the appliance works, and they've read scare stories. It may be proven someday that there are too many radio-wave frequencies in the air altogether from broadcasting, police radar, telephone operations, etc. But in the meantime, I have read or heard nothing that makes me fearful about the microwave in my kitchen, since no one in our house has a Pacemaker. The oven won't operate with the door open, so hands won't cook.

I asked the audience how many had ever burned themselves on a conventional gas or electric stove. Everyone raised a scarred hand.

Process This One
January 16

Early in the year, supposing a share of readers had found a food processor under the Christmas tree, I tried two simple processor recipes, including Celery With Brandied Blue Cheese, with a filling so good "just give me a bowlful and a spoon." I told readers:

Is it indecent to be in love with a machine? I guess if men can be passionate about cars, women can love their Cuisinarts. I wonder about my husband, though. He's nuts about his car and the processor. The only thing the machine couldn't do for this recipe is pull strings from celery.

Why are these machines going to be popular? Because I reckon there are lots of lazy cooks in the world. Like me ... happy that I'll never again have to bulge my biceps or skin my knuckles on a hand grater. To perfectly shred a pound of cheese in seconds, to have carrots ready for carrot cake in five seconds, to never again chase errant walnuts when hand-chopping them makes converts mighty fast.

CELERY WITH BRANDIED BLUE CHEESE
Makes 1 cup filling

1/4 cup walnuts
1/2 cup (2 ounces) crumbled blue cheese
1 tablespoon cream
2 tablespoons butter, cut in pieces
1 tablespoon brandy
Salt and pepper
Celery, cut in 1 1/2-inch lengths

With metal blade in place, add walnuts to bowl of food processor. Process only until coarsely chopped. Remove. Set aside. Add all remaining ingredients, except celery, to work bowl. Process for 5 to 7 seconds. Season to taste with salt and pepper. Add walnuts. Turn machine on and off several times to distribute nuts evenly. Transfer to storage container. Cover. Chill. Spoon into celery to serve.

"Town Chocoholic" Continually Led Astray
March 20

I tell you, it's murder to have a reputation as the town chocoholic. Here's what happened to me in one week — a binge, all because people know my proclivities.

A loyal reader, visiting San Francisco, airmailed 1 1/2 pounds of absolutely glorious Findley's Fabulous Fudge. "Thought you might enjoy this. It's supposed to be San Francisco's best," she wrote on the enclosure card. Of course, I enjoyed it — too much. And was I popular with Aric when I arrived home with that package of brown gold. (He has the same affliction I do. I've caught him guzzling straight out of the Hershey's syrup can.)

The day before that feast, I'd found, propped on our mailbox, a slice of chocolate-covered, pastry-wrapped toffee torte made by a gourmet friend. Ecstasy! It lasted about as long as a snowball in the Sahara. Thank goodness he didn't send the whole cake.

Then another friend called to say she had just found a fabulous chocolate dessert recipe, and she's going to make it for me. I'm flattered. And getting fatter — just in anticipation.

That's not all, folks. Reader Dorothy Mahood of St. Paul sent her favorite pudding recipe "because I have the same feeling about chocolate as you." She wrote that her formula is "absolutely foolproof, quick, easy and so delicious that you want to run your finger around the 'pot' to get the last lick! PLEASE try it," she urged. Now, Dorothy, do I need urging?

She's right. It's the ultimate recipe for anyone who likes to eat chocolate by the spoonful. Making it takes all of two minutes, and it was ready to eat immediately.

The Mint That Ate My Back Yard
July 3

Several years ago, I mentioned that I was having trouble finding mint for a recipe. A kind reader from St. Paul's East Side appeared at my desk the next day with a bunch of mint for transplanting. I plunked it in a planter filled with evergreens alongside our garage.

Now it's hard to see the trees for the forest of mint that's all but taken over. I have this hang-up about uprooting the fragrant weed because it's edible. But one can drink only so many mint juleps.

So I pounce on any recipe calling for fresh mint, hoping to harvest some of my crop. Hawaiian Shortcake was chosen not only because of the potentially luscious pineapple-strawberry topping, nor because the shortcake sounded extra good, nor because the lemon-flavored whipped cream was unique. It was tested because it calls for two mint sprigs. They're optional, but not at my house.

Which is worse? To drink too many juleps or eat too much shortcake in a futile attempt to keep pace with an herb that grows like a weed. Anyone want some mint plants? Please?

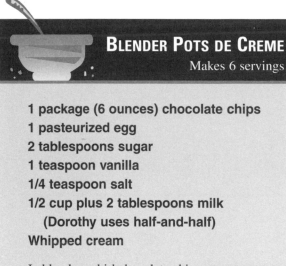

BLENDER POTS DE CREME
Makes 6 servings

1 package (6 ounces) chocolate chips
1 pasteurized egg
2 tablespoons sugar
1 teaspoon vanilla
1/4 teaspoon salt
1/2 cup plus 2 tablespoons milk
**   (Dorothy uses half-and-half)**
Whipped cream

In blender, whirl chocolate chips, egg, sugar, vanilla and salt at high speed to break up the chocolate pieces. Meanwhile, bring milk or half-and-half just to a boil. Pour into blender. Whirl at low speed for 1 minute. Pour into 6 pots de creme or demitasse cups. Chill until served. Top with dab of whipped cream.

A reader says . . .

Every time I use your recipes for company, I get many compliments.

— Diane O'Donnell, St. Paul

HAWAIIAN SHORTCAKE
Makes 6 to 8 servings

Pineapple-strawberry topping:
- 1 can (20 ounces) pineapple chunks
- 2 cups sliced strawberries
- 1/3 cup brown sugar
- 1/4 cup syrup from pineapple
- 2 mint sprigs (optional)

Rich shortcake ring:
- 2 cups all-purpose flour
- 2 tablespoons sugar
- 1 tablespoon baking powder

- 3/4 teaspoon salt
- 1/4 teaspoon cream of tartar
- 1/2 cup butter or margarine
- 1 large egg, beaten
- 2/3 cup half-and-half

Lemon cream topping:
- 1 cup whipping cream
- 2 tablespoons sugar
- 1/2 teaspoon vanilla
- 1 teaspoon grated lemon peel

To make pineapple-strawberry topping: Drain pineapple, saving syrup or juice. Rinse, hull and slice strawberries. Slightly crush 1 cup berries. Combine all fruit, brown sugar, 1/4 cup reserved syrup and crushed mint sprigs. Cover. Chill.

To make rich shortcake ring: Into mixing bowl, sift together flour, sugar, baking powder, salt and cream of tartar. Cut in butter or margarine until mixture resembles fine crumbs. Stir in beaten egg and half-and-half. Spoon dough in 6 to 8 mounds around edge of greased 9-inch cake pan. Brush dough with a little additional melted butter. Sprinkle with additional sugar. Bake in 400-degree oven for 25 minutes.

To make lemon cream topping: Beat whipping cream to soft peaks with sugar and vanilla. Fold in grated lemon peel.

To serve: Top portions of hot shortcake with pineapple-strawberry mixture and lemon whipped cream.

Bootlegging Mint
July 17

In the weeks that followed, more mint recipes and suggestions for drying my abundant crop poured in, but this solution to mint oversupply came in a truly unexpected manner:

Riding home on a packed bus one very hot night last week, we heard a bang and then S-s-s-s. Blowout. Hiking home with neighbor Buzz Cummins, we got to talking about mint, especially long, tall, cool mint drinks — wishful thinking at that point.

Buzz mentioned that his dad, Carl W. Cummins Jr., mixes a mean mint Philadelphia Bootleg. Here's the recipe: In a blender, combine equal parts sugar and fresh or bottled lemon juice (about 1 cup of each) "and as much mint as you have," explained the elder Cummins when I called him. "Beat the bejeebers out of it. Then pour equal shots of the mint mixture and gin into a glass, fill up with charged water, stir, and top with a mint sprig."

Of course, I tried his formula and found it dandy — if you don't mind sipping something that looks like swamp water.

Hot-and-Sour Soup: A Perennial
September 4

Rarely do I remake a recipe, no matter how much it was praised in the column. It's a matter of always trying something new rather than revisiting my repertoire. Hot-and-Sour Soup is one of the few exceptions. We've made it at home so many times that my recipe is stained and tattered. And the tangy soup is the ruler by which I measure a Chinese restaurant. This one was tried after I'd eaten my first true Chinese banquet, as Chinese restaurants were getting more complex in their cooking, and our interest was growing about food from the country gradually opening to the West.

Describing that Chinese feast in Honolulu:

We yum-yummed our way through exotic soups, appetizers, steamed buns and rice wine. Through the fish course and something rich with shrimp. Through several kinds of stir-fry, some wrapped in pancakes. "Enough already," our innards were pleading, but yet

---

A reader says . . .

Thank you for the pleasure I get from your column. Scratch cooks are the best!

— Shirley Nagle, St. Paul

---

to come were Peking duck and a couple of desserts — at least 12 courses in all. It was one time when I wasn't hungry an hour after eating a Chinese meal. Not even one day afterward.

HOT-AND-SOUR SOUP
Makes 4 to 6 servings

4 small Chinese dried black mushrooms
1/2 cup canned bamboo shoots, drained and slivered
1/4 pound boneless pork, slivered (use a pork chop)
4 cups chicken broth
1 tablespoon soy sauce
1 teaspoon salt
1 cup slivered soybean curd (tofu)
1 teaspoon ground white pepper
3 tablespoons red-wine vinegar
2 tablespoons cornstarch mixed with 3 tablespoons cold water
1 egg, slightly beaten
1 tablespoon sesame oil
1 whole green onion, finely chopped

Cover mushrooms with boiling water. Soak for 30 minutes. Drain. Remove and discard stems. Shred caps. In large saucepan, combine mushrooms, bamboo shoots, pork, broth, soy sauce and salt. Bring to a boil over high heat. Reduce heat. Simmer for 3 minutes. Add bean curd, pepper and vinegar. Return to a boil. Add cornstarch mixture. Stir until soup thickens. Slowly pour in beaten egg, stirring gently until egg is cooked. Remove from heat. Ladle into serving bowl. Stir in sesame oil. Garnish with green onions.

Tea at the
White House

— *With Rosalynn Carter* —

Would she or wouldn't she? Contradictory messages kept arriving prior to the food editors' visit to the White House about whether Rosalynn Carter would join us for afternoon tea. Well, she did, and this June 17, 1979, column told the story:

Abraham Lincoln, portrayed in oils, looked bemused as he gazed at the throng in the White House State Dining Room.

Perhaps it was the first time he'd seen a group of visitors more interested in taking notes about the lavish buffet goodies than in eating them.

America's newspaper and magazine food editors were invited to the White House for a reception to meet First Lady Rosalynn Cater. It was to be the icing on the eclair after a daylong session on food-price inflation issues. Just as there were pools betting whether chief inflation fighter Alfred Kahn would show up at the seminar (he did, but hours late), food editors wagered whether Mrs. Carter would arrive in time for the reception.

First, it was to be a morning coffee meeting with her, then she canceled, declining to return to D.C. from a vacation with the President. Word arrived shortly before our departure to the East Coast that she could join us at 5:30 p.m. But would she really?

The first question everyone asked when they learned I was going to the White House was, "What are you going to wear?" That required pondering. I settled on a ladylike blue and white tweed suit. Unplanned was the pink lipstick smudge front and center on my white blouse, acquired while getting dressed. Fortunately, I had a blue brooch along that nearly covered the Naked Pink, just as if I'd planned to wear it there all along.

Not that we all looked perfectly groomed. We'd sat through a seven-hour seminar in the steamy Old Executive Office Building next to the White House, the one that looks like a Victorian wedding cake.

At 5:15 p.m., a Secret Service agent arrived to escort us to the White House. "Follow me," he commanded. "If you don't stay with the group, you won't get in." No chance to stop for primping. Noses unpowdered, lipstick long gone, toting bulky packets of documents, we marched, 120 strong. A gust of wind as we entered the front portico demolished hairdos.

Once inside, we forgot about our dishevelment. Handsome White House aides (remember that Lynda Bird Johnson married one) greeted us. One of their number played the massive grand piano, supported by golden eagles, that dominates the foyer.

What to do with all those packets and with the suitcases some of us carried so we could eat and run to the airport? We were allowed to place them on and under sofas and chairs until the foyer was littered. "Tacky," said a food editor friend, surveying the debris.

The Red Room, the Blue Room, the Green Room were open to wander through leisurely, a wonderful

Rosalynn Carter speaks to food writers; Eleanor is at center, behind Janice Okun (who's wearing light dress).

treat. The last time I saw them was from behind a rope while taking the public tour.

But first things first — like food. We circled three buffet tables, scribbling notes, marveling at the display, certain that White House Chef Henry Haller had made good on his comment that if food editors were coming, he would have to do something special.

Floral cloths and garden bouquets of white, blue and yellow flowers decorated tables of hot, cold and sweet items. Glazed sliced salmon, proscuitto wrapped around bread sticks, hot crab cakes, almond pastry crescents filled with brie were piled on platters and chafing dishes. Also displayed were vegetables and dip, cheeses and crackers, which at most parties would be called finger food. At the White House, one tries to use a fork.

Everything was garnished and decorated by some brilliantly artistic culinarian. It tasted great, but to look at it was the real treat.

The dessert table was a "died and gone to heaven" experience. Pastry chef Albert Kumin is master of the petit four. Truly beautiful chocolates filled with dark chocolate mousse, miniature eclairs, tiny jellyrolls on macaroon rounds with almond cream frosting — pardon while I gush, but it was all too lovely. One food editor was seen tucking a few pastries in her purse.

Pity the poor waiters and butlers who were interviewed relentlessly about the food, despite their protests that they were only there to serve it. "We're not surprised. They told us you were food writers," one said. They're certainly accustomed to such receptions. A butler said ours was the second that day, to be followed by an evening dinner for SALT (Strategic Arms Limitation Treaty) negotiators.

Energy-conserving Americans will be happy to know that the White House is not overly air conditioned. It soon became just plain hot in the State Dining Room, where wines and orange juice quenched the parched. Marble-topped consoles supported by more golden eagles soon were stacked with empty plates and wineglasses.

At 6:15 p.m., Mrs. Carter entered the gold and white dining room and went to podium set against windows overlooking the Washington Monument. A description of what she wore, in food writer terms, would be a vanilla-colored cardigan suit with an apricot blouse.

"Hello, everybody. Welcome to the White House," she began, then told us she was sorry to be late, but she had helicoptered in at 5 p.m. from "fishing with Jimmy" and she had to fix her hair.

"I was just talking with Chip (her son), and he told me to tell you the story about the first time I toured the White House with Mrs. Ford before we moved in," she said. "We walked into the kitchen where I overheard a chef say he thought he could please the Carters. 'After all, they're from the South, and I cook like that everyday for the help.'"

Mrs. Carter said that, indeed, the food is good, especially those tempting desserts created by Chef Kumin. Chefs Haller and Kumin were introduced and joined Mrs. Carter at the podium for pictures. "How about looking this way?" one food editor called. When the chefs turned her direction, she said, "Attaboy."

Mrs. Carter suggested the administration "needs the active participation of the public" and she urged, "Let us hear from you. It's very easy to become isolated in Washington."

She wasn't isolated in the crowd, as she pressed flesh in a receiving line. We may have thought we were expected to say something cleverly grateful to Mrs. Carter, but the real purpose was for the White House photographer to snap a quick picture of each of us with the First Lady.

As she and I shook hands, she said we should turn toward the photographer. Before I could, the camera flashed, Mrs. Carter positioned for a flattering full face view, and me a startled double-chin side exposure. Several editors refused to go through the receiving line, not because they didn't want to meet the President's wife, but because they objected to "meat line" photos.

Sure, we were part of a constant parade of reception guests. But it was lovely to be invited. I had a final petit four and a goblet of orange juice (the same size glass

that had cost $1.75 when I breakfasted at the Capital Hilton that morning). After one more stroll through the Red, Blue and Green rooms, I retrieved my packet from under a red-brocade sofa in the foyer and reluctantly left what was probably a once-in-a-lifetime party.

That same Sunday, we ran Mrs. Carter's recipe for Plains Special Cheese Ring, and the following:

Prerequisites for First Ladies are charm, commitment, a travel-ready wardrobe — and a recipe.

Mamie Eisenhower became famous for her fudge, Lady Bird Johnson for her Strawberry Ice Box Pie and Deer Meat Sausage. Every time a church cookbook committee asked for a presidential favorite, Pat Nixon sent Crab Bisque and Betty Ford dispatched Cream Cheese Roll. Jackie Kennedy preferred French recipes.

Rosalynn Carter's recipe is Plains Special Cheese Ring, which has been reprinted dozens of times, including appearances in two of the many Carter-inspired cookbooks. One, "Miss Lillian and Friends," reveals a member of the Carter clan brought the ring recipe to Plains, Ga., where it has become a party staple. It was served at the $5,000-a-plate dinner at Miss Lillian's Pond House in Plains, which raised money for son Jimmy's presidential campaign.

Sure enough, when food editors attending a White House seminar Monday opened their packets of complex government price and inflation data, tucked in the front was Rosalynn Carter's cheese ring recipe on impressive White House stationery.

I didn't see the ring on the buffet tables at the reception in the State Dining Room, which is a good thing, because strawberry preserves are sticky and there would have been 120 food editors with White House paper napkins glued to their fingers. Makes it rather difficult to shake hands in a receiving line.

So I hauled the fancy recipe card home for testing. Certainly is simple to put together. I dosed it liberally with freshly ground pepper, which I adore but may bring tears to some eyes.

Mrs. Carter suggests finely chopped nuts, which could be peanuts. I prefer pecans, which are also abundant in Georgia. You can hardly see Plains for the pecan trees.

Office tasters were divided on the recipe, not because of politics, but over the sweet-and-savory issue.

Most liked the combination of cheese and jam, but some campaigned against it.

That's what makes America work — a two-party system.

"Plains Special" Cheese Ring

1 pound grated sharp cheese
1 cup finely chopped nuts
1 cup mayonnaise
1 small onion, finely grated

Black pepper
Dash cayenne
Strawberry preserves, optional

Combine all ingredients except preserves, season to taste with pepper. Mix well and place in a 5 or 6 cup lightly greased ring mold. Refrigerate until firm for several hours or overnight.

To serve, unmold, and if desired, fill center with strawberry preserves, or serve plain with crackers.

With best wishes,

Rosalynn Carter

1978

— After a decade, the column introduces computer gremlins, klutzes, "cuising," spaghetti sauce and squash —

Computer Gremlins Get Us

July 30

As technology relentlessly marched, the 10th anniversary Tested Recipes column encountered the computer age. It hadn't been so long before that we'd began using electric typewriters at the newspaper, and they seemed daunting at first. Now, it was computers, and I hoped it would mean the end to recipe errors, the rotten eggs in any food writer's life. Those errors had been the gremlins bedeviling my job, though they hadn't been jumping up to bite me too often of late, I wrote for that anniversary column:

Saying that, of course, is going to unleash those gremlins, some of whom reside in the video terminal on which I will be setting recipes directly into print, starting this week. I am terrified.

I know there are gremlins in these terminals because when my co-workers who are already trained (I am resisting until the last possible moment) hit the wrong key, an electronic somebody in there squawks as though he'd just been kicked in a tender spot. That somebody also eats copy.

Furthermore, under this new direct system, if 1/2 teaspoon salt comes out as 1/2 cup salt in the newspaper, it will be my fault and mine alone. No longer will I be able to blame some faceless printer. I contemplate early retirement a lot.

Sure enough, new technology, new problems. For the 10th anniversary column, I selected a spate of favorite recipes, and Appetizer Oat Balls appeared with garbled instructions. With computers, we had transitioned from hot type to cold type involving sheets of waxy-backed paper that have to be cut and pasted. While making corrections, a printer stuck two lines of type from the first paragraph of meatballs directions over the top two lines of sour-cream sauce. When I peeled them away after learning of the error, correct directions were underneath. Foiled by a scissors-happy printer. When I cried on his shoulder, he said I was lucky he got those errant two lines in the right recipe. I was not consoled.

Processing a New Word

January 29

A new addition to the culinary vocabulary has been coined in St. Paul. My friend Jayne Trudell decided she needed a food processor to add zest to her declining interest in cooking. After she researched the brands available and dropped appropriate hints to her husband, George, she was presented with a Cuisinart on Christmas morning. Now, her husband's first question each night is, "What have you cuised today?"

Almost Everybody Cooks
February 5

The rage of '78, starting in California, of course, was the "everybody-cooks" dinner party. We hosted one, inviting women friends in the food business and their husbands. The guys were capable cooks, too, except for one whose last culinary attempt was making popcorn 10 years ago. His wife swears he needs detailed instructions to fill water glasses. But even if experience was limited, his enthusiasm was boundless. He was soon separating eggs and caramelizing sugar for sherried flan. He told his wife on the way home that maybe cooking wasn't so tough after all.

Aric's Cookbook
April 9

Flatterers will sometimes tell our son, Aric, in my presence, that he'll have a hard time finding a wife who can cook like mom. I appreciate their compliments, but I assure them that Aric's tastes are simple. Were he to elope tomorrow, his intended could write a cookbook of his favorite foods on the back of a McDonald's napkin (since they'd probably be there anyway, eating a Quarter Pounder with Cheese, on which he could exist, given the opportunity).

On the napkin would be recipes for tuna salad, meatloaf, broiled steak and a few other straightforward favorites. Nothing too exotic, nothing too challenging for a new bride.

One would hope, by the time he's of matrimonial age, that his tastes in food would be as sophisticated as his taste in women. Meanwhile, he's a plain-food kid stuck in a household where the chief cook tests crazy things, such as Spaghetti With Tuna Sauce.

Let me assure you it was declared delicious by everyone — except Aric who viewed it with wrinkled nose.

I tried the old "The whole is equal to the sum of its parts" argument.

"You like tuna, don't you?"

"Yes."

"You like spaghetti, don't you?"

"Yes."

"You like cheddar cheese, don't you?"

"Yes. But not all together."

Foiled again. So I made him a bowlful of tuna salad. Plain.

I was telling a friend about this 8-year-old of mine with his stubborn taste buds. When her boys behaved similarly, she'd look 'em in the eye and say, "Do you want to be 9?" They'd eat. Gotta try that.

Since writing that column, two decades have gone by, Aric has married lovely Jennifer and he never eats Quarter Pounders anymore. He rarely eats meat, and likes his fish raw, sushi style, or yellow fin tuna barely cooked. In their household, he does a good share of the cooking, and Jennifer never says, "Yuck." But wait until they have kids!

A reader says . . .

What fun to win the food writers' category and have lunch with Paul Newman! Thanks for taking us along. I am one of your devotees and have enjoyed your column and recipes for years.

— Helen Lawson, Stillwater, Minn.

Food Writers' Funnies

June 18

Every food writer has funny tales to tell about calls from readers. On that June Sunday, I told a few of my own and others collected from my sisters in the business:

A woman was upset because the newspaper's recipes were too large. "I want a pickle recipe using just one cucumber," she told one of my startled colleagues. "After all, I live alone."

And then there was the call from a person wondering about recipe directions that stated the food should be kept "under refrigeration." Queried the reader, "If I put it under the refrigerator, won't it spoil?"

My favorite is the request for a turtle soup. After I'd given the caller a recipe, I asked her why she wanted it. "I'm so darn sick of the kids' turtle," she replied.

Salad Scorchers Anonymous

October 15

I am officially registered as Kitchen Klutz of America, number 2,809.

You may have suspected the klutz part, but did you realize there were so many of us willing to carry a union card?

The "klub" was started by a food editor friend of mine, Joy Gallagher of the Flint (Mich.) Journal, who doesn't assume pretension of perfection, either.

We have an official motto: Sorry, I burned the tossed salad.

And an official prayer based, through no small accident, on the Alcoholics Anonymous plea: Grant me the serenity to accept the fact that I am a kitchen klutz, the courage to march into any potluck with my

latest disaster borne proudly on a silver platter, and the wisdom to tell anyone who makes a snide remark to go stuff a green banana up his nose.

We Go Batty

August 27

How I spent my summer vacation, or why it's sometimes more restful to go to the office:

On the first blissful day, the bank called to say we were $1,000 overdrawn, which was eventually traced to new incorrectly coded checks. Not our fault.

But since I wanted to prove that I surely wasn't amiss by a thousand bucks, I thought I'd better do a little financial housecleaning. So from 7 p.m. to midnight, I kept company with an adding machine, working at the kitchen table, re-entering hundreds of checks and recomputing all my figures. Nice way to spend a vacation.

After the "Tonight Show" monologue, husband and son headed for bed, while I toiled with my accounting. Just as I'd finished my last calculation, two bats as big as B-29s, flying in formation, whooshed into the kitchen. I grabbed the checkbook and dashed out the back door.

If I'd grabbed my purse instead, I would have had a dime to call home and wake my husband. Instead, I tried pounding the front door knocker and yelling for him in the direction of the upstairs bedroom windows.

Next time he tells me he's a light sleeper, I'm going to laugh hysterically. I'd hit the huge brass knocker so hard that I thought the oak door would break, then run to the windows and holler. Back and forth for what seemed like forever, and still he slept. I bet the neighbors didn't.

Finally, he appeared at the door, stark naked, carrying a tennis racket. When I visualized that later, I realized how hilarious the moment was. But all I could do was holler, "The house is full of bats!" I tend to exaggerate under stress.

"I know. They're both up in the bedroom," he informed me. "Well, I'm not coming in until they're gone," I informed back. While I paced the porch, he practiced his backhand and did away with the midnight visitors.

Later, I asked him how he would sleep through all my pounding and banshee screams. That didn't wake him, he said. What did, was the sound, mind you, the **sound** of bats winging around the bedroom.

Keeping Our Cool
February 12

Readers took a weekly trip into my kitchen. If they came to our 1902-vintage house (built with thick brick walls but no insulation) during the miserably cold winter of '78, parkas were the required mode of dress:

HAM 'N' CHEESE LOAF
Makes 2 loaves

6 to 7 cups unsifted flour, divided
1 teaspoon sugar
1 tablespoon salt
2 packages active dry yeast
1 cup plain yogurt
1/2 cup water
2 tablespoons margarine

6 eggs, at room temperature
1/2 pound muenster cheese, shredded, divided
1 cup sliced boiled ham, cut into julienne strips
1 egg, slightly beaten
1 tablespoon milk

To make bread: In large bowl, thoroughly mix 1 1/2 cups flour, sugar, salt and undissolved active dry yeast. In saucepan, combine yogurt, water and margarine. Heat over low heat until liquids are very warm, 120 to 130 degrees. (Note: Margarine does not need to melt.) Gradually add to dry ingredients. Beat for 2 minutes at medium speed of electric mixer, scraping bowl occasionally. Add 6 eggs, 1 cup flour and all but 1/2 cup cheese. Beat at high speed for 2 minutes, scraping bowl occasionally. Stir in enough additional flour to make a stiff dough. Turn out onto lightly floured board. Knead for 8 to 10 minutes, or until smooth and elastic. Place in greased bowl. Turn to grease top. Cover. Let raise in warm place, free from draft, for 1 hour, or until doubled in bulk. Punch dough down. Turn out onto lightly

floured board. Knead in ham. Divide dough in half. Shape each half into round ball. Place on greased baking sheets. Cover. Let raise in warm place, free from draft, for 1 hour, or until doubled in bulk.

To bake bread: Combine beaten egg with milk. Brush over loaves. Sprinkle with remaining 1/2 cup cheese. Bake in 350-degree oven for 30 minutes, or until loaves are golden brown. Remove from baking sheets. Cool on wire racks.

Note: In 1978, finding unflavored yogurt was a challenge. "I must have rummaged through 200 containers trying to find some unflavored stuff. No success," I told readers. "I settled on some vanilla yogurt, and it seemed to blend well with all those eggs, cheese and ham into mighty rich loaves. Hardly needs butter."

The weatherman doesn't have to tell me we've had a record-breaking below-zero spell. I just count the layers of wool sweaters and socks I wear around the house, because we keep our home very cool. How cool? I'll tell you:

We put butter in the refrigerator to soften it.

Face cream is applied in lumps to melt from my body heat before I can smooth it on.

Ice cubes don't disappear in drinks. In fact, a bottle of pop stored in our house hardly needs ice cubes.

Wine kept at room temperature is chilled.

And we don't take saunas to get clean. We take saunas to get warm.

The only thing that gets us steamy is reading the monthly heat bill. We could go to Nassau for what we're paying for gas this winter.

That chilly assessment led up to testing of a ham and cheese bread:

In a house where the temperature hovers between 55 and 60, any excuse to heat the oven is welcome. When we get two delicious Ham 'n Cheese Loaves and a warmer kitchen, well, that's wintertime bliss.

Finding a place for bread to rise in a cold house is a problem. There's always the oven. But even better is our one warm room, the den, where, if the door is kept shut, the temperature will creep up past 70, and yeast has a chance to thrive. That's where we hibernate winter evenings. To step out of that room is like taking a giant step from Florida to Alaska.

Actually, a cold house isn't so bad. The cooler indoor climate is keeping us healthy while those around us are sniffling. But that doesn't mean I'm not praying that the ground hogs are all nearsighted. Let's hear it for a record-breaking warm spell! Let's just skip the next six weeks and move right into April.

Spaghetti Sauce Second to None

July 23

Recipes came from all sources, this one from Perry the Printer (Perry Cucciarella, who spent his career in the newspaper's composing room). He calls it Second Best Spaghetti Sauce in the World because he swears his mother makes the world's best spaghetti sauce. One of the happiest moments of his life, Perry said, was the day his father couldn't detect any difference between mother's and son's spaghetti sauces.

I confessed to readers that I usually doctor a jarful of Ragu when making spaghetti for the family, "but now I fear that Perry's recipe has spoiled me forever more. The balance of sweet basil, pepper and garlic is magnificent. Anyone who dares add oregano gets a meatball in the eye."

Pork, Perry told me, kissing his fingertips, makes the best sauce base. "But braciola — ah-h-h." That beef treatment rated kissed fingertips and a "Mmmmm" from Mr. Spaghetti Sauce.

More than anything, Perry's sauce, made by generations of his Italian foremothers, needs unquestioning, unlimited patience. I spent the better part of a Saturday afternoon in the kitchen, stirring and tasting, tasting, tasting — it's addictive.

Perry had advice about cooking spaghetti, as well. He brings salted water to a boil, adds spaghetti, brings the water back to a boil, then turns off the heat and lets the spaghetti sit, covered, for 10 to 12 minutes. Then, he blanches it in cold water.

How does he know it's done? "Throw a strand against the wall, and if it sticks, it's done," he said. "Wonder what Mrs. Cucciarella says about that when she has to wash starchy kitchen walls," I mused.

SECOND BEST SPAGHETTI SAUCE IN THE WORLD

Makes 8 servings

Sauce:
A piece of meat, such as a small pork roast (or the braciola listed below)
1 can (29 ounces) tomato puree
1 can (12 ounces) tomato paste

1 tablespoon salt
1 teaspoon black pepper
1 teaspoon garlic powder
4 tablespoons sweet basil
4 tablespoons parsley

To make sauce: In saucepan, 5-quart Dutch oven, or large cast-iron frying pan, brown meat (pork is best, but any meat will do). After meat is brown, remove it but leave drippings in pan. Add remaining ingredients. Fill tomato puree and paste cans with water. Add water to other ingredients. Stir well. Bring to a boil. Reduce heat to simmer. Return meat to sauce. Simmer, stirring occasionally, for 2 to 3 hours, or until dark grease appears on top of sauce. When sauce gets too thick, add a little water. (Note: Any cooking after dark grease appears is a waste of time, effort and energy. Unless the meat is unusually large or tough, it will be done when the sauce is ready.)

To make braciola: Season a large thin round steak with 1/2 teaspoon salt, 1/4 teaspoon black pepper, 1/2 teaspoon garlic powder, 1 teaspoon sweet basil, 1 tablespoon parsley flakes and 1 1/2 tablespoons grated parmesan cheese. Roll up jellyroll-style. Secure with string or toothpicks. Brown meat. Follow instructions for spaghetti sauce. When sauce is done, remove string or toothpicks from meat. Slice meat into 1/2- to 3/4-inch thick portions.

Meatballs:
6 slices bread
2 pounds ground beef
1 teaspoon salt
1/4 teaspoon black pepper
1/2 teaspoon garlic powder

1 heaping tablespoon sweet basil
1 heaping tablespoon parsley flakes
2 heaping tablespoons grated parmesan cheese
3 to 4 eggs

To make meatballs: Use old, hard Italian or French bread that has been dried out in paper bag. Soak about 6 slices in cold water. Squeeze out as much water as possible. Break up bread. Place in bowl with other ingredients. (Note: Number of eggs used depends on how dry mixture is. If it's dry and sticky, add another egg.) Mix all ingredients thoroughly. Roll into balls about the diameter of a half-dollar.

To brown meatballs: Cover bottom of cast-iron frying pan with oil (any kind). Heat pan. Place meatballs in pan to brown. (Note: If they stick when turned, let them brown some more. They won't stick when fully browned.) Turn them over only once. (They are ready to be turned when you see a little gray at the oil line and a little dark brown just below that.) When browned, remove from pan to be served with spaghetti and sauce. Grease from pan can be used for sauce base. Store grease in uncovered jar in refrigerator until making another batch of sauce.

If You Can't Say It, Eat It
November 19

An old saying, coined by some suspicious type, suggests that if you can't pronounce it, don't eat it.

Well, try rolling isquouterosquash around the tongue. As intimidating as the word looks and sounds, the last syllable is the one we know and love. Good old squash.

When I brought Squash Spice Bars to the office, only one taster guessed squash. The wise one was fashion writer Georgann Koelln, a gardener at heart. "I grew up on a farm, and I know the ways people use up all that stuff," she said of seasonal abundances. All others guessed pumpkin, or were so mystified they had to have another piece for further investigation. Likely excuse.

The original recipe called for 1 3/4 cups sugar, but after trying the bars, I suggested that 1 1/4 cups would make them adequately sweet, and let the isquouterosquash shine through.

SQUASH SPICE BARS
Makes 36 bars

Squash bars:
- 4 eggs
- 3/4 cup salad oil
- 1 1/4 cups sugar
- 1/4 cup unsulphured molasses
- 1 package (12 ounces) frozen squash, defrosted, or 1 1/2 cups mashed cooked squash
- 2 cups unsifted flour
- 2 teaspoons baking powder
- 1 teaspoon baking soda
- 1/2 teaspoon salt
- 1/2 teaspoon ginger
- 1/2 teaspoon cloves
- 1/2 teaspoon nutmeg

Orange cream icing:
- 1 package (3 ounces) cream cheese
- 2 tablespoons soft butter or margarine
- 1 teaspoon orange juice
- 1 teaspoon grated orange peel
- 1 teaspoon milk
- 2 cups powdered sugar

To make bars: In large mixer bowl, beat together eggs, oil, sugar, molasses and squash. Sift together flour, baking powder, baking soda, salt and spices. Add to squash mixture. Beat until well blended. Pour batter into greased and floured jellyroll pan or 2 (9-inch) square pans. Bake in 350-degree oven for 35 minutes, or until edges pull away from sides of pan and center springs back when lightly touched. Cool. Frost. Cut into bars.

To make icing: Beat cream cheese, butter and orange juice, grated orange peel and milk until fluffy. Add powdered sugar, beating until smooth.

1979

_Eating on the cheap, meeting
the animal kingdom and animated klutzes,
"keeper" lasagna and cookies —_

Meeting Meatless

March 5

Beef prices blipped upward in 1979, so testing emphasis turned to chicken and meatless meals:

"Economize" is ringing in our ears so loudly these days that a new Excedrin headache has come throbbing into the world.

My tasters for Meatless Manicotti were Aric and his school buddy, Dean, who's a plate polisher any cook would love. Aric should take lessons. They seemed happy to eat anything Italian so I didn't go into details.

The boys agreed they smelled pepperoni. Should I tell them it was meatless? Of course not. Neither noticed zucchini. Should I point it out? Absurd. When two skeptical 9-year-olds are pronouncing something good, they don't need specifics.

We all have our methods to cut food costs. Take author and talk-show combatant Truman Capote. He writes in the forward to "The Potato Book" by Myrna Davis about how he saves money by roaming the potato fields surrounding his Long Island house after harvesting is done.

"I amble out through the empty rows collecting small, sweet leftover potatoes for my larder," he said. Oh, goodie. Free potatoes. Such economy!

If only he stopped there. But Capote continues in the next paragraph, "Imagine a cold October morning. I fill my basket with found potatoes and race to the kitchen to create my one and only most delicious ever potato lunch."

On those free potatoes, his guests pile sour cream. Then he whisks out "the big tin of caviar, which I forgot to tell you is the only way I can bear to eat a potato. Caviar — the freshest, the grayest, the biggest Beluga — is heaped in mounds over the potatoes."

On those scavenged potatoes, he squanders supreme caviar, which, since the upheaval in Iran, is selling for about a dollar per little fish egg, or hundreds of bucks per pound.

One way to avoid the high price of beef was to eat tofu, which was just becoming familiar to those of us without Oriental parentage or an earlier venture into vegetarianism. Later in the year, the column said:

Timing for tofu was perfect. The phone tip about a Roseville firm that manufactures tofu (soybean curd) came just as I returned from China, where I'd eaten the stuff in every conceivable form. I'd had it liquid, dried, fried, smoked, cubed, rolled, slivered, shaped and mashed. And there was one memorable dish I'd rather forget called Stinking Bean Curd, which lived up to its name and looked like charcoal briquets.

A Squirrelly Tale
January 21

Neighbors — all kinds — became part of the column. Writing, somewhat belatedly after post-Christmas travels, about Bombe Noel, of which I'd made two, overestimating the capacity of guests invited for a holiday party:

The second bombe was planted in a cardboard box and stored in our outdoor freezer: the back deck. The next day, I cut a wedge to give to neighbors who couldn't come to the party.

A couple of days later, I noticed another "neighbor" had helped himself. The foil cover had been torn away and a squirrel had happily eaten the chocolate cake layer and part of the raspberry mousse. He isn't a pistachio fan, apparently.

I spoke too soon. Updating readers a few weeks later:

Friend squirrel just needed more time. By now, the entire bowl, which contained a half-gallon of ice cream and a quart of raspberry mousse under the chocolate layer, is licked clean. He must be the fattest, glossiest critter in the neighborhood.

Getting Hooked
March 11

Call me the Unhappy Hooker. We do — and eat — some kinky things in our house, all in the name of recipe testing, but I've just spent a day unkinking paperclips and sticking them into Chinese spareribs.

For months, a box of giant paperclips was in plain sight in our house. But when I needed them, where were they? Not anywhere I looked. If the ribs hadn't already been marinated, I might have abandoned the whole Chinese project, which directed that the meat must be hung from oven racks.

Should I use fishhooks? What about cutting a hanger apart? Could I sew the meat to the rack? My most brilliant thought was to use drapery hooks, but I didn't have enough without taking down the living-room curtains.

By rummaging through drawers, I found enough paperclips to continue. In the book of psychotic behavior, there must be a chapter devoted to people who twist paperclips compulsively. Now, if anyone questions such a quirk, just say you're making Chinese spareribs.

Ladybug, Ladybug, Fly Away Home
April 22

Aric always dives into the grocery bags when I come home from the store, hoping to find edible treasures. Last week, he found something not so snackable.

Just as he pulled out a package of spinach, a ladybug decided to stroll from under a green leaf for a promenade visible through plastic wrapping.

"Yuck," he said.

"She won't eat much," my husband consoled.

"Free protein," I suggested.

"I don't care. I'm not eating any spinach," Aric insisted. That may be the end of a little charade we've been playing. Our little Popeye likes fresh spinach salads. When spinach isn't available, I've been able to pass off romaine as spinach. Now, he probably won't eat that, either, for fear of biting a bug.

King of the Klutzes
November 4

After I wrote about the Kitchen Klutzes in 1978, people in the St. Paul area leapt to fourth place in national membership, which had rocketed to 7,000. When the national Grand Klutz award was announced, the most kitchen-inept people in America proved to be the Barnett family from Afton, 20 miles east of St.

Paul, who made exploding root beer and on another occasion, even managed to burn down the house. That disaster happened when a Barnett or two got engrossed in a Frankenstein movie while heating oil for deep-frying a snack.

Other contenders for the national award included a 94-year-old who was "determined to make one pan of decent gravy before I die."

A woman named Sharon "proved that you cannot open a fresh coconut with an aluminum saucepan, or even by flinging it repeatedly at the curb in front of your house after you have bent the saucepan all to hell." She also learned that 18-pound watermelons do not bounce. And, alluding to the Kitchen Klutz creed, which states, "Sorry, I burned the tossed salad," Sharon confessed, "I have burned a salad, and it was tossed — tossed out. It was to be wilted lettuce, but it went up in smoke."

Her masterpiece was a turkey trussed with plastic dental floss which melted completely into the bird.

Give It a Second Chance
March 18

It pays to advertise. Weeks earlier, I'd mentioned how everyone raved about the spinach lasagna on the potluck table at Aric's school, but by the time we got there, only a few green strands remained in the pan. No one knew who had donated it. After my plea, I heard from the lasagna-maker, who gave me the recipe on the promise of anonymity. While she was at it, she also shared the recipe for Hamburger Soup, which was the rage of Mendota Heights that year.

Since then, this lasagna has become a family classic. Sometimes, for Christmas, I add a layer of chopped fresh tomato. But the first time we made it, eager to taste what we'd missed at the potluck, we sampled it fresh out of the oven. It was so rich, so buttery that both my husband and I felt queasy afterward. We could only make a small dent in the large panful. What to do with the rest? Take it to the office, he suggested; they'll eat anything.

SPINACH LASAGNA
Makes 8 servings

2 pounds cottage cheese
Salt, pepper and garlic powder to taste
1 tablespoon parsley
2 eggs
1/2 cup soft butter
8 ounces lasagna noodles, cooked
1 pound Monterey jack cheese, grated
2 packages frozen chopped spinach, thawed and drained
1 cup grated parmesan cheese

Mix cottage cheese, seasonings, parsley, eggs and butter. Grease lasagna pan. Place 1 layer of noodles in pan. Add layers of cottage-cheese mixture, Monterey Jack cheese, spinach and parmesan. Repeat layers. Bake, uncovered, in 350-degree oven for 30 minutes.

The joke was on us. After the lasagna had a day to absorb the butter and cheese, and after it was reheated for a half-hour, it was absolutely sensational. Two office-mates fought over the last morsel.

Moral: This lasagna is definitely better the second time around.

We Could Eat These Everyday
June 3

After attending the funeral of Martha Peters, a friend and neighbor both in St. Paul and at the lake, I decided the most appropriate memorial would be sharing one of her best recipes.

A wonderful cook, Martha made the most delectable cookies I've ever tasted. She called them Everyday Cookies and took no credit for originating the recipe, which was soon circulating among my relatives and friends.

I suggested that Martha should enter Everyday Cookies in the State Fair. She was suffering from cancer, but she accepted the challenge, taking some from the freezer to the Fairgrounds. They won third place. If she'd baked a fresh batch, they would have taken a purple ribbon, I bet.

EVERYDAY COOKIES
Makes 10 to 12 dozen

1 cup margarine
1 cup white sugar
1 cup brown sugar
1 cup corn oil (Mazola)
2 medium eggs
1 teaspoon vanilla
3 1/2 cups flour
1 teaspoon soda
1 teaspoon salt
1 teaspoon cream of tartar
1 cup Rice Krispies
1 cup quick oatmeal
1 cup coconut
1/2 cup chopped nuts (use pecans so cookies taste like Pecan Sandies)

To make cookies: In mixing bowl, cream together margarine, sugars and oil. Add eggs. Beat well so oil won't separate. Add vanilla. In another bowl, combine flour, soda, salt and cream of tartar. Add to egg mixture. Stir in Rice Krispies, oatmeal, coconut and nuts.

To bake cookies: Drop by teaspoonfuls onto ungreased cookie sheet. Flatten slightly. Bake on lower shelf of 350-degree oven for 5 to 6 minutes. Move pan to shelf at middle of oven. Bake for 5 minutes, or until lightly browned. Remove from cookie sheet. Cool.

Note: Martha Peters suggested having another sheet of cookies ready to bake so when the first pan is moved to the middle shelf, the second pan can go on the bottom shelf to speed up baking. She admonished to "watch carefully" so the delicate and crisp cookies don't overbrown.

HAMBURGER SOUP
Makes 6 servings

1 medium onion, chopped
3 tablespoons butter
1 1/2 pounds lean ground beef
1 can (28 ounces) tomatoes
2 cans beef consomme
2 soup cans water
4 carrots, sliced
4 celery tops, chopped
Parsley to taste
1 1/2 teaspoons thyme
10 peppercorns
1 tablespoon salt
1/2 cup barley

Saute chopped onion in butter. Add ground beef. Cook until browned. Drain. Add all remaining ingredients. Simmer, covered, for 1 hour or more.

Double Dose of Peking Duck

— *She Crashed a Dinner at China's Great Hall* —

The greatest coup of my food travels occurred on my first day in China in 1979, where I led the pioneering group of food writers to venture into that still-mysterious nation.

"She crashed a dinner at China's Great Hall" appeared on this recount. After I was done "crashing," I rode a taxi through black-as-midnight (actually, it was midnight) streets of Beijing to our distant hotel, wrote this story longhand, and mailed it the next morning with enough stamps on the envelope to carry a letter three times around the globe. It arrived in St. Paul in time to appear in the next Sunday's paper, September 9, 1979. Just at that time, China was changing its geographical spellings, from Westernized versions to a closer reflection of its own language. That's why I still referred to Peking in the story.

Peking (Beijing) — How I talked my way into the Great Hall of the People without speaking one word of Chinese, to eat Peking duck twice in one night.

There it was, Vice President Walter Mondale's Air Force One plane, parked on the runway when our group of newspaper food editors arrived in Peking on a sultry Saturday night.

How coincidental. Mondale was among those to whom I'd appealed during the disappointing days when it looked like the People's Republic of China would never give visas to a group of food editors hungry to learn about real Chinese cooking.

An opportunity to take this trip arose from another source shortly after I'd written to the Vice President. But how unique that he and I would arrive in Peking hours apart, both on our first trips to this new tourist mecca. I determined, walking across that dark runway illuminated only by the glow from the late Chairman Mao's immense portrait, to look up my fellow Minnesotan.

Sunday afternoon, while touring the Summer Palace, I called the American consulate to leave word for Al Eisele, Mondale's press secretary and a former reporter for the St. Paul Dispatch. Peking's phone system is a one-way thing, I gathered from my several attempts. I shout because I can't hear the person at the other end, and he has his eardrums battered because he can hear fine.

I think, from what little I could hear, that the secretary assured me he'd pass along messages, but the call from Eisele didn't come at the appointed hour. So I went off with my group to eat a 20-dish Peking duck dinner, from jellied feet to split head cradling cooked brains. Nothing is ignored in Chinese cuisine, except the squeamishness of certain American food writers.

After eating the last bit of duck I could manage, I thought I'd take a solitary stroll across Tiananmen Square to see what was happening at the welcoming banquet for Mondale.

The stroll was far from solitary. Peking residents streamed through the streets, most of them on bicycles.

Vice President Walter Mondale gets a lesson in chopstick usage from China's Vice Premier Deng Xiaoping at a welcoming dinner at the Great Hall of the People in Peking in 1979.

They have learned if they slow down for the hapless pedestrian, they'll get mowed over from behind, so strollers must be swift when crossing streets. Pedestrians have no rights here. Motor vehicles are lords of the roads, sovereign over bike traffic. Cars and buses honk their way through traffic, miraculously missing most of the bikes. The overall din is deafening.

There's no such thing as a "quick stroll" across the square, either. Spaces are vast, and streets are dark. I was unsure which of the immense buildings was the Great Hall, but I came upon a young Chinese fellow, standing under a streetlight, practicing his English by reading out loud to a fence post. He pointed to the Great Hall, and I dodged bikes to get there, only to be met by two smiling but insistent army guards who wouldn't let me advance to the doors.

I could have given up then. But where were the limousines? Maybe this wasn't the right entrance.

Around the massive building I went, and sure enough, there were the black limos — and more army guards. The language barrier was impenetrable. I made

sign language attempts by scribbling on my note pad and pointing to my camera to indicate I was a journalist. They made gestures to ask for my official invitation. No ticket, no dinner.

Finally, persistent gestures to the great golden doors got me an escort that far, with stern warnings to stay put. Would I try an uninvited entrance when there were three guards — bayonets fixed — between me and the door?

While I watched a clock on a nearby tower inch toward 9 p.m., I waited and waited. At last, an American Associated Press correspondent came outside for a smoke. He passed word to a Chinese press aide who took my credentials, telling me, "Wait here" as he disappeared. The guards and I watched each other. They weren't smiling.

The chief Chinese press officer appeared. How did I know the Vice President? Why was I here trying to crash a Chinese state banquet?

More minutes evaporated. The guards were still grim. But then the press officer reappeared and escorted

A year after we ate Peking Duck at the Great Hall of the People, Vice President Mondale serves me his backyard barbecue in Washington, D.C. Taking a bite is Mary Hart of the Minneapolis Tribune. At center is Charlotte Hansen of the Jamestown (N.D.) Sun. Both have recipes in this book.

me past the bayonets. Good ol' Al Eisele had vouched for me.

I asked only to observe from the sidelines, but I was ushered to a table in the cavernous banquet hall. On my right was Rod Rodriguez, who manages the vice presidential mansion in Washington, D.C. On my left was a Chinese foreign-affairs officer.

At the head table were the Mondales, Chairman Hua and Vice Chairman Deng Xiaoping. In a socialist country where all are nominally equal, the head table is not elevated, so it was difficult to see how international relations were progressing.

I arrived just as official toasts were ending, so I didn't have to "gom-bei" (bottoms up) the choking Mao-tai liquor.

But I did get there in time for the foreign official to serve me roast duck in brown sauce wrapped in pancake "doilies," just what I'd eaten only an hour before.

An orchestra played stirring music. Waiters glided about filling glasses with red wine and orange soda.

Decor and service weren't elegant, but they were efficient.

Platters of red and yellow watermelon on the tables, to be served family style, were followed by Ice Cream of Three Flavors (we call it Neapolitan), which had a canned-milk flavor.

I'd missed the Cream of Three Delicacies (fish maw, pigeon eggs and sea cucumber). Who's complaining?

All of a sudden, with no announcement or closing speeches, everyone stood up. Handshakes were exchanged, and the dignitaries filed out.

I spotted Eisele and went over to thank him for approving my impromptu gate crashing. "You're pretty brassy," he grinned at me.

During a final handshake with Mondale before he climbed into his limousine, I reminded him of my letter begging help to get into China. "I see we both made it," he said.

Global Gourmets

— *Eating Our Way Around the World* —

Barbara Bush was my inspiration. Her urging propelled me into organizing world travel for food writers, 34 trips thus far.

Before she and George settled into the Vice President's residence, and then the White House, they were U.S. emissaries to China. She spoke at a seminar during the 1978 Pillsbury Bake-Off about her experiences in a then very unknown country. "Food writers better get to China before there's a McDonald's on every corner," she prodded.

That did it. I decided to organize a trip (I was president of the Newspaper Food Editors and Writers Association at the time, and offering travel opportunities to our members was one of my goals).

In 1979, one didn't just call a travel agent and book a trip to China. Visas were only issued via official invitation from the Chinese government, or through a very limited favored list of China-friendly organizations. It took months, but we finally gained permission via the U.S.-China People's Friendship Association. Before we could enter the country, we underwent a two-day "orientation" in Chicago, indoctrinating us for the experience. We were the first group of U.S. food writers to gain entrance.

In the August 26, 1979, column, written just before the trip, I told readers that we hoped "to see everything from soy sauce factories to chef-training schools. I say 'we hope' because nothing is guaranteed. The Chinese are, indeed, inscrutable. We will negotiate day by day

For the third time, on the 1991 trip, Eleanor climbs China's Great Wall.

Eleanor and husband Ron don Imperial duds in Hong Kong.

to visit the places that will make the best stories for food-writing journalists."

This "journey into the mysterious" carried certain worries about the food I'd be eating. I'd read about menus featuring sea slugs "and, of course, people are delighted to tell me stories like, 'This person I know went over there and had to eat fish eyes.' Maybe if they were chocolate-covered ..."

A reader says . . .

I have enjoyed reading your delightful inside stories on what the great chefs are whipping up in Hawaii. It must be great fun for you to visit and sample their creations. Thank you for sharing those experiences with your readers
— Cindy Svering, St. Paul

I confessed to readers that a decidedly squeamish streak runs through me, so I will eat first and ask questions later. That determination is what sustained me through all the duck brains, sea slugs and yes, fish eyes on that trip — and the countless world food experiences to come.

At one point, it was suggested that our group might want to wait until 1985, when the country would "be ready" for us. By then, there could be a McDonald's on every corner in Peking. "I think we'll wager to see who's first in our group to see a Chinese person drinking Coca-Cola," I told readers just before that great adventure began.

We did find Coke at the largest hotel in slightly Westernized Canton and at the Summer Palace near the capitol, but the average Chinese couldn't afford to drink it. Those two weeks, with no news from the outside, were equivalent to falling off the edge of the world, but I wouldn't have traded a second of them.

The first McDonald's didn't open in Beijing (as it was spelled by then) until just before our fourth trip to China in 1991. By the fifth trip in 1995, American franchises, even the Hard Rock Cafe, made the larger cities seem all too familiar. On the 1979 trip, only those of us with foreign currency were allowed to enter the Friendship stores, set up to sell tourists arts and crafts. I

Janice Okun, food editor for the Buffalo (N.Y.) News, and Ron Aune sample street food in Suzhou on the 1991 China trip.

recall buying a tablecloth in the Changsha Friendship store, my friend and I the only customers, while dozens of Chinese watched us through the windows. Now, anyone can shop in those department stores, and the one in Beijing is flanked by a Baskin-Robbins store and Pizza Hut.

Sea Slugs, Yes; Snake, No
September 23, 1979

Recipes were hard to come by in China, but while sharing some we acquired in Hong Kong, I prefaced with accounts of our Chinese food encounters:

Squid, fish maw, sea slugs, duck feet, platters of chicken with heads intact staring dolefully at diners. Stinking Bean Curd, which looked like lumps of charcoal and was said to be Chairman Mao's favorite — the things I ate in the name of research!

I drew the line at eating snake, though many in our group tried it. They were able to eat it after they'd watched three writhing snakes slither around their feet in the restaurant, one killed and skinned before their eyes. Such dedication.

I managed to miss that revolting scene, dining in Canton's best noodle restaurant, arriving at the snake restaurant just in time to watch my colleagues eat reptile. It was man bites snake: from bile, to shrimp balls on cobra skin, to soup in which the snake bone structure floated, to several forms of stir-fried snake. They told me it tasted OK, though seemed rather greasy.

Being in a snake restaurant made me so jumpy that when a cat darted from behind a chair, I almost had heart failure.

(On subsequent trips, I did, indeed, eat snake, bamboo rat, even shrimp with french-fried scorpions. And I didn't always eat first and ask questions later, either.)

"American Gourmets" Dine on "Junk Food"
September 23, 1979

The Chinese may not have grasped the role of food writers, but our reception once we left China's border behind us was wildly enthusiastic. We were transformed into "The Delegation of American Gourmets" the instant we entered Hong Kong.

We were rather embarrassed to be given such a lofty title. Everywhere we went, signs read, "Welcome the American Gourmets." If those in Hong Kong only knew how many of these tested recipes have bombed over the years under my "gourmet" touch.

One evening, we were invited by Sir Kenneth Ping-Fan-Fung, industrialist and dedicated gourmet, to his private Nautilus Club. Over cocktails, he mentioned that he owned the McDonald's franchises in Hong Kong and told us it would be years before one could open in China, until that country's beef for burgers and wheat for buns improved. So much for Barbara Bush's warnings.

Hong Kong was a feast for "American Gourmets," Eleanor among them.

CHICKEN IN LEMON SAUCE
Makes 4 servings

1 pound chicken meat
3/4 teaspoon salt, divided
1 egg yolk
6 1/2 tablespoons cornstarch, divided
3 cups oil plus 1 tablespoon
Half of a lemon
1 tablespoon white vinegar
1 tablespoon sugar
7 tablespoons water
Small cucumber and tomato for garnish

Cut chicken into 12 pieces. Combine 1/4 teaspoon salt, egg yolk and 1 tablespoon cornstarch. Stir well. Use to coat chicken. Dredge chicken pieces in 5 tablespoons cornstarch. Heat 3 cups oil in work or deep pan. Add chicken. Deep-fry until golden brown. Remove and drain. Meanwhile, slice lemon. Combine with vinegar, sugar, 1/2 teaspoon salt and water. Boil lemon mixture. Add remaining 1/2 tablespoon cornstarch dissolved in 1 tablespoon oil. Stir until slightly thickened. Pour sauce over chicken. Garnish with tomato and cucumber slices. Serve atop rice, if desired.

Sir Kenneth's Chinese chef had been bestowed the highest French culinary accolades, and this is what he presented:

Opening the meal were stunning individual ice carvings, each lit from within, adorned with a perfect red rose, and cradling a plate bearing a pink butterfly fashioned from salmon, caviar and crabmeat rounds.

White-gloved waiters, one for every two diners, presented turtle soup in cups completely encased in puff pastry. Wonder after wonder arrived: pheasant quenelles in cognac sauce, tart orange sherbet in marzipan-decorated orange baskets, butter-tender U.S. beef filet with artichokes Florentine and souffle potatoes, artfully arranged cheeses, strawberries Romanoff nestled in pastry baskets adrift with spun sugar.

Centering the open rectangular table was a jungle of greenery and a towering ice carving of a Chinese junk, sails and all. My dinner partner marveled, "If this is junk food, I'd die happy eating it."

Chef Wong Kai Ming of the Hong Kong Hilton Hotel, where we reveled in Western luxury after enduring the basic accommodations in China, showed us how to make this tangy, quick chicken, then seldom seen on Midwest Chinese menus.

One Trip is Never Enough
October 12, 1980

"That was fun. Where are we going next?" the China group said. So the next year, I put together an Italian trip to study with two pasta masters, Giuliano Bugialli in Florence, the queen city of Tuscany, and Marcella Hazan in Bologna, central to Emilia-Romagna, the "fattest" province for its lavish use of butter, cream and its own Parmigiano-Reggiano, king of cheeses. On this side of the Atlantic, especially in the Midwest, Italian food was all tinged with tomato. We went to the land of white sauces, and the revelations were shared with readers:

My husband has diagnosed the cause of the shakiness we've felt after returning from a food trip to Italy.

"Pasta withdrawal," he said quaveringly.

Not once in the weeks we devoted to learning about Italian food the best way — by eating and more eating — did we have what Americans think of as Italian fare. Not once did we even see spaghetti heaped with red meat sauce, lasagna layered with more of the same, pizza so thick with cheese that it could stretch to Sorrento.

Our explorations were in northern Italy, land of creamy white sauces. Oh, the tagliatelle, the agnolotti, the tortellini, the cappelletti and the garganelli! Day after day, we pasta'd out.

We took lessons from Giuliano Bugialli, who festoons the room with swoops of paper-thin pasta emerging from the machine he vigorously cranks, while bobbing on one leg stork-style.

Scholar of the Renaissance and admirer of Catherine di Medici, Bugialli is a cooking classicist, yet he demonstrated pasta using the machine.

Marcella Hazan chronicles the food of Italy today, but in her classes, nervous students are taught to roll pasta by hand.

Hazan sets the stage for her "sfoglina," Giovanna, who kneads and rolls pasta by hand, so thin that Hazan's cigarette package can be read through it. No newfangled mechanical contraptions for grandmotherly Giovanna, who has practiced her floury craft eight hours a day since she was 14. She attacks kneading the newly formed ball of dough with a rock'n'rolling motion of feet and body, a doughy dance with pasta as her partner. Pressure is always from the heel of her hand, fingers closed.

Giuliano Bugialli rolls pasta stork-style.

Marcella Hazan inspects the work of her "sfoglina" Giovanna.

Though Florence and Bologna are only a few driving hours apart, their pastas are quite different, reflecting the unyielding regionalism of Italian food. Bologna's pasta contains only eggs and flour, measured not by volume or cups, but by "two-egg pasta" or "six-egg pasta," whatever meets mealtime needs. In Florence, olive oil and salt are added.

When queried if she ever adds oil or salt, Hazan said sharply, "No! We're in Emilia-Romagna. That would be a crime."

Pasta, she said, "is found all over Italy. Ours here in Bologna is soft, the traditional kind against which all others are measured. Factory-made pasta is good, but it's different. Think of silk and wood. They're both beautiful, but they're different things."

The Epitome of Pastas
October 12, 1980

It got to be a joke on the Italy trip that 25 food editors would swoon so over the food. Meal after meal,

we'd say, "This is the best one yet." But if we had to choose one dinner as the epitome, it was the one at Ilbarrino on Via de'Biffi in Florence.

Anyone who thinks of Italian food as heavy should have been there to taste the delicacies: airy Bavarian of bell pepper coated with aspic, fresh green beans topped with cream and finely chopped nuts, a pasta pocket filled with spinach and ricotta centered with a perfectly

FLORENTINE PASTA PIES
Makes 6 servings

2-egg batch of fresh pasta:
    2 cups unbleached flour
    2 extra-large eggs
    2 teaspoons oil
    1/4 teaspoon salt
Filling:
    1 cup cooked fresh spinach, drained and
        pressed dry

1 cup ricotta cheese
1/2 cup freshly grated Parmigiano-
    Reggiano cheese
Salt and pepper
6 egg yolks
Melted butter
Finely chopped flavorful mushrooms (or
    white truffles for the real experience)

To make pasta: Pile flour on board or countertop. Make a well in center of flour. Add eggs, oil and salt. Keep pushing flour into eggs and oil, mixing with fingers, until dough forms. Knead on floured board until smooth.

To shape pasta: Roll out 2 sheets of pasta on hand-cranked pasta machine set on second to last notch (1/8 inch thickness if rolling by hand). Cut pasta into 12 large squares. Precook pasta sheets quickly, allowing 20 seconds after water returns to a boil. Blanch in cold water quickly. Rinse under cold water. Separate sheets.

To make filling: Clean and cook spinach. Drain well. Press dry. Measure 1 cup. Add spinach, ricotta and Parmigiano cheese to food processor fitted with

plastic blade, or put in large bowl. Mix well, but do not chop too fine. Season to taste with salt and pepper.

To fill pastas: Spoon one-sixth of spinach mixture onto 1 sheet pasta. Form spinach into a ring. Place 1 egg yolk in center of ring. Season lightly. Top with 1 sheet of pasta. Using ravioli cutter, pan lid or sharp-edged bowl, cut 6-inch circle. Press edges of pasta together, moistening with egg white, if desired. Form 5 more pasta packages.

To cook pasta: Place on rack. Immerse into pan of boiling water. Cook for 2 minutes, or until egg yolk seems set. Place on buttered baking sheet. Bake in 350-degree oven for 5 minutes, basting with melted butter to which chopped mushrooms have been added. (Note: If desired, saute mushrooms first.) Serve hot with butter-mushroom sauce.

baked egg and drizzled with butter and white truffles. Those truffles from Italy's Piedmont region sell for about $500 a pound, so we got only a smidgen.

On and on we dined, on chicken breast wrapped in lettuce, on a salad of julienne carrots, on blackberry custard tarts. Perfection — without one shred of mozzarella or touch of red tomato sauce.

Of all my food memories anywhere in the world, those egg and spinach pasta pockets, fragrant with white truffle butter sauce, remain a high point. Once home from that Italy trip, I tried to re-create them with a small measure of success, but alas, without white truffles.

Ilbarrino Revisited
November 30, 1980

What a guilt trip to travel in Italy with Barbara Gibbons.

Don't misunderstand. She's a lovely person. Good looking, too. A sylph, a shadow of her former 208 pounds. Millions of newspaper readers know her as the "Slim Gourmet" for the syndicated column she writes several times weekly.

Sitting next to Barbara at a Florence restaurant for one of the most exquisite meals I've ever had, I suddenly realized that while the rest of us were practically licking our plates, she was eating only half of every portion. Pure anguish was etched on her face when she stopped halfway through a pasta dish that was totally out of this world.

I knew by the near tears in her eyes that she wanted to eat it all. It was the greatest demonstration of will power I have ever witnessed.

"I don't have to eat the whole thing to know how it tastes," she said. The rest of us could see our reflections in our perfectly cleaned plates, but she refrained: "That's why I don't weigh 208 anymore." She admitted later that part of that anguish was fear that someone was going to stab her hand with a fork, trying to spear her leftovers.

Halfway through the trip, in Venice, Barbara and her roommate started weighing themselves on every scale they could find to discover what damage all that food was doing. "I've lost five pounds," she said triumphantly. "We've taken all the readings, divided by 2.2 (Italian scales weigh in kilos), taken the average and I've lost five pounds!"

She practically danced through St. Mark's Square, then decided after depriving herself, she needed a treat. We took the launch over to the classy Cipriani Hotel for after-dinner coffee, and she ordered a great big piece of banana cake. And she didn't leave half on her plate.

Maybe it was the banana cake. Maybe she relaxed her will power the second half of the trip, but the scale back home in New Jersey said she'd gained a pound. Not bad, considering what a knife-and-fork marathon we'd completed. I'll tell you, though, if I ever see an Italian scale, I'm buying one. Maybe I'll be five pounds lighter the minute I step on it, and I can eat banana cake, too.

Hamming It Up in Smithfield
June 22, 1980

What's a pig's favorite ballet? Swine Lake.

What two plays do pigs like best? "Pygmalion" and "Hamlet."

Who is a pig's foremost hero? Richard the Loin-Hearted.

What's a pig's favorite meal in basket? A pignic.

Food writers were giddy with piggy puns during a visit to Smithfield, Va., home of the world-famous hams. The column went into deep detail about how the salty hams are produced, then sliced translucently to be eaten on feathery biscuits for classic Southern munching.

Maybe it was the salt. Maybe it's that Southern hams aren't that frequently eaten in the North, but the recipe I liked best in Smithfield, where Southern hospitality is alive and thriving, was Picnic Tea, served to us on the lawn of the town's 1750 courthouse after a hot day of touring smokehouses. We drank it from silver Thomas Jefferson drinking cups borrowed from homes throughout the town for our visit.

SMITHFIELD PICNIC TEA
Makes 1 gallon

3 to 4 lemons
1 cup sugar
1/2 cup water
3 quarts strong tea
Mint sprigs (optional)
Small bottle of ginger ale (optional)

Thinly slice lemons. Sprinkle with sugar. Add water. Squeeze lemons well with hands until sugar is dissolved. Add lemon mixture (peels, too) to tea. Add more sugar, if desired. Dilute with water, if necessary. For an extra touch, add crushed springs of mint and ginger ale. Serve over ice cubes.

Parmigiano-Flavored Notes
January 11, 1981

Should you, in about two years, buy a piece of Italian Parmigiano-Reggiano cheese that's colored Bic blue, blame it on my friend, Janice Okun, food editor for the Buffalo (N.Y.) News.

Janice was standing on a raised platform overlooking vats at a cheese-making cooperative in Parma, Italy, when food writers visited there.

She felt her notebook slipping, falling ...

"It was like being in an accident, when you realize you're going to hit another car, but it seems like an eternity before the moment of impact," she said.

Janice knew her notebook full of freshly-penned information was going to splash into that vat, and after time stood still, it did, much to her embarrassment. Co-op officials were not bothered. They fished it out of the curds, dried it off and returned it to her later, forever impregnated with the aroma of Parma's cheese.

On that same trip, one of our cooking teachers, Marcella Hazan, lectured us about the American version of "parmesan cheese" for which she has the greatest contempt. "Buy sawdust. It's cheaper and tastes the same," she claims.

Parmigiano-Reggiano cheesemakers looking for the Bic blue.

Well-Balanced Lunches in France
December 20, 1981

On a trip to France to study with French cooking virtuoso and author Madeleine Kamman, we faced this dining dichotomy:

We were a group of food editors, dining in two- and three-star restaurants at night. But our lunches were much less formal, some of them eaten picnic-style on the bus as we rode between destinations.

They were well-balanced meals — balanced on our laps as the bus lurched around corners and up and down the foothills of the Alps. Not too many pieces of pate or slices of salami tumbled to the floor, but woe to those who tried to pour wine as the bus took a bump. You could pick us out of any crowd. We were the ones with red splotches on our coats.

HAWAIIAN BANANA MUFFINS
Makes 24 to 30 muffins

2 cups sugar
1/2 cup shortening
2 tablespoons salad oil
2 cups mashed bananas
3 large eggs
2 1/4 cups pastry flour (or cake flour)
2 1/2 teaspoons baking soda
2 1/2 teaspoons baking powder
3/4 teaspoon salt
3/4 teaspoon vanilla
1 1/2 teaspoons lemon juice
1 cup buttermilk

In mixing bowl, cream sugar, shortening and salad oil well. Add bananas. Cream well. Add eggs. Mix well. Combine dry ingredients. Add to mixing bowl with vanilla and lemon juice. Mix at low speed until ingredients are incorporated. Add buttermilk gradually until smooth. Scrape bowl. Mix at medium speed for 3 minutes. Put batter into greased or paper-lined muffin pans. Bake in 375-degree oven for about 20 minutes.

Luau-Sized Batch of Muffins
April 19, 1981

Before I left for Hawaii in 1981, readers asked me to bring back a recipe for banana muffins, a standard at many Island hotels. Hans Weiler, pastry chef at the Ilikai Hotel, Honolulu, gave me a recipe, cut down from his usual batch to what he calls "home size." "Home size" I said, "if you're baking for the Brady Bunch." I cut it down further and got 30 muffins. If you want fewer, you do more math.

About Clam Chowder, Mo Knows
July 4, 1982

After the 1982 food writers' meeting in Portland, Ore., we journeyed south along the Pacific highway and met Mo Niemi, who I dubbed "seafood queen of the Oregon coast." She often served 2,000 customers a day in her two Newport restaurants, and nearly all of them ordered her famous clam chowder.

Mo knows clam chowder.

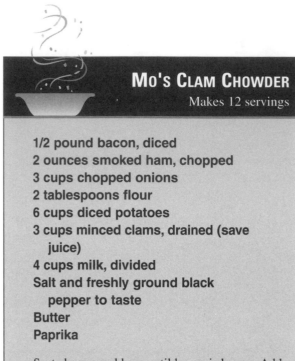

MO'S CLAM CHOWDER

Makes 12 servings

1/2 pound bacon, diced
2 ounces smoked ham, chopped
3 cups chopped onions
2 tablespoons flour
6 cups diced potatoes
3 cups minced clams, drained (save juice)
4 cups milk, divided
Salt and freshly ground black pepper to taste
Butter
Paprika

Saute bacon and ham until bacon is brown. Add onion. Saute until limp. Drain off some fat, if desired. Stir in flour. Add potatoes and clams (with 1 cup drained clam juice and 1 cup milk, adding more liquid as necessary). Cook for 15 minutes, or until potatoes are very soft. Add 3 cups milk. Season to taste with salt and pepper. Serve hot with dollop of butter and sprinkle of paprika. (Slightly revised from Marian Burros' version to match Mo's formula.)

When I asked for the recipe, she told me that Marian Burros had it. Burros, former food editor of the Washington Post and now at the New York Times, is a longtime colleague. She shared this chowder formula, which had also appeared in "Pure and Simple," one of her many books.

Marian's food philosophy is not predisposed to fats, so she suggests draining off all the bacon grease. Mo had told us to blend the flour with at least part of the fat to make a roux that will thicken the soup. For sure, don't drain off the fat until the onions are cooked, and then keep as much as your conscience allows.

Our testing came to a sudden halt when Marian's version of Mo's chowder said to cook the potatoes until tender, but there was no liquid in the pot. The fragrance of burned potatoes wasn't something we wanted perfuming the house, so I added 1 cup of drained clam juice (saved because my husband said, "They sell clam juice in bottles — don't throw it out") and a cup of milk. Later, he stirred a cup of water into the pot, and still later, we added more milk.

What you should get is a thick soup, floating with butter and pink with sprinkled paprika, which you could eat with a fork. "I have my cooks put butter in the bottom of the bowl before they add the chowder," Mo told us. "That way I can be sure they're keeping the soup hot enough to melt butter." That attention to perfection is how she's stayed in business for 40 years.

Chefs at Romantik Hotel Schlosswirt in Anif, near Salzburg, whip up a nockerl for note-taking food writers.

SALZBURGER NOCKERL SCHLOSSWIRT
Makes 2 to 3 servings

12 pasteurized egg whites
6 tablespoons sugar
1/4 cup flour
8 pasteurized egg yolks
1 teaspoon finely chopped lemon zest
For pan, a walnut-size piece of butter
    and a little sugar

Rub ovenproof or stainless-steel round cake pan with butter. Sprinkle with sugar. In large mixing bowl, combine egg whites and 6 tablespoons sugar. Beat until stiff peaks form. By hand, fold or whisk in flour, egg yolks and lemon zest. Pour into prepared pan. Sprinkle with additional sugar. Bake in 450-degree oven for 5 minutes, or until top turns a "nice color." Serve immediately.

The Most Romantik Desserts
October 3, 1982

Our 1982 Alpine trip, visiting historic Romantik inns nearly every night, introduced us to the most airy of desserts, from gossamer strudel at the Vienna Hilton to the classic meringue desserts of Salzburg.

While in Salzburg, we saw Nockerl made by the chef at the top-rated Goldener Hirsch hotel and also at the charming Schlosswirt, a Romantik inn housed in stables of a castle centering a nearby lake, said to have inspired Walt Disney's Cinderella's castle. The Schlosswirt's Nockerl was the easier and more flavorful fluff. The eggs bake briefly, but perhaps not long enough; therefore, I would suggest using pasteurized eggs, but be aware that beating those whites into a meringue takes extra effort.

Confederate Cake Favored by Union First Lady
June 26, 1983

Today, we're going to restage the Civil War, not with cannons, but with cakes, said a column written after a trip to Lexington, Ky.:

Wearing Union blue over suspected Confederate gray petticoats is Mary Todd Lincoln, competing with her white cake. Opposing her is Gen. Robert E. Lee,

MARY TODD LINCOLN'S WHITE CAKE
Makes 1 tube cake

1 cup butter
2 cups sugar
3 cups cake flour
2 teaspoons baking powder
1 cup milk
1 cup finely chopped blanched
    almonds
1 teaspoon vanilla
6 egg whites
1/4 teaspoon salt

To make cake: Cream butter and sugar lightly. Sift flour and baking powder together. Add alternately with milk to butter mixture. Toss almonds with a little additional flour. Add almonds and vanilla to batter. Add salt to egg whites. Beat until stiff. Fold into batter.

To bake cake: Bake in 10-inch tube (angel-food) pan in 350-degree oven for 40 to 45 minutes. Ice with boiled frosting to which 1/2 cup finely chopped candied cherries and pineapple have been added.

commander of the Southern cause, going into battle with his orange-lemon cake.

Though Abraham Lincoln is the favorite son of Illinois, he was actually born in Kentucky, as was his wife, whose childhood home in Lexington food writers visited. There, we tasted a genteel cake that was said to be her favorite. It was originally created by a French baker in Lexington for the 1825 visit of French General Lafayette to that Southern city. The recipe was treasured

FOURNOU'S OVENS' SALAD
Makes 4 servings

Dressing:
- 1 pasteurized egg yolk
- 1 tablespoon Dijon mustard
- 1/4 cup red tarragon vinegar
- 1 cup salad oil
- Salt and freshly ground pepper

Salad:
- 1 head butter lettuce
- 1 head Belgian endive
- 2 ounces small shrimp
- 2 ounces Roquefort cheese, crumbled
- 1 small carton enoki mushrooms
- Chopped parsley

To make dressing: Whip egg yolk and mustard. Add vinegar. Slowly pour in oil while whipping. Add salt and pepper to taste.

To make salad: Wash lettuce and endive. Toss lettuce with some dressing, sprinkling with coarsely ground pepper. Place 3 lettuce leaves on each salad plate. Cut endive into thin strips. Toss with some dressing. Sprinkle on lettuce. Toss shrimp with remaining dressing. Sprinkle on lettuce. Garnish with Roquefort cheese, mushrooms and parsley.

by the Todd family, who thought it was the best white cake they'd ever eaten.

Frosting isn't essential; just a dusting of powdered sugar will do. The cake slices perfectly into almost transparent pieces.

Salad, San Francisco Style
June 24, 1984

"Salad perfection" was the consensus when this recipe from one of my favorite San Francisco restaurants, Fournou's Ovens in the Stanford Court Hotel, appeared. It was built with threadlike enoki mushrooms, which I'd first experienced six years earlier at a picnic on the grounds of Domaine Chandon winery in Napa Valley. Years went by before they were available in St. Paul, but they were worth the wait.

Parmigiano Forever
May 19, 1985

I once defined eternity as two people trying to finish a 10-pound ham. New definition: Eternity is 2 kilos of Parmigiano-Reggiano. That's 4 1/2 pounds of cheese, enough to last nearly forever in our small household.

My two souvenirs of a recent trip to Italy were Parmigiano, purchased right in the heart of north-central Italy, where it's made, and a quarter-kilo of dried Italian supersize wild mushrooms called funghi or porcini, bought in Florence's magnificent market.

Funghi/porcini affront the taste buds with flavor that one learns to love slowly, but ultimately crave. They're available in precious packets in local Italian markets. To stretch their costly flavor, soak them with white mushrooms, which adopt the wild essence.

The last time we were in Italy, we also bought Parmigiano-Reggiano, but instead of getting on the

SPAGHETTI WITH DRIED WILD MUSHROOMS AND PARMIGIANO-REGGIANO

Makes 4 servings

**1 ounce dried wild mushrooms
    (funghi, also known as porcini)**

3 tablespoons butter

3 tablespoons olive oil

2 cloves garlic, peeled

12 ounces spaghetti

Salt

**3 ounces freshly grated Parmigiano-
    Reggiano cheese**

To prepare mushrooms: Soak mushrooms in 2 cups lukewarm for 30 minutes. Lift out. Rinse. Filter mushroom soaking water to remove any grit. Reserve liquid.

To prepare mushroom butter: In medium saucepan, combine butter, oil and garlic. Saute over medium heat, stirring frequently, until garlic becomes pale brown. Remove garlic. Transfer mushrooms and filtered soaking water to saucepan. Cook over medium heat, uncovered, until almost all liquid has evaporated.

To prepare pasta: Cook spaghetti in boiling salted water until al dente (still firm). Drain. Mix spaghetti thoroughly with mushroom butter. Add cheese. Toss thoroughly.

plane within 48 hours of purchase, we hauled it for another dozen days of Alpine touring. I remember that cheese as pungent — and so was my suitcase.

Giorgio Fini, patriarch of that Modena food empire, taught us about balsamic vinegar, still largely unknown in the United States. He also gave me this recipe for spaghetti to use up my stash of cheese and mushrooms.

Eleanor toasts her group at the end of another astounding trip.

Quick, Everybody Duck!

October 19, 1986

My trip to France was just ducky.

We ate duck with peaches, with cherries, with figs. That ever-present French fowl appeared with black currants, with pears, with oranges and raspberries. We downed duck cooked country-style in its own juices, duck with brown sugar, duck with sherry vinegar sauce (and more that I can't remember). We even had pressed duck in which the meat and carcass, except for its very rare breast filets, are cranked in a silver press to extract the juices (read that blood) for a sauce so rich that one ladleful per lifetime is sufficient.

For this white-meat eater, it was duck overdose, but my food-writing colleagues were better sports than I was. When top-flight chef Michel Rostang suggested wild duck for our $75 lunches at his Paris restaurant, four of the six at our table didn't duck that opportunity. My husband and I had rack of lamb, thank you.

It was getting to be a joke after about the 10th duck dinner. But French chefs cook what's in season, and duck, even the domestic bird, is very much a September and October critter.

Our last evening in France was amid the luxury of La Cote St. Jacques in Joigny, the latest French restaurant and hotel to receive a coveted third Michelin star. Chef Michel Loraine proposed a special menu. Something told me to ask what the meat dish would be. "Canard sauvage," he stated proudly, and couldn't understand why I started laughing. I'd translated that to mean more duck.

PRINCESS MARIE-BLANCHE'S DUCK WITH RASPBERRIES
Makes 10 servings

5 duck filets
7 tablespoons butter, divided
1 1/2 cups raspberry vinegar
5 lumps of sugar (about 1/4 cup)
4 cups chicken or duck stock
Salt and pepper
1/2 pound fresh raspberries
Watercress for garnish

To prepare duck: Remove tendons from filets. Lightly score skin. In skillet, saute filets over high heat in 5 tablespoons butter. Remove from skillet. Keep warm in 300-degree oven.

To make sauce: Remove grease from skillet. Deglaze pan with raspberry vinegar. Add sugar lumps. Simmer until mixture is reduced by half. Add stock. Simmer again to reduce by half. Correct seasoning with salt and pepper.

To serve: Slice filets into 10 to 12 slices each. Over heat, whisk sauce, slowly adding remaining 2 tablespoons butter. Correct seasoning, if needed. Arrange slices of duck on serving plates. Top with sauce. Sprinkle with raspberries. Decorate with watercress.

Of all the duck dinners on that trip, the best was prepared by Princess Marie-Blanche de Broglie, our traveling companion throughout Normandy. Princesses are imbued with grace under pressure, no more evident than the morning we arrived late at her family's country estate near Rouen for a cooking lesson in her school there. Typical Norman September morning fog obscured the landscape, and our driver was unsure of the road. Suddenly, a figure, bright green coat flapping, emerged running through the mist, waving us to stop. A regal apparition, our princess.

This is the duck she made for us that morning. Scoring the breast skin discourages shrinkage during sauteeing.

Home Cooking in Hawaii
April 5, 1987

On food-editor trips to Hawaii, we always tried to have a group cooking session, but mostly we dined out. When we took Aric and a buddy to Hawaii during their senior-year spring break, we knew feeding two teen-agers in restaurants would be prohibitive. The condos we stayed in had great kitchens, so we mostly cooked in, feasting on papayas from the farmers' market and the recipes I tested, such as this chicken salad sent by the Hawaiian Ginger Commodity Group just before we got on the plane.

Knowing that ingredients would be costly, we took along a very large carton packed with seasonings, peanut butter, lots of mixes and condiments and staple items I'd need for testing recipes. What we didn't eat on Maui was reboxed and transported to Oahu. A bottle of oil came uncorked during that short journey, making for some slippery groceries.

By the end of our stay, we'd eaten almost everything. "Leave the rest," my husband pleaded. But I'm too frugal. So he stuffed spice bottles into his suitcase, and I put the remaining nonperishables into a plastic bag for carry-on luggage. We now have, returned safely to our home cupboards, the best-traveled box of macaroni and cheese in Minnesota.

HAWAIIAN CHICKEN SALAD
Makes 4 servings

4 large half-breasts of chicken, boned and skinned (about 1 1/2 pounds)
1 tablespoon finely chopped or grated fresh ginger
1 teaspoon pressed fresh garlic
1 tablespoon soy sauce
1/2 teaspoon liquid smoke (optional)
1/4 teaspoon finely crushed red pepper
1 tablespoon sugar
1/2 cup light salad oil
1/4 cup white-wine vinegar

1/2 cup mayonnaise
2 tablespoons oil for sauteing chicken
1/2 cup thinly sliced celery
1/2 cup thin strips red and yellow bell peppers
1 small cucumber, pared and cut in small strips
1 1/2 quarts small leaves of butter lettuce or romaine
3 tablespoons toasted sliced almonds

To marinate chicken: Pound chicken breasts lightly between wax paper to flatten slightly. Combine fresh ginger, garlic, soy, liquid smoke, red pepper, sugar, oil and vinegar until well blended. Blend 1/4 cup seasoning mixture into mayonnaise. Set aside for dressing. Rub 1/4 cup seasoning mixture over both sides of chicken breasts. Cover. Refrigerate for 1 hour or longer.

To cook chicken: Lightly brown chicken in 2 tablespoons oil. Turn. Cook over medium heat for 10 minutes, or just until tender (being careful not to overcook). Cool. Cut or tear into generous strips. Toss vegetables with lettuce and remaining seasoning mixture. Arrange on 4 large salad plates or in shallow bowls. Top with chicken. Sprinkle with almonds. Serve with seasoned mayonnaise.

Bring Your Appetite to Big Easy
December 6, 1987

Every trip to New Orleans is a food adventure, with new chefs to meet, their restaurants to savor. We operate according to this "Old Nawlins" saying: When the stomach is full, it sends a message to the brain: "Tell Mouth to stop eating." Mouth retorts to Brain: "Tell Stomach to make room. We may never pass this way again."

These crepes were discovered at a restaurant called George IV, created by a chef named George Rhode IV:

Ours was a brief visit. We promised ourselves we'd order only appetizers because we'd soon be in another cab, tearing back to the French Quarter for dinner at Paul Prudhomme's restaurant, K-Paul. Food writers tend toward such insatiable insanity. One writer from the Washington Post told me she tried 20 restaurants during one unforgettable day in New Orleans.

LEMON CREPES
Makes 10 servings

20 crepes, 6-inch size
Cream-cheese filling:
3 packages (8 ounces each) cream
   cheese, softened
1/2 cup sugar
3 tablespoons lemon juice
1 tablespoon light rum
2 teaspoons vanilla
1 teaspoon grated lemon peel
Lemon sauce:
3/4 cup sugar
2 tablespoons cornstarch
1 1/4 cups cold water
3/4 cup lemon juice
1/4 cup (1/2 stick) butter or margarine
Dash of vanilla
Thin slices of lemon for garnish

To make cream-cheese filling: In large bowl, beat all filling ingredients together until smooth. Chill for at least 30 minutes.

To fill crepes: Make crepes with batter seasoned with nutmeg (see His, Hers and Ours chapter for crepes recipe). When crepes are complete, spoon 3 tablespoons filling on edge of each crepe. Roll up to 1/2-inch diameter. Place crepes in single layer in shallow baking dish. Cover. Chill until ready to serve.

To make sauce: In small saucepan, combine all sauce ingredients. Bring to a boil, stirring constantly. Boil for 20 seconds. Remove from heat. Keep warm.

To serve: Bake filled crepes in 375-degree oven for 10 minutes, or until hot. Place 2 crepes on each individual serving plate. Spoon 4 tablespoons warm sauce over each serving. Garnish each plate with a lemon twist.

When I got home, I made Rhode's crepes, this vignette proving how irresistible they are: An Edina couple, famous for the desserts they market, had just left our dinner table, stuffed to the teeth, bearing a paper plate of leftover crepes for a next-day treat.

She admitted later, "It was disgusting. We ate them cold on the way home. We were fighting over them." No forks, no plates, just crepes dipped in the jar of sauce, eaten with their fingers while driving the Crosstown highway. What a sticky trip that must have been.

Delving Into Dumplings
September 27, 1987

Back to China for the third time, our 1987 trip had its amazing food memories, including dining on bamboo rat in Guilin (it tasted like overdone roast beef). The most memorable edible of the entire three weeks — scorpion. It was in Qingdao (Tsingtao), famous for its beer, that we were served french-fried scorpions as garnish for a shrimp stir-fry. Believe me, it took a hearty swig of Tsingtao brew to wash down those little ticklers.

All the way across country in Chengdu, capitol of westerly Szechuan province, we learned the nuances of that fiery fare:

Americans hear "Szechuan," and they start to sweat. In our vernacular, it's synonymous with "Hot!" We were prepared to breathe fire for four days. But we found a subtle quality to the food that surprised us, until our escort, Mandarin-speaking Rusty McLagan of St. Paul, explained. "Not every dish is — or should be — hot," he said. "It's the chef's challenge to make each course taste different. One will be sweet, the next salty, the next sour, the next hot. Contrasts in texture and appearance are also important."

Sophisticated Szechuan chefs use the flower of the red pepper, which is more aromatic and creates a numbing rather than a burning sensation. But down on the farm, at the Golden Horse township commune near

Chengdu, cooks aren't as subdued. My mouth was not only numbed; my lips actually vibrated. That's hot!

Then we went to Xi'an, tracing the steps of Marco Polo, the first foreign tourist to visit that city of the terra-cotta warriors and dine on the city's famous dumplings:

Marco Polo may have introduced dumplings to Italy, where they transcended generations until they reached the Paulucci family, who boarded a boat to America and a train to Minnesota. Could Polo's edible souvenir have influenced young Jeno Paulucci's entry into the Chinese and Italian food business?

"Jeno's Pizza Roll," I said when the first deep-fried appetizer arrived at our table at De Fa Chang restaurant, which specializes in 130 types of dumplings.

We looked like dumplings by the time we'd finished eating 25 varieties, plus soup, noodles and the inevitable watermelon for dessert. But only that first dumpling looked like a refugee from an American grocery-store freezer case.

A waitress in De Fa Chang restaurant in Xi'an brings yet another round of dumplings.

Every other bite-sized delight was steamed succulence, each unique in shape and filling. My soy-sauce-and-vinegar-stained notebook is decorated with

HAR GOW (SHRIMP DUMPLINGS)
Makes 30 dumplings

Filling:
    3/4 pound fresh shrimp, shelled
        and halved
    2 tablespoons lard, cubed
    3 tablespoons bamboo shoots,
        shredded
    1 1/2 teaspoons salt
    White pepper to taste
    1/2 teaspoon sugar
    2 teaspoons cornstarch
Har gow wrappers:
    1 pound flour
    2 pounds cornstarch
    1 pint boiling water

To make filling: In electric mixer, combine shrimp, lard, bamboo shoots, salt, pepper, sugar and cornstarch. Beat until creamy, but not pureed. Let mixture rest for 30 minutes. If desired, add 1 teaspoon sesame oil for additional flavor.

To make wrappers: Combine flour, cornstarch and boiling water. Mix into dough. Knead until elastic. Place small round of dough, about 1 scant tablespoon, on board. Press with side of Chinese cleaver into 2 1/2-inch round. Using cleaver blade, lift dough off the board so it can be filled.

To fill dumplings: Place 1 teaspoon shrimp mixture in center of each wrapping. Fold in half. Pleat edges together. Arrange dumplings in greased steamer basket or on plate in covered pan. Steam for 10 minutes. Serve with hoisin sauce.

sketches of meat-filled, nearly transparent dough twisted into bowknots, fashioned into printers' hats, looking like mushrooms, like incredulous eyebrows, like pig's eyes, like chrysanthemums, like Hershey's Kisses. One had the ridged backbone of a triceratops. Miniature meat dumplings, as small as pearls, floated in broth served from a flaming cauldron. That dish was a favorite of the Empress Dowager, we were informed.

Disappearing Dumplings
August 30, 1987

I'm sad to report that, on the 1995 China trip, when we again visited Xi'an, we tried to return to De Fa Chang restaurant, but it was a pile of rubble, the victim of urban development, and no one knew if it had relocated. On that '87 journey, we had a lesson in dumpling making from Chef Lung Wai Shar at the Hong Kong Hilton Hotel. That hotel has also been torn down, but this recipe survived.

What remains is Luk Yu, the oldest teahouse in Hong Kong, and my favorite:

Dim sum dumplings are served from metal boxes suspended from the necks of Chinese women who look as if they'd served Luk Yu's patrons since the doors opened a hundred years ago.

Lucky you if you can eat dumplings and steamed buns at that venerable house, where it's darn hard for a tourist to get a table. So many faithful customers come daily to read the Hong Kong Standard and nibble breakfast dumplings that the drop-in foreign patron is usually shooed away.

For this recipe from the Hong Kong Hilton, Testing Results said placatingly: Pleating dumpling dough is a lifetime occupation for some Chinese. Novices shouldn't be distressed if a first attempt looks like a seventh-grade sewing project. If all else fails, buy a plastic dumpling press, which automatically pleats the dough perimeter.

The Perfect Margarita
August 6, 1989

Though all margaritas we met on a food writers' Southwest trip were enchanting, the drink was most sublime at La Casa Sena, a 300-year-old structure near Santa Fe's historic plaza. Jose Sena built the house for his wife and 23 children, but I bet it's much more tranquil today as a restaurant than it was with all those kiddies tearing through its adobe rooms.

Owner Gordon Heiss promised to teach us how to make the perfect margarita, and after sipping his potion, we agreed he wasn't bragging.

Heiss gave us his recipe adequate to make 140 drinks. Not expecting 100 thirsty guests anytime soon, I translated his recipe into proportions that will allow you to make a pitcherful or even one frosty glassful. A shot glass will make one generous drink or two average ones; a cup will produce enough for a small party.

LA CASA SENA'S MARGARITAS
Makes 2 drinks

2 parts Cuervo Gold tequila
1 part Triple Sec
1 part Rose's lime juice
3 parts fresh lime juice
Sugar to taste, from 1 to 2 parts

Shake ingredients with ice. Pour into glasses rimmed with salt or sugar. Garnish with short straw and lime wedge. (Note: The secret of a small batch is to dissolve the sugar first in a small amount of hot water. Using large end of a 2-sided shot glass to measure, you'll have enough for 2 drinks.)

Husband Ron Aune and Eleanor were king and queen of a feast at Bunratty Castle in Ireland, where brown bread was on the menu.

Ireland's Staff of Life
May 28, 1989

Yes, it is possible to spend nearly two weeks in Ireland and never eat corned beef and cabbage. Never even see it on a menu. But our food-writers group encountered one Irish inevitable — brown soda bread. We found it in castles and country restaurant, even afloat on a Galley Cruise luncheon en route to Waterford.

I'm not referring to the white soda bread that appears in St. Paul on St. Patrick's Day. I mean whole-grain, treacle-sweet, heavy-textured bread that tastes best when slathered with sweet Irish butter. It's a one-bowl, one-spoon, one-step bread that couldn't be easier. This version came from Ferrycarrig Hotel near Wexford, featuring one of the most ambitious organic menus I've seen anywhere.

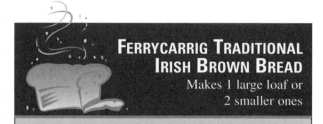

FERRYCARRIG TRADITIONAL IRISH BROWN BREAD
Makes 1 large loaf or 2 smaller ones

1 cup bran
2 cups plain white flour
4 cups whole-meal flour (whole wheat with a little wheat germ)
1 teaspoon baking soda
Pinch of salt
1/2 cup porridge (dry oatmeal)
2 tablespoons sugar
1 quart buttermilk

Mix all dry ingredients together. Add buttermilk. Place mixture into greased loaf tin. Bake in 475-degree oven for 15 minutes. Reduce temperature to 350 degrees. Bake for 60 minutes. Remove bread from oven. Wrap loaf in damp cloth. Allow to stand for 3 hours before cutting.

Bali High Cuisine
April 15, 1990

Bali Belly can be the scourge of tourists in paradise, but instead of suffering tummy rumbles, we were happy tummy rubbers — savoring everything we ate in Bali, our last stop after nearly a month in Southeast Asia.

There are two Balis, though many tourists know only the one at beach level with its aggressive commercialism and aggravating traffic.

I prefer Bali high.

Head for the hills should you ever visit that Indonesian island. Our driver handed a wad of ruppiah out the window of our minicoach so we could take the back road to Ubud. The instant the gate was lifted and we rolled onto the one-lane road, we began to see the other Bali of terraced rice paddies, family compounds, temples at every turn.

Meeting another vehicle was a squeeze play, and we were often eye-to-eye with a load of pigs en route to their fate. But we were silently enthralled by scenes right off the pages of the National Geographic: women winnowing rice in the paddies, temples piled with offerings as the Balinese version of Christmas approached, and greenery at its most intense hue.

Homemade
Peanut Sauce
April 15, 1990

Throughout our Southeast Asia travels, especially at the ethereal Mutiara Beach Resort on Malaysia's Penang Island, we collected recipes for peanut sauce, but found them impossible to successfully duplicate at home. Not long after returning, I received a press release containing the perfect peanut sauce recipe. It came from Hawaii-based chef Peter Merriman, whose mother, Woodene Merriman of the Pittsburgh Post-Gazette, was on the trip and had also been trying to make peanut sauce at home with those indecipherable recipes. She should have just asked her son for the solution.

PETER MERRIMAN'S PEANUT DIPPING SAUCE (SATAY SAUCE)
Makes about 2 cups

1 tablespoon shallots or onions, chopped
3/4 teaspoon oil
1/4 cup fresh basil, chopped
6 ounces creamy peanut butter
1/4 cup lemon juice
1/4 cup soy sauce
1/2 tablespoon hot Oriental chili paste
1/3 cup unsweetened coconut milk
2/3 cup water
1/4 cup firmly packed brown sugar

Saute shallots in oil until transparent. Add basil. Mix thoroughly. Add all remaining ingredients, except sugar. Cook over low to medium heat for 3 minutes, stirring constantly or it might burn. Add sugar. Cover pan. Cook, stirring frequently, for 10 minutes. Pour into dipping bowl. Serve warm with beef or chicken satay.

And What Is Satay?
June 17, 1990

Satay is a Southeast Asian specialty of skewered and grilled marinated meat strips that I first learned to love in Singapore on our 1979 trip, when we were surrounded by a rising heap of used wooden skewers piled by our elbows as we indulged in the meat treats.

The only hazard of a satay orgy is skewering one's tonsils. A practiced satay artist tugs meat off with front teeth without poking the sharp stick any farther back than the molars.

Hawaiian Chef Peter Merriman with mom, Woodene Merriman, our frequent traveling companion.

Peter the Great
April 2, 1995

Visiting Hawaii in 1995, again with Woodene Merriman of the Pittsburgh Post-Gazette in our group, we dined at both of Peter Merriman's restaurants, Merriman's in the high country of the Big Island and Hula Grill on Maui's Kaanapali beach. While eating his Coconut Creme Brulee, this is what Woody had to say about Peter, who has become a food force in Hawaii:

"He amazes me," says his mother, whose own career may have inspired Peter's interest in food, but who assumed no credit for his creativity. "I never cooked this way at home when he was a kid."

According to Peter, his food pursuits were spawned by an inner need. "I've been hungry all my life. I like to eat a whole lot," he says, stretching to emphasize his considerable stature. "Mom was at the office, so I had to learn how to cook."

Woodene grimaces at his forthrightness, but she's mollified when Peter makes it clear that she educated his palate from a very early age.

"When I lived in Mary McKee's house — that was Woody's byline when she was food writer for their hometown McKeesport (Pa.) Daily News — we had to eat some new recipe every day because she was always testing things," Peter told us. Woody's late husband, Steve, the gentlest of men, would kindly comment on any disastrous outcome by saying, "We won't print this one, will we?"

When Peter was in college, living in a house with 14 guys, "he'd call me 10 times with questions about some recipe he was making," Woody recalls. Now, he's a food star in the family, too, and she's delighted to let him do the cooking on visits back to mom's kitchen in McKeesport — no questions asked.

Once a mother, always a mother. Woody told us, as we were savoring Peter's cuisine at Merriman's, "When this restaurant first opened, Peter needed 40 customers a night to make it. On our visits to Hawaii, Steve and I would come in each night and count...37, 38, 39, 40. Whew!"

Now, the count might be of celebrities who come into Merriman's on the Big Island: Kevin Costner, Dennis Hopper, Joe Pesci, Priscilla Presley and Wolfgang Puck among them. At Hula Grill, Woody couldn't possibly count the customers fast enough. They come in droves.

Ahoy There, Aric
August 19, 1990

Our Aric has been a "galley slave" all summer, though don't feel sorry for him. He's been sailing New York-Bermuda-New York weekly aboard the Royal Viking Star, not bad duty. To visit Aric on his summer cruise, we had to treat ourselves to a week aboard the Star, not bad duty, either.

He's rotated among different departments in the ship's kitchen, gaining experience required to complete his major in hotel management at the University of Denver. The first week of August, when we were aboard, he was in the pastry area, dishing desserts. He decorated his dad's 55th birthday cake — the first time he'd ever worked with marzipan roses or etched "Happy Birthday" in icing. Believe me, I was impressed. That

THE REEF'S COCONUT CREAM PIE
Makes 6 to 8 servings

Sugar paste (pastry):
  2 tablespoons sugar
  1/2 stick butter
  1/2 cup flour
  1/2 egg yolk
Cream pie filling:
  3 tablespoons sugar
  1 cup milk
  1 tablespoon cornstarch
  2 egg yolks, beaten
  1 cup whipped cream
  5 ounces grated coconut
  A few drops of Malibu coconut rum
      liqueur (CocoRibe or plain rum will
      do)

To make pastry: In mixing bowl, blend sugar, butter, flour and egg yolk. Press mixture into 8- or 9-inch pie plate. Bake in 375-degree oven until browned. Allow to cool.

To make filling: In top of double boiler, combine sugar, milk and cornstarch. Stir until thickened. Pour some hot mixture into egg yolks. Return egg yolks to double boiler. Stirring constantly, cook until mixture coats back of spoon. Cool. Stir in whipped cream, coconut and liqueur (or rum). Spread filling over crust. Bake in 375-degree oven for 40 minutes, or until top is browned and filling is set.

cake was more elaborate than anything I've baked for my son's 21 birthdays.

Despite the rigors of 70-hour weeks and a tendency toward sea-queasies, Aric says he's absorbed considerable knowledge during his summer afloat —

including the firm realization that he doesn't want a career in the kitchen.

As I watched him in the ship's Bergen Lounge, resplendent in crisp white chef's jacket and towering toque, deftly carving beef and ham for a luncheon buffet, I could see he wasn't the same kid we'd sent off to sea in June. I can hardly wait for him to come home Saturday. My galley could use a new chef.

While exploring Bermuda during that cruise, we found Coconuts, a thatched restaurant balanced between boulders overlooking a pink sand beach at The Reef, a classy resort on Bermuda's south shore. Before we went back to the ship, I left my card at the front desk with a request for the restaurant's wonderful coconut pie. Sure enough, the recipe was waiting on my desk when I returned to the office, thanks to the miracle of fax and the courtesy of The Reef's executive chef, Kim Canteenwalla.

A Bite of New England History
November 11, 1990

Joe Froggers sound like marine critters, but guess again, Kermit. They're cookies — and they were our first taste of New England, passed around by Betty Hunt, who guided visiting food writers through the crooked streets of her beloved Marblehead, Mass. She's one smart cookie when it comes to hometown history, and she gave us the cookie recipe, too, one that had been found tacked to the kitchen door of an old Marblehead house.

In Colonial days (when 8,000 calories a day was the normal intake), Marbleheaders ate Joe Froggers that were 8 to 10 inches in diameter. Dainty cookies may have been served to ladies at 18th century tea parties, but Froggers were "a man's cookie," Betty Hunt says. Wives made them for their fisherman husbands going off to sea. The cookies had marvelous keeping qualities. "They take about a year to truly harden," Hunt says.

Every early Marblehead kitchen had the main ingredients: molasses and rum. Local cooks were quick to copy the cookie recipe of a certain Joseph Brown who owned a tavern on Gingerbread Hill in that seacoast town. Part black, part American Indian, Brown was known as "Black Joe," and the pool beside his tavern (it's still there) was known as Black Joe's Pond. The cookies were named for him and for the frogs occupying the pond's lily pads.

A pitcher of milk and a plateful of Froggers were a favorite Sunday-night supper in Marblehead of yore, when bakeries sold the cookies for a penny apiece.

JOE FROGGERS
Makes 4 to 5 dozen cookies

1 cup shortening
2 cups sugar
2 teaspoons baking soda
2 cups dark molasses
1 cup rum
7 cups flour
1 tablespoon ginger
1/2 teaspoon allspice
1 teaspoon nutmeg
1 teaspoon cloves
1 teaspoon salt

To make cookies: In large bowl, cream shortening and sugar until light. In another bowl, combine baking soda and molasses. Add rum. Into another bowl, sift flour with ginger, allspice, nutmeg, cloves and salt. To creamed shortening, alternately add rum mixture and flour mixture. Stir well between additions. (Note: Dough will be sticky.) Chill overnight.
To bake cookies: Flour board and rolling pin. Roll dough 1/2-inch thick. Cut with large cutter. Bake in 375-degree oven for 10 to 12 minutes, or until done.

Raclette Updated
May 19, 1991

Some years ago, a herd of us food writers traipsed through the high pastures of Switzerland, stopping to munch in the utterly picturesque village of Murren. One of my companions, Betsy Balsley, food editor for the Los Angeles Times, whose ancestors were Swiss, was aching to taste raclette.

If you've never dug into a plateful, raclette is a Swiss dish traditionally made with cheese melted by an open fire that's drizzled over boiled potatoes, tiny pickles and onions. Betsy was thrilled to see raclette on the menu of an outdoor restaurant on Murren's main street. Envisioning cheese turning liquid on a warm hearth — or at worst, softening under glowing heat rods in a modern raclette machine — she inquired of the waitress, "How do you make your raclette?"

"In le mick-ro-wave," the Swiss miss told her.

The Day I Almost Went to Jamin
November 17, 1991

I once had a chance to lunch at Jamin, the epitome of Paris restaurants. A friend with connections had wangled an impromptu table for four (getting a reservation usually requires a two-month wait). But a fifth person in our group expressed interest, and I, perhaps in a moment of frugality, stepped aside.

Instead, I went to a two-star restaurant, spent $70, and couldn't tell you now what I ate that day. The four who went to Jamin spent $100 apiece and have enjoyed a thousand dollars' worth of pleasure recounting their experience to anyone who understands that Jamin is to food what the Arc de Triomphe is to France: a national monument.

That recollection was in a column about the cookbook sharing Joel Robuchon's recipes from Jamin. He has since closed the restaurant, so now I'll never eat there.

A Marvelous Mess
March 31, 1991

Dale Curry, food editor for the New Orleans Times-Picayune, cooked this local classic for a dinner party we shared with friends in the Crescent City. Flavor was electrifying in this dish credited to a New Orleans restaurant called Pascal's Manale. Marvelously messy though it was to peel and eat jumbo shrimp dripping brown butter sauce, and then swab the bowl with French bread, we just reached for more napkins and kept eating. Head-on shrimp adds richness because the shrimp's fat is in the head; if you can't get them, use headless shell-on shrimp. Seasoning amounts are adjustable, to taste.

NEW ORLEANS BARBECUED SHRIMP
Makes 8 servings

3 sticks butter

3 pounds jumbo shrimp, heads on if possible

Lots of Worcestershire sauce

5 huge garlic cloves, crushed

8 shots liquid smoke

12 to 15 shots Tabasco

Juice of 2 small lemons

Salt

Lots of freshly ground pepper

Tony Chacherie Cajun Seasoning

In baking pan, melt butter (not margarine). Add remaining ingredients. Mix to blend. Bake in 400-degree oven, stirring occasionally, for 20 minutes, or until shrimp have pulled away from shells.

A New View of American Life
September 27, 1992

Four times I've seen China through my American eyes. Now, I am seeing America through Chinese eyes.

Professor Zhong Jiazhen is living in our home this school year while she is a visiting scholar at Macalester College. She teaches English at Shaanxi Teachers University in her home city of Xi'an, a mecca for tourists who flock to view the vast 2,000-year-old royal tomb filled with an army of terra-cotta warriors guarding the emperor Qin Shi. I've seen them and been awed.

Do you know what awes Professor Zhong as she encounters American life on her first trip out of China? Hot water. Any time of day.

"Who tends it?" she asked.

"No one. It's automatic," I said, showing her the hot-water heater, which she touched, surprised by its cool surface.

As I introduced her to the automatic washer and dryer, microwave oven, toaster, dishwasher, disposal, icemaker in the refrigerator — appliances we take for granted — she marveled. "You Americans have machines for everything. Life must be so easy for you."

She watched as my husband turned on a gas burner, and, hearing the clicking of the automatic ignition system, the professor said, "Ah, even a machine to light the flame."

Large cars and homes are an astonishment, but she wondered, as she explored our St. Paul Crocus Hill neighborhood, why so many houses belonged to someone named Edina or Burnet. Those are the "for sale" signs of local real-estate companies, we told her, another new concept for someone who comes from a country were city dwellings are usually government owned and assigned.

Most telling are the simple things. "I sat outside and looked at the blue sky and clouds," she said one early September day. "I remember blue sky when I was a child," says this 50-year-old woman who has lived most of her life under the persistent grayness of China's thick urban atmosphere.

She was fascinated to note that my husband is adept in the kitchen. "In my home," says this mother of three grown children and wife to another English professor, "my husband and I share the work: I cook and he eats."

Pizza was something else entirely new. "This is what Americans order when we don't feel like cooking," I told her.

She was hesitant at first to pick it up with her fingers, but we assured her that was the way we eat it. She folded a partial piece in half, and it reminded her of the most famous food of Xi'an: Chinese dumplings.

"Here you have a similar crust made with flour and water, and you have meat and vegetables, as we put in our filling," she said.

It's a small culinary world.

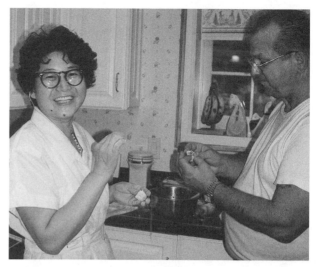

Professor Zhong Jiazhen shows Ron Aune how to pleat dumplings.

ANZAC BISCUITS
Makes about 36 cookies

- **1 stick butter**
- **1 tablespoon golden syrup**
  (available in better-quality grocery
  stores, or use corn syrup)
- **3/4 cup flour**
- **1/2 cup sugar**
- **3/4 cup rolled oats**
- **2/3 cup coconut (desiccated,**
  not long shred)
- **1 teaspoon ground ginger**
- **1 teaspoon baking soda**
- **1 tablespoon hot water**

In saucepan, melt butter and syrup. In mixing bowl, combine flour, sugar, rolled oats, coconut and ginger. Add melted mixture. Stir thoroughly. Dissolve soda in hot water. Stir into dough. Drop large teaspoonfuls of dough onto lightly greased oven cookie sheet, about 1 1/2 inches apart. Bake in 350-degree oven for 15 minutes.

Tea Time at Tui's
April 25, 1993

My good friend Tui Flower is one of New Zealand's rare birds.

This delightful dumpling with the sometimes tart tongue is revered for her influence on New Zealand's food scene. Tui, named for one of her native country's exotic birds, was not only food editor of the Auckland Star, but also of New Zealand Woman's Weekly, so she was read by the majority of that country's cooks.

She invited our touring contingent to her home in the Mount Eden district of Auckland, where she hosted a morning tea. Now officially retired but busier than ever, she'd arisen at dawn to bake shortbread, assorted scones and Anzac biscuits. Of course, with a group of food writers milling round her dining-room table, she had recipes to distribute.

We were especially delighted to have Anzac directions because on every airplane flight and coffee stop in Australia, we'd been getting little packs of the cookies made with such unfamiliar ingredients as wattle seeds. Tui's version is not quite the same as the commercial kind we'd been munching, but it's a perfect reflection of her own personality — sweet and gingery.

Golden syrup is available, but the recipe works with plain corn syrup. With no egg, I wondered if the dough would cling together, but as those Down Under say, "No worries." Anzac was a wartime term referring to the Australia-New Zealand Army Corps, whose members probably received a lot of these cookies from their moms and sweethearts back home.

Crepes of Many Countries
October 10, 1993

What was this? Chocolate sauce and ice cream melting and mingling into the anticipated orange sheen of my favorite shipboard dessert, crepes Suzette?

"They're crepes Alaska," said Giovanni Bolzani, our ever-beaming headwaiter aboard the Crystal Harmony sailing amid the Greek islands.

CREPES ALASKA
Makes 4 servings

Suzette butter:
1/4 cup butter
Grated rind of 1 orange
2 tablespoons Cointreau or
   Grand Marnier
2 tablespoons powdered sugar

Sauce:
1/3 cup sugar
Juice of 2 oranges
12 crepes
Additional Cointreau or Grand Marnier
Cognac
Vanilla ice cream
Chocolate syrup

To make Suzette butter: Grate orange rind into butter. Using fork, mix well. Add Cointreau and powdered sugar, stirring until blended. Set aside.

To make sauce: In large nonstick skillet over medium heat, allow sugar to melt until it begins to caramelize, turning medium brown. Add Suzette butter, stirring until melted and well-combined with sugar. Very slowly, add orange juice, stirring until bubbly.

To assemble: Place 1 crepe flat into sauce. Quickly flip to other side. Sprinkle center of crepe with 2 drops of Cointreau or Grand Marnier. Quickly fold it into

quarters, pushing to side of pan. Continue until all crepes are soaked, sprinkled and folded.

To flame crepes: Add approximately 3 tablespoons Cognac to sauce. If cooking on gas burner, tilt pan to ignite Cognac. On electric burner, ignite Cognac with a long match. In either case, stand well back when Cognac ignites.

To serve: Allow flames to subside. Place 3 crepes on each dessert plate. Top each serving with a scoop of vanilla ice cream. Drizzle with chocolate syrup. Serve immediately.

"I could make you crepes Hawaii or crepes Creole some other night," he offered.

"Of course, that's after I make you peaches flambe," he grinned.

How we ever got off that ship without gaining more than two pounds I don't know.

When we were again landlubbers, using Bolzani's directions and suggestions from several cookbooks, this is the crepes facsimile that I compiled. I told readers: It works just fine, but if you want to make it easier on yourself, simmer the sugar, Suzette butter and orange juice together until it's syrupy without caramelizing the sugar first. Whatever technique you use, don't do the dumb thing I did — use a rubber scraper to tend the caramelizing sugar. B.F. Goodrich might have appreciated the results, but my husband didn't enjoy picking bits of melted spatula from his crepes.

Days of the Iguana
February 6, 1994

We ate our way around Aruba, which doesn't take much doing since the island, just a dozen miles off the coast of Venezuela, is about the size of St. Paul. Like its ABC neighbors — Bonaire and Curacao — Aruba is a dry isle where about the only thing growing, besides aloe plants and cactus, is the tourist industry.

Despite the internationalization of the island, there's a definite Aruban cuisine built on the isle's two most common meats: goat and iguana. The latter is supposedly protected now, but islanders occasionally manage to make a pot of iguana soup with the stately reptile. We had a taste of it at Mi Cuchina, the most authentic of Aruban restaurants.

Don't let this critter chatter deter you. Every familiar fast-food franchise can be found on Aruba, and the fine hotels have fabulous restaurants. At the Radisson Aruba, Chef Greg Carroll created posh bread pudding, revised here for a smaller group and for a stronger chocolate kick.

The island's most elegant restaurant is L'Escale in the Sonesta Hotel. Strolling Hungarian musicians played "Golden Earrings" with such plaintiveness that I practically wept into my excellent lobster bisque.

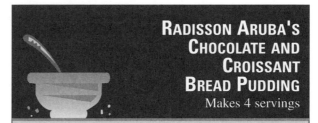

RADISSON ARUBA'S CHOCOLATE AND CROISSANT BREAD PUDDING
Makes 4 servings

4 day-old croissants
1/2 cup semisweet chocolate chips
4 large eggs
1/4 cup granulated sugar
1 teaspoon vanilla
2 cups heavy cream
1 cup whole milk

Dice croissants. Divide evenly among 4 ovenpoof soup plates or baking dishes. Divide chocolate chips evenly among soup plates or dishes. In mixing bowl, beat eggs until light and frothy. Add sugar. Beat for 3 minutes. Add vanilla, cream and milk, mixing well. Evenly divide egg mixture among soup plates or dishes. Place plates in large baking pan. Add 1/2 inch hot water to create water bath. Bake in 350-degree oven for 35 minutes, or until custard is firm. Serve puddings hot from oven. Or cool, refrigerate and serve cold with a dusting of powdered sugar.

What a Jerk!
April 24, 1994

I'll tell you how hot Scotch Bonnet peppers are. After handling the ones I brought back from Jamaica, I washed dishes, then later showered and shampooed my hair. The next morning, after several intervening hand-washings, I put in my contact lenses, and my eyes burned from pepper fire still lingering on my fingertips.

JAMAICAN JERK CHICKEN
Makes 4 servings

**2 whole chicken breasts or
    1 cut-up chicken
Jerk marinade:
1 onion, chopped
1/2 cup chopped scallions
2 teaspoons fresh thyme leaves
1 teaspoon salt
2 teaspoons sugar
1/4 teaspoon ground nutmeg
1/4 teaspoon ground cinnamon
1 teaspoon ground allspice
1 hot pepper, chopped (Scotch bonnet,
    habanero or jalapeno)
1 teaspoon ground black pepper
3 tablespoons soy sauce
1 tablespoon cooking oil
1 tablespoon cider or white vinegar**

To prepare marinade: Mix all marinade ingredients in blender or food processor, combining well. Rub chicken with about half of marinade. Reserve remaining marinade. Refrigerate chicken at least 4 hours.

To grill: Arrange chicken, skin side down, on grill over white coals. Baste frequently with reserved marinade. Turn chicken every 10 minutes. Over slow fire, chicken will cook in about 1 1/2 hours. Over hotter grill, it will take about 40 minutes. Chicken is done when flesh feels firm and juices run clear when pricked with fork.

To serve: Hack chicken into pieces.

Yes, they're hot, but the flavor is more complex than heat alone. It has soul and flair, like the music of Jamaica — and it's just as catchy.

At the Pork Pit in Montego Bay, jerk meat was hacked with a cleaver any which way, across bones. My husband hacked his grilled chicken breasts into very tasty chunks. Definitely finger food. Very lickable. Very likable.

This recipe, brought back from a chicken seminar in Jamaica, is the way Hans Schenk, chef-owner of the Sugar Mill restaurant near Montego Bay makes it, and our home-testing proved his version was as good as any tasted on the island.

Roosting for Wings in Buffalo
June 26, 1994

Many years ago for this column, we tested a recipe for supposedly authentic Buffalo chicken wings. But how would I know for sure, never having tasted the real thing. Finally getting to Buffalo, N.Y., we planned an obligatory visit to the coop from which the wings took flight: the Anchor Bar.

But we didn't get there, and maybe that wasn't much of a loss. The Anchor Bar, according to former New York Times food editor Craig Claiborne, is "raffish." My friend, Janice Okun, food editor for the Buffalo News and, by rights of location, America's leading expert on Buffalo chicken wings, describes the bar as very dark, rather dingy, decorated with license plates from every state of the Union.

But such decorative deficiencies are forgiven in consideration of the Anchor Bar's utter finesse with chicken wings. "Everyone goes there for take-out," Janice says, and that's how we got to taste the real thing.

Foregoing the experience of sitting amid all those license plates, we polished off five orders of take-out wings — three medium, two hot — in the elegant living room of Sydney and Jerome Goldstein, Janice's good friends. Buttery fingers were a danger to the Goldsteins' damask upholstery, and blue cheese dressing tended to drip onto their plush carpeting, but we tried not to create an environmental disaster as we did the wing thing.

Let me tell you, going to the source is best. Eating chicken wings from the Anchor Bar in Buffalo rates right up there with having pizza in Naples or fajitas in San Antonio. They're best on home turf.

Chocolate-Lover's Nirvana
June 26, 1994

The urge to dive headfirst into a vat of Hershey's chocolate and roll around until I was coated head to toe almost overcame me during a tour of the home of Kisses and Crunch Bars. But an inner voice argued that would be unseemly and probably ruin 100,000 Hershey's Bars in the process.

Six hours of determined driving from Buffalo, N.Y., is Hershey, Pa., the town that chocolate built, where street lamps are shaped like foil-wrapped Kisses. The aroma of chocolate hangs in the air, the kind of industrial pollution few would disdain.

With watches off, lest they fall into a chocolate vat, and dowdy caps totally covering our hair, we stepped into the 90-year-old main factory (where tourists are no longer allowed) to watch Hershey's Bars go from liquid chocolate to wrapped candy. Something like 33 million candy bars a day make that journey.

Chocolate-filled molds, jiggled to remove air bubbles, spend 20 minutes on a conveyor turning the bars from soft to solid. At the end of that belt sits an inspector with a suction wand to pluck out any defective ones. We watched for a long time, and none had to be rejected.

Then we beheld Kisses coming off the line by the thousands. They have to be jiggled, too, so the tiny curls at their tips fall off.

On the wall, we saw a quality-control chart that identifies missed Kisses, those that droop, lean, are too high or too flat. None of those continues the trip to be embraced by a paper "plume,' that slim slip printed with the Hershey name, then wrapped in foil.

Czech This Out!
October 30, 1994

Here's a title for a food thriller: "Death by Dumplings."

We almost succumbed to dumpling overdose during Eastern European travels, eating bread dumplings and potato versions the size and weight of junior bowling balls, cut into thick rounds and drenched with gravy.

Potato pancakes were a relief from all our well-rounded meals. Beggars' Pockets, a pancake folded over goulash, were our lunch during the craziest wine festival I've ever waded through.

Visiting Melnik castle in the Czech Republic to talk with Princess Lobkowitz about her reacquisition of the family's heirlooms after 40 years of Communist dispersal, we arrived in the midst of a wine bash. Forty thousand young people, drunk on the new vintage, thronged narrow streets and the castle courtyard, where a rock band blared against ancient stone walls.

What a relief to escape such pandemonium, retreating to the quiet of the castle restaurant. We were late, food had to be prepared quickly, but in 20 minutes, waiters served Beggars' Pockets. Cooking 42 huge potato pancakes so fast amazed us, as did the goulash that filled them, coming one country before we expected it. (Hungary was our next destination).

In Prague, a posh cookware shop called Potten & Panen gave us a demonstration of cooking chicken-breast filets in potato-pancake batter. I adapted the store's recipe to use as "pockets" for my version of the goulash filling we ate in Melnik castle.

BEGGAR'S POCKETS
Makes 4 servings

Pork filling:
1 pound lean pork (such as boneless pork chops)
1 onion, diced
1 green pepper, seeded and diced
1 long red Hungarian pepper, seeded and diced
2 tablespoons cooking oil
1 yellow squash, diced
1/2 cup tomato sauce or ketchup
1/2 teaspoon salt

2 tablespoons paprika paste, or
1 tablespoon paprika
1/2 cup water
Potten & Pannen's potato pancakes:
5 medium potatoes, peeled
1 small onion
2 cloves garlic, minced
1 egg
3/4 cup milk
1/4 cup flour
Salt and pepper
Cooking oil

To make filling: Cut pork into cubes. Prepare 1 onion and peppers. In large saute pan, heat oil. Add pork. Saute over high heat until lightly browned. Add onion, peppers and squash. Saute until slightly softened. Add tomato sauce, salt, paprika and water. Reduce heat to medium low. Simmer, covered, for about 30 minutes, stirring occasionally. Add water if mixture become dry. (Note: Liquid should be nearly gone by the time pancakes are ready to serve.)

To make pancakes: Grate potatoes and onion into bowl. Add garlic, egg, milk, flour, salt and pepper, stirring until blended. Heat low-sided saute pan or griddle over high heat. Coat with oil. Spread a round of batter about 10 to 12 inches in diameter onto pan. Cook until bottom is browned. Carefully flip with 2 spatulas, or by inverting pancake onto a plate and sliding it, uncooked side down, back into pan. Cook until other side is browned. Repeat until all batter is used. Keep cooked pancakes warm.

To serve: Place pancake on plate. Place some filling on one side. Fold.

No Bones About It
June 12, 1994

Northern Minnesota Finns all know about kalamojakka, that rudimentary fish soup flavored with allspice, milk and butter. My mother made kalamojakka when she got her hands on a nice northern pike, but I never liked it because of the bones.

The night Pekka Korpinen made dinner for us in his castle in the Finnish woods, his fish soup had bones and eyes, all too reminiscent of what I refused to eat as a kid. But, being a good guest, I picked out the ribs and enjoyed the flavor of Pekka's potful.

Eeva Salonen, food editor for the Helsingin Sonomat, Finland's largest newspaper and a longtime friend, was at Pekka's dinner table that night, also trying to eat around the fish bones. She most politely

EEVA'S FISH SOUP
Makes 4 to 6 servings

1 freshly caught fish, such as a
   "keeper" walleye, or several pan fish,
   filleted, saving all bone structure
Cold water
6 to 8 whole allspice
1 bay leaf
1 small onion, sliced
A sprig of fresh dill
2 carrots, cut into large chunks
2 potatoes, diced
1 cup milk
2 tablespoons flour
1 tablespoon butter
Fresh dill
Cream
White wine

To make broth: Fillet fish. Set aside. Put head or heads and ribs in large pot. Add 5 to 6 cups cold water, allspice, bay leaf, onion, dill and carrot chunks. Bring to a simmer. Cook, covered, for 30 to 60 minutes. Strain broth. (Note: There should be 4 to 5 cups liquid.)

To make soup: To clear broth, add diced potatoes. Boil until potatoes are nearly done. Combine milk and flour (instant-blending Wondra, if possible). Stir into hot broth. Add fish and butter. Simmer for 5 minutes, or until fish is done. Stir in generous amount of fresh dill, a little cream and some white wine. Serve hot with good rye bread.

declined to mention that the very next day, on the cover of her food section, she would be running a color photo and recipe for her version of Finnish fish soup — sans bones. She later translated her recipe for me, and it's going to become a classic at our lake dinner table.

Lingering on Lanai
April 23, 1995

In Hawaii, a brief misty shower is known as "pineapple rain." That occasional rain doesn't kiss many Hawaiian pineapples anymore, as the industry is moving to Malaysia, Mexico and other tropical sites where labor costs are lower.

Lanai, near Maui, has been a private pineapple island for decades, rarely visited by vacationers. On previous trips when I've inquired about going to Lanai, the usual response was there wasn't much to see or do. That's still somewhat true, but now two glorious places to stay lure those who want private paradise and don't mind paying $300 or more per night for a pillow.

We didn't sleep there. We just ate and got back on our chartered boat. But when the Powerball prize is in my pocket, I'm going back to Lanai and stay awhile.

As our boat neared the island, it skirted craggy vertical cliffs, then docked in a small bay alongside a few other craft. No harbor village — not even a gift shop at the wharf — was an indicator that tourism has yet to taint the island. A small bus hauled us up the hill and into a vast plain, the crater of an ancient volcano that proved the perfect incubator for pineapple. Now, there's more red soil than green plants visible in that huge basin, so we could only imagine it in its pineapple prime.

We bounced through the town of Lanai built for field workers. Utilitarian housing and communal-bath structures were sheltered by towering Norfolk pines, proving how long Lanai had been settled. No stops at the gift shop here, either — we didn't even see one. "This is how old Hawaii must have looked," my seatmate observed.

A few miles beyond town, down a long lane edged with pines, velvety lawns hinted we were about to experience new Hawaii. Dole Food Co., owner of the island, now develops elegant resorts instead of pineapple plantations. The Lodge at Koele in the central uplands and Manele Bay Hotel by the coast, where we had lunch on our way back to the boat, are take-your-breath-away luxurious. Both are built around vast Great Halls, the Lodge's decorated in early Hawaiian plantation opulence, and Manele Bay themed Oriental-style. I've never seen so many comfy chairs and sofas — and so few people sitting on them.

At the Lodge, Chef Edwin Goto dazzled us with a bowl of sunshine-yellow soup, served chilled, yet warmed by the fire of jalapeno peppers. When Goto gave us the golden gazpacho recipe, we were amazed

how simple it was. On that hot morning, we also cooled ourselves with his spiced tea. Both showcase the island's former star player, pineapple.

LANAI SPICED ICED TEA
Makes 2 quarts

4 cups water
1/4 ounce loose tea (about 2 tablespoons)
1 cinnamon stick
3 whole allspice
3 whole cloves
4 cups pineapple juice

Boil water. Tie tea, cinnamon stick, allspice and cloves in cheesecloth. Place cheesecloth bag in water. Turn off heat. Steep for 20 minutes. Remove cheesecloth. Refrigerate tea until well chilled. To serve, mix spiced tea with equal parts of pineapple juice. Serve over ice cubes. (Note: If you don't want to spice your own tea, use a commercial spiced tea mix, such as Constant Comment, and blend it with equal parts of pineapple juice.)

Much Was Lost in Muffin Translation
November 26, 1995

Halfway around the world, home seemed very near. The Minnesota Vikings were playing Green Bay on TV when we arrived in our hotel room in Kunming, the remote southwest China city that was the start of World War II's Burma Road.

LANAI PINEAPPLE GAZPACHO
Makes 4 servings

1 cup peeled and seeded cucumber
1/4 cup red bell pepper
1/2 cup yellow bell pepper
1/2 jalapeno pepper
2 tablespoons sweet Maui onion, or other sweet onion
1 tablespoon Italian parsley
1 cup pineapple, skin and core removed
1/2 cup pineapple cider or pineapple juice
Pinch of salt

Coarsely chop cucumber, peppers, onion, parsley and pineapple. Place in blender. Add pineapple cider or juice and salt. Blend until mixture is smooth. Chill before serving.

Buses in Beijing were emblazoned with 3M ads.

At Dan Ryan's Grill in Hong Kong's Ocean Terminal, our first destination for steak sandwiches and hot-fudge sundaes after three weeks of eating China's food, I thought the manager looked vaguely familiar, and, indeed, I'd seen her before — in St. Paul. She was Manling Wong, who'd worked in several area restaurants before she and her husband returned to Hong Kong's hospitality industry.

This so-far-yet-so-near syndrome also surfaced on the Victoria II cruise ship gliding along the Yangtze River between Wuhan and Chongquin. Claudia Sutherland of Edina, part of our food-explorer group and noted for the Twin Cities dessert business she founded, noticed on a galley tour that the ship's pastry chef had a Xeroxed sheaf of American baking recipes with Chinese notations in the margin. They looked familiar, and when Sutherland studied them more closely, she realized why. In 1988, she had consulted with General Mills on several recipes that were later included in a "Country Baking" cookbook.

There, in a Chinese floating kitchen, Sutherland was staring at her own recipes.

The ship's pastry chef, Zhao Dong, was eager for advice about how he could bake her recipes using Chinese ingredients, achieving results that would please mostly American cruise-ship clientele.

Claudia and I and professional caterer Bob McElroy of Augusta, Ga., promised to return after dinner for a baking session. We shanghaied the cruise line's director, Richard Hayman, to be interpreter.

The 26-year-old pastry chef was adept at what he already knew. His breads and coconut macaroons were superb (I'd give you the macaroon recipe, but he wrote it for me in Chinese). His breakfast croissants were excellent, too, although in China, the crescent rolls are named for their shape, "cow horn biscuits."

Zhao was curious about an unknown — muffins— and he asked us to show him the procedure for the Hawaiian Chocolate version in his limited recipe collection (given to him by the wife of the Chinese-American who owns the cruise line).

"Get rid of the cocoa powder," Sutherland advised when the galley's larder proved to lack that ingredient.

Eggs were no problem. Chinese chickens supply them aplenty, and the chef professionally cracked them one-handed.

But other familiar-to-us ingredients called for in the recipe proved foreign in the galley. Sugar is raw, brown in color, large in grain. More is needed to attain the sweetness of our granulated white kind. When it was time to add flour, Zhao asked us, "Bread or pastry?" We guessed that he should use pastry flour.

Crushed pineapple in syrup is probably available in China, but didn't happen to be in the ship's pantry. We suggested he pluck pineapple out of a can of fruit cocktail.

Macadamia nuts? None to be had. Walnuts, somewhat rancid, were produced, but we rejected them. Try raisins, we suggested, but soak them in fruit cocktail juice first.

Zhao did have baking powder, a huge red canful, but we were unsure of its strength.

Since cocoa powder had been omitted, we suggested that cinnamon might flavor the muffins. Did he have some? Yes, but the Chinese term for it is "old jade powder," poetically named for its brown hue.

Measuring, so important to American recipes, was a problem. The chef had no American-style cups and spoons, so we guesstimated amounts.

"Because Chinese cooking is an oral tradition, it isn't based on measurements," Hayman said. Perhaps that's why Chinese fare is so spare on cakes. Proportions of ingredients in a stir-fry aren't so critical, but baking is technical and chemical, requiring precise quantities.

Once everything was in the bowl, Zhao mixed them with those all-purpose tools, chopsticks. To portion batter among paper baking cups (which, remarkably, he had), he squeezed it through his hands in exact dollops.

Considering all the substitutions and inexact measurements, we couldn't blame Betty Crocker when the muffins emerged from the oven somewhat tough and sticking to the paper. Were our blushes caused by the heat of the kitchen, or from shame that three baking "experts" couldn't turn out a decent muffin?

Maybe we should have told him to use bread flour.

1980

— Beginning an eclectic decade with French chefs, Herman, zucchini, flan, wild-rice soup, a toasted terrine – and a last bite for the original Office Hungries —

Claiborne is Converted

July 6

The 1980s began with a cavalcade of visiting chefs and food personalities. Among them was Craig Claiborne, then recently retired as New York Times food editor, touting his "Gourmet Diet" cookbook, which endorsed cooking without salt (he was far ahead of that trend):

On the verge of a stroke, Claiborne saw a doctor who put him on a low-salt diet. It was the instant conversion of a salt sinner to a sodium saint, and in the process, he lost 20 pounds of puffiness.

Claiborne had been a salt addict with a passion for sauerkraut juice over ice and all the peanuts within reach at New York's Plaza Hotel's bar. You and I might eat chips. His sodium style was several notches higher, in the caviar class.

I tried several of his high-heat, ultra-spicy recipes designed to compensate for no salt, and they were the perfect diet food — no one wanted to eat them. But nearly two decades later, our taste buds have caught up with Claiborne's, and we wouldn't think his low-sodium foods overly seasoned at all.

Translating French Recipes

February 3

French chefs paraded into the Twin Cities as if it were Bastille Day on the Champs Elysees, and we tested their oft-complex recipes for bouef en croute, vegetable terrine and other extravagances. After one particularly lengthy effort, for which I'd encouraged readers, "Don't be frightened. Take a deep breath and plunge ahead, taking it section by section," the last paragraph said:

You did it! You're a hero or heroine with the folks around your table. No recipe we ever run in this column will daunt you. Congratulations.

Writer and readers had both clambered over a hurdle, from hassled to haute.

La Varenne Cooking School in Paris, which I'd visited several years before, sent its premier chef, Claude Vauguet, to the Twin Cities. He was assisted in his demonstration by a then-unknown student of French cooking, Stephen Raichlen, who has since become a magazine columnist, cookbook author and frequent teacher himself:

La Varenne, when it first opened, promised to be a Paris cooking school where teaching was done in

English. The founders apparently never let the chefs in on that secret, for they're still speaking French.

Translators (as Raichlen was that February day) are intermediaries, though often the chef and translator chatter on for minutes, and the interpretation takes seconds. One suspects, as the saying goes, that something gets lost in the translation.

Despite the language barrier, Vauguet was a comedian, answering in response to an audience question, that he "couldn't give a hoot about when Escoffier lived or died." To another question about how to keep from crying when chopping onions, the chef replied, "Have someone else do it."

Going on the road is always troublesome, especially when cooking on makeshift equipment. Vauguet's late-afternoon demonstration was in a lobby lounge outside 510 Haute Cuisine restaurant in Minneapolis, which occupies the first floor of an apartment building. As residents of the building came home from work, they turned on their television sets, stoves and lights, creating such an electricity drain that Vauguet couldn't get water to boil on his portable burners.

Hello, Herman
August 3

Herman came into our lives. He's a sweet sourdough starter who needs to be fed daily:

After 10 days, you're either emotionally involved with Herman, or sorry you started the whole affair. Herman is meant to be shared with friends, who must also feed some, give some away, and so on, and so on, like a gooey, smelly chain letter.

Wok Talk
January 6

Like many of my readers, I began experimenting with wok cookery as China's cuisine was becoming familiar to a growing legion of Orient travelers. My wok was a Christmas gift, and on the first Sunday of 1980, as we repented holiday excesses ("My veins are running pure fudge and Tom and Jerry batter"), I tried some sensible wok dishes:

How does a food writer who's been to China exist without a wok? It hasn't been easy. We've stir-fried in a skillet that tends to litter the stovetop with debris. What a luxury to have a huge, heavy wok to contain all those little chopped tidbits, no matter how briskly we stir.

That pan was still in frequent use by the time The Year of the Monkey swung in during February: You probably didn't hear any tin horns and noisemakers. The loudest sound was the click of chopsticks, because the Chinese have the good sense to celebrate their new year with feasting.

Forgive Me, Food Editors
November 2

People often say to me, much to my dismay, "I wouldn't dare invite you to dinner. You're a food editor. What if my dinner was a flop?"

If these people worry about inviting one food scribe, imagine how I quaked when asking 40 newspaper food editors from across the United States and Canada to my house when they were in the Twin Cities for a conference. It felt like the San Andreas fault line moved to the middle of St. Paul's Lincoln Avenue.

What to serve? My food-editor buddy and foreign traveling companion Janice Okun of the Buffalo (N.Y.)

News said she'd contribute. And she did, holding on her lap during her flight an ice-packed box of fancy hors d'oeuvres made by a Buffalo catering firm. She arrived slightly frost-bitten. But then, Buffalo gals are used to the cold.

I decided to make, with Janice's help, a classy terrine of turkey, ham, bacon and chicken livers, which was put to bake after we spent a night on the town with our colleagues. At midnight, I went to bed, setting two alarm clocks, the clock-radio for 6 a.m., and a wind-up model for 1:30 a.m., when the terrines would be done baking. At 1:15, I opened one eye, looked at the clock, and went back to sleep. At 2:30, I awoke again, this time smelling the aroma of toasting terrine.

Are you reading this, you folks who worry about inviting me to your house for dinner? I took one groggy look at the terrines, inhaled one charred sniff, put the loaves in the refrigerator and cried myself back to sleep.

All was not lost. Under the char, the terrine was quite delicious. Nobody complained about the crusty edges. Food editors are a forgiving lot, all having had their share of kitchen fiascoes. They ate a lot of it, and what leftovers remained were packed for Mary Hart (longtime Minneapolis Star-Tribune food writer) to take to her newsroom. She was going back to work that night, and she said that the Tribune staff "will eat anything, even if it comes from (the competition) the Pioneer Press."

I'm a Flan Fan
January 30

Flan is my all-time favorite dessert, and I've eaten it all around the world. The flan of my dreams was spooned warm from huge panfuls, swimming in caramel, at El Bodegon restaurant in Cartagena, Colombia, which we visited twice in the early 1970s, before it became impolitic to go to that South American nation.

CARTAGENA CARAMEL FLAN
Makes 12 servings

Caramel:
 1 cup sugar
 1/2 cup water
Custard:
 8 eggs
 3 3/4 cups whole milk
 2 cups sugar
 1 teaspoon vanilla
 1/4 cup sherry, rum or favorite liqueur

To make caramel: In heavy saucepan, combine sugar and water. Cook without stirring until mixture becomes caramel-colored. Coat bottom and side of large ring mold or spring-form pan with caramel.

To make custard: While caramel cooks, in mixing bowl, beat eggs lightly, just until yolks and whites are mixed. Add milk, sugar, vanilla and sherry (if liquor is not used, increase milk to 4 cups). Pour custard mixture into caramel-coated pan.

To bake: Place custard-filled pan in larger pan. Add water so it comes halfway up side of flan pan. Bake in 325-degree oven for 1 hour, or until flan tests done (when silver knife inserted into custard comes out clean). Refrigerate. Let flan set in its baking pan for a day, or it may not hold its shape. Invert to serve, or spoon out of baking dish.

Before our first trip there, we conferred with Trudy and Fernando Torres, who represented Colombia in the Twin Cities. Trudy gave me this recipe then, and I repeated for 1980 readers. It's the closest to Cartagena flan we've ever made.

VEGETABLE PASTA SUPPER

Makes 4 servings

1 jar (6 ounces) marinated artichoke
    hearts (oil reserved)
1/4 pound thin noodles, such as
    fettuccine or linguine
1 clove fresh garlic, pressed
1/3 cup chopped onion
1 cup sliced fresh mushrooms
2 cups thinly sliced zucchini
1/2 cup grated romano cheese, divided
1 tablespoon butter
2 tablespoons finely chopped parsley

Drain artichokes, saving oil. Cook noodles as directed on package in boiling salted water until just barely tender. While noodles cook, saute garlic and onion in 2 tablespoons oil from artichokes (add more, if needed). Cook until soft but not browned. Add mushrooms, zucchini and drained artichokes (cut larger ones in halves, if desired). Cook, stirring, over moderately high heat for 1 minute, or until tender-crisp. (Note: Take care not to overcook.) Remove from heat. Gently mix with 1/4 cup romano cheese. Drain noodles well. Toss with remaining oil from artichokes, butter, remaining 1/4 cup cheese and parsley. Serve on heated platter with vegetables alongside, or toss both lightly together. Serve with additional cheese, if desired.

Original Office Hungries Eat Their Last

February 10

After a dozen years of writing about the Office Hungries — at least the original group — I said farewell to them, telling readers that our women's department (also known as Trends, Family Life and Accent over the years) was being cleaved, half of us going to write for the Pioneer Press only, the others assigned to the Dispatch:

It's like a divorce or death in the family — the breakup of a mostly cohesive, usually happy Trends group that was consistent about one thing: They were always willing to taste the week's cooking effort and never feared being brutally frank in their assessment.

My culinary ego carries scars from their frequent jabs about my cooking, but their comments enlivened the column. Other Office Hungries, a new mix of mouths, may take their place, but with my luck, half of those mouths will belong to career dieters and be clamped shut.

Our Zucchini Crop: Zilch

April 20

When a zucchini recipe wins $40,000 in the Pillsbury Bake-Off, you know the ubiquitous green squash with the odd Italian name has really become part of American cookery.

I dusted off recipes, such as this zucchini-artichoke pasta, in anticipation of our first attempt at growing backyard zucchini. Later that summer, and in subsequent years, I had to admit that while everyone else was overloaded with the vegetable, we didn't harvest a single one. Seems the backyard squirrels knew all about the tender pleasures of baby vegetables years before those infantile edibles became the rage. Our zucchini crop, year after year, was nipped right after the bud.

Summer Soother
July 13

Relatives from Massachusetts were tasters for this quick, cold soup served on a long, hot summer night. "Rather a thick, sweet soup tempered with just enough tang from yogurt," was my assessment.

COLD LEMON AVOCADO SOUP
Makes 6 servings

1 large ripe avocado
2 cartons (8 ounces each) lemon yogurt
1 cup milk
3 tablespoons minced green onions
1/2 teaspoon salt
Mint leaves

Peel avocado. Remove pit. Cut avocado into chunks. Place avocado chunks in blender with yogurt, milk, onions and salt. Blend until smooth. Sprinkle with fresh mint leaves.

Minnesota's Official Soup
November 23

Recounting adventures at the very first Crocus Hill neighborhood progressive supper we attended (over the years, that twice-annual supper inspired a

continuum of recipe testing), I first printed this soup recipe that became a column classic and a repeat favorite at our house. It was the house soup at the Radisson South Hotel in Bloomington, Minn., and is very simple, very good. For a party, the soup can be prepared up to the point of adding the cream, then reheated and finished just before serving.

MINNESOTA WILD RICE SOUP
Makes 12 servings

2 cups cooked wild rice (about 1/2 cup uncooked)
1 large onion, diced
2 large fresh mushrooms, diced, or 1 small can sliced mushrooms, drained
1/2 cup (1 stick) butter
1 cup flour
8 cups hot chicken broth
Salt and pepper to taste
1 cup light cream or half-and-half
1 to 2 tablespoons sherry or dry white wine (optional)

Prepare wild rice using 2 cups water. Simmer for 35 to 40 minutes. Saute onion and mushrooms in butter for 3 minutes, or just until vegetables soften. Sprinkle in flour, stirring. Cook until flour is mixed in but do not let it begin to brown. Slowly add chicken stock. Stir until mixture is well blended. Add rice. Season to taste with salt and pepper. Heat thoroughly. Stir in cream. Add sherry or white wine, if desired. Heat gently, but do not boil.

1981

— In a racy year, we delve into sex, French Silk, the layered look, rising dough and smooth gravy —

Better Than Sex? Only If You're Hungry
June 14

Better Than Sex cake was making the rounds. I brought the recipe back from a food-writers meeting in St. Louis and inflicted it on readers:

Patting the cake pan I carried, I said, "Better Than Sex" to columnist Bill Farmer as we met in the newspaper office elevator. "More calories, too, I bet," he retorted, fleeing before he'd have to sample a slice and give an opinion on such a subjective title.

Never, never has such hilarity and smirking greeted a Tested Recipe brought to the office. You've got to admit that the name is a grabber. In more genteel circles, the cake is also known as Better Than Robert Redford. Could anything be better than Robert Redford?

Every food editor at the conference scribbled down the ingredients when a staid panel on regional foods suddenly got raucous as we heard that Better Than Sex was the big thing in Charlotte, N.C. I couldn't resist testing, despite warnings by author and regional-food expert Bert Greene that we shouldn't further circulate such an atrocious recipe.

Greene was absolutely right. The cake is a soggy version of trifle, without the sherry (sherry might have improved it). Hot yellow cake is soaked with crushed pineapple simmered with sugar and then swathed with a double-size package of vanilla pudding cooked with milk. Then, the whole thing is buried under whipped cream and coconut.

That version may not have been the best, but in the years since, several versions of Better Than Sex have surfaced. It's a name that will not die.

Laying It On
July 5

The Layered Look filtered from fashion to the food world. Testing several examples of layered salads, "the latest cutesy culinary kink," I told readers:

It's all for effect, layering. A way to please the eye before everything gets mixed up anyway. If you don't have a clear glass salad bowl, forget it. The effect would be totally lost hidden deep in the dark confines of a wooden container.

Vegetarian Variations
March 1

Vegetarianism, espoused by hippies in the '70s, was drifting into mainstream dining in the early '80s, and recipes were tested for those who were eschewing rather than chewing meat. I tried to untangle the confusion over vegetarian choices:

Vegetarians tout so many philosophies about their food styles that a food writer gets nervous testing recipes for them.

Our 13-year-old niece doesn't eat meat because her college-age sister doesn't, but she will eat chicken — and an occasional Big Mac when the urge overtakes her. She calls herself a vegetarian.

You've probably heard the term "ovo-lacto" vegetarians. They eat eggs and drink milk, but stay away from meat. And I know people who are committed to a totally nonanimal diet, subsisting by careful mathematical accounting of proteins and nutrients from vegetables, seeds, nuts, sprouts and grains. They're the ones who know what they're doing. Some don't.

I remember the phone call from the anguished mother of a college-age son who had adopted

---

A reader says . . .

I have read everything you have written unless I was out of town. I admire your style: full of wisdom, wit and always very professional. The idea that impressed me most was long ago, when you mentioned, ever so gently, that Jello-O wasn't a proper item to serve at a company dinner.

— Martha Saul, St. Paul

---

vegetarianism to save money. He was eating mostly carrots and apples, which are fine, but not enough to maintain a grown man. He was getting sick, his mother was getting worried, and neither understood what vegetarianism is.

Nightmare in a Dream Kitchen
March 15

Do you know what a brand-new "dream home" with all the amenities and furnishings cost in 1981? KTCA-TV was hoping someone would pay $110,000 for the North St. Paul home they were offering as a fundraiser. To make buyers drool enough to whip out their checkbooks, they invited me to bake something during an open house. I thought the aroma of whole-wheat cinnamon rolls would waft wonderfully. The rolls were a huge hit, but baking in an unequipped kitchen meant hauling everything from home:

I made lists of everything down to the last paper towel and packed it all in the car. When I pulled up to the Dream House, Miss North St. Paul and a contingent of dignitaries were waiting — not for me, but for the suburb's mayor who was to give his official blessing.

I opened the back door of my car and my big mixer fell right onto the road. Crash, rattle, bang! What an entrance. "Here comes Julia Child," someone in the crowd catcalled.

Dumping sand out of my mixer bowl, I went right to work in the new kitchen and discovered I'd packed everything but water. The faucets were not hooked up. Instead of asking to borrow a cup of sugar from the neighbor, I begged for a pitcher of water.

With people watching and waiting for the rolls to finish, we were all bored during the dough-rising process. The only excitement was when I poured some water into the bright red sink and then looked down later to find it had all run onto the floor. The drains weren't connected, either.

Mayor Raises Dough
October 18

Around the country, bread-in-the-bag seminars were encouraging people to bake bread the easy way (long before bread machines made it really effortless). At the Minneapolis Auditorium (before it became a convention center), my Bread Fair baking partner was Minneapolis Mayor Don Fraser:

"Mr. Mayor, do you bake bread often?" I asked somewhat hopefully. He admitted to being inexperienced but willing to try. "Actually, I'm here because we need all the dough we can get at City Hall."

Oo-la-la, French Silk Pie!
January 18

Arboretum French Silk Pie is among the most frequently repeated Tested Recipes at our house. We have friends who want it every time they come to dinner.

I tried it for the first time while I was in Florida visiting my widower dad. It was his first winter alone in the vacation home near Fort Myers that he and my mother had bought the year before she died. (He, too, died in November 1981, also of cancer.)

I'd gotten the recipe from a reader, Diana Oas of River Falls, Wis., who responded to a Household Forum request for French Silk. Oas said it was the one served at the Minnesota Landscape Arboretum in Chanhassen. I thought my dad would enjoy it as a reminder of a divine buttery chocolate pie we'd adored in a New Orleans French Quarter coffee shop on our first family trip to Florida when I was in high school:

ARBORETUM FRENCH SILK PIE
Makes 8 or more servings
(a small slice suffices)

Crust:
- 1/4 cup melted butter
- 1 cup vanilla wafer crumbs (30 cookies, crushed)
- 1/2 cup pecans, finely chopped

Filling:
- 3 squares unsweetened chocolate
- 1 cup butter
- 1 1/2 cups sugar
- 4 large pasteurized eggs
- 2 teaspoons vanilla

To make crust: Mix melted butter, vanilla wafer crumbs and pecans. Reserve 1/4 cup. Press remaining mixture into 9-inch pie pan. Place reserved crumbs in another small pan. Bake both pans in 350-degree oven for 15 minutes. Watch carefully so they don't scorch.

To make filling: Melt chocolate. Cool. Cream butter and sugar. Add cooled chocolate. Add eggs to filling, 1 at a time. After each egg is added, beat for 5 minutes with mixer on medium speed. Stir in vanilla. Pour mixture into 9-inch pie shell. Sprinkle with reserved toasted crumbs (a ring of crumbs about 2 inches from edge looks attractive). Freeze pie until ready to serve.

We'd never forgotten that marvelous pie. We'd never forgotten that trip, either, when we took the mail boat to Sanibel and Capitva Islands before the bridge was built. We were the only ones on the beaches, gathering shells, watching whales spouting in the Gulf. Some memories, like that pie, can be recaptured, but have you been to Sanibel lately? You can't even see the beach for the condos.

Al, You Make Doggone Good Pancakes
October 25

Minnesota's Governor's Residence, not far from our own house, has been the setting for many an event we've attended, from parties for visiting royalty to the introduction of cookbooks that raised money to renovate the classic Tudor-style Summit Avenue mansion. "The Governors' Table" was published in 1981 and featured recipes from the state's first families. Gov. Al Quie's feathery pancakes became one of the column's most frequently requested recipes. Baking powder is the reason they're so light, but it leaves its distinctive flavor in your mouth after the sweetness of syrup subsides. If you have buttermilk and can follow that variation, you won't notice the baking powder as much.

AL's BEST DOGGONE PANCAKES
Makes 9 (4-inch) pancakes

1 cup milk
2 tablespoons vegetable oil
1 egg
1 cup all-purpose flour
1/2 teaspoon salt
2 tablespoons sugar
2 tablespoons baking powder

Combine milk, oil and egg. Beat well. Combine dry ingredients. Add to egg mixture. Stir to make a smooth batter. Grease griddle as necessary. Cook pancakes over low heat.
Variation: Use buttermilk in place of regular milk. Decrease baking powder to 1 1/2 teaspoons and add 1/2 teaspoon soda.

Awesome Aric, the trophied BMX racer.

Fuel for a Racer
August 30

"Awesome Aric" his racing shirt reads, and, indeed, he must be something incredible, for he keeps coming home with trophies. Our 12-year-old son has become a BMX racer. I'm not sure what that means — something like bicycle moto-cross, I guess. But I do know that it means bike parts are all over our entry hall.

To keep up his energy, I tested these bars, and they became one of his childhood favorites. As an adult now who seldom eats sweets, he probably wouldn't race for a piece, but when he was younger, he insisted I make them as part of our household's Christmas-candy collection. The first time they appeared, I told readers: I'd figure the calories in a batch of these, but I can't count that high — and I really don't want to know.

NUT GOODIE BARS
Makes about 120 pieces

12 ounces chocolate chips
12 ounces butterscotch chips
1 jar (18 ounces) peanut butter
1 jar (16 ounces) dry-roasted peanuts
1 cup butter
1/4 cup regular vanilla pudding mix (dry
    from box)
1/2 cup milk
2 pounds powdered sugar
1 teaspoon maple flavoring

Melt together chocolate and butterscotch chips with peanut butter. Spread half of mixture in jellyroll pan. Refrigerate. To other half, add peanuts. Set aside. In saucepan, combine butter, dry pudding mix and milk. Boil for 1 minute. Remove from heat. Add powdered sugar and maple flavoring. Beat. Spread over first layer. Cool in refrigerator. Spread remainder of chocolate-peanut butter mixture on top. Keep in refrigerator. Can be frozen.

Grappling With Gravy
November 22

Just before Thanksgiving, the column revealed:
I am coming out of the closet. After all these years of testing exotic recipes, I now admit that I cannot make gravy.

'Fess up. There are lots of you, like me, who suddenly get very busy cooking vegetables and setting the table when it's gravy-making time, We're more than willing to let a mate step up to the stove. Is there something macho about making gravy? Every man I know who cooks at all considers it the male prerogative to scrape the pan and perform that final touch to the meal.

During 16 years of marriage, I have never made gravy. My mother-in-law trained her sons right. My husband and his two brothers are all gravy-making masters. We wives mash the potatoes.

Take heart, timid gravy makers. This recipe is foolproof if you follow the measurements and use Wondra flour, which guarantees lump-free gravy.

EASY WAY PAN GRAVY
Makes a generous cup of gravy

2 tablespoons meat drippings
2 tablespoons instant-blending flour
    (Wondra)
1 cup cold water, milk or meat broth
Salt and pepper

Remove meat to warm platter. Pour drippings from pan into bowl, leaving brown particles in pan. Skim excess fat from drippings. Measure 2 tablespoons drippings back into pan. Sprinkle flour evenly over drippings. Pour in liquid. Blend thoroughly. Heat to a boil over medium heat, stirring constantly. Boil, stirring, for 1 minute. Stir in salt and pepper.

To make mushroom gravy: Stir 1 can (4 ounces) mushroom stems and pieces, drained, into meat drippings. Cook until light brown.

1982

— Of salt, plaster, pasta, fudge, fondue and other worldly visitors —

Don't Pass the Salt Shaker
March 28

Time magazine wondered in a cover story, "Salt: A New Villain?" and my column took note, commenting: Millions of salt shakers hit the garbage cans of this country shortly after its publication.

Salt is the cholesterol of the 1980s. During the last decade, national concern was over fats in our diets, and Americans started cutting back. Sure enough, the rate of heart attacks has been declining in this country.

Now, salt is getting scrutinized as we worry about stress and salt's relationship to hypertension.

Hills and valleys. Now in the late '90s, salt is less of a concern, and we're back to being fat phobic, verging on national vegetarianism.

We're Fondue You
October 10

Another trend prediction, this time mine, which may have been ahead of its time:

Mark my words. Fondue is on the rise.

Did you get so tired of moving your fondue pot every time you wanted to get at the pressure cooker that you put the fondue equipment in your last garage sale? I hope not, for food editors on our recent Alpine adventure said that fondue is resurging in every part of the country.

We all may have been ahead of the actual trend, for it wasn't until a decade later that fondue really took off again.

A reader says . . .

I enjoy your writing, advice and wit. Testing Results are almost the best part of the recipes. I have a cookbook that I got as a bride 55 years ago, and very seldom refer to it.

— Mary Hampl, St. Paul

E.T. Returns
December 19

Chefs, food writers, contest entrants and readers were usually the ones interviewed for the column, but on a December Sunday, readers met an extra-terrestrial returned home. She was actress June Lockhart, who I'd first written about when she and her family were grand marshals for the 1967 St. Paul Winter Carnival parade. This time, she was back in town touting microwave ovens, warmly wrapped in a custom-made Hudson Bay blanket coat because the Californian remembered how bitter Minnesota winters can be.

Lassie's plate of leftovers was never warmed in a microwave oven down on the farm. The same-name television series was too early for the modern cooking method.

"Lost in Space" was way beyond microwave cookery. On that futuristic TV show, food instantly whizzed out on a conveyor belt at the command of a touched button.

June Lockhart was Mom in both of those TV families, and despite her image of rural or otherworld domesticity, she candidly admits, "I don't cook."

So why was the actress in St. Paul on behalf of the new General Electric Dual Way microwave oven? "I'm very much into instant gratification," she said, a trait nurtured, no doubt, during the "Lost in Space" days, when she'd push buttons and the prop man would shove food onto the conveyor belt.

Aric Gets Plastered
July 25

The summer of 1982 was the longest we've ever endured, especially for 13-year-old Aric who underwent back surgery and spent his school vacation recuperating in a body cast from chest to knees:

I baked cookies for him and his friends who came to visit — cookies full of wheat germ, raisins and oatmeal. Anyone who's had to take care of a bed-bound person soon learns that it's important to feed lots of fiber to keep the patient's plumbing functioning. I keep shoveling fresh fruit into Aric, and he's eating a more sensible diet now than when he was able to raid the refrigerator.

Any time I ask Aric what I can bring him, his answer is "a saw so I can cut this cast off." But he's learned to cope with his plaster undies, though his most often used word about the experience is "bo-o-o-r-r-ing."

The last words we heard from the surgeon before we took Aric home from the hospital were, "Don't overfeed him. I've seen kids outgrow their casts."

That thought haunted me while Aric, bed bound, ate voraciously. I was sure he'd pop the plaster. As in "Hansel and Gretel," each day we checked to see if he was getting fatter. The fairy tale witch was perplexed why Gretel always seemed bony. I wondered why Aric, eating his favorite foods and getting no exercise, seemed to stay the same circumference around his middle.

We got the answer on the blessed day the cast came off, a plastic body brace went on, and he stood on wobbly legs for an instant. He'd grown as tall as I am, adding at least three inches during those six weeks in bed. A nicely timed growth spurt nearly had him outgrowing his cast in a direction we hadn't expected.

Fudge of my Fantasies
February 7

"What are you reading?" my husband asked, seeing me engrossed in a paperback book. He must have suspected it had been sold in a plain brown wrapper, judging by the lascivious look on my face.

No, it wasn't a sexy novel, I assured him. It was something else to inspire lust, however — a collection of fudge recipes. I tested three selected from among the 10,000 responses received by the editors of Farm Journal magazine, authors of that juicy book. Of those three, in fact of all the fudge recipes I've ever made, Velvet Chocolate is the smoothest and most foolproof. Cornstarch makes it velvety — and I still indulge in it every year at Christmas.

Lemon-Aid for Breakfast
February 14

Weekday breakfast at our house is a layered event. I usually fix something for myself while Aric hogs the bathroom, taking his eternal morning shower. The joys of mothering a teen-age boy are just beginning. When he finally emerges in a cloud of steam, hair blown dry,

VELVET CHOCOLATE FUDGE
Makes 8 dozen pieces

4 1/2 cups sugar
1 tablespoon cornstarch
1/2 teaspoon salt
1 can (13 ounces) evaporated milk
1/2 cup butter or regular margarine
**16 ounces regular marshmallows (about
   1 1/2 bags)**
**1 package (12 ounces) semisweet
   chocolate chips**
**1 milk-chocolate candy bar (then 8
   ounces; now about 7 ounces), broken
   up**
2 teaspoons vanilla
2 cups chopped walnuts

In heavy 5-quart Dutch oven, combine sugar, cornstarch and salt. Stir in evaporated milk and butter. Cook over medium heat, stirring constantly, until mixture comes to a rolling boil. Boil for 8 minutes, stirring frequently. Remove from heat. Stir in marshmallows, chocolate chips, chocolate bar and vanilla. Beat until smooth. Stir in walnuts. Pour into buttered 10-by-15-inch jellyroll pan. Cool. Cut into 1 1/4-inch pieces.

BOARDING HOUSE LEMON PECAN BREAD
Makes 4 large loaves

3 cups butter
5 cups sugar
12 eggs
9 cups flour
3 tablespoons baking soda
1 teaspoon salt
3 cups buttermilk
**Grated rind of 4 lemons (reserve the
   juice)**
Grated rind of 2 oranges
2 cups chopped pecans
1 1/2 cups sugar (for glaze)

Cream butter and sugar. Beat in eggs. Add dry ingredients alternately with buttermilk. Add lemon and orange rinds and juice from 2 lemons. Stir in pecans. Pour into 4 greased loaf pans. Bake in 350-degree oven for 1 1/4 hours. Mix remaining sugar with juice from 2 lemons. Glaze bread while still warm.

he eats. My husband usually skips the morning meal altogether, saying that if he breakfasts, he's ravenous by 10 a.m., but if he doesn't eat, he's not hungry all day. He ought to patent his stomach and sell the secret to dieters.

That column tested variations on a breakfast theme, and as an aside, included the enticingly tangy lemon pecan bread served at a neighborhood Grand Avenue restaurant, The Boarding House, where we sometimes brunched. Owner Dennis Smith, who made the bread himself, was willing to reveal his recipe, which became another of the column's all-time favorites.

What you see here is the proportions he sent for a four-loaf batch. "Do you ever halve it?" I asked. "Actually, I double it," Smith answered. He'd have to mix a double batch in a washtub, because this one practically overflowed my mixer. If you do make this entire recipe, it will be one of the first recipes on record to nearly use up nearly a quart of buttermilk — hooray!

Add the Peas, Please
May 2

In a small garden restaurant in Venice, I fell in love — with Paglia e Fieno (Straw and Hay), a northern Italian pasta dish that has become my all-time favorite. The creamy cheesy pasta may be out of style in this low-fat era, but for eating pleasure, it's unparalleled.

When asked to do an ethnic cooking demonstration at the Iron Range Interpretative Center near Chisholm, Minn., I made this recipe and the lemon chicken found in the Global Gourmets chapter of this book. Cooking and talking at the same time, I learned, takes considerable skill. But the audience had copies of the recipes, and when I forgot to put the peas into the pasta sauce, they quickly reminded me.

STRAW AND HAY
Makes 4 to 6 servings

1 pound fresh linguine or egg noodles, half plain, half spinach (or use dried linguine)
1 tablespoon oil
1/4 cup butter
1 garlic clove
8 ounces fresh mushrooms, cleaned, trimmed and sliced
1 1/2 cups cooked ham, cut into thin strips
1 cup whipping cream
1/2 cup half-and-half
1 cup fresh or frozen peas
1/8 teaspoon freshly grated nutmeg
White pepper to taste
Freshly grated Parmigiano-Reggiano or asiago cheese

To cook noodles: Bring a gallon of salted water to a boil. Add oil (flavored with garlic clove, if possible). Cook fresh noodles for 4 to 6 minutes. (Follow package directions if using dried linguine.)

To make sauce: Meanwhile, rub large frying pan with halved clove of garlic. Add butter. Heat until melted. Saute mushrooms in garlic butter until lightly brown. Add ham. Stir in cream, half-and-half and peas. Cook until sauce is reduced by about a third. Add nutmeg and pepper to taste. Add cooked pasta. Using 2 forks, toss pasta and sauce lightly, sprinkling with grated cheese while mixing. Serve with additional freshly grated cheese.

Goulash, Castle-Style
November 21

We had recently returned from an Alpine trip, and the column opened:

Goulash soup is the chili of Austria. We've had it in nearly pure gravy form and as a spicy stew with meat and potatoes. Either way, it's a traveler's tonic against the lethargy created by too much whipped cream and wine sauce.

This soup recaptured the flavor of a lunch at Schloss Kapfenstein, an 11th century castle that stood as a fortress against invading armies from the east and now welcomes invading tourists. They served Hungarian-style pork and vegetables with lots of paprika and no cream. This soup is a liquid version of that meal, and though it doesn't call for paprika, you could surely add some. Make sure it's red, fresh and potent, not rusty, oxidized and flat.

SAVORY PORK SOUP
Makes 3 quarts

2 pounds boneless pork shoulder, trimmed well, cut into 1-inch cubes
1/4 cup all-purpose flour
1/4 cup cooking oil
1 bunch green onions, sliced
2 cloves garlic, minced
2 cans (16 ounces each) tomatoes
2 cans (10 1/2 ounces each) beef broth
1 jar (16 ounces) small boiled onions, drained
1 can (6 ounces) vegetable cocktail juice (V-8)
1/2 cup water
3 ribs celery, sliced into 1-inch pieces
2 medium yellow squash, sliced
1 bay leaf
1 tablespoon dried parsley flakes
1 teaspoon salt
1/2 teaspoon seasoned pepper

Dredge pork cubes in flour, coating well. Heat oil in Dutch oven. Brown cubes on all sides in hot oil. Add green onions and garlic. Cook over medium high heat for 1 minute, stirring constantly. Add remaining ingredients. Bring to a boil. Reduce heat. Simmer, covered, for 1 to 1 1/2 hours, stirring occasionally.

A reader says . . .

I dearly love your column, and it's the first thing I read. It has been great to follow your son's growing up, your disasters and successes, your husband's diets, your remodeling, and, yes, the dogs, dear souls. Your columns are like a visit with a dear friend.

I'm preparing for our Norwegian church bake sale coming up, and beside my Norwegian cookies, I am preparing the cardamom cookies and cardamom toast that I got from your column. Last year, the cardamom toast was the first to run out. Thank you for all the testing, eating, humor — and just you.

— Irene Small, Detroit Lakes, MN

My Mother

— Saying Goodbye —

The Saddest Column, the Sweetest Memories

August 24, 1980

The best cook, the best person I know died two weeks ago.

My mother lost her eight-year battle with cancer, but not without a fight that amazed her doctors and gave her more years than they thought possible. Despite the blight of disease, they were good years of travel, of fulfilling retirement dreams, because my mother never let cancer control her lifestyle. She laughed so those around her didn't have to cry.

Perhaps she protected us too effectively. She did so well for so many years that when the last treatment was under way, her optimism that it would fend off the disease kept her family buoyed even as her pain increased.

To me, it seemed that the end came so fast. I was not prepared, but she was. She died with total calmness, worried more about those who stood at her bedside than about herself. "I just want you to be happy," she murmured.

Anyone who has ever watched a loved one dying knows the heartbreak tied to the ultimate realization that there is nothing left to do, no hope that another medical miracle will delay the inevitable. The decision to accept her death and let it come peacefully —

without more tubes and technology — was the most difficult for me, but the kindest for my mother.

My dad knew that. But I could only be at ease with it when she died so quickly and I realized that she would not have survived desperate last attempts at treatment.

I do not mean to cloud your Sunday morning with my sadness. In fact, my own sorrow came in the days before her death, and it is now softened with sweet memories. I would have wished her many more years — she was only 65. But no regrets mar my thoughts, only a lasting happiness that fate made her my mother.

And what a mother she was. A neighbor retold me the story recently of how, during the famous Armistice Day Blizzard of 1940, my mother trudged quite some distance on foot through the storm to borrow oranges, because baby Eleanor needed her juice.

Her doctor called her "The Champ" because she kept winning round after round in her battle with cancer. She was able to meet the end with strength and courage, just as she had fought to live, aided by her Finnish "sisu" — sheer determination.

As she floated in and out of a morphine haze during the last days, sometimes lucid enough to help us plan her funeral, sometimes speaking out what she was dreaming, she suddenly looked at me and said, "You know, I could never carry a tune, but I could always carry the food."

Good cooking and my mother were synonymous. Nearly everyone who contributed thoughts for the memorial service I wrote mentioned the joys of being at Ellen Ostman's table. Her skills were honed as a lumber camp cook early in her marriage, then as the operator of a Keewatin boarding house during the waning days of World War II, fixing meals and lunch pails for Iron Range miners.

Thereafter, most of her cooking was for family. Sudden realizations that I didn't write down some of her traditional recipes, that Aric will never again eat Grandma's cinnamon bread or potato sausage, renew our missing her, day after day. Aric may balk at some of my recipe testing, but he loved every morsel my mother made for her only grandchild.

There was usually a fresh batch of bread or rolls, a luscious cake to go with coffee she offered the moment anyone dropped in.

One of her longtime friends wrote,

"I'll remember her cheerful, 'Hello, anyone home?' as she came to our door. I had to accept for the hundredth time a gift of produce or flowers from her garden, delicious baked goods, even health foods to feed my man. I don't believe she ever came empty-handed."

Others wrote of her gardening talents, the flowers that flourished, the abundance of her vegetables. Strawberries and raspberries that she grew to the epitome of ripeness and sweetness have forever spoiled me for accepting pallid facsimiles in grocery stores.

The day she died, the night sky was ablaze with falling stars. A rare meteor shower brightened our lives nearly a century after the demise of the comet whose remains flashed through the heavens. That which died can still be with us. My mother brightened many lives and continues to do so in our memories.

You Can Go Home Again
May 9, 1982

I expected to get misty-eyed the first time I walked into our family home near Hibbing now that it belongs to another family. My dad left it in an ambulance on the first Wednesday of last November. New owners moved in Thursday, and my dad died on Friday. All so fast.

In April, I sat in the kitchen of my mother's best friend, peering across the road at the house, wondering how it would be to take that short walk backward in time, to confront a lifetime of memories.

Once the journey was made, actuality wasn't nearly as painful as anticipation had been. It was still my mother's kitchen, but the pictures on the walls, the knickknacks were unfamiliar, and there were matching highchairs for the twin daughters of the new owners. Different furniture in the living room erased the feeling that I should see my parents sitting there.

I didn't look into the bedrooms because I knew, then, that the house would never be the same. Acceptance was easier than it had been after my mother died but her things were still there.

New life fills those rooms. Two little girls will grow up in the house my dad built.

On their 40th anniversary, Ero and Ellen Ostman.

I Remember Mom's Cooking

— *She Made Great Plain Food* —

Dredging Mother's Recipe Files
October 28, 1984

At first, it was too painful.

Then, the box got shoved out of sight.

Four years after I brought that carton of memories home, I was asked to teach a cooking class to benefit the school my son attends. Any subject, the organizer assured me. Chinese? French? What would I like?

"Mother's," I told her. Finally, I would sift through my mother's recipe collection and teach a class inspired by the world's greatest cook.

World's Greatest Plain Cook would be a better description, because my mother's specialty was substantial but unfancy food, the kind my dad liked. As long as she had his meals ready and a fresh batch of goodies for his coffee breaks (his business was a few steps away from the house), all was right in his world and hers.

Sitting down at my St. Paul kitchen table with that stack of recipes was a sentimental journey 190 miles north to Hibbing, evoking images of that cozy kitchen so often filled with aromas of fresh bread and cooling cookies.

I regret, in this era of working mothers, that my son, Aric, doesn't come home from school to chew on a heel of warm rye bread, as I did. I adored those after-school treats and the hot breakfast every morning before I boarded the school bus. Mother's love was expressed through food.

My mother was a recipe clipper, and I pawed through assorted yellow scraps of newsprint, a lot of them Tested Recipes columns from years past. What an irony: I considered her the best cook I knew, yet she clipped my recipes.

Some were jolting. There was a cookie recipe on which a very young Aric had practiced his signature while his grandma baked. And there was a recipe written on a sheet of note paper backed by her handwritten list of chemotherapy medications that battled her cancer for so long — but not long enough.

What startled me is that so many of the recipes I remember her making weren't in that box. They died with her, because she was a woman who cooked more by instinct than instruction. I don't think she ever exactly followed a recipe. If a cake called for two eggs, she added three. Her palm was her measuring spoon. In all things, she was generous.

Food was the focus of her life, and she was always curious about trying something new. Newspaper clippings bore dates right up to the week before she went into the hospital, never to return.

Her Table Overfloweth
October 28, 1979

We arrived just in time for a northern Minnesota weekend to sit down to a big company dinner for which my mother had been cooking for days: Homemade potato sausage, cabbage rolls, her own cracked-wheat bread, squash baked with apples and prunes, green rice casserole flavored with broccoli — it was a harvest-season feast.

Devilishly Difficult Angel Food
July 22, 1984

Among my earliest childhood memories is of my mother hand-whipping egg whites to make angel-food cake. It was during World War II, and my parents kept a few chickens to augment rationing. Electricity would

not be strung to our new house, built during the early part of the war, until peacetime made available the wiring diverted to the war's ships and planes. With an abundance of eggs but no electricity, angel-food had to be a handmade treat. And my mother baked magnificent ones, whipping those whites so fast her arm was a blur, baking them in a wood-stoked oven (no electric stoves in wartime, either).

Yogurt, Finn-Style
July 18, 1982

My mother was always interested in new food trends, but in one case, she was way ahead of the mode.

In all my growing up years, I remember her nurturing a stretchy concoction that she called by its Finnish name, viili. It was yogurt in its most elementary state, hardly resembling the fruit-flavored gelatinous stuff we now buy in cartons.

Everything, as I recall, depended on a starter. My mother and her friends of Finnish heritage shared. Anyone who allowed her culture to expire would be over with a jar to get another spoonful from my mother's milky lode.

Personally, I would never touch the stuff. To me, it always looked like white glue. Now, I regret having been so finicky because as my Aunt Impi, another viili culturist, says, "Store-bought yogurt just doesn't taste as good."

Requisite for enjoying viili is that one must appreciate buttermilk, for that's how Impi describes the homemade yogurt's flavor. To make it, she said, add a teaspoon of starter to 1 1/2 cups milk warmed to about 110 degrees. (Raw milk is best, but any kind will do.) Set it on the counter, and the next morning, it should have jelled. Then, it goes into the refrigerator. It's much lower in calories than the sugared, fruited commercial varieties. My mother used to make it constantly when she was on a diet.

Please don't call me for a starter. I don't have any. Ask the next nearest Finn.

A reader says . . .

You've supported women (and men) who chose to provide comfort to family and friends through cooking and entertaining. You've kept the community abreast of cooking trends and helped us explore other cultures through columns on Thai, Chinese, Mexican and other cuisine. I would venture to say that your columns created harmony and understanding among the races, because you presented the culture, not just the food.

— Patricia Jorgensen, Maplewood, Minn.

Forget the Salad, Just Eat Dressing
November 16, 1980

I can't remember at how many holiday dinners my mother forgot to take her carefully molded gelatin salad out of the refrigerator until the meal was done. But it was often enough that when she opened the 'fridge to stash leftovers and cried, "Oh, no!" upon seeing the salad, it became a family joke.

But nobody missed pineapple and cranberry-studded Jell-O because we stuffed ourselves with my mother's brown-rice turkey dressing. Sometimes, she used part wild rice. I've never found one I like better.

ELLEN OSTMAN'S BROWN RICE STUFFING
Makes enough to stuff a 20-pound turkey

- **1 pound brown rice (part wild rice, if desired)**
- **2 pounds ground pork shoulder**
- **1 cup chopped onion**
- **1 cup chopped celery**
- **1 cup mushroom pieces**
- **2 to 3 cups fresh bread cubes (whole-wheat preferred)**
- **Sage, salt and pepper to taste**

Cook rice as directed on package. (If desired, replace 1/4 pound brown rice with 1/4 pound wild rice, cooked separately.) Brown pork in frying pan. Add onion, celery and mushrooms. Cook until tender. Mix rice with pork mixture, adding enough soft bread to hold the mixture together. Add sage, salt and pepper to taste. Use to stuff turkey, or bake in casserole.

Pulla: The Staff of Finnish Life
March 1, 1970

My mother didn't need directions to make pulla or "biscuitia," as it was called by northern Minnesota Finns speaking "Finnglish." I never did get her recipe, which she made so effortlessly and frequently, but I tested this recipe, thinking it would be close.

According to my mother, the really proficient Finnish ladies made their coffeebread so that it had a wonderfully fine texture. I'd match this bread against any of them.

This version, which came in a press release from a yeast company, was fancified with lemon peel in the dough and almonds on top, but it omitted the most necessary flavorant, crushed cardamom. My mother always shelled whole cardamom, then pounded the black seeds in the corner of a dishtowel to release their pungent flavor. As far as I'm concerned, that's still the best method. Powdered cardamom will never produce the flavor or the flecks that make Finnish pulla perfect. For a batch this size, you'll need a teaspoon of pounded seed.

Ellen Ostman on one of her proudest days, when her Finnish Beet Salad won a prize in the State Weight Watchers' recipe contest.

FINNISH PULLA
Makes 1 large braided loaf

4 1/2 to 5 1/2 cups unsifted flour
1/2 cup sugar
1/2 teaspoon salt
2 teaspoons grated lemon peel
1 package active dry yeast
2/3 cup milk

1/4 cup water
1/2 cup (1 stick) margarine
3 eggs, at room temperature
Milk
2 tablespoons sugar
Slivered blanched almonds

To make bread: In large bowl, thoroughly mix 1 1/2 cups flour, 1/2 cup sugar, salt, lemon peel and undissolved yeast. Combine 2/3 cup milk, water and margarine in saucepan. Heat over low heat until liquids are warm (margarine does not need to melt). Gradually add to dry ingredients. (Note: This is when cardamom should be added.) Beat for 2 minutes at medium speed of electric mixture, scraping bowl occasionally. Add eggs and 1/2 cup flour, or enough flour to make a thick batter. Beat at high speed for 2 minutes, scraping bowl occasionally. Stir in enough additional flour to make a soft dough. Turn out onto lightly floured board. Knead for 8 to 10 minutes, or until smooth and elastic. Place in greased bowl, turning to grease top. Cover. Let rise in warm place, free from draft, for about 1 hour, until doubled in bulk.

To shape bread: Punch dough down. Turn out onto lightly floured board. Divide dough into 4 equal pieces. Set 1 piece aside. Shape remaining 3 pieces into 20-inch ropes. Braid ropes together. Pinch ends to seal. Place on large greased baking sheet. Divide remaining piece of dough into 2 equal parts. Roll into 12-inch ropes. Twist together. Pinch ends to seal. Place on top of braid. Brush loaf with milk. Sprinkle with 2 tablespoons sugar and almonds. Cover. Let rise in warm place, free from draft, for 1 hour, or until doubled.

To bake bread: Bake in 350-degree oven for 40 to 45 minutes, or until done. Remove from baking sheet. Place on wire rack to cool.

Mom's Best Bread
May 30, 1982

All recipes come to those who look long enough. For all of you who have ever lost recipes, you may be comforted to know that food writers lose them, too.

The one I couldn't find was very important to me — my mother's recipe for molasses raisin rye bread.

I remembered the day that I had enough sense to ask her what she put in her bread. So many times I've heard people say they wished they had gotten a favorite recipe for Mom or Grandma, but that it died with the one who knew how to make it.

I don't know where my mother got her recipe. Perhaps it was one she invented, adding a little of this and that to rye bread. Getting directions down on paper was hard because she made the bread by "feel" rather than measuring. But she came up with a list of ingredients, though not always quantities. What she told me was "some" powdered milk, and "a dollop" of honey and "white flour" without saying how much.

Vague as it was, I wanted to find that recipe, and so did others who wanted to savor it again. The bread was the cornerstone of all my mother's Christmas dinners. Her niece's husband loved it so much that all he wanted for Christmas was a ribbon-tied raisin-rich loaf.

But the recipe was lost, and my mother had died. I searched all my recipes boxes at home and thought it was gone forever, until I found it tucked in a file at the office just a couple of weeks ago. Timing was providential, for it surfaced just a week before we would be going to the North Shore to have a memorial service for my dad, and to disperse his cremated remains in his favorite trout stream. Those who would be there had all tasted my mother's bread, and it had also been my dad's favorite.

Greatest joy of all, even more than finding the lost recipe, was slicing into the warm loaf and reliving a flavor memory. A lost tradition in our family had been regained.

At our picnic lunch on the North Shore, which gave us strength to carry out my dad's wishes, everyone wanted the bread so they could remember my mother, too.

I'm not the baker my mother was, but with some experimentation, her sketchy instructions became this workable and truly delicious recipe.

MY MOTHER'S MOLASSES RAISIN RYE BREAD
Makes 3 loaves

2 packages yeast, soaked in 1/2 cup water (120 degrees)
3 1/2 cups liquid (add 1 cup powdered milk to water for richer bread)
2 cups raisins
2 cups rye flour
1 cup oatmeal
Dollop of honey (about 1/4 cup)
2 tablespoons caraway seed
3 to 4 cups white flour, as needed
1/2 to 3/4 cup molasses
1/2 cup oil
4 teaspoons salt

Combine soaked yeast, liquid, raisins, rye flour, oatmeal, honey and caraway seeds. Add enough white flour, about 2 cups, to make batter for sponge. Let rise until fluffy. Stir in molasses, oil and salt. Add enough additional flour, 1 cup at a time, to make a kneadable dough. Knead until soft and elastic. Divide dough into 3 parts. Form into round loaves. Place on greased baking sheets. (Or, flatten dough, roll tightly, seal ends. Place in greased 9-by-5-inch bread pans.) Let rise, uncovered, for about 1 hour in warm place, until doubled in bulk. Bake in 375-degree oven for 10 minutes. Reduce heat to 350 degrees. Bake 30 to 35 minutes. Cool on wire racks.

This P.S. appeared in the August 22, 1982, column:

Mom would have been so proud. Doris Huebscher of Frederic, Wis., writes that my mother's recipe for raisin rye bread was entered by her 16-year-old son, Kevin, in the 4-H foods and nutrition division of the Polk County Fair. "He not only got a blue ribbon, but an exceptional exhibit ribbon. The judge liked your mother's bread, too."

Another Lost Recipe Recovered

September 14, 1980

I thought my mother's potato sausage recipe died when she did, but her dear neighbor and friend, Milly Sorenson of Hibbing, triumphantly waved a recipe card when we saw each other during the Labor Day weekend.

"I read in the column about your mother that you thought you'd never taste her potato sausage again. The last time we made it together, something made me write down the measurements your mother used," Milly said. And there they were, neatly typed. "Your mother was a handful-of-this, pinch-of-that kind of cook. I'm so glad we measured everything that last time." So am I, Milly. You saved a tasty piece of my past.

When my mother and Milly made this 15-pound batch, they'd split the results. "Your mother made this sausage for as long as I can remember," said Milly, who was mom's neighbor for more than 40 years. She recalled the early days, before electricity was strung to their rural Hibbing neighborhood, when all the grinding was done by hand. They preferred a fine grind, too. Milly suspected the recipe was "part of your mother's Finnish heritage," though she added, "it tastes just like the sausage my Swedish grandmother made."

The two usually ground their own pork, using shoulder stringently trimmed of fat. Lean ground beef

MY MOTHER'S POTATO SAUSAGE
Makes about 15 pounds

Sausage:
- 7 pounds peeled potatoes
- 7 pounds mixed ground beef and ground lean pork, such as pork shoulder (use more pork than beef)
- 1 1/2 pounds ground onion
- Pork casings

Seasoning mixture:
- 5 tablespoons salt
- 1 teaspoon whole peppercorns
- 1 teaspoon marjoram
- 1 teaspoon summer savory
- 1/2 teaspoon sweet basil
- 1 teaspoon whole sage
- 3 teaspoons monosodium glutamate (optional)

To make sausage: Combine spices in blender. Blend well until peppercorns are ground. Soak pork casings. Run water through them. Grind meat and potatoes and onions alternately through meat grinder. Combine them. Mix meat mixture with about half the spices, combining well. Fry patty of mixture. Taste. Add more spice, if desired.

To stuff and bake sausages: Stuff meat mixture into casings. Tie off (with cotton string) into portion sizes. Prick casings with a toothpick to eliminate air. Place sausages in roaster. Add about an inch of water. Bake in 325-degree oven for 1 hour, or until they are steamed done but not browned. (Note: Cooking the sausage in this manner permits them to be frozen without turning black. It also prevents sausage from bursting.)

To serve: Heat sausages, browning slightly in skillet.

from the store was acceptable. The rest of the project — peeling, mixing, stuffing and baking — was the kind of automatic effort that allowed these two friends ample time for gabbing.

When my husband and I tried the recipe, using our Kitchen Aid mixer with a sausage attachment, I agreed it required teamwork. One person just doesn't have enough hands to stuff filling into one end of a machine and catch the sausages coming out of the other.

Mom, the Guest Tester
June 4, 1978

My husband and I were busily and itchily cutting triangles of insulation for the lakeside geodesic dome we were building, so my mother became pinch-hit tester, taking an oath to follow the recipe exactly.

"If I hadn't sworn that oath, I wouldn't have shelled pecans," she admitted. "I would have used walnuts."

BROWNIE PUDDING CUPS
Makes 10 servings and 1 cup syrup

Crust:
- 1/4 cup butter, melted
- 1 1/3 cups shredded coconut
- 1 1/3 cups finely ground pecans

Filling:
- 1/2 cup (half of 6-ounce package) real chocolate chips
- 1/2 cup butter
- 4 eggs
- 1 1/4 cups sugar
- 3 tablespoons light corn syrup
- 1 teaspoon vanilla extract
- 1/4 teaspoon salt

Chocolate-cinnamon syrup:
- 1/2 cup real chocolate chips (half of a 6-ounce package)
- 2/3 cup sugar
- 1/3 cup water
- 1/2 teaspoon cinnamon
- 1/8 teaspoon salt

To make crust: In small bowl, combine butter, coconut and pecans. Stir until well-blended. Press evenly on bottom and half way up sides of 10 6-ounce custard cups, using about 1/3 cup for each. Set aside.

To make filling: Combine over hot (not boiling) water chocolate chips and butter. Stir until chocolate melts and mixture is smooth. Remove from heat. Set aside. In small bowl, beat eggs, sugar, corn syrup, vanilla and salt until well blended. Gradually beat in chocolate mixture. Blend well. Pour 1/3 cup mixture into each custard cup. Place on 15-by-10-inch baking pan. Bake in 350-degree oven for 45 minutes.

To make chocolate-cinnamon syrup: Combine over hot (not boiling) water chocolate chips, sugar and water. Stir until chocolate melts and mixture is smooth. Stir in cinnamon and salt.

To serve: Serve pudding cups warm or cool with scoops of vanilla ice cream drizzled with cinnamon-chocolate syrup.

Never in her cooking career has she made such a rich and gooey dessert. Or one as sticky. "I learned how to pack the crust into the custard cups by about the eighth one," she said.

Topped with ice cream and sauce, the brownie cups were a chocolate worshiper's ticket to heaven.

My dad asked how many calories the dessert contained. "Take a last look at your waistline," my mother advised him.

Best From Mom's Boxful

May 20, 1979

My mother was a recipe clipper all her life, trying most of them on her family, saving the ones she liked (accumulated in a big boxful by the time she died). Grandma's Casserole was clipped from a Florida newspaper after my parents moved south for the winters. Because wide noodles didn't have to be precooked, it became one of her favorites. After I included it in a column, it became a St. Paul perennial. I still get requests for it. You can use a few more noodles than the recipe suggests to soak up all the liquid. The casserole could also be made with lasagna noodles.

Grandma Ellen, with Aric, her only grandchild.

GRANDMA'S CASSEROLE

Makes 8 to 10 portions

1 cup chopped onion
1 green pepper, cut into strips
2 tablespoons butter or margarine
1 1/2 pounds lean ground beef
1 teaspoon seasoned salt
1/2 teaspoon pepper
1 tablespoon sugar
1 quart whole tomatoes
1 can (15 ounces) tomato sauce
2 cups water
1 package (8 ounces) uncooked wide
  egg noodles
8 ounces mozzarella cheese, sliced

In Dutch oven, saute onion and green pepper in 2 tablespoons butter for 3 minutes. Add ground beef. Brown. Add seasoned salt, pepper and sugar. Stir in tomatoes, tomato sauce and water. Heat meat mixture to a boil. Reduce heat. Simmer for 15 minutes. In 9-by-13-inch baking pan, layer tomato-meat mixture and noodles. (Note: Make certain noodles are well covered with sauce.) Top with mozzarella. Cover pan with aluminum foil. Bake in 350-degree oven for 45 minutes. Cut and serve as for lasagna.

Three Old Favorites Revived

October 28, 1984

At the cooking class where my mother's recipe box provided the menu, as described in the opening segment of this chapter, we tried so many recipes that they had to appear on two Sundays.

GLAZED HAM LOAF

Makes 8 to 10 servings

3 cups (1 1/2 pounds) ground smoked ham
2 cups (1 pound) ground pork
1 cup fine dry bread crumbs
2 eggs
1/2 cup apple juice
1 tablespoon minced onion
1/2 teaspoon dry mustard
1/4 teaspoon pepper
1/2 teaspoon Worcestershire sauce
Glaze:
3/4 cup dark corn syrup
1/3 cup vinegar
2 teaspoons dry mustard

In large bowl, combine ham and pork. Add bread crumbs, eggs, apple juice, onion and seasonings. Mix well. Shape into loaf. Place in pan. Bake in 300-degree oven for about 2 hours, basting occasionally with glaze.

To make glaze: Combine ingredients in small saucepan. Bring to a boil, stirring occasionally. Boil for 2 minutes before pouring over ham loaf.

DANISH PUFF

Makes 16 slices

Pastry:
1 cup all-purpose flour
1/2 cup butter
3 tablespoons water
Filling:
1/2 cup butter
1 cup boiling water
1 teaspoon almond flavoring
1 cup all-purpose flour
3 eggs
Icing:
1/4 cup butter
1 teaspoon vanilla
1 heaping cup flaked coconut
1/4 cup milk
2 cups powdered sugar

To make pastry: Cut flour into butter until fine crumbs form. Using fork, stir in 3 tablespoons water to form a soft dough. Divide dough in half. Form into 2 oblongs about 4 inches wide and as long as a cookie sheet. Using your fingers, pat dough into shape onto sheet.

To make filling: Melt butter in boiling water. Remove from heat. Immediately add almond flavoring and flour, all at once. Stir until dough leaves sides of pan. Put in small mixing bowl. Beat in eggs, 1 at a time. Spread on the oblongs. Bake in 350-degree oven for 50 minutes. While still warm, frost puff with toasted coconut icing.

To make icing: Melt butter in skillet. Stir in vanilla and coconut. Heat in skillet, stirring, until coconut is golden brown. Add milk. Thicken with powdered sugar. Spread on puffs.

It's easy to remember my mother's desserts because she made so many of them. She had a ceaseless sweet tooth, though her stated reason for baking was that my dad expected treats with his several daily cups of coffee and dessert after every dinner. It was a symbiotic, mutually satisfying arrangement, though it necessitated dozens of diets for my mother. She used to say that she'd lost a thousand pounds, 20 pounds at a time.

Baking was my mother's pride and joy, and if the angel-food or sponge cake rose taller than the pan, it was a mark of accomplishment. Before the advent of the box mix, she made those cakes from scratch. When Betty Crocker made it easy, she'd use a mix — but always she added extra egg whites to make it taste fresher and rise higher.

Included on the menu for the cooking class's dinner were Glazed Ham Loaf, one of my mother's dinner staples; Danish Puff, which she'd found in The Farmer magazine (the extent of my parents' farming was a vegetable garden and wonderful berries); and the first cheesecake we ever tried (shared by my mother's neighbor, Milly Sorenson; it became one of our favorites).

NO-BAKE CHEESECAKE
Makes 8 servings

Cheesecake:
- 2 envelopes unflavored gelatin
- 1 cup sugar, divided
- 1/4 teaspoon salt
- 2 pasteurized eggs, separated
- 1 cup milk
- 1 teaspoon grated lemon rind
- 1 tablespoon lemon juice (more if you like)
- 1 teaspoon vanilla
- 3 cups cream-style cottage cheese
- 1 cup whipping cream, whipped

Crumb topping:
- 3/4 cup graham-cracker crumbs
- 1 tablespoon sugar
- 1/4 teaspoon cinnamon
- 1/4 teaspoon nutmeg
- 2 tablespoons melted butter

To make cheesecake: Mix gelatin with 3/4 cup sugar and salt. Beat egg yolks and milk. Add to gelatin mixture. Cook, stirring constantly, for 10 minutes, or until gelatin dissolves and mixture thickens. Remove from heat. Add lemon rind, juice and vanilla. Cool. Beat cheese with gelatin mixture until smooth. Chill, stirring occasionally, until mixture mounds when dropped from spoon. Beat egg whites until stiff. Gradually add remaining 1/4 cup sugar. Fold in cheese mixture. Fold in whipped cream.

To make topping: Combine graham-cracker crumbs, sugar, cinnamon, nutmeg and melted butter.

To assemble pie: Line pie plate with a circle of wax paper. Sprinkle with crumb topping. Spread cheesecake filling into pan. Chill until firm. Invert to serve.

Who on Earth was Merk?

July 15, 1984

"Our favorite coffeecake is Merk's that I got from your mother," my sister-in-law, Ilene Aune, told me as we were eating blueberry buckle one morning in her Amherst, Mass., kitchen.

I could imagine my mother giving Ilene a coffeecake recipe, but who on earth was Merk? No one I ever knew among her friends. Ilene whipped open her recipe book, and there it was, Merk's Coffeecake, attributed to Ellen Ostman. "We had it for breakfast at your mother's house once," she said, remembering it better than I did.

The week after the coffeecake recipe appeared, my mail was full of answers, not about who Merk might have been, but where she came from:

I blush to admit it was the Minneapolis Sunday Tribune.

My parents, living in northern Minnesota, took the Sunday Tribune all their married life. I grew up reading Mary Hart's food stories, never dreaming I would become both a food writer and her friend one day. Clementine Paddleford's column in This Week magazine, tucked into the Sunday Tribune, was also delicious reading.

Paddleford was the first to publish Merk's Coffeecake, and that's where my mother must have gotten it.

Several readers commented on the sweetness of the cake. Indeed, in Testing Results, I suggested reducing the filling amounts by half. Some readers said that, according to the original, Ilene's hand-copied recipe should have listed 1 teaspoon instead of 1 tablespoon of baking powder. But she liked it that way, so use your own judgment.

MERK'S COFFEECAKE
Makes 16 servings

Filling:
- 6 tablespoons margarine
- 1 cup packed brown sugar
- 2 teaspoons cinnamon
- 1 cup chopped nuts

Cake:
- 1/2 cup shortening
- 3/4 cup sugar
- 1 teaspoon vanilla
- 3 eggs
- 2 cups flour
- 1 tablespoon baking powder
- 1 teaspoon soda
- Pinch of salt
- 1 cup sour cream

To make filling: Combine filling ingredients. Set aside.

To make cake: Cream shortening, sugar and vanilla. Add eggs, 1 at a time, beating well after each addition. Sift dry ingredients. Add to creamed mixture alternately with sour cream.

To bake cake: Spread half of cake mixture into well-greased 10-inch tube pan. Sprinkle with half of filling. Spread with remaining batter. Cover with remaining filling. Bake in 350-degree oven for 50 minutes.

A reader says . . .

I still have a heart full of gratitude for your wholesomeness, your food comments and recipes. Keep it up.

— Helen Manglos, Gilman, Wis.

Asparagus That Wouldn't Die
March 24, 1985

My mother was a gifted gardener. She cultivated asparagus for 20 years, and it grew verdantly, rising each spring from its protective garb of winter mulch. The first tender tips were joyously welcomed, but once it got going, my mother had so much asparagus that she gave it away by the bagful. Her summer flower bouquets were always arranged with asparagus fern.

STIR-FRIED ASPARAGUS
Makes 4 to 6 servings

1 pound asparagus
1/4 to 1/2 cup chicken stock
1 tablespoon soy sauce
1/2 teaspoon sugar
2 tablespoons oil
1/2 teaspoon salt
3 slices fresh ginger root, minced
1 tablespoon finely chopped celery
1 small can water chestnuts, drained
Sesame seeds

Cut spears diagonally into 1- to 1 1/2-inch sections. Combine stock, soy sauce and sugar. Heat oil. Add salt, ginger root and celery. Stir-fry for a few seconds. Add water chestnuts and asparagus. Stir-fry to coat with oil. Heat through. Add stock-soy mixture. Heat quickly. Simmer, covered, over medium heat for 2 to 3 minutes, or until asparagus is crisp-tender. Just before serving, sprinkle with sesame seeds.

After my mother and dad died, their home was sold, but I told the new owners that we would be back in the spring to dig up at least part of that well-established asparagus to be transplanted at our lake place. We drove up with shovels and buckets on Memorial Day weekend only to find that the beautiful patch had been roto-tilled by the young new owners two weeks earlier so they could plant carrots and peas.

"Nobody puts in a garden before Memorial Day in northern Minnesota," I wailed

"Well, we did, and besides, we don't like asparagus," they said stubbornly.

They liked it even less as, all summer, their garden was a disarray of emerging asparagus spears. Even roto-tilling couldn't kill those deep roots.

My mother didn't make this recipe, but she would have loved it as a way to consume her crop. I tested it in her memory.

Memories of Lumber Camp
September 20, 1987

I was told to bring dessert to dinner at a northern Minnesota lumber camp, where I was doing a story. It had to be Raisin Pie (this recipe found in "The Fannie Farmer Cookbook") because it was one my mother made when she cooked for lumberjacks:

Doing that story was a sentimental return to my childhood. When I was 4 years old, during the waning days of World War II, my dad built a logging camp somewhere in the Effie, Minn., area, and my mother and I went to spend the winter there, she as camp cook, me as the little darling of all the lumberjacks. They probably loved her cooking more than this bratty kid, but I still have the fairy tale book some of them gave me.

I remember a winter of deep snows, tall forests and the warmth of the cookshack. I slept in a bunk for the first time in my life, and I recall hearing a young singer on our battery radio. My dad called him "Frankie Snotnose" when my mom became dreamy-eyed listening to Sinatra's love songs crackling over the airwaves.

And now, two other mothers ...

RAISIN PIE
Makes a 9-inch pie

1 cup orange juice
2 cups raisins
Pastry for a 9-inch 2-crust pie
1 1/2 cups sugar
4 tablespoons flour
3 tablespoons lemon juice
1/8 teaspoon salt

To plump raisins: Put orange juice and 1 cup water in pan. Bring to a boil. Remove from heat. Stir in raisins. Let stand for 2 hours.

To make pie: Line 9-inch pie pan with half of pastry dough. Add sugar, flour, lemon juice and salt to raisin mixture. Cook over low heat, stirring frequently, for 10 minutes, or until well thickened. Pile filling into lined pie pan. Roll out remaining dough. Make a lattice top. (Note: Hot filling will singe fingertips if you try to weave lattice; just lay strips in criss-cross pattern.) Crimp edges. Bake in 425-degree oven for 10 minutes. Reduce heat to 350 degrees. Bake for 35 minutes, or until top is browned.

Grandma's Rose-Colored Cookstove
October 8, 1978

I remember my grandmother, Suoma Ostman, standing beside the wood cookstove in her snug little home near Angora, north of Virginia, Minn.:

"Stove" is too lowly a name. It was loaded with chrome and had a cooktop about the size of an aircraft carrier's flight deck, lording over one entire side of her kitchen.

Its color was divine, a rosy pink that was about the shade one's cheeks turned if standing too close when its fires were roaring.

Perhaps, in memory, it has gained in stature, but it really was big. My grandmother knew how to tame that monster. She could stoke it so her weekly batches of Finnish coffeebread were golden perfection. I can still see her putting her hand in the oven to test for temperature. I especially remember Christmas turkeys and venison roasts, cooked until the meat and bones parted. Rare meat was never, ever served on my grandmother's table.

Of course, it was always very warm in my grandma's small house. Rheumatism bowed her legs until she was much shorter than that stove. She and her knees liked it toasty. The rest of us would gasp at the heat and take frequent strolls outside to cool off.

The warmest spot was the white rocking chair next to the stove. Sitting there, one not only basked in the rosy glow but also inhaled the aroma of Grandpa's wool socks drying behind the range.

I have that rocker now, but the stove was left in the house when it was sold after my grandmother's death in 1966. Nobody wanted it then. Nobody wanted to think about having to budge it.

A few years ago, when woodstove nostalgia bit me, we inquired about buying the stove from its new owners. No luck. They knew what they had. When they built a modern house on the property, they moved the glorious pink Duesenberg-of-the-stove-world into their new kitchen.

Jacques' Mentor was Mom

May 14, 1978

Over the three decades of this column, I've written about many moms, but one of the most memorable was Madame Jeanette Pepin, mother of French-born Jacques Pepin, who has become one of America's cooking stars. On Mother's Day in 1978, Madame Pepin was introduced to readers:

Don't you just love this? Jacques Pepin — who has been personal chef to three French presidents including DeGaulle; who is in demand as a food consultant, a teacher, an author, a magazine columnist (and since then, a television chef) — gets taken down a few notches when he visits his mother in Bourg-en-Bresse near Lyon, France's gastronomic epicenter.

"When I am at home, my mother and my aunt say, 'Look at that. You use too much butter. You use all the pots,'" Pepin says.

Jacques Pepin, without his mom, came to our house for lunch — which he cooked.

His mother, a former restaurant owner who serves good but unfancy food, says Jacques' cooking "is like a Dior dress, whereas mine, although not a Dior, comes from a good dressmaker."

Testing Results enthused: Voila! A souffle that doesn't require separating eggs. ("That's a lot of work. French housewives can't be bothered," Madame Pepin says firmly.) It works perfectly, and the light Swiss cheese flavor leaves a pleasant aftertaste. Bake until the top of the souffle is deep brown and an inserted knife comes out quite dry.

MADAME PEPIN'S SOUFFLE AU FROMAGE

Makes 4 servings

1/3 stick unsalted butter
1/3 cup flour
1 3/4 cups milk
1/2 teaspoon salt
1/4 teaspoon ground pepper
Dash of nutmeg
1 1/2 cups grated Swiss cheese
5 large eggs, slightly beaten with fork

Butter and flour 5- to 6-cup souffle mold. Set aside in refrigerator. Melt butter in small saucepan. Add flour. Cook, stirring with whisk, for 1 minute. Add milk. Bring to a boil, stirring as mixture thickens. Cook for a few seconds. Remove from heat. Add salt, pepper, nutmeg and cheese. Mix well with whisk. Cool for a few moments. Mix in beaten eggs. Pour into prepared mold. Set aside for 40 to 45 minutes before baking. Bake in 375-degree oven for 50 to 60 minutes. Serve.

1983

— *Tracking trends for fish, croissants and deadly desserts* —

Julia Asks *Me* for Recipes
October 16

Despite a steamroller year of food news and trend watches, the biggest event as far as I was concerned was when Julia Child leaned across a lunch table and asked *me* for recipes. She wanted wild-rice ideas:

Who could refuse the Godmother of Culinary Arts? I extended the invitation to readers. A thick collection was mailed to Julia's Cambridge, Mass., home, and in the December 4 column, an excerpt from her letter of response appeared:

"I have just received your large packet of wild-rice recipes and think it is perfectly marvelous. I shall go over them with great interest. We are just about to leave for California, so I will read them with pleasure on the plane." Can't you just hear her saying "per-r-r-fectly mahr-r-r-velous"?

I can't recall if any of those Minnesota recipes ever landed on one of Julia's TV shows or made it into her books, but some did make it into my column. Testing was delayed until after the holidays, so you'll have to turn to the 1984 chapter to get the best wild-rice soup recipe we ever printed.

During our lunch together, Julia got testy when the subject of Nouvelle Cuisine arose, then the darling

We sent Julia Child enough wild rice recipes to fill her biggest bowls.

topic of food magazines. "Hogwash — and you may quote me," said Julia about Nouvelle Cuisine and its chefs, "who fool themselves if they think they're cooking light." When Swiss restaurateur Fredy Girardet, hailed as the greatest chef in the world (whose restaurant I had visited the year before), prepared a dinner in New York, "there were 800 calories of butter in the first three dishes," Julia fumed.

"I do think Nouvelle chefs are getting over their season of silliness, however. I believe in fresh food, good food, in moderation but in great variety. An awful lot of our trends are faddy. If you don't have any salt in your food, you're going to faint in a hot climate."

Vintage Julia.

Beautiful Fish, Ugly Face
January 23

New foods were being added to our plates and shopping lists. Orange roughy was just being introduced to Minnesotans, and the column remarked on party conversation regarding the "cheap, boneless, delicious fish from New Zealand." Everyone was trying it, and we did, too, baking it with almonds, parsley, butter and lemon juice.

A reader says . . .

I faithfully read your column, and I appreciate your honesty when you state that you have a failure. Some authors make it sound like every cooking experience is perfect.

— Frances Hillier, St. Paul

Turned out that Minnesota was one of the first markets in the nation to get the deep-water fish with an ugly face only a mother roughy could love. It soon became so popular here and elsewhere that it no longer could be classified as "cheap."

Learning New Food Speak
June 5

"What's this too-foo stuff?" a reader asked, which prompted a column on meatless diets — a harbinger of changing food styles.

"Primavera" was a new word for others, who saw it attached to pasta dishes on restaurant menus. On June 19, as a not-fond farewell to the coldest spring on record, we tested two recipes with primavera in the title, with this definition: From the Italian, it translates as "springtime." In food, it signifies a collection of vegetables.

In the chocolate department, the words "Decadence" and "Mort du Chocolat," (Death by Chocolate) were attached to the most potent desserts, and we "decadenced" ourselves to death during 1983 testing.

Trying a multilayer torte called Chocolate Death for the July 17 column, I wrote:

Just by reading the recipe, I knew this was a cake that demanded an occasion. My father-in-law's 80th birthday was approaching. Considering that his siblings who would be at the party are all in their 70s and 80s, bringing a birthday treat called Chocolate Death was a bit morbid. The name wouldn't kill anybody, I figured, but after tasting the cake at the party, I must warn you not to serve it to anyone in delicate health. It has such an intense flavor that it could send a fragile person into chocolate shock.

Definitions of a "chocoholic" included: You consider vanilla somebody's idea of a joke. M&M's never have time to melt in your hands. You would campaign to have Sara Lee's birthday declared a national holiday.

A Crumby Trend
March 13

Croissants were leaving crumbs all over the place, from bakeries to sandwich shops: An Embers restaurant proudly shouts on its outdoor sign board "We have croissants." Aromas from croissant shops perfume the air in both Twin Cities. My husband and I stepped into Croissant Express in that trendy part of Minneapolis, near Hennepin Avenue and Lake Street, and we could hardly elbow our way to the counter on a Saturday afternoon.

Any trend is usually bashed by backlash. I later wrote about a KTCA-TV parody, which derided my column discussing the croissant craze. The TV-type said they were too fancy for him, and he was doing his own survey on where to find the best buttered toast in the Twin Cites.

Confirming Aric's Choices
November 6

Aric graduated to a teen-age appetite, but he still had his preferences. I wanted to test recipes when it was my turn to cook supper for his confirmation class at House of Hope Presbyterian Church, but he insisted on spaghetti and brownies, which he knew everyone would like. I snuck in a couple of extra tested desserts, but he was right. Brownies disappeared while the other sweets stayed put. The report:

Well, friends, the spaghetti feed went well, except for one incident when two boys decided to go, at the same moment, through a swinging door between the kitchen and dining hall from opposite directions. One of those boys was carrying a full plate of dinner. What didn't land on the floor stained his shirt front so red that he looked like walking wounded, giving his mother one heck of a laundry problem.

Give Them Their Daily Bread
November 20

Later that month, the growing national awareness of hunger was covered in a column about cooking for the Dorothy Day Center, in St. Paul, which feeds the homeless and hungry. A team of us from House of Hope learned the vagaries of quantity cooking and realized a greater need:

You've relinquished chocolate bonbons or big beef steaks for Lent, and you're feeling righteous. But do you realize there's something wrong in this holy season? People are deprived, not just of the expendable, but of basic needs, of their daily bread.

Because We're Not Bocuse
April 24

Recipes tested became more exotic. After tasting French chef Paul Bocuse's mussel saffron soup both at his restaurant near Lyon, France, and at one bearing his name in Hong Kong, we tried a facsimile. Aric amazed us by eating every drop of broth after carefully picking out the mussels, inspecting them closely, and deciding they were too gruesome to eat. This home-cooked version was the third best of the three mussel-saffron soups we've tasted, but then our last name is not Bocuse.

Crust and Yeast Quandries
Sunday after Sunday

Ongoing for months were two controversies: Lola Perpich's oil pie crust, which worked for me but turned into crumbles for readers, and the newly marketed quick-rising yeast, which barely rose at all for me and many readers, but worked for others. We made batch after batch of pie crust (see Lola's recipe in this chapter) and baked goods, talked to the experts, used all varieties of flour, oil, techniques, and never could make everyone happy. But both issues certainly kept the column pot boiling.

Lola's Persnickety Pie Crust
October 2

Oh, what controversy Minnesota First Lady Lola Perpich's apple pie created. Hers, based on a recipe she got from her sister Ann Stanisich of Keewatin, Minn., was hailed by Ladies Home Journal magazine as one of America's best gubernatorial apple pies. I tried it, liking the simple crust so much that I vowed to give up lard.

Then, mail and phone calls rolled in from readers who tried the pastry and ended up with a pile of

Lola Perpich cuts her controversial apple pie.

LOLA PERPICH'S MINNESOTA APPLE PIE
Makes 8 servings

Pastry:
- 1/2 cup corn oil
- 1/4 cup cold whole milk
- 2 cups all-purpose flour
- 1 teaspoon salt

Filling:
- 5 large Minnesota Haraldson, Rome Beauty or Golden Delicious apples (about 2 1/2 pounds)
- 3/4 cup granulated sugar
- 1/4 cup firmly packed brown sugar
- 1 tablespoon flour
- 1 teaspoon cinnamon
- 1 teaspoon lemon juice
- 2 tablespoons butter

To make pastry: In 1-cup measure, combine oil and milk; do not stir. In bowl, combine flour and salt. Add oil and milk. Mix. Shape pastry into a ball. Divide into 2 pieces, 1 slightly larger than the other. Place larger piece between 2 sheets of wax paper. Roll out to 11-inch circle. Peel off top paper. Invert into 9-inch pie plate. Remove paper. Dust pastry lightly with flour. Roll out remaining pastry between 2 sheets of wax paper to 10-inch circle. Set aside.

To make filling: Peel and slice apples. In bowl, mix apples, sugars, flour, cinnamon and lemon juice. Spoon into pastry. Dot with butter. Cover with top pastry. Flute edges. Sprinkle with sugar. Slash top for steam to escape. Bake in 425-degree oven for 20 minutes. Reduce temperature to 350 degrees. Bake for 30 minutes.

crumbs. I tried it again and again, with various kinds of flour and brands of oil, and it always worked for me. But for months, the column printed letters from those who were still having problems. We even involved the pros at the Betty Crocker Kitchens who invented the stir-and-roll crust concept, continuing to insist the crust should be more of a boon than a boondoggle.

In the November 13 paper, my favorite response to the problem came from "A Range Reader" who wrote, "Have tried the Perpich pie crust two times — no problems. Suggestions: Maybe it only works for Iron Rangers or Democrats. Maybe readers who are neither should play a polka record while attempting to make the crust. That might help."

Conclusion to that column in which readers suggested that measuring, that using skim instead of whole milk, that using unbleached flour might be problems: So that's it, pie bakers. Follow the recipe exactly. Measure liquids carefully. Don't pack the flour into the cup. Put on a polka record. Pray for success. Good luck!

But that wasn't the end of it:

We heard from Lola Perpich, whose ultra-simple pie crust started this controversy. "I enjoyed your recent article on the Perpich Pie Recipe. I was especially amused by the comment, 'perhaps one should be a Ranger — a Democrat — or play polkas to master it.' If things should ever get dull, I want you to know I would be happy to provide you another Perpich recipe."

Thanks you very much, Mrs. Perpich. I will, um-m-m, think about that offer.

Muchos Nachos

January 9

Nachos were newcomers in this area far from the Mexican border. When cooking teacher and "Chili Madness" author Jane Butel came to teach a class at St. Paul's Th'Rice cooking school (now known as Cooks of Crocus Hill), all of her students, including

me, couldn't get enough of her Pecos River-style snack.

Jane gave us general instructions. I put together specifics for this appetizer, which we made for a chili

JANE BUTEL'S NACHOS GRANDE
Makes enough for a crowd

2 tablespoons lard
1 cup chopped onions
1 can (16 ounces) refried beans
3 cups grated Monterey jack cheese
3 cups grated cheddar cheese
1/2 cup sliced black olives
1/2 cup canned jalapeno pepper slices, drained
1 bag (1 pound) taco chips
Guacamole
Sour cream

In skillet, melt lard. Saute onions. Add refried beans. Cook until well blended with onions and heated through. Spread taco chips on 2 large baking sheets, leaving a space at center of each tray. Heat chips in 350-degree oven briefly. Remove from oven. Place strip of refried beans at center of each tray. Sprinkle Monterey jack and cheddar cheeses over chips. Sprinkle with olives and jalapeno slices. Bake for 5 to 10 minutes, or until cheese is melted. Remove from oven. Spoon guacamole and sour cream in mounds on either side of refried beans. Eat by dipping cheese-topped nacho chips in refried beans, guacamole and sour cream.

Note: Butel's guacamole is made with mashed avocados flavored with lemon or lime juice, finely chopped scallions, chopped tomatoes, minced garlic and salt.

party held during a 16-inch blizzard. Fifty were invited. Twelve couldn't get out of their garages. Ones who braved the storm had plenty to eat, including three styles of chili made with 30 pounds of beef. My husband had blisters after hand-chopping all that meat.

I suggested, to disperse the fire of jalapenos in these nachos, to chop them very fine. The timid could replace them with diced canned green chilies.

We had heaps of sizzling Southwestern food left over from that snow no-show party, including cornbread studded with chilies:

Think I'll feed it to the blizzard-stranded birds. They'll probably want margaritas as a chaser. That's one way to keep the bird bath from freezing solid.

Recipes Are Our Business
October 9

Like shoemakers and their children's shoes, food writers can be just as slow producing their own cookbooks, but after seven years of planning, we are published. Perhaps it was during my presidency of the Newspaper Food Editors and Writers Association beginning in 1976 that a committee was first appointed to produce our own cookbook. My memory is dim on the exact date, but we were a fledgling professional group whose business was recipes, so why not put out a cookbook?

A reader says . . .

I read your column almost every week, and I've clipped many recipes with which I have had great success.

— Alta Olson, Hastings, Minn.

When the project finally got rolling, so many recipes came in that we had sufficient for a book and a sequel. From the very first "Food Editors' Favorites," published by the Newspaper Food Editors and Writers Association, here's an easy, flavorful pot roast. It was contributed by one of my best foodie friends, Charlotte Hansen, who then edited food pages for the Jamestown (N.D.) Sun.

The gravy is more sweet than sour (adjust the sugar, if you wish), but the marriage of lemon juice, honey and cloves is a happy one. Aric identified the flavors as "Chinese." In that case, you might want to serve the beef and gravy with rice instead of mashed potatoes.

CHARLOTTE HANSEN'S SWEET-SOUR POT ROAST
Makes 6 servings

1 tablespoon solid shortening
4 pounds chuck or rump beef roast
2 onions, sliced
1/4 teaspoon pepper
1/4 teaspoon ground cloves
1/4 cup honey
1/4 cup granulated sugar
Juice of 2 lemons
1 teaspoon salt or to taste

In Dutch oven or heavy skillet with tight-fitting lid, heat shortening. Add meat and onions. Brown well, turning frequently. Add pepper, cloves, honey, sugar, lemon juice and salt. Cover tightly. Simmer slowly over low heat, or bake in 300-degree oven for 3 to 3 1/2 hours, or until meat is tender.

1984

— When food celebrities come to dinner, dazzle them with your footwork —

Paul, a Cheeky Guy
February 19

New Orleans chef Paul Prudhomme came upriver to St. Paul (though I'd known him since 1978, I would finally get to his K-Paul restaurant in New Orleans later in the year). As he cooked in a Mendota restaurant, someone asked Prudhomme if creole food is influenced by Nouvelle Cuisine:

Paul Prudhomme blackens anything.

"There is no Nouvelle in New Orleans. It's all Vieux — old. We like things as they have always been. Our food has been there for 200 years."

He left Minnesota with a package of walleye cheeks, though he told the lunch crowd he had walleye throats. A member of the crowd inquired if Prudhomme's famous technique of blackening fish would work on lutefisk? "Only if you step on it first," he said.

James Beard: No Worries
March 25

While he was still breathing, James Beard's best friends wrote a cookbook about his favorite foods and threw a dinner of homage, at which they all told their favorite James Beard stories. Writing about that book, I told some of my own tales about the famous epicure:

He wasn't feeling well and went to visit the doctor. On his return, a colleague asked what the doctor's verdict was. "I guess I ate too much," said Beard, for whom food has always been the greatest pleasure, bringing on the necessary pain of dieting. But when he diets, he drinks champagne to ease the agony. My kind of guy.

James Beard with a really big fungus find.

Another story I've told countless times: Beard and I were at an event in Colorado in 1969, and during a free afternoon, while most everybody else explored ghost towns or went trout fishing, he gathered wild mushrooms. His harvest was prepared for the first course of our dinner. In an era when few knew mushrooms beyond the button variety, the rest of us watched Beard eat his share, alert for signs of distress, before we put a fork into the fungi.

A year or so later, when I saw him again, I mentioned our hesitation.

"Why would you worry?" he said, looking totally perplexed. After all, he was James Beard and he knew his mushrooms.

A reader says . . .

My secretary tells me over 60 cookbooks have been sent out as a result of your influential column. That's might impressive.

— George C. Weinman, senior pastor
Roseville Lutheran Church

He Doesn't Trifle With Truffles
February 12

In the candy world — and Lord knows, this column pays attention to anything chocolate — truffles were trendy:

Our resident teen-age chocolate addict can smell chocolate at 40 paces. Nothing is safe in the house. If he can't find candy bars or brownies to satisfy his craving, he eats chocolate chips or baking chocolate. Or swigs Hershey's syrup.

Nothing escapes his choco-detectors, except the fancy little gold carton imprinted "Truffles" in our house just before Christmas. "I read that word on the top, and I thought they were those smelly black mushrooms that pigs dig in France, dipped in chocolate," said Aric, who hates mushrooms as much as he loves chocolate. I'd wondered why that box of goodies lasted so long.

Cravings Between Covers
April 1

Chocolatier magazine first appeared in 1984. I asked Editor-in-Chief Joanne Steuer how the premier issue had been received. "Absolutely phenomenal," she said. My take: A half million copies have been snapped up from newsstands like M&M's at a kindergarten picnic.

Steuer says she hates the term "chocoholic." "It's negative. It sounds like a person needing a fix, like he wears a raincoat and sneaks into 7-11 to buy a stash."

In that first issue, readers were astonished to find a recipe that satisfied both chocolate and pasta cravings. We tested chocolate fettuccine for that April Fool's Day.

Buenos Dias, Fajitas
December 9

No foolin'. Fajitas were suddenly taking hold, and we tried several varieties. I'd first tasted them the previous year at Mi Tierra restaurant in San Antonio's Old Town, and I came back to write about this fiery food unfamiliar in St. Paul. About two years later, a locally based restaurant chain put fajitas on its menu, and everyone became smitten.

Here, Julia, Have a Spoonful
January 15

When Julia Child asked me for wild-rice recipes in 1983, I asked readers to contribute. Before a thick packet was sent off to her, I made copies of several for testing, and this soup earned a "Wow!"

It was the creation of Connie Halverson of North Oaks, Minn., who was trying to replicate a wild-rice soup she and her husband had tasted at the Orion

WILD-RICE SOUP
Makes 10 or more servings

**2 to 2 1/2 pounds smoked pork hocks, or
  1 large meaty ham bone**
3 quarts water
1 large white Bermuda onion, chopped
1 1/2 cups raw wild rice, rinsed and drained
6 tablespoons butter
6 tablespoons flour
2 cups whipping cream

3 egg yolks
2 to 3 cups milk
**3 jars (2 1/2 ounces each) sliced
  mushrooms (or use fresh)**
**3 chicken bouillon cubes (or 3 individual
  envelopes of Wyler's Chicken Broth
  Break, if available)**
Salt and pepper to taste

To cook wild rice: In heavy 8-quart Dutch oven or heavy kettle, simmer pork hocks in water with chopped onion for 4 to 5 hours. Add wild rice. Continue simmering for 1 1/2 to 2 hours. Drain broth through colander into large bowl. Add water to broth to make 8 cups liquid. Reserve broth. Reserve wild rice and ham hocks in colander.

To make soup: In Dutch oven, melt butter. Stir in flour. Cook slowly for a couple of minutes without browning. Pour in warm ham broth. Beat vigorously with wire whisk to blend thoroughly. Bring to a boil.

Boil for 2 to 3 minutes, stirring well. Remove from heat. Pour whipping cream into medium bowl. Beat in egg yolks with wire whisk. Gradually dribble in 2 cups hot broth, beating continuously. Add cream mixture to broth in Dutch oven. Return to heat. Add cooled wild rice and any meat picked from ham bones. Stir in milk, drained mushrooms and chicken broth. Add salt and pepper to taste. Heat through. Serve steaming hot with dab of butter on top, if desired.

Room, then the restaurant atop the IDS Tower in Minneapolis. She borrowed a technique from pea soup, and advice from — who else — Julia Child to get the creamy, rich consistency. Expect a huge batch (which can be frozen). When first cooking, or when reheating, do not boil the soup after adding eggs and cream, or it will curdle. Taste before seasoning with additional salt; it might not need a speck. Devote a day at home to this project.

Until I tried Halverson's wild-rice soup, I thought I had a pretty good recipe, the creamy Radisson Hotel version tested earlier in this book. But that was suddenly pallid and bland compared to her fabulous formula.

Cookbook P.S.
July 1

The 1983 chapter mentioned the Newspaper Food Editors and Writers Association's first cookbook, written to float our fledgling organization out of red ink. Here's what happened to that revenue:

Novelist Nora Ephron had tossed a few recipes into her achingly funny book, "Heartburn." For that reason, she was invited to speak at our association's meeting in Montreal.

Ephron didn't look like A Famous Writer when she first arrived, dressed in green paratrooper jump suit and ankle-high laced tennis shoes.

For her speech, wearing understated black: She doesn't dress like someone who commanded $3,250 to enlighten us (not much) for 30 minutes, draining in that half-hour the entire proceeds from our cookbook that had involved dozens of people and several years of work. Oh, well, excruciatingly come, easy go.

Speaking Naturally
January 29

"Natural foods" was a term food writers were struggling to define for themselves and for readers:

Confusion among "natural," "organic" and "health" foods has some of us consoling ourselves with Twinkies.

MARINATED VEGETABLE BOWL
Makes 8 to 10 appetizer servings

1 bunch broccoli, cut into florets
1 head cauliflower, cut into florets
2 cups diagonally sliced carrots, cut 1/4 inch thick
10 large mushrooms, halved or quartered
1 red bell pepper, cut in thin strips
2 large cloves garlic, pressed
3/4 cup vegetable oil
1/4 cup plus 2 tablespoons red-wine vinegar
2 teaspoons sugar
1 teaspoon salt
1 teaspoon dry mustard
1 teaspoon sweet basil, crumbled
1/2 teaspoon pepper
1/8 teaspoon ground nutmeg

Place broccoli, cauliflower, carrots, mushrooms and red pepper in airtight container. Combine remaining ingredients. Whisk together. Pour over vegetables. Cover. Refrigerate for 6 hours or overnight. Turn vegetables occasionally to coat with marinade. Serve with toothpicks.

One of my colleagues, Pat Hanna Kuehl of Denver's Rocky Mountain News said, " 'Natural' has become such a buzz word that it's lost its magic. I even get so-called natural recipes using canned soup."

Marian Burros of the New York Times had already leapt ahead, as usual. "Natural foods are not in the front of everyone's minds anymore. They're another fad. People have picked out what they like, whether it's tofu or sprouts, and discarded the rest, except for the fringe that has always been interested in health foods."

In the midst of the colorless winter season, a little "natural" was added to the column with this multihued marinated appetizer. Needs more garlic and mustard, I thought at the time. Those more devoted to healthful eating could use honey instead of sugar and a salt substitute or more herbs to replace salt.

A reader says . . .

The world may have been mourning Diana and Mother Theresa, but I was more concerned with what happened to your column. I don't relate well to princesses or saints, but I feel as if you are an old friend. I don't pause at the headlines or even comics. I just go straight for your column, and really appreciate your testing and tasting results. Like many people in this area, I have read, clipped and tried many recipes, but mostly I have enjoyed watching Aric grow up, your husband tasting recipes, and stories of friends and the Office Hungries.

— Jean Shinn, Cottage Grove, Minn.

Party Food
May 20

When it comes to cookbook sales, few can beat the record set by a good friend, Mable Hoffman, who wrote a book on crockery cookery just at the time in the 1970s when everyone was buying a slow-cooker or

MABLE'S PEPPERED CHEESE
Makes 1 5-inch ball

- **2 cups (8 ounces) grated Monterey jack cheese**
- **1 package (8 ounces) cream cheese at room temperature**
- **1 teaspoon fines herbes (French herbs)**
- **1 teaspoon minced chives**
- **1 teaspoon Worcestershire sauce**
- **1 garlic clove, crushed**
- **2 to 3 tablespoons seasoned pepper**
- **Plain or bacon-flavored crackers**

In medium bowl, combine Monterey jack cheese, cream cheese, fines herbs, chives, Worcestershire sauce and garlic. Shape cheese mixture into 5-inch ball. Slightly flatten 1 side. Cut 12-inch square of wax paper. On it, spread seasoned pepper in even, thick layer. Roll cheese ball in pepper until completely covered. Refrigerate for 6 hours or overnight. (Note: Cheese ball can be stored in refrigerator for several days before serving.) Cut into thin slices. Serve with crackers.

crockpot. That simple book sold millions of copies. Mable and her late husband, Gar, continued creating books to match the way America cooked. When I last spoke with Mable, she was working on her latest, a healthful crockery cookbook. Maybe, like the fondue pot, the slow-cooker is resurging.

Many columns recounted our St. Paul Summit Hill neighborhood progressive dinners. For the '84 spring event, we had the appetizer course, and I made Mable's Peppered Cheese. Describing the party, this aside about the multicourse, multihouse dinner:

Another host, a bachelor living in one of the showplaces in our area, served chicken baked with rice. He tells organizers of the twice-yearly dinners to never send him the same guests twice because he only knows how to cook that one party dish.

CHINESE ALMOND CHICKEN SALAD
Makes 4 to 6 main dish servings

Vegetable oil
1 1/4 cups lightly packed threadlike rice sticks (about 2 ounces)
Five-spice dressing:
  1/4 cup vegetable oil
  1 teaspoon salt
  1 teaspoon dry mustard
  1 teaspoon deeply flavored sesame oil
  1/2 teaspoon five-spice powder

Salad:
  2 cups cooked skinless chicken, cut in thin strips
  3 1/2 cups shredded iceberg lettuce
  1 cup lightly packed fresh cilantro sprigs
  3 green onions, with tops, thinly sliced
  1 tablespoon sesame seeds, toasted
  3/4 cup sliced almonds, toasted, divided
Lettuce leaves

To fry rice sticks: Pour oil into heavy 8- to 10-inch skillet to depth of 1/2 inch. Heat over high heat until very hot. Drop rice sticks into oil, a small handful at a time. Rice sticks will expand to about 4 times their original size. (Note: Oil is too hot if they immediately turn brown and don't puff.) Remove immediately with slotted spoon to paper toweling. Set aside. Continue until all rice sticks are fried.

To make dressing: Thoroughly whisk 1/4 cup oil with salt, dry mustard, sesame oil and five-spice powder (available in Asian grocery stores or larger supermarkets).

To make salad: Pour dressing into large bowl. Add chicken. Toss. Add lettuce, cilantro, green onions, sesame seeds and all but 2 tablespoons almonds. Toss thoroughly. Add rice sticks. Toss lightly. Arrange lettuce leaves on serving platter. Mound salad on lettuce leaves. Sprinkle with remaining almonds. Garnish with cilantro sprigs, if desired. Serve immediately.

A Little Soft Shoe
May 27

"Dazzle them with your footwork," my husband always says in situations that could be intimidating. So we do the unexpected at times when the expected might not be perfect.

When Pierre Franey, French chef and New York Times columnist, sat in my living room, did I offer him a glass of French wine? No. I poured a Minnesota vintage, telling him it's made "where the grapes suffer." He was surprised and impressed. Impressed that we can make a decent wine where winters reach 30 below.

It would have taken a costly bottle of French wine to create the same interest. He was dazzled by my footwork.

When Italian cooking teacher and author Giuliano Bugialli, in town to teach cooking classes, came directly from the airport to our dinner table, did I cook pasta for him? No way! He's the pasta expert, and he might be sick of it by now. We dazzled him with Texas-style shrimp bisque served with giant popovers, Chinese chicken salad and our favorite cheesecake.

Worth Any Price
October 7

"I love to say bu-u-t-t-er-r r. I make it sound sexy. And sinister," says the man known as the Merchant of Menace.

Sexy, sinister and buttery describe Vincent Price, one of America's most durable and recognizable actors, who was spokesman for the American Dairy Association when he was interviewed this time. On another occasion when he visited St. Paul, we were so besieged by his fans in the restaurant where we were lunching that I could hardly ask enough questions for a story.

For all his evil roles, he loves to talk about the homey joys of cooking. Price grew up in a well-to-do St. Louis household. His parents went to Europe every year, but only to one country per trip so they could study the food. When they returned, they'd teach their brood of four how to make the dishes.

"We learned to cook, sew and clean up. My mother was a one-woman home-economics class. Our parents taught us to respect food. We even ate spinach. My mother used 'Florentine' under everything."

I would put his easy, velvety Hollandaise over everything.

VINCENT PRICE'S PROCESSOR HOLLANDAISE SAUCE
Makes 1 cup

4 pasteurized egg yolks
1 tablespoon fresh lemon juice
1/8 teaspoon white pepper
1/2 cup (1 stick) butter

Place egg yolks, lemon juice and pepper in processor work bowl. Mix just until well combined. Melt butter in saucepan over low heat. Turn processor on. Gradually add butter in steady stream. Mix until well blended and thickened.

1985

— California Cuisine, grazing, and
we hear fewer "yucks" —

California, Here We Go
February 3

My heart belongs to Minnesota, but my taste buds have moved to California.

This recently identified collection of food concepts known as California Cuisine gets my juices flowing. It's an ethnic blend with eclectic overtones of Asian, Mexican and Continental Nouvelle, plus homage to the foodstuffs that grow and swim so abundantly in that state and off her shores.

It's a colorful paean to fresh ingredients, and most of all, it's lively and imaginative. Sometimes new-style California Cuisine is outrageous, but it's always energizing to tired palates.

Food writers worth their herb-seasoned salt, with still enough verve to cut the gewurztraminer mustard, continually seek new flavor experiences. When I read the menu of a new Twin Cities ultra-expensive restaurant last year, it was so cautiously classic that nothing elicited an "I really want to try that" reaction.

But a short time afterward, I was at Chef Wolfgang Puck's new Chinoise-on-Main restaurant in Santa Monica, Calif., where French, Asian and California food styles blend with such pizzazz that I wanted to order absolutely everything.

A Lot of Hot Air
October 6

By the time the year was over, we'd been to San Francisco and Napa Valley, and came back with enough recipes from Wine Country to fill several columns. One opened with this breathtaking vignette:

Ron Aune readies the balloon for his perilous ascent.

Whew! I've survived a high point in my life, riding a hot-air balloon over the Napa Valley. It was truly a wondrous experience, except for one scary moment. When the balloon carrying my husband rose out of the parking lot at Domaine Chandon, its basket tangled with the upper branches of an ancient oak. For a minute, I thought I was a widow. But that airborne rainbow safely continued its upward flight as its passengers picked leaves out of their hair.

The Grass Isn't Greener
March 3

Class, have you been paying attention to my lectures on food trends? Then, you remember that "grazing" (also known as browsing, snacking or noshing) has become the meal pattern of the 1980s.

I want you to turn to the New York Times, which recently surveyed some younger-than-35 Manhattan corporate climbers. One starts the day with a freshly opened can of Nutrament, "sort of grown-up baby formula." Another skips lunch in favor of a late breakfast of Chinese takeout food purchased the day before.

An investment banker never eats breakfast, tries not to eat lunch and exists on nibbles during his 12-hour day. Whatever happened to the three-martini lunch?

A self-described entrepreneur lives on Lean Cuisine, sometimes three or four of the frozen diet meals in a day.

Not one of the interviewees boiled an egg for breakfast, ate a decent lunch or heated the oven for dinner. They opened cupboards or refrigerators and wolfed down whatever fell out first. That's grazing.

Muffins, American Style
May 26

If anyone had shouted "Author!" half the folks on our bus bumping along in Italy would have stood up. We were a group of food writers, and most food writers eventually produce cookbooks.

Elizabeth Alston, food editor for Woman's Day magazine, added to the list (of the many I'd mentioned as cookbook authors earlier in the column) by telling us, in her quiet manner, that she'd just finished another volume. "On what?" we asked as Sicilian scenery flashed by the bus windows. "On muffins," she said simply, and then we started talking about fava beans or couscous or whatever our last meal had been.

Her cookbook was waiting when I returned home, and we tried several recipes:

Muffins bounced in among last year's crop of food trends, and they haven't lost their momentum yet. Elizabeth's fondness for them goes far beyond their recent revival.

"When I was growing up in England, muffins were, for the most part, a romantic treat of the Victorian past. During their heyday, they were usually made in bakeries, carried home and toasted in front of an open fire. They were buttered lavishly and served under a silver dome at all proper breakfasts and teas.

"I knew what they were supposed to be like: round, flat, yeasty and craggy on the inside.

"Imagine my surprise, as a young adult 3,000 miles from the land of muffins, on a sunny Long Island porch, when I was served a basketful of what appeared to be warm, delectable, golden cupcakes, but were introduced to me as muffins. I naively assumed a mistake had been made," she wrote.

Elizabeth, we call your childhood treat English muffins on this side of the Atlantic. Muffins to us, as you've discovered, mean anything American ingenuity dreams up.

Pure Lust
June 30

On the cookbook scene, the "Silver Palate" gals, Julee Rosso and Sheila Lukins, visited to promote their second cookbook, which needed little hype, but I gave it some, anyway:

Supreme Court Justices just ruled that lust is OK by them, so there's no need for me to be embarrassed about telling you that I lust for just about everything in "The Silver Palate Good Times Cookbook."

Those of us who read cookbooks with a passion do it to indulge in page after page of food fantasies. This is not exactly furtive pleasure. I've never known a cookbook addict to cover a volume with a plain brown wrapper. But we do get our jollies by fantasizing the silken touch of a perfect sauce, the thrill of meeting a gorgeous stranger ingredient, the voluptuousness of a forbidden dessert.

Cold Pasta? Basta!
July 28

Italians take no credit for cold pasta salads. "Americans invented them," we were told on a recent trip to Italy, and I may have detected a slight sneer in that statement. From Sicily through almost the entire length of Italy's peninsula, I saw only one cold pasta salad. Ideas cross the Atlantic in both directions, and while we Americans embrace most anything Italy sends us, that country doesn't seem eager to adopt our chilled macaroni.

Without extensive research, I would guess the cold pasta craze can be credited to the salad-bar explosion in this country. Those salads gained popularity because they're colorful, filling and inexpensive. What people tasted while eating out soon became a homemade phenomenon. Italians, however, remain unconvinced, preferring their pasta hot.

New Thrill on the Grill
June 2

Another trend had us roasting exotically hot peppers as we tried to capture the best of authentic Southwestern food. In a particularly scorching column, I suggested: Do try these well-stuffed peppers on the summer barbecue grill when brats and burgers have lost their thrill.

Sundae Best
July 14

Some unknown wit named Anon. said, "An ice-cream cone can solve any problem, even if only for a few minutes." I say a sundae might make a person forget the problem entirely.

The Morel of the Story
September 8

Minnesotans officially have fungus among us. The morel has been designated our state mushroom, to join the lady-slipper as flower, the walleye (and some say the mosquito) as official representatives of our state's proudest (or most prevalent) flora and fauna.

Will He Remember Mom's Cooking?

June 2

Aric no longer says "yuck" to my experiments, as he did when he was a grade-school gourmet preferring peanut butter. Now, he just declines, sometimes not so politely, to eat the odd assortment of tested recipes that pass through our kitchen. He's usually not hungry, anyway, because he makes his own dinner the minute he's home from school.

Sometimes, I wonder what he'll recall, when he's old, about Mom's cooking. There certainly hasn't been much repetitive pattern to our meals on which to build fond flavor memories.

Monster Pudding

December 12

Though they were becoming rarer, utter disasters still occurred during recipe testing:

Somewhere in our house, in a place so obvious I can't see it, is a 2-quart covered steamed-pudding mold, one of those utensils used about every three years and in the way the rest of the time. I've seen it lately, but I don't know where. As with all temporarily lost items, it will show up within days after I don't need it anymore.

On that mold hinged the success of a recipe I wanted to try from what will likely be the cookbook of the year, "Glorious American Food," bearing the price of the year, too — $50.

But the preferred mold had disappeared. I found another coverless mold I thought would work. The ginger pudding batter fit with plenty of space to spare, and a top was made with foil tightly tucked around the upper lip. I did not, I confess, measure how many cups that mold held until later. Then, I discovered it was only a 6-cupper.

My husband peeked into the pot after the pudding had been simmering for a while and said, "Good God, what are you growing in here?"

Undulating in the roiling water were brown dough gobs that had escaped from the mold and expanded dramatically in that moist environment. The foil was loose and bulging. There was nothing to do but let the pudding complete its simmering time.

What I didn't realize until later was that some law of cooking physics says, "What goes out may be replaced by an equal measure of something coming in." When the foil was removed, we saw a soggy mire caused by incoming water. I hoped it would congeal overnight. It didn't. Instead, the pudding shriveled into itself, poor thing. It still had a nice spicy flavor, despite its water infusion. Fortunately, whipped cream can cover any dessert disaster.

Dream Entree Nightmare

January 13

For the second time on a New Year's Eve, we hosted a Dream Entree dinner party. Guests brought their own main course, based on what they'd order if they were in the best restaurant. The collection this time: three lobster tails, two live lobsters, five steaks, two noisettes of lamb in champagne sauce and two shrimp crepes.

We heard that Coastal Seafoods, a small (in 1985) fish shop in Minneapolis, had wonderful bay scallops for $3.99 a pound. So my husband went there to buy scallops for this recipe and also my Dream Entree lobster tail.

Word was out about the seafood bargains. He waited in line for over an hour — agony for a man who swears he endured enough lines in the Navy to last him forever. He was certain that, like tickets at the movie theater on a Saturday night, they'd run out of scallops before he could get to the counter. Fortunately, they had plenty.

SAFFRON SCALLOPS WITH VEGETABLE MEDLEY
Makes 4 servings

- 3/4 cup blanched, slivered almonds
- 3 tablespoons butter, divided
- 2 carrots, peeled and julienned
- 1 large rib celery, julienned
- 1 small turnip, peeled and julienned
- 1 teaspoon olive oil
- 2 tablespoons finely chopped shallots
- 1 clove garlic, chopped finely
- 2 tablespoons dry white wine
- 1 pound scallops (if large, slice into medallions)
- 2 tablespoons heavy cream
- 2 tablespoons sour cream
- 1 tablespoon chopped fresh tarragon, or 1 teaspoon dried
- 1 teaspoon salt
- 2 large pinches saffron threads, or 1/4 teaspoon powdered saffron dissolved in 1 teaspoon hot water

Saute almonds in 1 tablespoon butter until golden. Reserve. Plunge carrots, celery and turnips into boiling salted water. When water returns to a boil, remove vegetables. Drain. Reserve. In remaining 2 tablespoons butter and olive oil, saute shallots and garlic until translucent. Add white wine. Scrape up any bits in pan. Add scallops. Simmer gently for 1 minute. Add cream. Simmer for 1 minute, or until cream is reduced. Stir in sour cream, tarragon, salt, saffron, vegetables and almonds. Heat through before serving.

Michelle Schmidt, writing a book on behalf of California almond growers, was one of the first to interpret vegetable-rich, high-flavor California Cuisine. That's where I found this party-worthy first-course idea, better than any fancy restaurant could muster on a New Year's Eve.

A Whole New Processor
August 11

Not long ago, I wrote about my antique food processor, so aged that the work bowl had lost its handle, and we couldn't buy parts anymore. Carolyn Vale, local representative for Cuisinart, called to convince me that I should have a new one. It was like shopping for a car. There were model choices and accessories to consider, then we traded in our old clunker (which still had a lot of miles left in it) and gave a chunk of money to boot.

My old machine, the first model Cuisinart introduced, had two slicing blades (thick and thin), a grater and a metal blade that my husband had sharpened several times but was long past the stage where it bloodied unwary fingers in the dishpan.

Our new processor is equipped with blades and graters and julienners and french-fry cutters and plastic scrapers and prongs and — best of all — a pasta-making attachment. Compared to our uncomplicated vintage model, it's so complex that Vale had to train us how to operate it. The transition was like going from a manual typewriter to a computer keyboard. So many new buttons to push and gizmos to master.

With the new equipment, we made this colorful, delicious salad. The finest shredder disk instantly produced perfect haystacks of zucchini, carrots and radishes. But I shouldn't have used the thinnest slicing blade for the mushrooms. Had they been cut thicker, they might not have broken when tossed with the dressing.

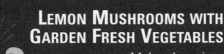

LEMON MUSHROOMS WITH GARDEN FRESH VEGETABLES
Makes 4 servings

1/2 cup vegetable oil
2 tablespoons chopped green onions
2 tablespoons lemon juice
1 1/2 teaspoons grated lemon peel
1/2 teaspoon sugar
Salt and pepper to taste
8 ounces mushrooms, sliced
2 cups assorted shredded fresh
    vegetables (carrots, zucchini,
    radishes, beets, etc.)

In mixing bowl, whisk together oil, onions, lemon juice, lemon peel, sugar, salt and pepper. Add mushrooms. Toss to mix well. Arrange choice of vegetables on serving plate. Spoon mushrooms and vinaigrette over vegetables.

Kissing Up
June 23

June. Weddings. Anniversaries. Hugs and kisses.

These are much on my mind because on Thursday, my husband and I celebrated two decades of wedded bliss. I thought it would last — but 20 years?! My only regret is that my wedding dress won't zip, even if I were pinched into a Scarlett O'Hara corset. Seventeen years of testing recipes have left their deposit, the most recent addition from kissy cookies about which I was passionate. They were tested for summer wedding and anniversary parties, but also because who can resist a (Hershey's) kiss? Not this romantic in love with chocolate.

Peeling silver foil from chocolate Kisses is like picking berries. One to keep, one to eat, one to keep ...

COCONUT CHERRY KISS COOKIES
Makes about 4 1/2 dozen

1/3 cup butter or margarine, softened
1 package (3 ounces) cream cheese,
    softened
2/3 cup sugar
1 egg yolk
1 teaspoon vanilla
1 1/4 cups unsifted all-purpose flour
2 teaspoons baking powder
1/4 teaspoon salt
1/2 cup chopped maraschino cherries
5 cups (14-ounce package) flaked
    coconut
54 milk chocolate Kisses (9-ounce
    package), unwrapped

To make dough: In large mixer bowl, cream butter with cream cheese and sugar until light and fluffy. Add egg yolk and vanilla. Beat well. Combine flour, baking powder and salt. (Note: A touch of almond extract intensifies cherry flavor.) Gradually add to creamed mixture. Stir in chopped cherries and 3 cups coconut. Cover tightly. Chill for 1 hour, or until firm.

To bake: Shape dough into 1-inch balls. Roll in remaining coconut. Place on ungreased cookie sheets. Bake in 350-degree oven for 10 to 12 minutes, or until lightly browned. Remove from oven. Immediately press 1 chocolate Kiss in center of each cookie. Cool 1 minute. Carefully remove from cookie sheets. Cool completely on wire racks.

That's not a job for the kids if you ever want to plant Kisses on the cookies. Even after the cookies are baked, beware of stolen Kisses. I noticed that the teen-age kissing bandit in our household had snitched the chocolate but left the cookies.

Cooking at the Lake

— Casual Cabin Cuisine —

Why We Love the Lake
August 29, 1993

Life in the North Country doesn't get much better than:

... when blueberries dangle like five-carat sapphires, so thick they can be "milked" from branch to bucket.

... when wildflowers cover unmowed spaces in such glorious profusion that Monet would run out of paints and canvas.

... when three pairs of loons on our lake trill day and night, creating a slightly hysterical northwoods serenade.

... when a doe and her fawn calmly survey us as we drive down our lake road, when a young timber wolf races in front of our truck on the road to our secret blueberry patch, and when we manage to miss clipping a black bear galloping across Highway 65 at dusk.

... when my husband is putting the last logs on our new summer home, and I'm painting a door "cloudless sky" blue, an exact match to what's overhead.

... when at night, shooting stars lace the sky during a meteor shower's apex.

... when we feast on salmon grown in former iron-ore pits on the Range, a creative reuse for the ravished land, which once supported a booming industry.

... when not even the voracious mosquito crop this summer can suck any luster from Minnesota North in August.

We used some of the pit-raised salmon (that producer, sadly, is no longer in business) to make this recipe, a variation of one sent to me by my favorite French champagne house, Taittinger.

Baking in parchment is a superb means to achieving moist salmon, and with leeks, sparkling wine and tarragon, oh, so elegantly flavored.

The dome before it gets an overcoat of shingles.

SALMON BAKED IN PARCHMENT
Makes 8 servings

1 pound fresh mushrooms, sliced 1/4-inch
   thick
12 tablespoons unsalted butter, divided
1/2 to 3/4 cup sparkling wine
   (or dry white wine)

4 medium leeks, white part only,
   thinly sliced
Salt
8 salmon fillets (6 ounces each), skinned
8 sprigs fresh tarragon
Freshly ground white pepper

To prepare mushrooms: In skillet, melt 2 tablespoons butter. Saute mushrooms over high heat for about 30 seconds. Add 4 tablespoons sparkling wine. Saute until liquid is absorbed. Remove from heat. Set aside.

To prepare leeks: In skillet, melt 2 tablespoons butter. Add leeks. Saute for 5 minutes, or until leeks are transparent. Remove from heat. Set aside.

To wrap salmon: Cut 8 sheets of parchment paper, 12 by 18 inches each. (Note: Reynolds Microwave Wrap works wonderfully and is more readily available.) Divide leeks evenly among the 8 sheets. Place salmon fillets on top of leeks. Divide mushrooms equally atop each fillet. Place tarragon sprig on top (or sprinkle with dried tarragon). Dot each serving with 1 tablespoon butter (use less if you wish). Sprinkle with sparkling or dry white wine. Season with salt and freshly ground white pepper. Starting at 1 corner, fold and twist edges tightly to other end. Fold last corner securely under.

To bake salmon: Bake in 400-degree oven for 10 to 12 minutes (about 10 minutes per 1-inch thickness of fish). Packets will inflate as they bake. When fish is done, carefully open packets. Using metal spatula, gently lift fish and components onto plate. Serve with garlic mashed potatoes, if desired.

Summertime, and the Cookin' is Easy
June 9, 1985

Know why I love to spend weekends at the lake? Because it's such mindless time. I can play 10 games of solitaire without guilt. I can sit and read without the washing machine singing a siren song. I can indulge in laziness usually forbidden by my city schedule. There are no pressures, no deadlines except the moment, always too soon, when we must load the car and start pounding the pavement back to St.Paul.

My cabin cooking falls into two categories. Either I'm testing recipes, usually making them part of dinner for the neighbors, or it's the leisurely breakfast, quick sandwich, uncomplicated stuff that takes no concentration or effort. Easiest of all on this cook is getting invited next door for a meal.

Prose on Being Prone
July 10, 1988

Thoughts while floating on a slowly-leaking air mattress ...

The lake last weekend was idyllic. Even the loons, who usually save their warbling for nighttime, were trilling their delight at a perfect afternoon. As long as I kept my left index and little fingers pressed tightly to two bubbling pinholes in a brand-new air-mattress, I could lay prone for hours between blue sky and blue water.

One benefit of northern Minnesota's dry weather is the dearth of mosquitoes. During an entire week in the woods, not one buzzer bit me, so I took courage and went floating on the lake. Still no mosquitoes, although a dragonfly mistook my city-white legs for runways. Despite their fearsome name, dragonflies don't bite.

Free Goodies in Goodland
August 9, 1981

We had guests with us one weekend, dear friends from Edina, city folks to the core. After we ate, I announced the evening's entertainment: We'll go to the dump to watch bears dig up some dinner. That's the most exciting event in Goodland Township on a Saturday night.

I'd never been, but I'd heard plenty about it from our lake neighbors, Betty and Wally Peters of St. Paul. Several times, they'd driven the two miles to the landfill to watch the bears, usually a mother and two cubs, sometimes joined by a massive male.

Betty knew she was ready to go back to the city "when the biggest thrill in my life is going to the dump."

Dusk, we were told, is the best bear-watching time. When we got to the dump, we were not alone. Twenty cars were parked amid the refuse. Those in them, trying not to breathe through their noses, were watching a single black male select his evening repast. It was Yellowstone Park East.

Our Edina guests were both revolted and fascinated. Watching the bear rip into a garbage-filled Hefty, city-raised kid Jared Jordal said, "Now, that's what I call a bag lunch."

The new log home — retirement, here we come.

New Cabin, New Cook
July 27, 1980

Our lake dome home has been housewarmed, and the kitchen has been christened, but I wasn't the first one to test a recipe there. Aric was.

It was an absolutely euphoric feeling, after three years of building, to be able to sleep in our dome for the first time. My husband was thrilled to be able to use indoor facilities after three summers of enduring a spider-filled outdoor biffy. He hates spiders.

Several of the kitchen cabinet drawers are still filled with electrical parts and tools, but the stove works. So do the disposal and dishwasher. A couple of people have "harrumphed" about having a dishwasher at a lake place, but I don't like to wash dishes any better in the north woods than I do in the city. This is a vacation cottage, and that includes vacations from dishpan hands.

TURKEY PARMESAN

Makes 6 servings

1 pound fresh or frozen turkey cutlets, thawed

3/4 cup enriched cornmeal

1/3 cup all-purpose flour

1 teaspoon garlic salt

1/8 teaspoon pepper

2 eggs, beaten

1/4 cup milk

1/4 cup vegetable oil

1 jar (15 1/2 ounces) prepared meatless spaghetti sauce

1 cup (4 ounces) shredded mozzarella cheese

1/4 cup grated parmesan cheese

To prepare cutlets: Pound cutlets with meat mallet or rolling pin to 1/8-inch thickness on cutting board or between 2 sheets of wax paper. Combine cornmeal, flour and spices. Combine eggs and milk. Dip cutlets into egg-milk mixture. Coat with cornmeal mixture.

To cook cutlets: Heat oil over medium-high heat in 12-inch skillet. Pan-fry cutlets in 2 batches for 5 to 8 minutes, or until light golden brown on both sides. Drain on absorbent paper. Arrange cutlets in 9-by-13-inch baking dish. Spoon spaghetti sauce evenly over cutlets. Sprinkle with cheeses. Bake in 375-degree oven for 15 minutes, or until cheese melts.

While I finally had a chance to lounge, and my husband actually wet a fish line, Aric was looking for something to do.

"I'll cook," he ventured.

"Would you like to test a recipe?" I suggested, sensing an opportunity to lounge a little longer. He took the bait, adding confidently that anyone who can read a recipe can cook.

No mother whose son is testing his first recipe can remain in the lounge chair very long. I hovered a little, but let him plow through preparations of Turkey Parmesan by himself. Reading a recipe is one thing; understanding it is another. "I knew I had to saute the turkey first, but then I thought I was supposed to put all the cheese in the frying pan, too," he later admitted. But with a little help from Mom, this first meal at the cabin turned out fine.

Everyone who came for that first dinner praised the meal. Later, I saw Aric in the kitchen earnestly telling his grandmother, one of the world's better cooks, how to make Turkey Parmesan.

A few days after that I asked him if he would he make the cutlets again. By then, the adulation had died down and he was again a typical 11-year-old blase boy. "Make them again? I don't know. If I had to, I suppose," he said.

Mosquito Anti(pasto)dote

June 7, 1981

Move over, Cutters and Deep Woods Off. I've found a new antidote for northern Minnesota mosquitoes: antipasto.

After two lovely years with barely any bugs, they were buzzing when we drove into our lake place for Memorial Day weekend. Friends once gave us, as a joke, a miniature metal trap that was supposed to catch Minnesota's giant mosquitoes. This spring, that trap suddenly seems practical, for I've never seen bigger, meaner, more numerous mosquitoes than the current hatch. One advantage of big mosquitoes — they fly slower, making swatting easier.

I've never been fond of Eau de Off, so I usually just flail my arms a lot and run fast during bad mosquito years. This time, I discovered that every time I dipped into the bowl of antipasto I'd tested, mosquitoes left me alone. Maybe it was the garlic. Maybe the peppers made my blood too hot.

Every taster raved about this antipasto, which is said to have originated with Loni Kuhn, a San

SICILIAN ANTIPASTO
Makes 20 side-dish servings

Olive oil
4 ribs celery, sliced
4 to 6 carrots, sliced
2 to 4 onions, coarsely chopped
6 to 8 garlic cloves, minced
1 head cauliflower, florets sliced
1 to 2 heads fennel, sliced (optional)
2 to 4 zucchini, sliced
2 cans (8 ounces each) tomato sauce
1 can (6 ounces) tomato paste
1 cup chopped parsley
1 to 2 tablespoons oregano
1 to 2 tablespoons basil
1/4 to 1/2 cup capers
1 to 2 jars (about 8 ounces each) pearl or
   cocktail onions, drained (more is better)
1 to 2 jars (about 16 ounces each) mixed
   sweet pickles, drained and sliced
1 can (about 8 ounces) pitted black olives,
   drained

1 jar (about 8 ounces) stuffed green olives,
   drained
1 jar (about 16 ounces) cherry peppers,
   mild or hot, drained
1 jar (about 13 1/2 ounces) pepperoncini,
   drained
1 to 2 jars (6 ounces each) marinated
   artichoke hearts and juice (cut hearts
   into quarters)
1/4 to 1/3 cup red-wine vinegar
1/4 cup sugar
Salt and lots of freshly ground black
   pepper
Choice of one of the following: 6 ounces
   anchovies, finely chopped; 2 to 3 cans (6
   1/2 ounces each) tuna packed in oil,
   undrained; or 1/2 pound salami, cut in
   julienne strips

To very large heavy pot with lid, add enough olive oil to cover bottom. Place over heat. Add celery, carrots, onions, garlic, cauliflower and fennel. Cover. Cook for 5 minutes. Add sliced zucchini. Steam for 5 minutes. Remove from heat. Add remaining ingredients, including choice of anchovies, tuna or salami. Stir gently to mix. Return to heat. Simmer for 3 to 4 minutes, just to blend. Refrigerate antipasto for 3 days, stirring daily. Can be served over next 10 days as an appetizer, with crackers. Refrigerate any remainder.

Francisco cooking authority. It mellows as it ages. The recipe allows latitude for amounts based on personal taste. If you don't like olives, just use more onions or artichokes. Julienne strips of mozzarella can be added, too. The hardest thing about the recipe is leaving it alone for the three days it should marinate.

Puff Piece
October 14

When my cousin Betty says, "Come for breakfast," we hope she's making puff pancakes, and she usually is, serving them with syrup or fresh fruit. They're a variation on kropsua, the Finnish baked pancakes that my Aunt Impi, Betty's mother, often made when I was a kid. Betty has a stack of 7-inch pie plates in which she can bake an ovenful of pancakes at one time, enough to satisfy all the Lake Hungrics around her table with a whole pancake apiece.

BETTY'S PUFF PANCAKES
Makes 1 large or 2 medium pancakes

1/2 cup flour
2 eggs
1/2 cup milk
Pinch of nutmeg
1/4 cup butter

Lightly beat flour, eggs, milk and nutmeg (some lumps can remain). Heat oven to 425 degrees. In 2 7-inch pie pans or 1 9-inch pan, melt butter. Pour batter directly on top of butter. Bake for 20 minutes, or until puffed and browned. Serve hot.

Heavy Meals
June 8, 1986

My cousin Betty was cutting rhubarb custard pie a la mode to cap a dinner of cheese soup, fried chicken, macaroni salad and several other fattening fixings, when it occurred to me that maybe there's a flaw in our summertime share-the-cooking plan. It's wonderful not to plan and cook more than one big meal during our lake getaways. But we have to eat more than one big meal. With each hostess putting all her energies into a single feast, calories do pile high.

Mosquitoes are so fierce that we couldn't do much outside to wear off our table excesses. My husband swore he put lead weights in his pockets so he wouldn't be lifted aloft by winged swarms, but I think the pork chops, mashed potatoes, gravy, salad and cake eaten at another neighborly dinner did an adequate job of keeping his feet on the ground.

Thrills on Blueberry Hill
July 27, 1986

Time stands still in the blueberry patches of northern Minnesota. Last weekend could have been 20 years ago. The sensations — pleasures and pains — remain unchanged when, plastic pail in hand, I gleaned the goodness of nature.

Sounds of berry picking do not change. On the granite hills behind my grandmother's farm north of Virginia, Minn., where berries were always the sweetest, I'll always remember the crunch of dried lichen and blueberry branches under my feet. There's another sound I always listened for but never heard, that of a bear snacking from blueberry bush to bush. My mother told of hearing it and of hightailing it off that granite slope so fast that half the berries rolled out of her bucket.

BLUEBERRY STREUSEL MUFFINS
Makes 12 large muffins

Muffins:
1 1/2 cups all-purpose flour
2 teaspoons baking powder
1/2 teaspoon salt
4 tablespoons (1/2 stick) butter or
   margarine
1/2 cup sugar
1 egg
1 teaspoon vanilla
1/2 cup milk
1 1/2 cups fresh or dry-pack frozen
   blueberries, rinsed and drained

Streusel-walnut topping:
2 tablespoons butter or margarine
2 tablespoons brown sugar
1/4 to 1/2 teaspoon cinnamon, to taste
1/4 cup finely chopped walnuts

To make muffins: Sift flour, baking powder and salt onto wax paper. In large bowl, cream butter with sugar until fluffy. Beat in egg and vanilla. Stir in flour mixture alternately with milk. Fold in blueberries. Place paper baking cups in each of 12 large muffin pan cups. Spoon batter into cups, filling each two-thirds full.

To make streusel-walnut topping: In small saucepan, melt butter. Remove from heat. Stir in brown sugar, cinnamon and walnuts. Sprinkle over muffins.

To bake muffins: Bake in 400-degree oven for 20 minutes, or until tops spring back when lightly pressed with fingertip. (Note: If blueberries are juicy, add another 5 minutes.) Remove from pan. Cool on wire rack.

I love to be in a berry patch and hear the wind through the pines. That soothing symphony of woodwinds played in the tranquility of our favorite picking grounds, not far from our lake house. It was tranquil until a carload of pickers, three generations strong, tramped into my domain.

"Oooh, I found some big ones," hollered a 7-year-old just starting to gather her first memories of blueberry picking. That could have been me, many summers ago.

Another sound is inevitable. Always, always, a single buzzing critter adopts me, dive-bombing my hair, undeterred by my flailing hand. I usually give up the battle before the insect does.

Whining mosquitoes discover all the patches on my person not sprayed with bug dope. They add to the exercise that is berry picking. This is how it goes: Jane Fonda, are you paying attention? Find a good spot. Squat. Pick. Swat. Pick. Scratch. Pick. Then stand up, stretch, move to the next laden bush and squat-swat-scratch all over again.

Despite the bugs, there's a compulsion to pick berries in a good year, to turn aside the green leaves and find a cluster of edible sapphires, at least three carats each. Blueberries are the jewels of a Minnesota summer, and muffins and pancakes are our reward for finding them.

These muffins, rated "perfection," were tested with my wild blueberry plunder.

Growing Into Fish Soup
August 14, 1986

When I was a kid, I turned up my nose at my mother's kalamojakka, a Finnish fish stew. This one I liked. A little maturity helps. So does having a neighbor like Looch of the Lake, who provided the panfish from his nightly catch.

ELEGANT FISH SOUP
Makes 6 servings

2 cups fish fillets

2 strips bacon, cut up fine

1/2 onion

3 potatoes, diced

1/4 cup fresh parsley

3 cups milk

Seasoned salt, regular salt and pepper
to taste

3 tablespoon butter

2 tablespoons flour

Cook fish fillets (panfish preferred) for several minutes in simmering water, or until fish turns white. Using slotted spoon, transfer fish to large plate to cool. (Note: Use as little water as possible for cooking fish, and keep water to use in soup.) Brown bacon. Pour off grease, leaving only enough to saute chopped onions. Add onions and bacon to fish broth. Add diced potatoes and parsley to broth. Cook until potatoes are tender. Cut fish into small pieces. Add to soup along with milk. Season with seasoned salt, salt and pepper. Mix butter and flour. Add to soup. Boil gently for several minutes. (Note: Add 1/3 cup potato flakes for thicker soup.) Serve with pats of butter and crackers.

Am I Blue?
July 23, 1989

It's that time of summer that makes me blue. Blue hands, blue lips, blue knees.

What really makes me blue this summer is that I'm heading for New Mexico just as the northern Minnesota blueberry crop is proclaimed the best in years. My cousin-in-law, Looch, the family's official berry scout, says this is a bumper year for blues. All I'm hoping is that the patches haven't been picked over by the time I get back to our lake place. A summer without at least one batch of wild blueberry pancakes is like a lake without a loon.

Crude Food? Hardly
June 24, 1990

Pounds have been accumulating in the last month. It must be because we've been going to the lake every weekend.

Let me tell you about last Sunday. That was the day after the clan gathered to celebrate the 40th wedding anniversary (with a restaurant steak dinner, followed by cake and champagne) of my cousin, Betty Rostvold, and her husband, Looch. That morning, I cooked breakfast for the gang: French toast made with cinnamon bread; eggs scrambled with mushrooms, onions, green pepper, cheese and sliced wild-rice sausages; hot baking-powder biscuits.

At midafternoon, grills started heating up at Betty and Looch's cabin next door. On one Weber, a lunker turkey smoked. On another, whole pheasant, frozen since last fall's successful hunting trip, got equal treatment. On the third, a butterflied and rolled venison roast, seasoned with a blend that Betty and Looch's eldest son, Paul Rostvold, keeps secret, achieved juicy tenderness.

Friends of the younger Rostvolds arrived, bringing salmon and halibut caught in Alaska. Some salmon steaks were reserved for grilling, but Nick Muhar of Chisholm cubed the remaining fish. His wife, Millie, dipped the pieces in egg, then in instant potato flakes blended with seasoned salt. Then, Looch cooked them in his propane-fueled deep-fat fryer. They were fabulous.

At least one of my extra pounds can be blamed on the Vidalia onion rings that Looch deep-fried. Betty has been experimenting with beer batters, and the one Looch approves of mixes 1 1/4 cups flour, 1/4 cup cornstarch, 1/2 teaspoon salt, 1 teaspoon baking powder, 1 egg and 1 can of flat beer.

While men tended the grills, the women were inside devouring hors d'oeuvres. Paul's wife, Suzy, brought a bowlful of tortilla roll-ups and recited the recipe while I simultaneously scribbled and munched.

TORTILLA ROLL-UPS
Makes 12 servings

8 ounces cream cheese
1/2 cup mayonnaise
1 package (8 ounces) Cheddarella (or 4 ounces each of shredded cheddar and mozzarella cheeses)
1 envelope Hidden Valley Ranch salad dressing mix
1 bunch green onions, sliced
1 green pepper, finely diced
1 package large flour tortillas

Mix all ingredients, except tortillas. Spread mixture on tortillas. Roll up jellyroll-style. Slice into 1-inch pieces. Secure, if necessary, with toothpicks.

When the grilled meats were ready for slicing, the table was suddenly laden with pasta and vegetables salads, cakes and bars, all contributed by guests. Everyone asked if I was going to critique the meal, so I had to sample everything. My rating: four stars.

I was teasing Paul Rostvold that if I'd done the venison, I might have made a citified sauce with balsamic vinegar and raspberries.

"Up here, we're a little more crude than that," he replied.

Crude? He only has to check prices in a city restaurant for smoked pheasant, venison and Alaska halibut to understand how elegantly we eat at the lake.

The Finn and the Feast
July 12, 1992

Cousin Betty, returning to our cabin compound after a trip to town last weekend, slammed on her brakes in surprise as she headed up her driveway. Stretched between two pines, forming a triumphal statement across the road, was a huge banner that read, "One Finlander Feeding One Hundred Norwegians."

Betty is the Finn, and the Norwegians are her husband's clan who came from a half-dozen states, even as far as Okinawa, for a Rostvold family reunion at our lake. The sign was the handiwork of Pat Filippi, a Keewatin Italian who married a Nashwauk Rostvold and became Norwegian by association.

Betty organized a feast on Friday that involved 40 pounds of pork loins, two buxom turkeys and a 10-pound venison roast on a bevy of grills. Usually, Rostvold parties revolve around a pig on a spit, but this time, the hosts reverted to whole pork loins with a few extra ribs attached to the outside, which made good pickings for Betty's husband, Looch, and the guys manning the grills. "I wasn't hungry by the time dinner started," admitted the Chief Grill Cook and Nibbler.

To that meal, I contributed Chutney and Curried Broccoli Salad. Kevin Streeter, chef at Naniboujou Lodge north of Grand Marais on Lake Superior's North Shore, gave me this recipe. It originally called for two jars of chutney. One does nicely for this size batch.

When everyone had eaten to capacity — and then some — Looch suddenly panicked. "You forgot to put out the potato salad," he said, remembering buckets of the stuff stashed in the porch refrigerator. "That's for tomorrow night," Betty patiently advised him.

After Saturday's Fourth of July parades in town, carloads of hungry people arrived for picnic fare, including that potato salad, beans and relishes. An 18-pound ham had baked in our cabin's oven. Knowing that she had leftover pork loin to peddle, Betty didn't even cook the second 18-pounder she'd bought.

This wasn't the biggest feed Betty ever put on at the lake. Wedding receptions for her kids and big barbecues involved more people, but only for one day.

The reunion went on and on, some relatives staying for a week, showing up at her table daily for meals.

Even with her years of experience, Betty said she'd wake up night after night thinking about the task ahead. "All those meals were cooked many times in my head before they were actually prepared," she said.

A few uninvited guests showed up. Bears have been patrolling our woods this summer, driving the dogs crazy at night. The aroma of grilled meat was an invitation they couldn't resist, which must have made the Californians sleeping in a tent trailer rather jittery.

Every night about sunset, bats in the eaves of Betty and Looch's cabin flap their wings as they head out for a mosquito feast. Wouldn't you know, on the first night when the cabin was full of sleeping relatives, a bat swooped in, creating middle-of-the-night hysteria.

Apparently, there isn't a creature alive that wants to miss Betty's hospitality.

When all had departed, Betty was seen on her way to town, her car's backseat heaped with towels to wash. That sign should have read, "One Finlander Cooking and Washing for One Hundred Norwegians."

CHUTNEY AND CURRIED BROCCOLI SALAD

Makes 16 servings

- 2 heads broccoli (florets and some stems), cut in small bite-sized pieces
- 1 1/2 pounds red grapes (about 5 cups)
- 1/2 red onion, diced
- 1 cup toasted slivered almonds
- 2 cups mayonnaise
- 1 jar (9 ounces) Major Grey's chutney
- 2 tablespoons curry powder

Prepare broccoli. Combine with grapes, onion and almonds. Mix mayonnaise with chutney and curry powder. Stir into broccoli mixture until blended. Refrigerate until served.

A reader says . . .

I have always admired your writing for its grace, simplicity and genuineness, and I've enjoyed following your food and life adventures. For the years that I lived out of state, my mother mailed me the best sections of the Sunday paper, and she invariably circled your column to make sure I didn't miss it.

— William Jack, Minneapolis

Cooking in a New Cabin
September 18, 1994

Five years ago, when we finished a major redo of our St. Paul cooking quarters, I thought I had sketched out my last culinary floor plan. But that was before my husband and I got the bug to build a new log home, to replace our geodesic dome that is about done in.

Northern winters have been rough on our round abode. It was built too early in the technology of dome construction, and several unforeseen factors have caused the structure to weaken, heave and leak. Carpenter ants are chewing away at it, and the floor is so uneven that a spill becomes an instant river.

Further, the kitchen that was quite spacious 17 years ago is now woefully inadequate. Cupboards are stuffed. Counters are piled high. The refrigerator is full of frost, and the dishwasher is about to die.

We've had good times and hundreds of great meals in that dome, but now that the log house is almost done, I can't wait to move out of the round into the rectangular.

Over Labor Day weekend, the glowing natural-finish knotty pine kitchen cabinets went in, and now we're awaiting the blue countertops — somewhere between the shade of summer sky and well-washed denim — and plumbing hook-ups to begin cooking with some elbow room. We're installing two double-bowl sinks, one below a window facing the lake, and one at the kitchen's opposite end, with a woodsy view. No more two-cook collisions at the sink.

While the kitchen was being installed, I was camp cook (in the old kitchen) for the workers. This he-man casserole was given a four-hammer rating by our building crew. I gave it four spoons for ease of preparation. To feed the hungry bunch, I doubled the batch and baked it in a 10-by-15-inch pan; it would have been rather wimpy otherwise. If sticking to a single recipe, use a 9-by-9-inch pan. You'll need to shovel the meat mixture from the pan, but the cheese layer keeps the "bun" from getting soggy.

SLOPPY JOE UNDER A "BUN"
Makes 8 small servings

1 pound ground beef
1 can (about 15 ounces) sloppy Joe sauce
2 cups shredded cheddar cheese
2 cups Bisquick baking mix
1 cup milk
2 eggs
1 tablespoon sesame seeds

Cook ground beef until brown. Drain. Stir in sloppy Joe sauce. Spoon into ungreased 9-by-9-inch baking dish. Sprinkle with cheese. Stir baking mix, milk and eggs until blended. Pour over beef mixture. Sprinkle with sesame seeds. Bake in 400-degree oven for 25 minutes, or until crust is light golden brown.

Aunt Impi Winters and her daughter, my cousin Betty Rostvold, on the deck of our new lake house.

Picking was Berry Good

July 9, 1995

Pickings were good. No, make that pickings were astoundingly great last weekend at Nordic Ridge Gardens, a berry and vegetable farm south of Calumet, Minn., not far from our lake house.

Every year, I watch for the simple sign to appear, a single red strawberry and an arrow pointing to the dirt lane. I've responded to that sign with Pavlovian regularity for the past three summers, following it past a neat updated farmhouse bordered with flowers to the fields where hundreds of rows of pristine strawberries beckon.

What booty to push aside a canopy of protective greenery and find a trove of ruby-hued edible treasures, often growing in plump clusters.

My friend, Jayne Trudell of Falcon Heights, Minn., who had never gone berry picking in her life, was dazzled, exclaiming over the fruit's size. "This is a prize," she'd say, holding up a supersize berry. "No, this one's even bigger."

On she went in her quest for behemoth berries, and, like the other three of us, she filled a 5-quart ice cream bucket to 6-quart height in 10 minutes. Those heaped buckets gave us about 24 quarts of berries, swapped for a $20 bill. We were done so quickly that my back and knees didn't have time to start complaining.

That berry bonanza was on the July 4th weekend, when the last picture had been hung and rugs had been spread on gleaming wood floors in the new lake house. We celebrated our own independence, at least for a weekend, from hammers and paint brushes. This coffeecake, based on a recipe distributed by Nordic Ridge, was served to a houseful of holiday guests.

STRAWBERRY COFFEECAKE

Makes 15 servings

- 8 ounces cream cheese, softened
- 1/2 cup butter, softened
- 3/4 cup sugar
- 1/4 cup milk
- 2 eggs
- 1 teaspoon vanilla
- 2 cups flour
- 1 teaspoon baking powder
- 1/2 teaspoon baking soda
- 1/4 teaspoon salt
- 3 cups fresh strawberries, sliced
- 1/4 cup brown sugar
- 1/2 cup chopped almonds or other nuts

Combine cream cheese, butter and sugar. Beat until light and fluffy. Stir in milk, eggs and vanilla. Sift together flour, baking powder, baking soda and salt. Add to cheese mixture. Mix until smooth. Spread half of batter in greased and floured 9-by-13-inch baking pan. Spread berries evenly over batter. Dot remaining batter over berries. Mix brown sugar and nuts. Sprinkle evenly over batter. Bake in 350-degree oven for 40 minutes. Serve warm.

A reader says . . .

I was using one of your recipes this morning, and it dawned on me that I've never written to thank you. Bothered you on the phone to get cooking advice, but never an honest "Thank You." You are a wonderful part of the Sunday paper.

— Jeanne Fischer, St. Paul

1986

— Confronting Midwest trendiness (finally!) and food mysteries, building gingerbread cottages —

Finally, We're "In"
August 24

"The Midwest is newly chic," according to cookbook author Margaret Guthrie. "I guess Garrison Keillor has done that for us," she said, crediting Lake Wobegon's master storyteller. Indeed, among the year's travels was a conference in Kansas City devoted to the emerging allure of Midwest farm fare, part of the comfort food craze. At last, we were getting our brief spin in the constant whirl of food trends.

Thank Goodness It's "Out"
September 14

Southern-style "white trash" cooking, explained by a tacky cookbook of that name, was given Sunday shrift, and for the first — and last — time, okra, right at the bottom of my list of acceptable vegetables, got tested, with pitiful results.

"Let's put poor Limpin' Susan out of her misery," I said about a pathetic fried okra and rice dish bearing that name:

Think of "White Trash Cooking" as a "look book." Kick off your shoes, sit down a spell and read it from cover to cover, just for the fun it is. And be thankful that it captures a food style that isn't around much anymore.

It's a Date
January 5

For the first Sunday of the year, a treatise on calendar art and recipes:

Some years, these annual calendars have been absolutely luscious. I'm thinking of a chocolate version that arrived several years ago, photos dripping temptation, one glance enough to erase New Year's resolutions. It was not the kind of calendar on which to note dentist appointments.

Aric, the Quotable
January 12

People always say to me, "You never write about Aric anymore."

Well, the finicky toddler you longtime readers remember is now 16 years old, and he's become quite the good cook. The counselor on his Rocky Mountain backpacking trek last summer commended his hiking skills, but was even more complimentary about his camp cooking. Guess all these years of recipe testing have rubbed off on the kid.

Aric is also of an age — and has been for several years — when he doesn't want to be quoted weekly so his classmates can read it and tease him Monday morning.

But then "The Bachelor Cookbook" arrived, promising "there is life after peanut butter and jelly," and Aric agreed (not enthusiastically, you understand) to be my guest tester, since he's the only bachelor in the house.

In the process of testing Hamburgers Deluxe — he cooked, I took notes — a whole new lexicon of teen jargon surfaced.

"Rude!" he said as he shaped the burgers, dripping with 1/2 cup of steak sauce. "I hate this," he muttered, looking at his sticky fingers.

Teen-age machos have an interesting way of forming burgers. He tossed a lump of meat from hand to hand, as if it were a baseball, until it rounded into shape. Then he flattened it.

As soon as the burgers hit the pan, they started releasing all that steak sauce. "Harsh!" said Aric as he poured off the first accumulation of juices in which the patties were stewing. The second time he had to drain the pan, when it became clear that the burgers were in trouble, he said, "This is a wreck and a half. They're so soupy, they're disintegrating. Two tablespoons of steak sauce would have been plenty. If a person was on a budget and this was the only thing for supper, he'd be hurting."

Any attempt to flip the burgers courted disaster. They crumbled at the slightest touch. "They're gross," he said, then finally announced, "This is pitiful. I'm not going to eat these."

The cookbook, he declared, "was obviously written by guys who didn't know how to cook and suddenly tried." Aric has never been one to sugarcoat his comments.

Bob Vila, Where Are You?
December 7

I'm barely literate when it comes to writing with frosting, managing, at best, a wobbly "Happy Birthday" in sugary scrawl. Frosting roses? I'm all thumbs (and not one of them is green) when "growing" flowers from pink icing.

So why would I tackle Santa's Workshop Gingerbread House? Because Mable Hoffman told me it was easy, and she and her husband, Gar, have developed a kit that's foolproof. It is for Mable, the nation's leading food stylist. For a certified cake decorating klutz like me, maybe ...

With the kitchen TV tuned to Channel 4, I began the project just as CBS "Sunday Morning" was ending. By the time Alfalfa had won the singing contest on "The Little Rascals," I had patterns pushed out (like reliving my paper-doll days), dough made, and I was rolling and cutting house parts. The first pan went into the oven when the Vikings pre-game show started. During the Tampa game, I kept cutting, baking, recutting and cooling pieces for the construction project.

My husband came into the kitchen to see where the dickens I'd been all morning. I let him sample the door I'd just cut out of the baked front of the house. "Are you sure you don't need this?" he asked before munching. No, it's a cut-out," said I. He'd eaten it and left before I discovered that door piece was really needed. Oh, well, cut and bake another one.

Five hours later, the football game was over and I'd mixed frosting, unwrapped candies, baked "stained glass" windows (made with crushed Lifesavers), glued the window shutters with icing mortar, affixed candy canes and M&M's decor on all sides, and frosted the chimney pieces together. Then I took my aching head up to bed for a short nap, telling my husband (who last summer erected a 40-by 24-foot garage at our lake cabin in a week) that he could finish the building project.

Forty-five minutes later, I heard him urgently shouting for me. I raced downstairs to find the house fully constructed. The chimney never did get attached, but Santa's hideout was just as cute as the kit's photographs promised.

"I wanted you to see it before all the candies fall off the roof," he said. Later, as we ate dinner in the dining room, we could hear the "plink" of mints bouncing on the kitchen counter. He'd raced through the roof project so fast that the frosting glue didn't dry hard enough to hold the mints in place once the roof was raised.

Mom:
Spuds Aren't Duds
February 16

If my mother had a soapbox subject — or better, a bushel basket topic — it was the food value of potatoes.

Though she spent a good part of her life trying to overcome the genetic curse of portly ancestors, it always irritated her that diets and dieters immediately eschewed potatoes. She could quote the vitamins B and C, mineral and calorie content of potatoes at the drop of a vegetable peeler.

Potatoes, she would expound, were unjustly branded as fattening for what was put on them. Under the butter and gravy, they were "darn good food," and the best ones of all were the potatoes she raised herself.

SHOESTRING WESTERN
Makes 2 servings

2 tablespoons butter or margarine
1 1/2 cups (about 5 ounces) frozen
   shoestring potatoes
1/2 cup coarsely chopped green bell
   pepper
1/2 cup chopped onion
2/3 cup cooked ham cut in julienne
   strips (about 3 ounces)
4 eggs
2 teaspoons water
Salt and pepper, to taste

In 8-inch nonstick skillet, melt butter. Add potatoes, bell pepper and onion. Saute over high heat, tossing occasionally, until potatoes are heated through and pepper and onion are tender-crisp. Add ham. Toss to heat through. Beat eggs with water, salt and pepper. Pour egg mixture over contents of skillet. Cook over medium heat until lightly browned on bottom. Invert. Cook again until lightly browned on the bottom. Cut in half to serve.

I don't think there was a national Potato Month when she was alive, but she would have celebrated it with gusto and probably with a low-calorie baked potato or two.

This perfectly simple, perfectly satisfying dinner ready in 10 minutes was tested for that column on potatoes. It tasted like potato omelets we'd had in Spain. Inverting it can be messy. The flavor will be the same if it's flipped in segments.

Saints Preserve Us

November 16

I know what I want to do when I grow up. I'll get a mini-motorhome, load it with road maps and word processor, and take off with my husband on whatever back roads that vehicle can maneuver, looking for funny and fascinating stories.

Two people had that idea first. Jane and Michael Stern, who had produced yet another cookbook on their road food finds, were the column's subject:

Since the book is divided regionally, I naturally turned to the Midwest section to see what the Sterns had discovered in our area. Iowa and Wisconsin are explored, and entire chapters are devoted to Chicago deep-dish pizza and to pasties from Michigan's Upper Peninsula. But not a mention of Minnesota, except an offhand reference to St. Paul in a sandwich called Shrimp St. Paul.

"St. Pauls are an unsolved mystery of St. Louis noodle parlors," the Sterns wrote in their section on Midwest Rude Food. "Every menu lists St. Pauls — pork, ham, chicken, beef or shrimp.

"The mystery is that no St. Louisian seems to know how St. Pauls got their name. Why aren't they called St. Louises? No such dish exists in St. Paul, Minn. Is

St. Paul the patron saint of noodle parlors? Even Howard Wong of the Lotus Room (in St. Louis), who grew up with St. Pauls, didn't have a clue. If anyone has an answer, we would like to know."

Well, Jane and Michael, I tried to solve this mystery. You're right, there are no St. Pauls on St. Paul menus. Joe Pollock, restaurant reviewer for the St. Louis Post-Dispatch, told me he doesn't know where the name came from. But he does know that the sandwich preceded the era of Chinese take-out restaurants there.

"I used to eat St. Pauls in regular restaurants when I was a kid, before the Chinese got hold of them and added bean sprouts," he said. "In St. Louis, a St.Paul is what you in St. Paul call a Denver sandwich. It was originally made with ham, onion and green pepper."

So there, we've had St. Pauls in St. Paul all the time, but we've given Colorado the credit.

SHRIMP ST. PAUL

Makes 2 servings

2 eggs
1/2 cup bean sprouts
1 tablespoon minced scallion
2 mushrooms, diced
1 water chestnut, diced
3 medium shrimp, peeled and diced
Salt and pepper to taste
1 tablespoon peanut oil

Beat eggs in bowl. Add sprouts, scallions, mushrooms, water chestnut, shrimp, salt and pepper. In wok or small frying pan, heat peanut oil. Pour in eggs. Fry for 1 minute, or until light brown. Turn and fry other side for 1 minute. When browned on both sides, scoot patty up side of wok. Squeeze out excess oil with spatula. Cut in half. Serve on toasted or untoasted white bread.

A reader says . . .

Thank you for all the years that you have given us, your loyal readers. I love your column and can't begin to tell you how many of those recipes I've tried. Your writing reveals your openness, friendliness and great sense of humor. You've been wonderful to read, and you've taught me a lot.

— Sandy Viney, River Falls, Wis.

Dinner With a Dividend

July 20

I thought it was a joke on Jayne and George Trudell. They'd paid a goodly sum at the St. Paul Chamber Orchestra's Fans and Fiddlers silent auction to buy dinner at our house — where, as friends, they have eaten many times before and could come anytime, for free.

It took them more than a year to collect on the dinner I donated to the auction, but by the time the evening had ended well beyond midnight, after the Trudells, my husband and I and six other invitees had cooked, wine and dined, I discovered the joke was one me.

"You know, we only bought a dinner for four," Jayne reminded me. Call the extra six people long overdue interest on your investment, Jayne.

For the dinner, each couple was given a newly published cookbook and asked to select a specific course to be cooked in our kitchen. We had a Chinese appetizer, an Italian pasta course, a California-style shrimp-avocado-pasta entree, a rice salad from Southern France, and a European cherry tart. In the photo accompanying the column, one guest, Jack Farrell, president of Haskell's wines and spirits stores, put a match to the vodka-soaked pasta. It didn't light, but we liked it, anyway. The recipe was found in "The Glorious Noodle" by Linda Merinoff.

A reader says . . .

I felt with your column I had a secret neighbor over the back fence. You gave me years of enjoyment, and I want to thank you for that. Your columns were a delight to one who had no kitchen, but could try out those recipes in my head and taste those flavors as surely as if I had stood over the stove myself.

— Sister Margery Smith,
College of St. Catherine, St. Paul

PASTA WITH VODKA SAUCE

Makes 4 servings

1/2 pound penne (diagonally cut short tubular pasta)
1 cup vodka
1 teaspoon hot red-pepper flakes
6 tablespoons unsalted butter, cut into 4 pieces
1/2 cup freshly squeezed orange juice
1 cup heavy cream
Salt and white pepper, to taste
3 tablespoons grated parmesan cheese
4 teaspoons grated orange rind

Drop penne into pot of boiling water. Cook until al dente. Drain. While penne is cooking, place vodka, red-pepper flakes, butter and orange juice in large saucepan. Cook over low heat until butter is melted. Simmer for 2 minutes. Stir in cream, salt and pepper. Bring to a boil. Return heat to low. Simmer, stirring often, for 7 minutes, or until slightly thickened. Stir in drained pasta. Cook for another 3 minutes. Stir in parmesan. Mix well. Sprinkle 1 teaspoon of orange rind onto each serving.

An Appetizing Task

December 14

"Just doing research," I said to someone who noted that I'd staked a spot next to the buffet at a features department holiday party. While others mingled, I watch appetizers being mangled, all in pursuit of a column.

It turned out to be slim pickings for actual recipes. Home economist Ellen Carlson pointed to her head when I asked her where she got the recipe for her Polynesian meatballs.

I asked copy editor Cheryl Burch-Schoff how she made her luscious miniature turnovers, and there wasn't much a recipe there, either. Just use standard pastry and fill rounds with a mixture of chopped chicken, green olives and taco sauce, she said.

"I got this recipe straight from Jeno," said a grinning latecomer who brought a plate of hot (and very familiar-looking) pizza rolls to the table. "I also got them straight from a Jeno's box," she admitted.

The fruited appetizer cheese log I contributed was lovely to look at, with alternating bands of parsley and chopped almonds covering its squat shape. But no one touched it. Perhaps it was too pretty.

Most hands reached out to rip at the contribution of columnist of Don Boxmeyer and his wife, Kathy: a cheese-laden, olive-studded bread loaf for which they're famous. Kathy said she has given the recipe to at least 200 people after getting it from a friend, Carol Peterson. Don once brought it to an office Christmas lunch and received an executive order from our top editor to put the recipe into the computer system so everyone could have it.

CAROL'S (OR KATHY'S) BREAD

Makes 1 appetizer loaf

1 loaf unsliced Vienna bread
1/2 pound (or more) butter
1 teaspoon dry mustard
1 tablespoon seasoned salt
2 tablespoons chopped onion
1 teaspoon (or more) poppy seeds
1 tablespoon lemon juice
3/4 pound Swiss cheese
3/4 pound cheddar cheese
1 small can ripe olives, drained and diced fine
Heavy-duty foil

To stuff bread: Cut bread into small diagonal slices, being careful not to slice all the way through bottom crust. In small saucepan, combine butter, mustard, seasoned salt, onion, poppy seeds and lemon juice. Stir until melted and blended. Cut cheese into julienne sticks about 3/4-inch long by 1/4-inch square. Place cut loaf of bread on large piece of foil. Starting in middle, stuff alternating sticks of Swiss and cheddar cheese into diagonal cuts, tucking them deep inside bread. Use foil to hold loaf in shape as it expands with stuffing. Drizzle butter mixture over loaf. Sprinkle with diced ripe olives.

To bake bread: Fold foil up and over bread, completely covering it. Bake in 350-degree oven for 1 hour.

To serve: Remove foil. Place loaf on board or plate. Place a sharp knife alongside to assist cutting pieces.

1987

— Winners, losers, graduations, empty nests and a trunk full of trends —

Doughboy Needs a Diet

February 8

For the pre-Valentine's Day column:

Even the Pillsbury Doughboy equates food and love when he says, "Nothing says lovin' like something from the oven."

The question is, does the Doughboy strike you as sexy? His ample middle likely resulted from too many biscuits and bundt cakes, when he should have been chewing whole grains, seeds and vitamin pills to find happiness at the aerobics class or the singles bar. Face it, Doughboy, how many cute chicks hang out inside ovens?

Instead of something chocolate or cherry or utterly gooey, we tried pasta flavored with three kinds of peppers as part of a Valentine meal for svelte romantics:

Peppers, especially hot varieties, produce a glow that attracts love partners. Stoking that flame in the recipe are garlic, considered a potent romance enhancer even in the days before Lavoris and Colgate, and tomatoes, nicknamed "love apples" by 17th century Europeans. (Funny, eating a stuffed tomato never made me feel particularly amorous.)

Chicken for Charity

March 1

Beef was getting bashed in the mid-1980s:

A trend is hatching. Within just one week, three women chairing major fund-raising dinners and charity balls told me chicken will be their entree. Not because of cost, but because of public demand.

Remember the days not so long ago when every social event fed its guests beef? The theory was that men hated to struggle into tuxedos, and they would really be ticked if the dinner didn't include a consoling steak. Ball food committees chafed under the sameness of their menus, but each year they discovered new ways to garnish the inevitable tenderloin.

My, how our eating attitudes have changed.

A friend who's chairing an upcoming event says beef is out, veal is too expensive (and controversial), fish is too tricky to serve to hundreds, so chicken it will be, perhaps with dill vodka sauce.

Frankly, I'd bet that in their efforts to enhance chicken with buttery embellishments, some of those events won't be as charitable with the cholesterol count as they think. A well-trimmed beef filet produced according to today's leaner standards, grilled, with no bearnaise, is probably better for the arteries than chicken breast dripping beurre blanc.

But public perceptions are like a runaway steamroller — pretty hard to make change course. We don't want you to chicken out if you're the benevolent type who supports local causes by attending expensive galas, but kiss the hope of tender beef goodbye.

Also in that column, another cooking trend: At a dinner in New York City prepared by the city's leading restaurant chefs, course after course, both fish and meat, were still quivering. All were seriously underdone on purpose. Chefs indicated that well-done is no longer done in top restaurants.

Man of My Dreams
March 8

Clint Eastwood starred in my dreams last week.

I was on a brief trip to the Monterey Peninsula of California, where Eastwood is mayor of the utterly quaint town of Carmel-by-the-Sea. Late one night, we made a pilgrimage to the restaurant he owns, as do most visitors, hoping for a glimpse of His Honor, who stops by frequently.

It's somehow appropriate that Dirty Harry would have a restaurant called Hog's Breath Inn. Walking in there at night is like descending into hell. The narrow

walkway slopes to a subterranean patio, where fires blaze in several rustic, open fireplaces. Customers cuddled by the hearths because it was chilly. On one side of the huddled masses was a very dark bar looking like it was lifted intact from a movie set — more like a Mexican cantina than a Western saloon. Fierce-looking boars' heads glare down on the timid.

Across the way is an equally unpretentious restaurant with a casual menu. That's for eating only, the hostess told us, and we had already dined.

Never mind. Suave Eastwood and I supped together in my dreams that evening. He made my night!

Can't Eat Just One
April 12

Chocolate, white and dark, was newsworthy.

Writing about just-introduced chocolate-covered potato chips: A hedonistic snack perfectly matched to the yuppie generation "because we've been raised on junk food but also know sophisticated dining," said the chocolate chips' marketer.

"Yes, and they're vegetarian," quipped an observer.

White But Not Light
August 9

We're into light foods. To some that means white foods. And that may be one reason America is going crazy for white chocolate — which certainly isn't light in the calorie department. Its light color is the shade of cocoa butter. But somehow, to the eye, which sends a message to the brain, white chocolate doesn't appear as damning to diets.

The Brunch Bunch
April 19

We were bunching for brunching during '87:

Not so many years ago, finding a Sunday brunch required determination. The Curtis Hotel in Minneapolis always had one, and, slowly, brunches spread to such restaurants as Lord Fletcher's on Lake Minnetonka and the old Commodore Hotel in St. Paul, if dimming memory serves me.

About the time the Curtis was imploded, the brunch concept exploded. It was hard to find a restaurant that didn't have Sunday brunch, and some even began offering the breakfast buffets on Saturdays, too.

On that Sunday, I wrote about testing brunch recipes in a Hawaiian condo. Trying Baked Eggs in Cheese Sauce:

Dropping raw eggs into a panful of cheese sauce is an act of faith. They plop out of sight, so you'll have to bake them by the clock rather than by eyeballing their firmness.

The same problems arises when it's time to retrieve the eggs for serving. They're down there somewhere. You'll have to grope with a spoon until you hit something solid.

Dangerously Fast Food
May 24

Home cooking was becoming an endangered activity. We were eating fast food, whether from the drive-in window, or quickly made in our own kitchens. I tried to comply:

Today's recipes are so quick that you couldn't drive to the grocery store or stand in line at the gourmet take-out shop in less time. Nor could you thaw and bake frozen ready-made dishes as fast.

These recipes are so quick that you could be eating warm chocolate pie before you have the chance to argue yourself out of craving it. Those calories will get you before you can say no.

In that column, discussing a new scheme for 20-minute baking, these dire statistics emerged: Only 41 percent of families enjoyed home-baked pies, cakes and cookies in 1984, a drop from 59 percent just three years before that. (As of this book's 1997 writing, I'd bet that percentage is drifting toward single digits.) In 1987, commercial products calling themselves "home-style" and "home-baked" were satisfying sweet tooths. With 50 million American women working outside the home, time — not vanilla — was the essence.

Chef to the Mob
April 26

Countless chefs wearing white toques had been pictured in the column during its first two decades, but now we meet a chef in a hat of another color:

Chef Rene's black hat could be considered the equivalent of a black arm band. He has buried nearly all of his colleagues.

"At the time I became a black-hat master chef in 1954, there were 134 of us. Now, I'm the youngest at age 75, and there's only one left in Greece, one in Paris and one in Washington, D.C.," he said. And there will be no more. According to the rules, a black chef's toque can't be earned until an aspiring chef has studied under the tutelage of five different black-hat masters for two years each.

Chef Rene, on his sixth wife and about to become a TV chef on public television, is lucky to be among the living.

Cardinal Cushing, the Kennedy clan and King Ibn Saud of Saudi Arabia have eaten Chef Rene's cooking, and he has been chef on the yacht of millionaire J. Paul Getty. His most dangerous client? "Once in New York, I dropped a tray of spaghetti on (Mafia kingpin) Albert Anastasia. I ran like hell. A week later, he shot his barber for cutting him during a shave."

Graduated Scale of Party Food

June 21

In the midst of a record-breaking heat wave, Aric graduated from St. Paul Academy-Summit School, and we cooked far too much food for his graduation party:

As the mother of only one, I have no experience on this subject. I know how much people generally eat when they come to our house for a party, but there's a glitch that graduation throws into planning. Pick a Saturday or Sunday in early June for your event, and you can be assured that your guests will have received several other invitations for that day. They'll hop from open house to house, nibbling a little here and there but never really biting deeply into anyone's buffet.

A friend with relatives in Taylors Falls, Minn., said that people there had attended so many graduation open houses and eaten so many cakes decorated in the school colors that everyone in town had blue teeth.

Aric graduates from SPA on the hottest weekend of the '87 summer.

If you ask a deli or bakery to estimate how much food you'll need for graduation, immediately cut their suggestion in half. I ordered a decorated sheet cake and told the clerk we were expecting about 50 people. "To serve 50, you'll need a whole sheet, and that will be $48," she said. Distracted by other desserts, I figure our guests ate about $8 worth of cake.

This is my advice: Check the long-range temperature outlook. Inquire in advance if your guests have several invitations. And if both numbers are high, adapt the traveler's maxim of half as many clothes and twice as much money. Only make that half as much food and twice as much liquid. If guests on a hot day don't eat much, they'll guzzle a lot.

The Scale Sometimes Lies

October 18

Spa Cuisine was the rage, and while testing low-fat but high-color recipes, I told this tale about the woes of watching my weight — usually going up:

It was such a pretty, match-our-bathroom-blue scale. On sale. So I bought it to replace the rusty white model I inherited from Grandma.

But it hadn't been out of its box for 30 seconds before I realized how much I despised this shiny streamlined model. It obviously lies. It had the gall to report a 5-pound reading above the more user-friendly results on our trusty, rusty old friend.

I rocked on my heels and stood on tiptoe, but it remained adamant. It's devastating to be told you've gained 5 pounds when haven't enjoyed a great meal in the process.

So now we have two scales in the bathroom, and guess which one gets used.

My cousin Betty mentioned that she'd just bought a new scale and it says she weighs 5 pounds less than her old one does. What we should do is trade these prevaricating poundage tattlers and then we'd both be back to normal.

Happy Mutual Anniversary, Johnny

October 4

From a column for which we tested a banana dessert for the Top Banana of the "Tonight Show":

Johnny Carson and I celebrated our silver anniversary Thursday. I've been with him longer than any of his wives.

On Oct. 1, 1962, I started working at these newspapers, and it's still my first job. That night, I went home to my newly rented bachelor-girl apartment and turned on the TV I'd inherited when my grandpa died (it was considered a "portable" though it weighed at least 20 pounds).

On that first night of living alone and being newly employed, I watched a young, thin, slightly nervous fellow, also newly employed as a talk-show host by NBC.

As the years passed, I would have forgotten to note the anniversary of my employment if I hadn't noticed Carson, dressed in a tuxedo, celebrating his annual salute to longevity.

Though we've both worked equally long, my compensation hasn't quite kept pace with his. Yes, my salary has increased tenfold, but considering where it started, that's not saying much. According to the current issue of Ladies Home Journal, Carson started at a meager $100,000 annually, but is now paid $7 million by the network, and that's not counting the other financial pies into which he digs his fingers.

Further, boss, there's the matter of vacation. After 25 years, Carson works three-day weeks and gets 15 weeks off a year. Can we talk?

With all that free time, I figured Carson must enjoy puttering around in the kitchen, so I called NBC in Los Angeles to discover if he had any favorite recipes. NBC referred me to the "Tonight Show" publicist, who referred me to Carson's personal publicist, Jim Mahoney. "Mr. Mahoney is in his Honolulu office," said a receptionist who sounded like she was auditioning to play nasally Agnes on "Moonlighting."

I finally got through to one Maggie Begley (never did find out if she's related to Ed) who told me, in our second conversation, that she had passed my request along to HIM.

"Who's HIM?" I said.

"Why, Johnny Carson," she said. "He handles this kind of thing himself." With all that high-priced publicity help?

Apparently he chose not to handle it, because my third, fourth and fifth calls were not returned. That old Hollywood put-off, "Don't call us, we'll call you," is still enforced.

Hold the presses! After this column was handed in, I got a call from Carson's P.R. office saying he doesn't cook.

Taking Asian Food to our Heartland

November 1

Probably the most significant culinary trend of the year was the amalgam known as East meets West:

That newfangled mingling of Asian and European-American cooking methods has come to the Heartland.

I hereby coin the newest phrase: East meets Midwest.

That was in a column featuring Vegetable Fried Wild Rice and Five-Spice Baked Acorn Squash created by New York author and Chinese cooking teacher Karen Lee (she's not Chinese, she's Jewish), who helped me explore the foods of China in 1979.

She told the cooking class that she was teaching at Thrice, a St. Paul cookware shop (now Cooks of Crocus Hill): "My book is not authentic (Chinese). It defies certain basic principles. But it's the most delicious food you've ever tasted."

Using her Chinese cleaver for emphasis, Lee proclaimed, "I'm the most expensive (bang) and the best (bang) caterer in New York."

Tie One On
December 20

What is this madness that besets us at the holiday season? When we have the least time and the most demands on our attention, an irresistible compulsion hits to do a really big creative food project. For some, it's 20 varieties of decorated Christmas cookies, or enough fudge to keep Clearasil in business well into 1988.

Last year, I decided to become a cookie carpenter, building and adorning a gingerbread cottage. My future, it became clear, is not in the construction business.

This year, because cooking-school owner and author Betty Rosbottom came to town, I tackled Chocolate Ribbon Cake (a showstopper created by Rosbottom for the cover of Bon Appetit magazine). All day last Sunday and until nearly midnight Monday, I labored, creating mountains of chocolate-besmirched pans and bowls and cups and spoons. By the time two-tone chocolate bows atop the cake were knotted, I was fit to be tied.

Shower Ends Kitchenware Drought
May 17

Any entertaining event at our house was cause for a column. This from a wedding shower for our niece:

If anyone could use shower gifts, it's Alison. Nearly two years ago, she arrived in her parents' native Minnesota, totally separated from all her worldly possessions. They'd been dropped off in Iowa by a hired driver who decided she didn't want to detour to Minnesota on her cross-country route.

So Alison had nothing with which to furnish the Duluth efficiency apartment we'd found for her. I gave her boxes of scuzzy castoffs from our North Country lake home. We donated mismatched silverware, a saucepan that wobbles on the burner, plastic bowls and assorted plates, glassware not much beyond the level of jelly jars, essential cooking tools, linens and a lamp that was so decrepit it tended to lean toward its eternal rest. As far as I know, though her own goods eventually arrived, Alison is still using those woebegone lake furnishings.

So for bride-to-be Alison to open prettily wrapped stainless-steel flatware, service for 18, all matching, was a thrill. She got towels with no holes. And brand-new bakeware. And a dish-drying rack, which she said would replace a wooden one now growing mold.

This shrimp spread was on the shower buffet table. Cook's prerogative: I made it without olives, which I consider definitely optional.

SPICY SHRIMP SPREAD
Makes 2 1/2 cups

- 1 package (8 ounces) cream cheese, softened
- 1/2 cup sour cream
- 3/4 teaspoon cumin
- 1 cup (4 ounces) shredded Monterey jack cheese with jalapeno peppers
- 1 bag (6 ounces) frozen cooked tiny shrimp, thawed and drained
- 1/2 cup chopped green olives (optional)
- 1/4 cup chopped pecans
- Paprika

Combine cream cheese, sour cream and cumin. Mix well. Add cheese, shrimp (save a few for garnish) and olives. Mix well. Spread evenly into 9-inch pie plate. Sprinkle with pecans. Bake in 350-degree oven for 20 minutes. Garnish with reserved shrimp. Sprinkle with paprika. Serve with crackers or tortilla chips.

A New Veggie in our Vocabulary
June 28

Increasing eclecticism in grocery-store produce sections had us constantly trying new recipes, such as this one from Greens, my favorite San Francisco vegetarian restaurant:

"What's this?" asked everyone who looked into the salad bowl. When I answered "jicama" (pronounced HEE-kah-mah), they still didn't know. But they were willing to try this new-wave salad, which gets its color from oranges and radishes and its crunch from potato-like jicama. Unfortunately, the main ingredient is pricey in this area, but if you can find a small jicama, you'll be able to notch a new food experience on your belt, which won't be tightened by too many calories.

A reader says . . .

The Tested Recipes column is the first thing I read. Your life, written in your food column over the past 30 years, has so closely paralleled mine. We did so many of the same things at about the same time — our travels, our children, our families.

I loved the stories of your mother and was saddened by her death. I "helped" build the northwoods cabin and picked blueberries for pancakes. I had four sons, so it was fun to read about Aric and his adventures. Ron — what a nice man — I loved him, too. I won't look forward to opening the Sunday PP with the same interest and enthusiasm.

— Kay Lyford, Shoreview, Minn.

JICAMA-ORANGE SALAD
Makes 4 to 6 servings

- 8 to 12 ounces jicama
- 5 tablespoons orange juice
- 6 tablespoons grapefruit juice
- 3 tablespoons lemon juice
- 1/2 teaspoon grated grapefruit peel
- 1/4 teaspoon salt
- 2 pinches cayenne pepper
- 1 tablespoon (or more) cilantro leaves, roughly chopped
- 1 or 2 oranges
- 4 large red radishes
- Sprigs of cilantro for garnish

To marinate jicama: Peel jicama with knife or vegetable peeler. Cut jicama in half. Slice each half into 1/8-inch-thick pieces. Cut slices into small cubes (or julienne strips, if you prefer). Place in large shallow bowl. Combine juices, grapefruit peel, salt, cayenne and cilantro. Pour over jicama. Let sit for an hour, tossing once or twice to distribute juice. (If it is to sit longer, cover and refrigerate.)

To serve: Peel orange or oranges. Remove each section from fine membrane surrounding it. Slice radishes into paper-thin rounds, then into narrow strips so each piece is tipped with red. Combine radishes and orange sections with jicama. Toss. Serve garnished with cilantro.

The Chick Has Flown

September 13

At 7 a.m. Thursday, our nest emptied.

We put Aric on a plane en route to his freshman year at the University of Denver. He was also accepted by the University of Puget Sound in Tacoma, Wash., and Lewis and Clark in Portland, Ore., both excellent schools. But he said he didn't want to be soggy.

The real deciding factor may have been Denver's proximity to enticing ski slopes. I fear his education may be all downhill.

For 18 years, I've written about that kid, his food likes and dislikes, his birthday parties, the hills and valleys of his adolescence, about "Awesome Aric" of dirt-bike racing. Because of his column notoriety, he has endured teasing from friends and comments from teachers, such as one who said, "Aric, those fajitas that your mother wrote about made me sick. They were so good I ate 10 of them."

That may be one reason he refused to consider Minnesota colleges. Out in Denver, no one knows him, and for Aric, that may be a blessing.

Now, it's just my husband and me, alone again — except for the dog. So, can a Schnauzer be taught to say "yuck" and "gross"?

Once the melancholy fades, we'll realize some advantages. No more waiting for Aric's leisurely morning showers to end so we can get into the bathroom. Our water bills should recede dramatically.

Our electric bill should drop, too. It must take a lot of juice to play a stereo that loud. And we can turn off the lights when we go to bed at a sensible hour, instead of leaving them on until the night owl rolls in.

Were phone bills calculated on the number of incoming calls, we'd be able to pay a good share of his tuition when our phone stops ringing a dozen times a night. It will be so peaceful. But too quiet, I fear.

His room looks so empty. We've gained a guest room but lost our star boarder. As if I weren't depressed enough, my husband said, "He'll probably get a job out West and marry someone from out there

after he graduates." Let me cope with one downer at a time.

When I was a college freshman, away from home for the first time, someone's mom regularly sent Dream Bars to Macalester's Bigelow Hall. I always

DREAM BARS

Makes 48 bars

1/2 cup butter

1 1/2 cups firmly packed brown sugar, divided

1 cup plus 2 tablespoons all-purpose flour, divided

1 1/2 cups flaked coconut

1 cup chopped walnuts

1/4 teaspoon salt

1 teaspoon baking powder

2 eggs

2 teaspoons vanilla extract

Powdered sugar (optional)

To make crust: In medium-sized bowl, mix butter, 1/2 cup brown sugar and 1 cup flour with fingertips or fork until crumbly. Pat into 12-by-8-inch baking pan, covering bottom evenly. Bake in 375-degree oven for 10 minutes. Cool.

To make filling: In small bowl, mix coconut, walnuts, 2 tablespoons flour, salt and baking powder. In medium bowl, beat eggs, 1 cup brown sugar and vanilla. Fold coconut mixture into creamed mixture. Pour over cooled crust, spreading evenly. Bake in 375-degree oven for 20 minutes, or until golden brown and filling is set. Cool slightly. While still warm, using sharp knife, cut into 48 bars. Cool in pan. Sift powdered sugar over bars, if desired.

made myself available when that cookie package arrived, and I've often dreamed of them since.

Dream Bars were baked in a rush of last-minute motherly love, before I turned Aric over to college cafeteria cooks. I'm embarrassed how many times I reminded him during our last dinner together, "You're going to miss me when you're gone."

This recipe was adapted from a California State Fair winner in "America's Best State Fair Recipes," written by Catherine Hanley, who I'd known during her long career at Pillsbury.

Sweet's Success
November 8

The history of pralines could inspire a juicy potboiler novel or TV miniseries weaving together French nobility, American wealth, sex, religion, innovation and intrigue.

According to Louisiana chef John D. Folse (owner of Lafitte's Landing restaurant in Donaldson, La., whose recipe we tried successfully), the sweet was invented by Marechal duc de Choiseul Praslin, who lived during the reign of French King Louis XII and was famous for his battlefield and boudoir victories.

The Marechal wooed ladies by giving them bonbons. But one day, close to a conquest, he ran out of candy. So he ordered his chef, Jean Dulac, to the kitchen to stir up a batch, using what was in the cupboard — sugar and almonds.

The new candy worked the usual magic, and friends pressed the amorous one for the recipe, naming the new confection "Praslin" in his honor. The name evolved to praline because the French do not pronounce the "s."

Now comes the religious part. Ursuline nuns, familiar with classical cookery of France but probably unaware of pralines' lascivious origin, brought the recipe to Nouvelle Orleans. However, there were no almonds growing in what was to become Louisiana. Native pecans were substituted.

Pralines' reputation for romance was confirmed in New Orleans. They became the sweet staple in magnificent ballrooms where sons of Louisiana's wealthy planters danced with beautiful Creole girls called Quadroons, indicating traces of black heritage.

Today, pralines are ubiquitous in "Nawlins," as the natives say it. Before our weeklong food writers' conference was over, we had tasted pralines daily. Large pralines. Tiny pralines. Smooth pralines. Sugary pralines — unfortunately, mostly sugary pralines.

LAFITTE'S LANDING PRALINES
Makes 27 to 30 pralines

- 2 cups light brown sugar
- 1 cup white sugar
- 1 cup water
- 1 cup heavy cream
- 1 tablespoon vanilla extract
- 1 1/2 cups chopped pecans
- 1 1/2 cups pecan halves

In heavy-bottom saucepan, combine sugars, water and cream over medium-high heat. Cook to soft-ball stage, 238 degrees (not a degree more, or they'll sugar). Remove from heat. Using wire whisk, whip until creamy. Working quickly, mix in vanilla and nuts. Drop by spoonfuls onto buttered sheet pan. Let cool. Store in airtight container.

At Home on the Iron Range

— Tales and Tastes from My Red-Ore Roots —

Stirring the Melting Pot of Ethnic Cuisines

September 21, 1981

Hordes of former Iron Rangers have relocated to "The Cities," as we who grew up in Northern Minnesota's mining region called St. Paul and Minneapolis. Eventually, we shake the red iron dust from the soles of our shoes, but we never quite surrender, in our souls, fondness for the Range and its ethnic blend of citizens. Nor do we lose our taste for their cooking traditions.

A wedding on the Iron Range isn't considered sanctified unless the nuptial buffet is piled with potica, a walnut-filled sweet bread, or sarmas, those meat-stuffed cabbage rolls, both brought to the Northland by Eastern European immigrants. So many sarmas have been made on the Range that they'd pave Hibbing's Howard Street from end to end.

Pasties, porketta, pulla — we all grew up with them, no matter our ethnic heritage, because if our own families didn't make them, our friends did.

The Iron Range has often been called a Melting Pot. I'd term it a Stew Pot for all the flavors that have been stirred together by those hearty families who came to work the iron mines and stayed to build the

necklace of towns strung between the pits and the dumps.

Through good times, when the mines were at their most productive, and during bad times, when economic devastation depressed that rusty landscape, substantial and diverse food sustained people on the Range.

Monitoring Range Fare
July 26, 1987

Phyllis Hanes, food editor for the Christian Science Monitor in Boston and a longtime friend, asked me to give her a food tour of the Range for a series of regional stories she was writing:

The wonderful aspect of Iron Range food, the concept I wanted Phyllis to understand and experience, is that the Range of my youth — and still today— is an area without food prejudices. We all made and ate Italian porketta and Cornish pasties brought by Finns who migrated from Michigan's mines where they might have met a Cousin Jack (Welsh miner) or two, and Slavic potica and dozens of other foods that neighbors shared with neighbors, no matter what port the boats left from when they sailed to America.

Potica: Pastry on a Roll
December 5, 1981

Pronounce it po-teet-za.

We all knew how to say it, and many in my mother's generation knew how to make it. Mom was one of those Melting Pot citizens, a full Finn, who made both pasties and potica.

Just after she died in 1980, I tried a potica recipe sent to me by a food company. If my mother had still been alive, she never would have recognized the results:

I'm not saying the company's version is unworthy. But it's not the potica I watched Iron Range ladies make when I was a kid. A covey of them, none with long fingernails, stood around a dining room table covered with a bedsheet, stretching and stretching dough until it was strudel-thin and as big as the bedding.

Then they spread a filling of ground walnuts, honey, brown sugar, eggs, cream and maybe cinnamon over the sheet of dough. Lifting an edge of the bedsheet to urge the dough forward, the ladies would create a roll of potica of perhaps 30 layers. It was divided into pieces that would fit on baking pans. Sliced for eating, it displayed a whirl of filling separated by gossamer layers of pastry. A masterpiece.

A year later, I finally found potica as it should be:

While in northern Minnesota in November, I read the Duluth News-Tribune and Herald's holiday cookbook compiling recipes from regional luminaries. Included were three from a woman I've known of for years, "Big Helen," who now lives in Hibbing. Some say she's the best cook on the Range, a reputation she earned when she owned, for two decades, the Oreland Cafe in Nashwauk (a mining town between Hibbing and Grand Rapids).

She and my mother worked together there in the early '50s before Helen bought it. My mother cooked for about a year because my folks had bought a new Oldsmobile and she was determined to pay for it fast.

"Those were the days," Helen Drazenovich Berklich told me when I reached her via phone. "Your mom and I only had to look at a customer to know how he wanted his hamburger fixed."

I used to get giggling fits as a young teen-ager listening to orders at the Oreland, especially the morning miner's call for "graveyard stew," less sepulchrally known as milk toast.

Many a time I've written in this column that a wedding or a holiday is not officially celebrated on the Iron Range unless potica and sarmas are served. After testing Helen's potica recipe clipped from the Duluth paper, I called her for more details. It was the day before Thanksgiving, and she was making potica and sarmas for the next day's feast. It would be the last meal she'd cook in her Hibbing house, where for the last several years, now that her own four sons are grown, she'd opened her boundless big heart to care for young retarded men.

"My legs are giving out," she told me, admitting they're supporting 280 pounds of Big Helen. "I'm moving to a senior-citizens home in Grand Rapids, which is right across from a new YWCA where they have aerobic dancing and exercise equipment. When you see me next. I'll be like Venus de Milo with arms."

My rolled potica had spilled fillings from the ends while baking, and the recipe didn't say what size pans to use. I asked Helen for advice.

"Who the hell measures?" salty Helen said about pan size. She uses a heavy cake pan she got "when everybody on the Range was buying waterless cookware." Whatever pan you use, she advised in her deep voice, make sure it's a heavy one with sides, then cut the rolls to fit. To keep the filling inside, pinch the ends of the rolls.

The dough may require more than 5 cups of flour, but it turned out to be the loveliest, most elastic strudel dough I've ever experienced.

BIG HELEN'S WALNUT POTICA
Makes 3 loaves

Dough:
- 1 cup milk
- 1/2 cup sugar
- 2 teaspoons salt
- 1/4 pound (1 stick) butter
- 2 small cakes fresh yeast or 1 package dry yeast
- 1/2 cup warm water
- 2 tablespoons sugar
- 4 eggs, well beaten
- 5 cups flour

Filling:
- 1/4 pound (1 stick) butter
- 1 cup honey
- 1 cup sugar
- 1 cup milk
- 2 pounds walnuts, ground
- 2 eggs, well beaten
- 1 cup whipping cream
- 1 tablespoon lemon juice

To make dough: Scald milk. Add 1/2 cup sugar, salt and butter. Set aside to cool. Dissolve yeast in warm water with about 2 tablespoons sugar. Set aside until foamy. Add yeast mixture to milk mixture. Add well-beaten eggs. Add flour, 1 cup at a time, beating by hand or electric mixer. Keep adding flour until dough can be handled without sticking. Knead dough on floured board for about 20 minutes. Put dough in bowl. Cover. Let rise in warm place for 2 hours, or until doubled in bulk. (Note: Do not knead dough after it has risen.)

To shape dough: Spread dough on cloth-covered table sprinkled with flour. First roll out dough. Then pull with hands from center to outer edge of table until thin, as for strudel. Dough should be at least 3 feet square. Cut off thick edges.

To make filling: While dough rises, melt butter. Add honey, sugar and milk. Bring to a rolling boil. In another bowl, mix walnuts, eggs, whipping cream and lemon juice. Pour butter-honey mixture over nuts. Mix. Spread filling all over dough. Roll up as for jellyroll. Cut roll into 3 pieces about 12 to 14 inches long. Put into greased pans. Cover. Keep in warm place for about 1/2 hour. Bake in 325-degree oven for 1 hour.

Big Helen's potica is as authentic as any I've ever tasted on the Range. Like fruitcake, it needs a little aging to make it slice perfectly. If you can't eat it all within a week, extra loaves freeze nicely.

Porketta: We Rolled Our Own

Date unknown

Italians contributed porketta to the Iron Range menu, and now everyone has a favorite version, including my all-Finn cousin Betty Rostvold of Keewatin and Hart Lake. Those who don't want to make the fennel-flavored pork from scratch can get "store-bought," ready to bake, at practically any Range supermarket and even in some Twin Cities stores. After porketta is roasted to fall-apart doneness, shreds or thin slices are typically eaten in sandwiches. I tried other porketta recipes for the column, but this one is the most dependable.

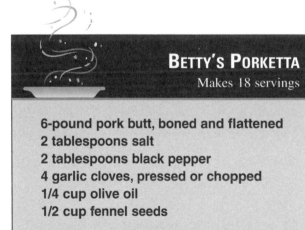

BETTY'S PORKETTA

Makes 18 servings

6-pound pork butt, boned and flattened
2 tablespoons salt
2 tablespoons black pepper
4 garlic cloves, pressed or chopped
1/4 cup olive oil
1/2 cup fennel seeds

Combine seasonings. Rub on both sides of pork. Roll and tie porketta. Roast in 350-degree oven for about 3 hours, until roast falls apart. Note: Some versions also add chopped parsley to seasoning mixture.

Pasties: Neat Meat Pie

September 12, 1982

Anyone who grew up on the Iron Range probably tasted pasties not long after being introduced to Pabulum. Brought to the Range by Cornish miners and their Finn co-workers who had previously toiled in northern Michigan's copper mines, the dough-wrapped meat-and-vegetable pies were soon carried by all nationalities in their lunch buckets.

On the Range, pasties are an institution, not only for good eating but for fund-raising. Ladies Aids at the Lutheran, Methodist and Catholic churches all had pasty day when I was growing up, selling the pies individually, or by the dozen to folks who filled their freezers.

Loyalties are still fierce on the Range, not only to a certain style of pasty, but to the people who make them. My cousin's husband told me about pasty day at the mines. On the Catholic church's day to sell pasties, Catholic miners sign up to buy, and when the Methodist ladies are bringing pasties, the Methodists are their best customers. If churches aren't selling, the Sunrise Bakery in Hibbing is a good source.

Variations on pasties are rife. Most people in northern Minnesota put fillings on half the pastry, fold over the other half and crimp the edges in a semi-circle. In Michigan, some bakers put the fillings in the middle of the dough circle and bring the sides up to the top. Minnesotans prefer cubed vegetables; in Michigan, they might grind them.

One Minnesota cook sautes her meat cubes and onion before adding raw vegetables. Another scoffed at that idea, but she uses hamburger instead of cubed raw meat. "Easier that way," she said.

There are two schools of pasty bakers: those who put their meat on the bottom and vegetables on top, and those who add meat last so its juices drip through the vegetables. I agree with the meat-on-top method.

Ah, the vegetables. Potatoes are a must with everyone. So are onions, and don't be afraid to use enough to flavor the pie. Nothing is more lackluster than a bland pasty. I grew up with carrots in pasties, but some bakers insist on rutabagas. You could use both, grating them if you wish. Never grate the potatoes, however. They should be tiny dice so they'll cook through but retain their shape.

Layering the ingredients may be esthetically pure, but it's easier to put all the vegetables in a bowl, add salt and pepper, and toss everything well before combining with meat and pastry.

THE REAL ELLEN OSTMAN'S PASTY

Makes 2 large pasties

Pastry for 2 large crusts
2 cups peeled and finely diced potatoes
1/2 cup peeled and finely diced carrots
1/2 cup finely diced onion
1 cup peeled and finely diced rutabaga (optional)
1 teaspoon salt
1/2 teaspoon freshly ground pepper, or to taste
1/4 pound round steak, cut into small cubes
Butter

Make pastry. Chill for 1 hour. Peel and finely dice vegetables (adjust proportions as you wish). Toss with salt and pepper. Roll half of pastry into large round. Place half of vegetables (drained first, if necessary) on 1 side of pastry. Top with cubed meat. Sprinkle with salt and pepper. Add a few bits of butter. Fold over other half of pastry. Tightly crimp edges so filling stays put. Carefully lift pasty onto baking sheet. Cut 2 or 3 small slits in top for steam to escape. Repeat with remaining pastry and filling ingredients. Bake in 375-degree oven for 50 to 60 minutes, or until pastry is nicely browned. Serve hot, with ketchup, if desired.

And now the crust. Lard crust is best, every pasty baker agrees. Ground suet is even more flavorful. And a few dabs of butter dotting the meat and vegetables won't hurt, either.

More than a decade later, when I received bound galleys of their work-in-progress, I was thrilled that Minneapolis co-authors Beth Dooley and Lucia Watson (chef-owner of Lucia's) had included my mother's pasty recipe in their book, "Savoring the Seasons of the Northern Heartland."

What a lovely memorial to a great cook. I immediately planned to buy Christmas copies for all my relatives until I read the recipe and realized my mother would have never recognized it. Garlic? Thyme? Nutmeg? Not in my mother's pasties! Further, my mother always used lard crust, and their pastry had two sticks of butter and two egg yolks in it.

I called Dooley, and she was apologetic. Though the offending ingredients couldn't be deleted, there was still time to print "optional" beside them. Watson told me later that she was the one who couldn't resist tinkering with the original, and Dooley said soothingly, "We hope it will be something your mom would have enjoyed."

So we tried it, and the northern pasty lovers who savored it said the touch of garlic could stay, and a hint of nutmeg wasn't offensive, but the thyme had to go.

Better to stick with the basics. Here is pasty in the style of my mother and countless other Iron Range cooks. Add garlic and nutmeg if you, like Lucia, can't leave it alone. My mother liked to put the meat on top so it cooked thoroughly and its juices could drift down through the vegetables.

We Knew Him When

August 15, 1976

Sentimental journey? Nostalgia trip? Big Bash might be the better description for the Hibbing High School All-Class reunion, which drew thousands, including this 1958 grad. The old town jumped like it never did in the days they were blasting for iron ore.

The class mixer was in a hall as hot as a sauna. Bob Dylan, nee Zimmerman, Hibbing's most famous alumnus, did not show up, but if he had, we probably wouldn't have noticed him in the crush.

Two decades earlier, my Hibbing High classmates and I heard Bobby Zimmerman's first public performance, at the school talent show. It offered no clue of his future fame. As I recall, the principal got the hook and yanked him offstage before he pounded the auditorium's Steinway into matchsticks.

Famous Rangers: Cooks and Others
December 27, 1981

Jeno Paulucci and his mother, Michelina.

The Iron Range has its share of Famous People beyond Bob Dylan, among them Boston Celtics basketball star Kevin McHale and food entrepreneur Jeno Paulucci, both from Hibbing. A column about Elizabeth Paulucci, Jeno's older sister and longtime business associate, told of her "Cookbook From a Melting Pot" describing the food of her Hibbing heritage. Here's what the column said about our shared experiences:

Hibbing is a hard town for returning to one's roots. This summer, I was showing a visitor the Hull-Rust mine, and I realized that more than a third of my life had been gouged from the earth. Washington Grade School, mentioned by Paulucci in her book, where both she and I learned to read, is gone, as is the lavish marble and muraled Carnegie Library, the hospital where I was born — the entire town of North Hibbing, in fact.

Also gone is Lincoln Junior High. Paulucci reminds me of its home-economics department where "each student had a miniature kitchen complete with cupboards stocked with ingredients and an individual little stove." That's where I learned the wonders of white sauce. To this day, I hate Eggs Goldenrod, lesson two in seventh-grade home ec.

Hibbing High School is still there, that castle dripping crystal chandeliers and opulence befitting its $6 million price tag in 1920. Paulucci recalls the home-ec department had sterling silver, beautiful linens and bone china. I don't remember those at all, but maybe we thought nothing of such luxuries when mining was at its heyday and schools were the foremost beneficiary of mining taxes. From somewhere, Paulucci dredged the statistic that when the high school was built, Hibbing spent as much tax money a year as the city of Minneapolis.

Paulucci learned to cook from her mother, Michelina (who is now immortalized by a line of Jeno-designed pasta products named after her). Not all the recipes in her book were Italian; she shared this one that she told me had been making the rounds of the Range for years. I loved the wine stew for its simplicity. Be sure to use totally trimmed stew meat, or make the stew a day early, cool it, lift off any fat, then reheat the rest. Adding some white pearl onions was suggested in Testing Results.

"GIVING A PARTY" BURGUNDY STEW

Makes 14 to 16 servings

5 pounds beef stew meat
2 cans (10 3/4 ounces each) golden
　mushroom soup
2 cans (10 3/4 ounces each) onion soup
　with beef broth
1 cup dry red wine (burgundy or chianti)
1 can (about 4 ounces) sliced
　mushrooms
Cooked rice, egg noodles or potatoes

Cut beef into uniform bite-size pieces. Put into covered Dutch oven with soups and wine. Cook, covered, in 315-degree oven for 4 hours. Remove cover near end of cooking time to allow gravy to thicken. Add mushrooms. Serve over wild rice, long-grain rice, egg noodles or creamy au gratin potatoes. After party, freeze any leftovers. (Note: Recipe can be cut in half.)

A Finn Cook Who Made Good

October 17, 1982

Duluth is where iron ore (now taconite pellets) from the Range is railroaded so it can ride to eastern mills via Great Lakes ore boats. This collection of Iron Range recipes expands its boundaries slightly to include one from my favorite Duluth cook, Beatrice Ojakangas, who has become a good friend over the years. "Peaches" and I share a northern Minnesota Finnish upbringing, hers near Floodwood. The very first loaf of bread I ever baked was her Chunk

BEATRICE OJAKANGAS' WILD RICE THREE-GRAIN BREAD

Makes 2 loaves
(or 1 braid or 4 baguettes)

1 package active dry yeast
1/3 cup warm water (105 to 115 degrees)
2 cups milk, scalded, cooled to 105 to
　115 degrees
2 tablespoons butter or lard, melted
1 tablespoon salt
1/2 cup honey
1/2 cup uncooked rolled oats
1/2 cup rye flour
2 cups whole-wheat flour
About 4 cups bread flour or all-purpose
　flour
1 cup cooked wild rice
1 egg beaten with 1 tablespoon water
1/2 cup hulled sunflower seeds, plain or
　salted

To make bread: In large bowl, dissolve yeast in water. Add milk, butter, salt and honey. Stir in oats, rye flour, whole-wheat flour and 2 cups bread flour to make soft dough. Add wild rice. Cover dough. Let rest for 15 minutes. Stir in enough additional bread flour to make stiff dough. Turn out onto bread board. Knead 10 minutes. Add more flour as necessary to keep dough from sticking. Turn dough into lightly greased bowl. Turn over. Cover. Let rise for 2 hours, or until doubled. Punch down. Knead briefly on lightly oiled board.

To bake bread: Shape as desired, either into large braided wreath, into 4 long French baguettes or into 2 loaves placed in 9-by-5-inch bread pans. Let rise for 45 minutes, or until doubled. Brush tops of loaves with egg mixed with water. Slash if desired. Sprinkle with sunflower seeds. Bake in 375-degree oven for 45 minutes, or until loaves sound hollow when tapped.

O'Cheese bread, with which she won second place in the 1957 Pillsbury Bake-Off. She was quite a heroine to northern Minnesota cooks back then.

Ojakangas has since written a shelf-full of cookbooks, and for years, she wrote "The Liberated Cook" column in the Duluth News Tribune. She's always testing, too, and she told me about the problems of feeding a family "ordinary food":

"Every day at our house, meals are essentially leftovers — food left from the day's experimentation. It could be three varieties of chicken salad, two rejects and one that worked. Or it could be six samples of barbecued food. Worst of all, according to my youngest daughter, it would be zucchini in almost every form."

I was impressed the first time I visited Ojakangas' rural Duluth home to attend a wild-rice seminar. Not only did she have two ranges, two regular refrigerators, two microwave ovens and enough pots and pans to run a small hotel, but she'd also installed a

MARY RANIELE'S SPAGHETTI SAUCE
Makes 6 or more servings

Sauce:
- 1/2 cup oil
- 6 big country spareribs with some fat on them
- Salt, pepper and garlic salt
- 5 cans (6 ounces each) tomato paste
- 1 teaspoon sweet basil
- 3 large garlic cloves
- 1 can (29 ounces) tomato puree
- 1 can (29 ounces) tomato sauce
- 1 can (8 ounces) tomato sauce
- 3/4 teaspoon oregano
- 4 teaspoons fresh parsley
- 4 tablespoons real romano cheese, grated

Meatballs:
- 1 pound hamburger (use pork, if desired)
- 3/4 cup bread crumbs
- 2 tablespoons milk
- 2 eggs
- 3 small garlic cloves
- 1/2 teaspoon sweet basil
- 1/2 teaspoon oregano
- Salt and pepper to taste
- 3 heaping tablespoons Romano cheese

To make sauce: Heat oil in large pot. Brown ribs. Add generous amount of salt, pepper and garlic salt. Continue to brown ribs very slowly for 45 to 60 minutes. Add tomato paste, rinsing out cans with a little water and adding water to pot. Stir in basil. Cut in cloves of garlic. Cook slowly for 45 minutes. Add tomato puree and both cans of tomato sauce. Again, rinse cans with water and add water to pot. Stir in oregano and parsley. Let mixture come to a boil. Simmer slowly for 4 to 5 hours. During last half of cooking, add romano cheese. Sauce is done when oil comes to top. Taste sauce for seasoning, adding more basil or oregano as needed. Pour sauce over hot cooked spaghetti. Serve with ribs.

To make meatballs: Soften bread crumbs with milk. Add to hamburger along with eggs, garlic, seasonings and cheese. Mix well. Coat hands with oil. Roll mixture into balls. Brown in skillet. Add meatballs to sauce just before serving.

walk-in refrigerator. This woman is a serious cook. From that seminar, I shared this truly excellent Minnesota-style bread from one of the nation's great bakers.

Spaghetti Sauce, Raniele Style
July 15, 1984

Every Iron Range cook has a specialty. Some are secretive, but the late Mary Raniele of Keewatin willingly shared the spaghetti sauce she developed as a young (non-Italian) bride:

"When I married Mimi (her Italian husband, who in addition to working in the mines ran the Keewatin movie theater, where this writer spent much of her youth), I had to learn how to make spaghetti sauce. So I watched all the old Italian ladies in Keewatin making their sauces, and I picked up ideas here and there. When I finally made the sauce this way, Mimi told me to quit experimenting. I'd gotten it right." She knows the recipe so well that she recites it by heart. What you see here is what she told to me.

She also told my cousin, Betty, who frequently makes the sauce in memory of her dear friend. Betty replaces large spareribs with bite-size riblets.

Going to the Chappel's
February 19, 1989

Did you see the Valentine's Day television report about Gov. Rudy and Lola Perpich returning to the place their romance began? Chappel's soda fountain in Keewatin is where they fell in love. That's where I fell in love, too — with ice cream.

We lived close to Keewatin, and Chappel's, with its dark uncushioned wooden booths and twirling counter stools, was the source for the occasional pint of ice cream my folks would buy to treat their toddler.

We'd eat the vanilla brick (always vanilla, my dad's favorite) immediately because it was wartime and our new house couldn't be wired for electricity, so we had no freezer.

In later years, Chappel's was where I'd eat summertime sundaes, and maybe they were scooped by Lola Simic, the dark-haired Keewatin gal whose first job was at that old-time soda fountain. I didn't notice, so smitten was I with ice cream. But a Hibbing lad, Rudy Perpich, did take note of the girl behind the counter.

Chappel's was demolished last week, minutes after the Perpiches left with a souvenir, the booth in which they'd courted. A bulldozer destroyed the fragile old frame structure, creating yet another empty lot on Keewatin's main street. But the Perpiches' love endures. So does mine — for ice cream.

"Imported" Sarmas
February 26, 1989

The Perpiches helped make sarmas famous throughout Minnesota. When they moved from Hibbing into the governor's mansion, the Croatian specialty was sometimes on the menu.

Milly Sorenson, who lives across from my childhood home, also brought sarmas to the Twin Cities, to be served at a potluck wedding uniting her daughter, Anita Leach, to Don Pouchnik, originally from Eveleth:

On the Range, heritage is important. I heard one of the bride's relatives inquiring about the groom, "Just what nationality is he?" Iron Rangers keep track of such things.

Milly is a perfect example. She has Swedish blood in her veins, but she brought sarmas, Eastern European in origin. She rattled off the recipe to me at the reception, adding that she'd gotten it "from Mrs. Markovich in Keewatin," and that Pete Michelich, a since-retired grocer in Keewatin, "was the only one who really knew how to grind sarma meat." That's the Iron Range.

MILLY'S SARMAS
Makes 20 or more

1 pound lean ground beef
2 pounds lean ground pork
1 medium onion, ground
Scant 1/2 cup raw white rice
Salt and pepper
Garlic (optional)
1 head cabbage
1 package fresh or frozen sauerkraut

To make filling: Combine meats, onion, rice and seasonings. Mix well. Form into rolls about 2 inches long, using 1/2 cup of mixture for each.

To form rolls: Remove leaves from head of cabbage. Gently simmer for a few minutes until softened. Wrap cabbage leaf around each meat roll, tucking in ends.

To bake sarmas: In deep baking pan or slow cooker, alternate layers of sauerkraut and sarmas until all are used. Bake in 350-degree oven for about an hour, or until meat is cooked.

Mojakka: Here's Looking At You
August 20, 1989

Every Iron Range Finn knows the word "mojakka" (pronounced moy-a-ca), and when most of us hear it, we think of fish mojakka, made with northern pike, potatoes, onions and milk. True mojakka contains the fishhead. It's been called the stew that looks back at you.

"Mojakka" is a word unknown, linguists say, in Finland. It may be the "Finnglish" way of asking for more of the meat version of the stew served in northwoods logging camps, cooked on the back of a wood stove for so long that it looked like something unprintable in a family newspaper.

That treatise announced the first International Mojakka Cook-Off during Finnish ethnic day at Ironworld USA near Chisholm. Liha, or beef, rather than fish, was the specified main ingredient:

One of the prize-winning teams did something no old-time Finn cook would think of — they browned the meat. Now, I'm not saying that browning meat is a bad idea, and it undoubtedly gave the stew more flavor, but true mojakka is boiled beef and vegetables.

ELMA AND SONIA'S BEEF MOJAKKA
Makes 4 servings

2 quarts water
1/2 pound beef
Soup bone
10 whole allspice
4 small rutabagas, cut up
1 small onion, cut up
2 small carrots, cut up
4 medium potatoes, cut up
Salt and pepper to taste

Bring water to a boil. Add beef and soup bone. Cook, skimming pot occasionally. Remove meat when tender. Add allspice, rutabaga, onion and carrots to broth. Cook for 30 minutes. Add potatoes. Cut up meat and return to pot. Continue simmering until vegetables are tender. Season to taste.

Elma Salmi of Chisholm, the contest's most authentic cook, knows how to simmer Finlander mojakka. She made it every week of her working life for the residents of Pyrinto, the Finnish boardinghouse in Chisholm. She met her husband, Neil, at the boardinghouse, and he tumbled at first bite of her mojakka and rye flatbread.

True mojakka, Salmi says, "is made just plain." That some people add celery and tomatoes offends her. Salmi's one nod to "fancy" cooking is liberal use of whole allspice. But when the Duluth newspaper printed her recipe and indicated that she also used whole peppercorns, Salmi was not willing to go that far. "Just regular ground pepper," she told me.

Now widowed, Salmi tends her own large home and garden, and this summer, at age 73, she picked 70 quarts of wild blueberries. Mojakka comes from that part of the world where all the women are strong.

For the competition, Elma Salmi cooked with her friend, Sonia Johnson of Balkan township north of Chisholm.

Antipasto Passes the Test

September 9, 1990

To this day, Tom Commerford of Keewatin makes me quake. He retired from a 31-year career as a driver's license examiner in the Grand Rapids-Hibbing-International Falls region, when he had godlike control over area teen-agers dreaming of driving.

A gruff guy, he made that critical passage to adulthood even more terrifying. I don't remember if I passed my first behind-the-wheel attempt, but I do remember nudging the stanchions while parallel parking. Tom, you should see me parallel park now — you scared me into competence.

After that magic day when I turned 15 1/2 and that coveted license was mine (we could get them at a younger age in those days), Commerford and I didn't cross paths — until a luncheon for Keewatinites at the Governor's Residence earlier this year, nearly 35 years later.

"FOGARTY'S" ANTIPASTO
Makes 40 pints

- 1 bushel red bell peppers, cut into bite-sized pieces
- 2 1/2 cups olive oil
- 1 hot banana pepper, diced small
- 6 cans (2 ounces each) anchovies, undrained
- 2 cups white vinegar
- 1 bottle Heinz hot ketchup
- 44 ounces tomato sauce
- 1 1/2 cups sugar
- 6 cans (6 1/2 ounces each) tuna in oil, undrained
- 6 cans (4 ounces each) mushrooms, drained
- 2 packages (1 pound each) pickling onions
- 2 quarts green salad olives
- 2 quarts sliced black olives
- Cauliflower, blanched (optional)
- Sliced and blanched carrots (optional)
- Yellow or green beans (optional)

To make "juice": Blanch peppers in boiling water for 1 1/2 minutes. Immediately plunge peppers into ice-cold water. (Note: Don't wash peppers; just wipe them before blanching.) In saucepan, heat oil, hot pepper and anchovies over medium heat until anchovies dissolve. Add vinegar, ketchup, tomato sauce and sugar. Boil for 10 minutes, stirring constantly. Add blanched peppers, tuna, mushrooms, onions and all olives. Bring to a boil. When this "juice" is done, add all other vegetables (cauliflowers, carrots, etc.), but not too many; the more vegetables, the less flavor.

To process antipasto: Place mixture in sterilized pint jars. Seal. Process in pressure canner for 15 minutes.

When he and I met again, I told him how terrified I'd been of him when I took that driving test. "The way you kids drove terrified me, too," he admitted.

With that same stern tone that I remembered him using to command me to release the hand brake during that test, he now ordered me to stop at his house in Keewatin and get a jar of his antipasto. "Only if you'll share the recipes," I said bravely.

That's why you're meeting Tom Commerford, alias "Fogarty," and his antipasto today. Really, he's a sweet guy, and a great hunting-camp cook, I hear, who shares antipasto with all his friends.

"The very best antipasto" is what Commerford titled his red-pepper recipe written in Irish-green ink on a yellow legal sheet. This was followed by an underlined warning: "Do Not Deviate From This Recipe." Those

words hit me with the same dread as if he'd been lecturing me about not deviating from my lane and crossing the double yellow line. What would happen if I altered his instructions? Could he take my license away after all these years?

During Labor Day weekend, we labored. My cousin Betty contributed the canner and more than half of the work. A non-canner, I let Betty deal with the pressure gauges, rings and lids because she knows what she's doing. My Aunt Impi helped cut up all those peppers, which were wiped rather than washed to keep them from going mushy in the can (advice from Betty's husband, Looch, who has an opinion on everything).

Polka music playing on WMFG radio from Hibbing set the beat as we packed peppers and opened tuna cans. Parsimonious Aunt Impi was aghast at the price of anchovies, just six to the can. "It would have been cheaper to salt some minnows," she said.

Of course, I wouldn't think of such a thing. Commerford would revoke my cooking license for that.

MILLY SORENSON'S SYLTA
Makes 2 loaves

3 pounds lean pork butt, cut into 3 or 4 chunks
3 to 4 pork hocks (with skin and bones)
2 medium onions, ground
1 tablespoon salt (or more to taste)
Heaping teaspoon of whole allspice

To prepare meat: In large kettle, combine chunks of pork butt and pork hocks. Add enough water to cover meat. Bring to a simmer. Cover. Boil for 45 minutes, or until meat is quite well done. Remove meat from liquid. Allow liquid to cool. Skim off fat. Meanwhile, remove bones and skin from meat. Grind meat.

To form loaves: In kettle, return skimmed juice to a boil. Add onions, salt and allspice. Add meat. Pour mixture into 2 loaf pans. Allow to cool. (Note: Loaves will firm up after several hours.) Slice and serve. Refrigerate leftovers.

Sylta: Secret to Swedish Longevity?
September 13, 1992

Eleven silver-haired siblings lined up at the head table in Keewatin's Senior Citizens Center last weekend — a living testament to the value of good genes.

For the first time in recent memory, all of the surviving Lundin brothers and sisters were gathered to celebrate the 90th birthday of Esther Lundin Hunter of Hibbing. And she isn't the oldest living child of Peter Lundin and his wife, Albertina Norberg Lundin. Of those at the table, aged 91 to a tagalong 71, not one is in a nursing home. They all maintain their own residences, most of them in the Grand Rapids-Jacobson area, close to where they were born.

Aside from those common signs of aging — eyeglasses and snowy hair (the two brothers still have plenty to comb) — they are in darned good shape. Once there were 13, but one child died in infancy, and a brother, Victor, died at age 52. The rest keep perking as steadily as a potful of Swedish coffee.

I remember Grandpa Lundin, tall and gray-haired, who lived to be nearly 90 himself. He and Albertina met not in Sweden, but at the Swan River railway station near Jacobson. Peter Lundin had homesteaded in Minnesota for five years and accumulated enough prosperity that a friend was able to borrow $200 to send passage for his intended Swedish bride. He also designated Lundin to meet the girl at the train — and that was that. The other fellow had to look elsewhere for a wife.

At the 90th birthday party for her mother, our beloved Hibbing neighbor Milly Sorenson made the Swedish sylta that her mother and all the other children of Grandpa Lundin adore.

Note: As this book was being written, Milly made sylta for her mother's 95th birthday party — and all of those 11 Lundins were still alive to celebrate.

Is This the Real "Ting"?
July 11, 1993

Hibbing, my hometown, is celebrating its 100th birthday this summer. I had intended to note the occasion with an uncomplicated column based on the "Hibbing Centennial Cookbook." But instead, I've become mired in controversy over a barbecue sauce from Ting Town, near the current location of Iron World between Chisholm and Hibbing.

Rangers who've taken a bit of tread off their tires remember Ting Town, a summertime-only drive-in specializing in beef, pork or ham sandwiches dripping with hot barbecue or relish-like sweet sauces.

The claim has been made that Ting Town, built in 1930, was Minnesota's first drive-in. Save for three years during World War II meat rationing, it was open continuously until the mid-1970s.

Its demise is attributed to errant snowmobilers who, it is surmised, started a fire inside to warm up. That bonfire burned the octagonal building to ashes. As

owner Rose Portugue of Chisholm watched the flames, she decided that she'd served her last barbecue sandwich.

My St. Paul neighbor, Jayne Niemi, a Chisholm native, was a teen-age carhop during Ting Town's latter years, and she remembers riding to work in Portugue's car, sharing the back seat with pans of meat that had been roasting in Rose's home kitchen all day, ready for the 4 p.m. opening.

Before Jayne told me how it was done at Ting Town, I'd tested a barbecue sauce recipe, supposedly from the long-gone drive-in, found in that centennial cookbook. I added sliced roast beef to the tomato sauce.

"TING TOWN" BARBECUE SAUCE
Makes about 6 cups

1/4 cup butter
1 green onion, chopped
1 onion, finely chopped
1/4 cup sugar
1 teaspoon salt
2 teaspoons paprika
1 teaspoon Worcestershire sauce
3 cans (8 ounces each) tomato sauce
3 cups ketchup
1 cup wine or cider vinegar
2 teaspoons celery seed
2 teaspoons dry mustard
1/2 teaspoon pepper

Saute onions in butter. Mix onions with all remaining ingredients. Simmer for 2 hours, stirring occasionally. (Note: Thirty minutes is enough.) Serve with roasted ham, beef or pork for sandwiches.

"No, no," Jayne admonished, telling me beef or pork were shredded and ham was shaved, then loaded into a bun. That's when sauce was added by Rose, the only one who made the sandwiches.

Ting Town was tiny, just a few tables inside, and an outhouse across the parking lot. Rose didn't offer french fries. She'd make a hamburger only if someone insisted, "and she always made a face when we put in a burger order," Jayne remembers.

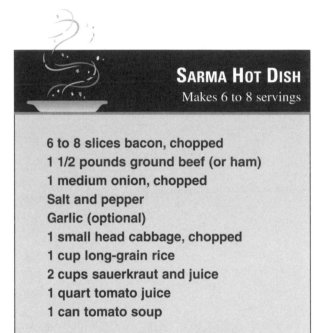

SARMA HOT DISH
Makes 6 to 8 servings

6 to 8 slices bacon, chopped
1 1/2 pounds ground beef (or ham)
1 medium onion, chopped
Salt and pepper
Garlic (optional)
1 small head cabbage, chopped
1 cup long-grain rice
2 cups sauerkraut and juice
1 quart tomato juice
1 can tomato soup

Fry bacon until crisp. Remove from pan. Add beef or ham and onion. Brown slightly. Add salt and pepper (and garlic, if you wish) to taste. Grease large casserole with butter. Line casserole bottom and sides with chopped cabbage. Add rice and bacon to meat mixture. Spoon into casserole. Top with most of sauerkraut and juice. Mix tomato juice and tomato soup. Pour over meat mixture. Top with a thin layer of cabbage and remaining kraut. Bake, covered, in 350-degree oven for 2 to 2 1/2 hours. (Note: During baking, check to see if there is enough liquid for rice to absorb as it cooks. If there is excess liquid, remove cover during last 20 minutes.)

Rose was most unbendale about the secret sauce recipes, which she and her husband, Elmer, had perfected over the years. She never, ever gave them out.

"She guarded them with her life," Jayne said. Which, of course, challenged inventive Iron Rangers to attempt to duplicate Ting Town's sauces, especially after the fire.

Vienna Sainio Hoberle donated to the Hibbing cookbook the recipe for Ting Town Barbecue Sauce, which she says she got "from a good source."

Her version may be close, but it's not the real thing, insisted Rose's son, Jerry Portugue. "Mother has never given it away. The sauces were a family secret," he insisted. "Nobody went into the kitchen when they were being made."

When I suggested he might like to make the cookbook's recipe to see how close it is to the original, Jerry said flat out, "I don't have to try it because I know they don't have it."

So I asked my neighbor Jayne to make the sauce, since she certainly served it and ate it often enough in her young life.

"It's close," she said of the impostor sauce, but added she would reduce the vinegar slightly. Follow that suggestion, and you probably won't have to balance the sauce with brown sugar, as I did.

The real secret, Jayne said, may be in the way Rose cooked those moist panfuls of meat that rode in the backseat on summer afternoons.

Shortcut Sarmas
July 11, 1993

Also from the Hibbing Centennial collection, I especially like this shortcut Sarma Casserole, contributed by Patricia Dillon Metsek, former director of the Hibbing Historical Society.

Her husband calls this "Lazy Person's Sarmas," but Metsek says, "My mother told me, why not put it all in one dish rather than go to the work of rolling individual sarmas?" Mother knows best.

1988

— Learning new words, losing loved ones, bearing up in the 20th anniversary year —

A Stack of Towels
January 3

I have computed a new method to measure the complexity of a meal. I call it the Dish Towel Quotient.

After the last Christmas guest had departed and clean-up was finished, I counted 11 used dish towels. Considering that two loads of dinner dishes were washed and dried in the dishwasher, that number of towels is measure of a meal requiring inordinant KP.

Factored into the quotient must be the number of friends who are willing to wield a towel. I don't expect guests to do dishes, but our friends were determined to help. Jayne Trudell said, "If I do these now, maybe I'll get invited back again." She would, anyway, but I appreciated her efforts at insurance.

Mashed Potatoes: New Love Potion
February 7

Testing chocolate recipes — what else? — for Valentine's Day, I tried one that we decided not to include in the column:

It would make a chocolate eater feel like he was consuming a square meal. Leftover mashed potatoes in my refrigerator were the impetus to test Mashed Potato Chocolate Cake swathed in fluffy white frosting. It was substantial eating, provoking one of the Office Hungries to ask, "Where's the gravy?"

Chefs Just Know How to Cook
June 5

This I have suspected for a long time. Chefs can't write recipes for home cooks. Chefs don't know how to write recipes for home cooks. Chefs don't want to write recipes for home cooks.

Before I am skewered with a French knife by a person in a tall white hat, let me explain. This theory doesn't mean that chefs can't cook. It's just that they can't deal with such diminutive tools as a half-teaspoon. A high-powered chef, the type who might presume to write a cookbook, usually has a squad of helpers and a larder stuffed with out-of-season rarities most grocery stores won't yield. He has a pastry chef to hand him a pound of puff paste, a salad girl to mince a heap of parsley.

Vocabulary Lesson
July 24

Though my husband frequently says, passing the buck when asked a question, "Ask Eleanor — she knows everything," sometimes a food term will trip me.

In the early days of this column, the word "bacalao" was mystifying. Readers of various ethnic persuasions wrote to tell me that, under assorted Mediterranean Basin spellings, the word refers to dried cod cooked with tomatoes.

Three years ago, I tasted a Tian of Vegetables during a Napa Valley lunch. Say what? My usually trusty "Larousse Gastronomique" skipped from "thymus" to "tiered plinth." But again, a reader added to our mutual education after I admitted ignorance. A tian, she told us, is not what goes into the dish, but the dish itself, a shallow oval or square ovenproof dish made of earthenware, china or even Pyrex.

So now we have "clafouti." The name first bit my attention when Gloria Kirchman of Eden Prairie won the Bay's English Muffin National Recipe Contest with Pear Clafouti. Shortly after, a recipe for

Blueberry Clafouti arrived. I still didn't know what this mystery word meant, but I sensed a trend in the making.

This time, Larousse had the answer: "Clafouti — a home preparation in Limousin, this is a kind of fruit pastry or thick fruit pancake made usually with black cherries."— From a column relating testing of pear and blueberry clafouti recipes.

Predictions Come True
September 11

California Cuisine, enthralling to us earlier in the decade, "has pooped out," San Francisco chef Joyce Goldstein told me:

Nowadays, grilling and baby vegetables, which so revolutionized American cooking, "are taken for granted," Goldstein said. What she sees becoming entrenched are Pacific Rim foods — Korean, Chinese, Japanese, Polynesian, Thai — tailored to American tastes. And diner food, that simple home-cooking substitute for people who don't want to cook at home.

A reader says . . .

Thank you so much for the wonderful article featuring the Christ Church cookbook. Everyone in the parish was thrilled. I spoke with a friend who has also read you for many years, and she said she feels you are our own local Erma Bombeck. Thought you should hear that.

— Jean Hoover, St. Paul

Two Decades of Sunday Madness
August 14

Tested Recipes' 20th anniversary was noted with a Sunday cover story. Under a headline, "She's tested about 2,500 recipes for you," this lede:

Twenty years of Tested Recipes are under our belts.

After a bit of column history, this comment: My question for the next decade — Is anybody out there cooking at all? When brownies are sold premixed in a disposable pan to bake 4 minutes in a microwave oven, will anyone "homemake" a 15-ingredient, three-layer brownie that dirties a stack of dishes?

Kudos for the Column
October 9

News item in the Sunday paper: Eleanor Ostman's Tested Recipes was named a winner in the recent Newspaper Food Editors and Writers Association column competition, topping 90 entries from the United States and Canada. It won a first-place award last year, as well.

Four and No More?
October 30

Sometimes, I fear for my job.

We recently invited some folks to assess our Wednesday food section. A chef on the panel said we shouldn't run any recipes at all unless they are specifically requested. "Nobody uses recipes, anyway," said the pro.

A home economist and young mother told us that any recipe requiring more than four items was suspect among her friends. "They aren't going to make something calling for 16 ingredients," she said.

At a conference in Providence, R.I., last month, food writers heard that we shouldn't assume (a) that anyone knows how to cook or (b) that anyone has time to cook.

I take all of this with a half-grain of salt, half believing, half realizing it's impossible to lump all cooks or noncooks into a single category. To counter the argument, cookbooks and food magazines are being published at a record rate. Someone must be buying all those books with the intention of stirring up more than four ingredients.

Bert Greene: A special radiance.

Goodbye to the Greene Man
December 18

Who knew it would be so soon? In 1985, one of my favorite foodies, New York cookbook author Bert Greene and I had been schmoozing on the phone, and I reported to readers:

Our conversation strayed to many topics, including James Beard's recent demise. "When I go, I hope people will say of me, 'He was a little quirky, but he was good,' Bert said, creating his own epitaph — not that he's teetering toward the grave."

Just three years later, Greene needed that epitaph, and I gave him this eulogy:

One less star is shining this holiday season, and I'm going to miss a guy who had a special warmth, whose radiance lighted those around him.

Bert Greene had the shoulders of a fullback. His crew-cut head rose right out of his clavicle. I never saw him wear a tie. He always sported a cravat tucked into an open shirt collar, not an affectation, but a necessity in a world where shirts with necks sizes larger than 18 are rare.

Bert loved food and everyone who revered it — from a simple country cook to a writing colleague. What I admired was his ability to focus. He was the funniest of men, so very entertaining himself. Yet he would look at me, his face alight, his interest in what I had to say so intense that I felt myself becoming more amusing, my conversation more dazzling. Bert was one of those people who could bring out the best in others. That's why everyone adored him.

I last saw Bert in Kansas City in March. He was in the process of finishing a book, and he said, "I guess I'll call it 'Greene on Grains.' Might as well continue what 'Greene on Greens' started." We sat at the dinner table designing titles for future books: "Greene on Grapes." "Greene on Gravy." "Greene on Gravlax."

Before the meal was over, Bert, who had done extensive research on American regional foods, and I were making plans for his visit to our northern lake place. "I'll introduce you to the best potica and pasty makers on Minnesota's Iron Range, and we'll take the canoe out after wild rice," I guaranteed.

But it was a promise I couldn't keep. Three months later, my 65-year-old friend was dead of heart failure. Such a big heart. He'd probably opened it to so many of his friends that he used it up far too soon.

Sticking to the Roof of Swedish Mouths

May 1

Food writers, no matter where in the world they're from, like to try new foods. Birgit Hemberg, editor of Sweden's leading glossy food magazine, Allt Om Mat (All About Food), was coming to our house for tea. I gave her peanut butter — in the form of an elegant pie that was to be served a few days later to those attending the St. Paul Chamber Orchestra gala at the Minnesota Club. Chefs Jim Klein and John Menson created this all-American pie:

What's more familiar to Americans than peanut butter? Europeans don't eat it, or even understand the American passion for such sticky, dreary-colored goo,

but it would be just the flavor a Swedish food writer might like to experience.

Hemberg liked the pie and asked for the recipe. Who knows, Turtle Pie may toddle into Sweden via the pages of Allt Om Mat.

Hemberg had been one of my sources, via telephone, for a story I was writing on modern Swedish

TURTLE PIE
Makes 1 9-inch pie

Cereal crust:
   1/4 cup corn syrup
   2 tablespoons firmly packed brown
      sugar
   3 tablespoons butter
   2 1/2 cups Rice Krispies
Filling:
   1/4 cup peanut butter
   1/2 cup fudge topping
   3 tablespoons corn syrup
   1 quart vanilla ice cream

To make cereal crust: In medium saucepan, combine corn syrup, brown sugar and butter. Cook over low heat, stirring, until mixture begins to boil. Remove from heat. Add cereal. Stir until well coated. Press evenly in 9-inch pie pan.

To make filling: Stir peanut butter, fudge topping and 3 tablespoons corn syrup together. Spread half of mixture over crust. Freeze. Allow ice cream to thaw slightly. Spread ice cream evenly over peanut-butter layer. Freeze until firm. Warm remaining peanut-butter mixture. Drizzle over slices of pie.

Note: You might want to make twice as much of the peanut-butter mixture and layer some amid the ice-cream filling.

food. When she arrived at my house, she showed me a recent issue of her magazine.

I laughed when I got to page 47. We were together because of the story I'd done trying to explain today's Swedish food to American readers — that it isn't all lutefisk and boiled potatoes.

There, in her magazine, was a story explaining American food to Swedes. The article's title: "America — It Isn't Just Hamburgers and Coca-Cola."

A reader says . . .

I just want you to know how much I appreciate your columns in the Pioneer Press. How much, you ask? So much that I can hardly wait for the Sunday paper. One week recently, our Sunday paper was missing the Express section. You can be sure it didn't take me long to get to the phone and ask a neighbor to save his paper's section for me.

Not only do I enjoy your recipes, but the columns you write, as well. It's enjoyable reading about the "Lake Hungries," what you served your son's future in-laws, etc. Your writing comes across as a good friend writing a personal letter. You report what results you had in testing recipes, what you would alter, even your dismay to see how someone altered your mother's pasty recipe.

Your columns are down-to-earth, homey, and written to ordinary me. Thank you!

— Luella Penner, Hudson, Wis.

A Salad Not Exactly Slimming
May 8

This broccoli-bacon blend was making the rounds of our St. Paul Crocus Hill neighborhood when two residents, Sara Struve and Jane McKim, included it in the cookbook they edited for the 100th anniversary of nearby St. Luke's Catholic Church. Another neighbor, Ann Dickinson, contributed the salad to the book, and though it was new to me at the time, I've seen it on countless buffet tables after it appeared in the column. Since then, low-fat salads have become the rage. This would never, ever qualify.

BROCCOLI-BACON SALAD
Makes 12 servings

Salad:
- 1 bunch broccoli, about 3 stalks
- 1 small red onion, thinly sliced
- 12 strips bacon, crisply fried
- 1 cup whole roasted sunflower seeds
- 1/2 cup raisins

Dressing:
- 1 cup mayonnaise (light or regular)
- 1/2 cup sugar
- 2 tablespoons vinegar

To make salad: Completely chop broccoli. (Note: If using food processor, cut up florets by hand so they don't get smaller than bite-size.) Add onion slices. Crumble in bacon. Add sunflower seeds and raisins.

To make dressing: Combine mayonnaise, sugar and vinegar. Mix with wire whisk until sugar is dissolved. Add to vegetables. Toss. Let salad steep for a while before serving.

Bear Grub
October 9

Are people afraid of bears? You bet!

The Office Hungries, informed that a gorgeous, pink-frosted cherry cake contained bear grease, ran away as if a grizzly was in pursuit. Courageous ones who took slices grudgingly agreed it was light and luscious, with no hint of "wild" flavor.

I have to admit hesitation about testing bear recipes, even through my first memory is of a bruin. It was a November during World War II, when my parents had a few chickens at our country home to compensate for meat-rationing. A soon-to-hibernate bear, who'd had slim pickings during a summer without berries, decided to raid the chicken coop.

My father shot him right between the eyes with a .22, and that monster didn't even blink. So Dad rousted the neighbors to form a hunting party, and by morning, they'd hung the raider by his heels from a tree next to the chicken coop. My mother took a picture of her 2-year-old standing next to the trophy. The bear was four times taller than I was.

Carol Suddendorf, who became Minnesota's only woman licensed bear hunting guide in the mid-1980s, lives not far from our lake house, in the

CHERRY BEAR LARD CAKE
Makes 1 9-inch layer cake

Cake:
2 eggs, separated
1/2 cup sugar
1/4 cup bear lard (or regular lard or shortening)
2 1/4 cups sifted cake flour
1 cup sugar
2 1/2 teaspoons baking powder
1 teaspoon salt
1/4 teaspoon baking soda
3/4 cup milk
1/3 cup cherry juice
1/4 teaspoon almond extract

Cherry buttercream frosting:
1/2 cup butter
3 cups sifted powdered sugar
1/4 cup cherry juice

To make cake: Grease and flour 2 9-inch round layer cake pans. Beat egg whites until frothy. Gradually beat in sugar. Continue beating until very stiff and glossy. In another bowl, stir lard to soften. Add sifted dry ingredients and milk. Beat for 1 minute, scraping sides and bottom of bowl constantly. Add cherry juice, egg yolks and almond extract. Beat for 1 minute, scraping bowl constantly. Fold in egg-white mixture. Pour into cake pans. Bake in 350-degree oven for 25 to 30 minutes. Cool layers in pans on rack for 10 minutes. Remove from pans. Frost.

To make frosting: Cream butter. Gradually add powdered sugar alternately with cherry juice. Cream until frosting is light and fluffy.

Baby Eleanor and the big black bear.

Balsam Lake area of Itasca County. She gave me the recipe (from her book, "Bears in My Kitchen") — and bear lard she'd rendered herself — to make this feathery, delicate cake.

Jo's Chicken Goes Hollywood

September 25

Back and forth to Sacramento I went, settling the estate of my departed Aunt Patsy. While there, I stayed with her friend, Jo Woodward, who lived in St. Paul before migrating to California:

Jo started talking about her fried chicken and how she used to run a Sacramento restaurant where the chicken became famous. And how she cooked it every year at the California State Fair, where Hollywood celebrities who appeared there would buy boxes of her chicken to take back to Los Angeles.

Jo started her restaurant back when a buck was a buck. She paid $250 for this secret fried-chicken formula, and the guy who sold it to her wasn't the Colonel.

Jo gave me directions for an entire gallon of coating mixture. What you see here is a third of a batch, as much as I made so I could provide chicken for the neighborhood potluck. It was twice as much as we needed for 16 chicken breast pieces and 16 drumsticks. If you're cooking for a family, cut the recipe in half.

Jo's Fried Chicken
Makes 5 1/2 cups buttermilk coating

1 1/2 tablespoons salt, or to taste
1/2 to 1 teaspoon powdered sage
1/3 teaspoon soda
1/3 teaspoon white pepper
1 quart buttermilk
1 cup milk
1/3 cup cream
Broiler-fryer chicken parts
Flour
Cooking oil

In large bowl, combine salt, sage, soda and white pepper with buttermilk, milk and cream. Mix well. Cut chicken into serving-size pieces. Wash. Pat dry. Dredge chicken pieces in flour. Drop into buttermilk mixture, immersing completely. Remove chicken pieces from liquid. Allow excess to drip off. Roll pieces again in flour. Heat cooking oil to 350 degrees. Fry chicken for 10 to 15 minutes, or until golden brown. Turn pieces in oil with tongs; do not pierce chicken with fork. Place chicken on paper towels to drain.

1989

— We survive, barely,
the Great Kitchen Remodel —

Out With the Old
June 11

I've just had the rug — more correctly, the linoleum — pulled out from under me. It went into the Dumpster along with the rest of the kitchen. What remains of my erstwhile testing facility are brick walls and rafters. Gaping holes give clues where magnificent new windows will be, but otherwise, we have hit the pits known as kitchen remodeling.

The last time we did this, about 18 years ago, it was so simple. Take down the old cabinets. Install new ones.

Two decades of collecting equipment and cookbooks and odd ingredients have overloaded those once-ample cupboards. Counter space kept diminishing, until available working space was measured in square inches.

This time, we're knocking out walls and building an addition. Our house is a 1902 model, and the architect who built it for his family lived in another era. It had, for instance, a maid's dining room.

During our tenure, for lack of maids, we've used that space as a home office, then as a cookbook library, and finally, as a catchall that I wouldn't let visitors see. Now, the maid's room will be the main

The new kitchen — white, light, bright.

work area of my new dream kitchen. What our house didn't have were such "back of the house" amenities as a broom closet or coat storage. They'll be built in now.

In the meantime, we're making do in the basement, washing dishes in the laundry tubs, and cooking with a hot plate, toaster oven and microwave. Finding a certain ingredient among those packed in boxes for the duration can take 20 minutes.

Aric came home from college just as the kitchen he's always known was going out the door. Now, more than ever, he has reason to complain, "There's nothing to eat in this house."

Sheetrock City
June 18

Readers commiserated, sending, when I requested, all their best ideas for kitchen efficiency, many of which were incorporated in our final plan:

My favorite letter so far is from Carolyn Salmanowicz of West St. Paul who is living through kitchen-rebuilding chaos, too.

"I am also adding an addition so my kitchen walls are knocked out, and I've begun doing my dishes in the basement laundry tub. Every meal has to be microwaved, even through it all tastes like Sheetrock or plaster dust." Salmanowicz had an added mess factor, children ages 4 and 2. "I have these little munchkins dragging sawdust and old plaster rubble. It is truly amazing how imaginative children can be with a few of daddy's tools and a little bit of dirt."

Got the Liver, Hungries?
July 2

Lucky me. I don't have a kitchen.

God must have known this was the right moment for Angie Reinbold Ibarra's cookbook to come into my life.

"Liver," said former newspaper colleague Betty Roney in a quavery voice when I asked what kind of book she was pitching for a Stillwater friend.

"Not in this Tested Recipes column," I vowed. A lifetime liver hater, the only way I touch the stuff is accidentally, when spooning Alpo into our dog's dish.

So what to do, with no kitchen and my prejudices? Aha! I'd ask the Office Hungries to do the testing. Like Mikey, they'll eat anything.

Not liver.

The only volunteer was Georgann Koelln, our fashion writer, who took liver on her honeymoon camping trip 24 years before because it was the one thing she knew how to cook. And her new husband ate it, night after night. True love.

After a bit of arm-twisting on my part and a little stalling on hers, she eventually tested Liver With Diable Sauce. Here is her report.

Dear Eleanor:

Our dog learned to eat from a fork last night.

Given that your test kitchen is in a major state of remodeling, and given that you have a new gourmet liver cookbook to review, and given that I've been known to consume liver smothered in onions at a certain Stillwater truck stop, it seems only logical that I volunteer to test a liver recipe for you. Heaven knows, I've consumed enough of your tested recipes over the years that I owe you.

I chose Liver With Diable Sauce, about as far from the liver I know and love as I could get, just for experimentation's sake. The recipe has everything going for it: It's quick, cheap and easy. And it might even be good for you, if you're guided by liver folklore, not current data about liver being a storehouse for chemicals.

Here are my family's tasting reactions:

Husband: "Tastes like liver in barbecue sauce. One good thing about the sauce; it takes away from the bad smell of fried liver." (Note from Eleanor: Guess the honeymoon is over.)

Teen-age son: "Seriously, Mom, I can't. It sticks to the roof of my mouth. Here, doggie, doggie, doggie."

Me: "Diable Sauce will never replace onions cooked in bacon grease."

Cooking hint: Have a pan of chicken thighs sprinkled with Lawry's Seasoned Salt baking in a 350-degree oven while preparing any liver recipe. You're probably going to need it.

Georgann

Cookbook author Angie Ibarra can understand our aversion. She doesn't like liver, either, but because there was no other cookbook on the subject, she decided to fill that niche.

Spouting "F" Words
April 2

How times and trends change, especially for those of us with enough personal mileage to map the undulating route of public opinion.

When I started writing about food, nobody had heard the word "cholesterol." Perhaps, they thought, at first encounter, that it had something to do with "chlorophyll." Now, everyone is aware of cholesterol, and everyone knows it isn't green.

We've added a string of "F" words to our eating vocabularies: fats (saturated, polyunsaturated), fungi (exotic mushrooms), flowers (edible) and, most basic to our inner workings, fiber.

Twenty years ago, when I began pounding the knife-and-fork beat for this newspaper, the only fats we considered were the thick rims on our T-bone steaks. Fungi came in one variety — white button mushrooms. And who would ever think of eating flowers?

Gossiping Border to Border
September 17

My elbows are propped on the back fence of the '90, and this one stretches across the nation. — From a column telling readers about Prodigy Interactive Personal Service (our first tangle with the Internet), coming to the Twin Cities. We asked for recipes, got them and tested them.

We Get Our Wires Crossed
January 29

Remember the old parlor game, Telephone? The object was to see how mangled a message could get after it passed through several sets of ears.

Boy, did I get tangled in a "telephone" connected to messages about Bailey's Irish Cream Cake.

Here's the directory of events:

At a pre-Christmas party for employees on this newspaper building's first floor, someone contributed a purchased cake soaked with Bailey's Irish Cream. Dave the Guard thought it was so delicious that he asked if I had a recipe. I suggested poking a pound cake full of holes and drizzling the creamy liqueur over the cake.

Dave discussed that procedure with Phyllis the Cashier, who, in turn, was discussing the cake with someone else when Teresa from Advertising happened by and said, sure, she had the recipe, which she got from Carol the Friend.

So Teresa from Advertising gave Phyllis the Cashier the recipe, which Phyllis gave to Dave the Guard, telling him it was the frosting for Bailey's Irish Cream Cake. Dave the Guard jotted the word "frosting" on the recipe and figured, with his pen, it would be enough for a "3 layer cake."

Then along comes Eleanor the Food Writer with an expense account to be redeemed by Phyllis the Cashier. "Hey, I've got the recipe for Bailey's Irish Cream Cake," she tells me, handing over a photocopy she got from Dave the Guard. We discuss the frivolity of any cake soaked with such good-sounding stuff lasting four weeks in the refrigerator, as the recipe directs. Phyllis the Cashier thought the three-layer cake to be put under this "frosting" just had to be chocolate.

So Eleanor the Food Writer goes home, bakes chocolate layers and puts the "frosting" ingredients in the blender. Ron the Husband, hearing the blender whirling, comes to investigate and wonders how something so pourable can ever be spreadable. He tries beating it with a gadget that can whip even skim milk solid, but the mixture won't thicken.

We decide perhaps it is not frosting, but rather the liquid for soaking the cake, so we put the layers in a flat-bottomed pan one at a time, pouring liquid as we go. We end up with soggy chocolate cake. Re-e-e-ally soggy.

So Eleanor the Food Writer goes back to the office to untangle the situation. She asks Phyllis the Cashier where she got the recipe. Then she tracks down Teresa from Advertising and asks her if she has ever made this Bailey's Irish Cream Frosting.

BAILEY'S IRISH CREAM CAKE
Makes 16 servings

2 cups cake flour
2 teaspoons baking powder
1/2 teaspoon salt
1/2 cup butter
2 cups sugar
2 eggs (3 would be better)
4 ounces (4 squares) unsweetened
   chocolate, melted
1 teaspoon vanilla
1 cup Bailey's Irish Cream liqueur
1/2 cup milk
1 cup chopped walnuts

Sift cake flour, baking powder and salt. Cream butter and sugar. Add eggs. Mix in chocolate and vanilla. Add flour mixture and Bailey's to creamed mixture. Add milk and nuts. Mix well. In 350-degree oven, bake in greased 9-by-13-inch pan or 2 round pans for 30 minutes, or in prepared bundt pan for 50 minutes.

"What frosting? That's a drink."

Dave the Guard later admits that the confusing notations about frosting and cake layers were his.

Mystery solved — almost. Does anyone have the bona fide recipe for a homemade version of the commercial Bailey's Irish Cream Cake? Please, please send it in.

Two weeks later, Mary Whalen from Stillwater came to the rescue. After trying it in bundt cake form, I suggested it might need an extra egg. And, going back to Plan A, poking holes into the cake and drizzling it with Bailey's will intensify flavor. Add a buttercream frosting flavored with Bailey's.

A Romantic Lunch for Other Lovers
October 29

A romantic picnic basket lunch I'd offered to the St. Paul Academy and Summit School Fanfair fund-raising auction was purchased as a wedding gift for a young couple. They finally collected many months later:

Perhaps the twosome had heard about our kitchen remodeling and didn't want vittles cooked in our "summer kitchen," the basement. Or maybe they just got lucky, planning a weekend at Bluefin Bay on the North Shore on the most beautiful weekend this autumn.

They knocked on our door Saturday, and I handed over a basket laden with smoked salmon mousse, a jar of golden caviar and a loaf of Wuollet's French bread. Digging deeper, they'd find Italian chicken salad, tomatoes stuffed with spinach and ham and, for dessert, almond-topped chocolate-mint bars. Also tucked in was a bottle of Piper Sonoma Cellars finest bubbly and two delicate flutes bearing that vineyard's logo.

I was tempted to ignore the doorbell, grab the basket and run out the back door for a romantic picnic with my own husband. Alas, nothing so elegant for us. We snacked on leftovers for lunch.

SAVORY STUFFED TOMATOES
Makes 6 servings

6 smaller-size tomatoes, such as Romas

4 ounces smoked ham

1 cup spinach leaves, washed and cut into thin ribbons

2 tablespoons low-fat plain yogurt

2 tablespoons mayonnaise

4 leaves basil, cut into thin strips

1/3 cup grated low-fat smoked mozzarella cheese

To prepare tomatoes: Cut tops off tomatoes. Using spoon, carefully hollow out insides. Turn tomatoes upside down to drain.

To make filling: Cut smoked ham into thin 1-inch-long strips. In mixing bowl, combine ham with spinach, yogurt, mayonnaise, basil and two-thirds of mozzarella. Stuff tomatoes with mixture. Sprinkle with remaining cheese. Bake in 350-degree for 10 to 15 minutes, or until cheese melts. Serve at room temperature.

Menu Multiphasic
September 3

For 20 years since he gummed his first spoonful of rice Pabulum at 1-week-old, I've been trying to figure out what Aric really likes to eat.

VEGETABLE MEDLEY TURKEY STIR-FRY
Makes 6 servings

1 package (about 1 1/4 pounds) fresh turkey breast slices or fresh turkey breast tenderloins

1/3 cup soy sauce

1 teaspoon dry sherry

1 clove garlic, finely chopped

1 tablespoon cooking oil

1 medium red or green pepper, cut into 1/4- by 1-inch strips

2 cups broccoli florets

2 cups sliced fresh mushrooms

3 ounces fresh pea pods

4 green onions, cut into 1-inch pieces

1 cup bean sprouts

1/4 cup chicken broth

1 to 1 1/4 teaspoons cornstarch

To marinate turkey: Cut turkey into 1/2-inch pieces. Mix soy sauce, sherry and garlic. Stir in turkey. Let stand for 15 minutes.

To stir-fry: In large nonstick skillet or wok, heat oil over high heat until hot. Stir-fry turkey in oil until no longer pink. Remove turkey from skillet. Add red pepper and broccoli. Stir-fry for 1 minute. Add mushrooms and pea pods. Stir-fry 1 minute. Add green onions and bean sprouts. Stir-fry for 30 seconds. Mix chicken broth and cornstarch. Add to skillet. Stir in turkey. Heat to a boil, stirring constantly. Boil, stirring, until sauce is thickened and clear. Add salt and pepper to taste. Serve immediately.

Now, I know what I should have done. Make him fill out a survey.

The new catering firm hired to feed his fraternity at the University of Denver sent a detailed questionnaire to be returned with the room-and-board payment. While I wrote the check, I sneaked a peek at his opinions. What a revelation! Why didn't I design my own Minnesota Menu Multiphasic long ago? I would have avoided lots of rejection and leftovers.

Chances are minuscule that even such a grandly named catering firm as Gourmet Creations would serve college students lobster, which was listed. It's safe as far as Aric is concerned. He X-ed lobster off as a food he didn't want. The company better not try to run meatloaf past him, either. That was X-rated, too.

I always thought he liked bratwurst, but that was X-ed out; so were bologna, pastrami, hard salami and ham. He likes quiches, croissant sandwiches and spicy foods, but he doesn't want to see liver on his plate or lemon meringue pie for dessert. All those years I urged, "Eat your broccoli" had an effect; he circled that as likable on the vegetable list.

Turkey is one of Aric's favorites, at home or away. While we were cooking in the basement during kitchen remodeling, he gave thumbs up to this quick, low-fat dinner featuring fresh turkey tenderloin or breast slices, now widely available in grocery stores. For more flavor in the sauce, you might add the remaining marinade to the broth and simmer that for several minutes before adding the cornstarch.

MARY HART'S POPOVERS
Makes 6

3 eggs, slightly beaten
1 1/2 cups milk
1 1/2 teaspoons melted butter
1 1/2 cups sifted flour
1/4 teaspoon salt

Beat eggs slightly. Add milk and melted butter. Sift flour. Measure flour. Add salt. Add to egg mixture. Beat until batter is smooth. Place in 6 very heavily greased custard cups. Bake in 400-degree oven for 1 hour.

I've always been fascinated by Mary's articles, and over the years, we've been the most cordial of competitors.

"The secret of these popovers is not to be chintzy with the batter," Mary wrote in her cookbook about this recipe she acquired from Jan Brautigam, proprietor of a Bloomington, Minn., reception hall. I've found it's easier to retrieve the custard cups from the oven if they're put onto a large baking pan. Don't crowd them.

Baking the popovers was one of the first efforts in my remodeled kitchen:

White cabinets to constantly wipe, brass accessories to polish, deep-blue marbleized countertops that announce every crumb and smudge may sentence me to a lifetime of cleaning, but I love the look — and the space.

Mary, Mary, Your Popovers are Never Contrary
December 3

As a tribute to the retirement of Mary Hart after 44 years as food writer for the Minneapolis Star-Tribune, we again printed the popover recipe I found in Mary's book published in 1979. It's never-fail (except for the time I used an insulated cookie pan to hold the custard cups, and the popovers refused to pop).

Mine, His, Ours

— *Putting Our Own Recipes to the Test* —

M ost Sundays for nearly 30 years, I tested recipes from other sources, but occasionally, I invented my own for contests and special occasions. My husband is also a creative cook, and our household repertoire is enriched with his food ideas, which almost always — with the exception of one memorable debacle — work flawlessly.

First Impressions
November 24, 1985

My husband was much more the gourmet than I when we met. It would be three years later that I became a food writer and learned about food on the job — and on him.

The night I met the fella who was to become my husband, he dazzled me by ordering, knowledgeably, fine French vintages for dinner. That was in the mid-1960s, a time in America when most people only knew that wines came in red, white or Portuguese rose. I was impressed.

After dessert, he requested snifters of Courvoisier cradled in flamers that heated the cognac, releasing its

essences. This child of the Iron Range had never had such elegant stuff. In fact, I'd never had cognac at all, but I was trying to appear as sophisticated as possible.

However, each time I'd lift the warmed liqueur to take a drink, fumes wafted over my contact lenses and my eyes watered. I certainly didn't want to appear tearful at sharing the evening with such an interesting man. Finally, when he wasn't looking, I dumped that expensive after-dinner drink into my coffee cup.

His Intentions Were Good
May 11, 1986

My husband tackles many recipes for the column, a boon to me when my schedule squeezes out testing time. And since he gets home from work earlier than I do, cooking dinner is often his duty, much to my delight. There's nothing more liberating for a working woman than to come home to dinner on the table.

But once, despite his cooking abilities, all went awry.

I'm trodding on a tender ego by telling this, and my husband has already threatened never to make another dinner for me if I do. But it's just too good a tale about kitchen pitfalls not to share. And it's told in the spirit of good-humored affection.

So forgive me, Dear, and promise you'll cook another day.

"Don't make me look like a dummy," he pleaded. Well, he's not. He's an inventive cook who usually doesn't need recipes. But sometimes, as for everyone, things go wrong.

Setting off the smoke alarms was one episode in that adventuresome afternoon. Bread he was oven-toasting to make croutons for French onion soup hit the incineration stage.

Recently, we had our house rewired, and several smoke alarms were connected directly into the electrical system. Trouble is, my husband didn't do the wiring himself, so he didn't know how to unhook four screaming sirens. He raced from cellar to attic, blowing on each one to disperse the smoke. When that didn't work, he yanked the circuit breaker.

Reaching for soup tureens, he knocked a ceramic fondue pot out of the cupboard. It sat, wounded, with its severed handle on the kitchen table as mute evidence of that mishap.

Hundreds of cookbooks are in our home, but none of them (he swore) had a recipe for chicken Kiev. So he improvised.

"I couldn't remember what flavored the butter, so I found this pesto seasoning in the cupboard," he said. Potent stuff it was, meant to be toned down with lots of fresh basil and pasta. He mainlined it into the butter filling.

Then, he couldn't remember what should coat the rolled chicken breasts, so he found a box of cornmeal and made a paste-like crust that so effectively insulated the meat that it was still pink inside when it reached the table.

And last of all, he couldn't recall if the chicken is deep-fried or oven-baked. He chose the latter, which baked that cornmeal to the consistency of a clay pot.

Baked stuffed potatoes would be nice, he decided, but where was the pastry bag to pipe the filling?

Nowhere that he could find it, so he went to the cookware shop and bought a new one.

And while he was there, he bought another springform pan for dessert. We already had two of them, but they didn't jump right out of the cupboard at him (as that fondue pot apparently had).

The potato-cheese mixture, he avowed later, was so stiff he could hardly push it through the pastry bug. But the cheese must have melted in the oven because the potatoes were soupy in their little shells.

I struggled through the meal because I'd had a huge lunch and wasn't hungry enough to forgive pink chicken and soupy potatoes. My husband could see that I was picking and pushing his efforts around on my plate. Even his salad, fresh strawberries in Jell-O, didn't slide down.

But he figured dessert would revive my appetite. He'd made it just for me. In the gleaming new springform pan, he proudly brought out his own creation: crumb-crusted chocolate pie.

But a strange look crossed his face when he took one bite. And then another. And then said to me, "Taste it and tell me what you think."

"I think it's burned," I confirmed.

Indeed, it was, though how that happened is still a mystery. It must have scorched when my husband was cooking the chocolate pie filling enriched with extra semisweet chocolate. Nearly the whole pie went down the disposal.

My husband's brother arrived late that night from Amherst, Mass. He was ravenous and thought the cornmeal-crusted Kievs were quite wonderful.

"If you write about my brother's dinner, you tell your readers that Bruce Aune, that well-known philosopher, noted gourmet and winemaker, thought the chicken was great," he said loyally.

I say it helps to be very hungry.

And the Winnah Is ...
Peanut Butter
Sandwiches?

June 25, 1981

Gala Cheesecake With Orange Macadamia Rum Sauce debuted at the 1981 Gourmet Gala to benefit the March of Dimes. My husband and I were among the guest chefs, joining Minnesota-born movie star Arlene Dahl, former Minnesota Viking Bob Lurtsema, beauty queen Shirley Hutton, and onetime Minnesota governor and U.S. senator Wendell Anderson cooking with his wife, Mary.

"How 'gourmet' can it be when peanut-butter and jelly sandwiches and meatballs draw the biggest crowds?" I wondered in print. Dahl made Norwegian meatballs — or rather watched as a chef from the Radisson South made her recipe. And Bob Lurtsema, in the "kitchen" next to ours, had everyone in hysterics as he demonstrated how to make "gourmet" peanut-butter sandwiches.

He arrived carrying a brown grocery bag from which he pulled a loaf of white bread and jars of peanut butter and jelly. "This is what I make best," he said, ignoring the Kahlua torte recipe he'd been assigned by the committee when he hadn't submitted his entry.

"You must always have fresh bread and peanut butter with no cholesterol," he lectured the crowd. "Never clean the knife between applying the peanut butter and the jelly, or you won't have as good a taste." With a spurt of inspiration, he grabbed

Eleanor and Ron make cheesecake with orange macadamia rum sauce at 1981 Gourmet Gala.

chocolate and a grater from the torte ingredients and gave the bread a dusting of chocolate as his "gourmet" touch.

For the $100-a-plate dinner at which our efforts would be tasted, "Benchwarmer Bob" said peanut butter sandwiches should be cut "elegantly" in triangles. Never mind the finger impressions in the oh-so-fresh bread. "That's the golden home touch," Lurtsema winked.

The recipes my husband and I prepared, a bit more seriously, were not totally my own, rather adapted from a New York department store cheesecake contest winner and from a orange-macadamia sauce tried during a food-writers' trip to Hawaii just a few months before the gala. Putting them together was my idea, and the judges liked the sauced cheesecake enough to award us first place in the dessert division. We've made the cheesecake more often than the sauce since then, for the rich, rich cake doesn't always require embellishment.

A reader says . . .

Everyone reads your column.

— Janet Martin, Hastings, Minn.

GALA CHEESECAKE WITH ORANGE MACADAMIA RUM SAUCE

Makes 12 to 16 servings

Cheesecake:
- 4 packages (8 ounces each) cream cheese
- 1 carton (16 ounces) dairy sour cream
- 1/4 pound (1 stick) butter
- 2 tablespoons cornstarch
- 1 1/4 cups sugar
- 1 teaspoon vanilla
- 2 teaspoons lemon juice
- 5 large eggs

Orange Macadamia Rum Sauce:
- 3 oranges, zest and juice
- 3/4 cup sugar
- 1/2 cup light corn syrup
- 1/4 cup dark rum
- 1/4 cup chopped macadamia nuts

To make cheesecake: Warm cream cheese, sour cream, butter and eggs to room temperature. In large mixing bowl, whip cream cheese until fluffy. Beat in sour cream and butter. Add cornstarch, sugar, vanilla and lemon juice. At high speed, beat mixture until well blended. Beat in eggs, 1 at a time. Continue beating until mixture is very smooth.

To bake cheesecake: Pour cheesecake batter into well-buttered 10-inch springform pan. Place pan into larger pan. Add enough water to come halfway up side of springform pan. Bake in 375-degree oven for 1 hour, or until top is golden and firm. Turn off oven. Let cake cool in oven for 1 hour with oven door open. Remove cheesecake. Let stand for 2 hours. Cover. Refrigerate for at least 6 hours before serving.

To make sauce: Using zester or vegetable peeler, remove only orange portion (zest) of peel from 3 oranges. Cut into very thin slivers to make 1/2 cup. Squeeze juice from oranges. Strain. In small saucepan, combine 1 cup orange juice and slivered peel. Simmer for 5 minutes. Add sugar, corn syrup and rum. Stir until sugar dissolves. Boil for 20 minutes, or until syrupy. Cool thoroughly. Stir in nuts. Serve in a bowl. Spoon onto cheesecake. Makes 1 1/2 cups sauce.

Ron, the Crepes King

April 13, 1980

My husband is the "ghost" cook of this column. He frequently helped me test, and he's eaten just about everything I tried. Some tasks were his alone, such as cutting up chickens or making crepes when a recipe called for them.

Early in our marriage, I went to a cooking class and came home with a crepe pan, eager to try a recipe for the French pancakes. My husband, who didn't know I was going to the class, had that same day a sudden urge to make crepes. When I got home, he was stoveside, flipping a stack that he incorporated into crepes Suzette. It was spooky to experience such mental telepathy.

This is his recipe for crepes. He always adds a touch of brandy or other liquor to make the batter silky.

Caviar, Anyone?
August 3, 1986

The Romanoff Caviar people asked me to contribute a recipe to their coobkooklet, "Recipes for the Caviar Lifestyle."

"Just tell us your favorite way of using caviar," they said, with a New York presumption that everyone has a favorite use for caviar. Rather than admit what a Midwest bumpkin I was, I agreed to invent a recipe, and this is the result. To showcase mild golden whitefish caviar from America's inland oceans, I used russets from the Red River Valley, Minnesota wild rice and yogurt (or sour cream) representing our dairy industry to concoct a regional meal in a potato.

RON AUNE'S COGNAC CREPES
Makes 2 dozen crepes

4 eggs
1 cup flour
1/2 teaspoon salt
3/4 cup milk
1/4 cup half-and-half
3 tablespoons melted butter
2 tablespoons "good" cognac

This is how the directions were written that Sunday:

After mixing everything well in the blender or with a beater, he lets it rest for an hour in the refrigerator, then strains the batter before making crepes. The hot saute pan is buttered after every second or third crepe. So he doesn't tear the delicate paper-thin pancakes, he uses a rubber scraper to turn them.

Or if he's feeling particularly giddy, he flips them and catches (most of) them mid-air. Are the ones he offers for samples those that hit the floor? I've often wondered.

GREAT LAKES SUPPER
Makes 2 servings

2 russet potatoes, baked
Salt, pepper and butter, as desired
1 cup cooked wild rice, seasoned
1 cup plain yogurt (or sour cream)
1/4 cup chopped green onions
1 jar (2 ounces) golden whitefish caviar

Slit hot baked potatoes. Push open. Mash lightly with fork. Season with salt, pepper and butter. Spoon 1/2 cup cooked wild rice into each potato. Add dollops of yogurt. Sprinkle with green onions. Top with golden whitefish caviar.

First Place With Second Try

February 15, 1987

Perhaps subconsciously, the "pepper" in Pepperidge Farm inspired me. That company revived the National Sandwich Contest by asking food writers who would be attending the International Food Media Conference

GRILLED PEPPER PACKETS

Makes 2 servings

12 thin slices jalapeno pepper cheese

4 slices whole-wheat bread (thin-slice preferred)

18 thin (about 1/4-inch) strips, 6 each of green, red and yellow bell peppers

1 tablespoon finely chopped green onion

Softened butter

To assemble sandwiches: Place 3 slices of cheese on 1 slice of bread. Alternating green, red and yellow pepper strips, place 9 pepper strips and half of onions on top of cheese. Cover with 3 more slices of cheese. Place 1 slice of bread on top. Build second sandwich in same way.

To grill sandwiches: Place saute pan or griddle over medium-low heat. Lightly spread 1 side of each sandwich with softened butter. Grill until browned. Spread untoasted sides of sandwiches with butter. Turn. Grill until browned and cheese has melted. Cut sandwiches in half diagonally to display the tri-color patchwork of peppers.

to design one. I adore colored peppers, especially the yellow ones we first tasted in Italy in 1980.

Pepper Packets, my first entry, incorporated a toss of red, yellow and green pepper strips and grated pepper cheese folded into puff-pastry dough and baked until golden. A couple of weeks later, Mary McGrath, public-relations director for Pepperidge Farm, called to say she loved the concept of the sandwich, but, oops, she hadn't absolutely specified that the bread division of the company was organizing the contest, so would I revise the recipe to make a bread sandwich?

More experimentation. When we finally hit on our favorite, my husband made two "just to make sure they're good." He was the one who discovered that if the peppers were arranged in alternating colors and the grilled sandwich cut diagonally, a red, yellow, green patchwork appeared.

That version made the finals, judged at the conference by the food editors themselves — those who could struggle into New York strangled by a January blizzard. Apparently, they were ready for something spicy to chase the New York chill, and my anonymous pepper-cheese creation — the only hot sandwich on the table — came in first. Our prize was a trip to a place where it never snows: Acapulco.

Flaming Shish Kebabs

Date unknown

My husband and I collaborated on an actual recipe after he came up with the idea of marinating beef in herbaceous Southern Comfort. We'll never forget the dinner party for which the meat was soaked in the high-test booze for 48 hours instead of just a brief bath. When Ron flamed the shish kebabs at the dining table, he could barely get the fire out. Our guests said it was the only time they ever got tipsy on meat.

RON AUNE'S SOUTHERN COMFORT SHISH KEBABS
Makes 6 servings

Marinade:
- 2 pounds beef sirloin or filet, cut into large cubes
- 1 tablespoon beef base dissolved in 1/4 cup hot water
- 2 cloves garlic, minced
- 1 small onion, minced
- 1 lemon, zest and juice
- 1 orange, zest and juice
- 1/2 teaspoon freshly ground black pepper
- 1/4 cup oil
- 1 cup (or more, if you dare) Southern Comfort

Shish kebabs:
- 3 slices fresh pineapple, cut into chunks
- Green pepper squares
- Pearl onions (bottled ones are best)
- Butter
- Cherry tomatoes
- Large mushrooms
- Thick zucchini rounds
- 1 teaspoon arrowroot
- Canned kumquats

To marinate beef: Dissolve beef base in hot water. Combine with remaining marinade ingredients. Add beef cubes to marinade. If you wish, marinate pineapple slices, green pepper squares and onions, too. Refrigerate, covered, for 6 to 24 hours.

To make shish kebabs: Broil meat pieces, green pepper, pineapple and onions under oven broiler, or cook over hot charcoal. Meanwhile, in pan atop stove, in enough butter to coat pan, briefly saute cherry tomatoes, mushrooms and zucchini. Simmer reserved marinade for at least 10 minutes to use as sauce. Strain. Thicken with arrowroot until it is syrupy. On skewers, thread meat alternately with assorted fruits and vegetables, including kumquats. Serve with sauce over platter of rice pilaf.

Tossing Salad Habits
April 29, 1990

My mother believed that it was her duty to decorate dinner with greenery, even in the dead of a northern Minnesota winter. So we had iceberg lettuce, sometimes with winter tomatoes, which seemed to be better back then.

Mom died 10 years ago without ever tasting — or even hearing of — radicchio, mache, arugula or sorrel. But her daughter, the iceberg maiden, grew up to eat manioc tops in Brazil and seaweed in China in a continuing exploration of the wonderful world of salads.

First tremors in salad shakeup of the past decade were felt, naturally, in California. I remember studying the salad course at Alice Waters' food-revolutionary

Chez Panisse in Berkeley about 10 years ago and thinking what was on my plate looked like lawn clippings. Now, those peculiar greens, fresh herbs and edible flowers are everywhere.

Look at the impact salad bars have had on the dining table. Now, salads are "composed." Or they come in dual temperatures, such as hot duck breast on chilled greens.

One of my favorite salad dressings from my younger years was tasted on a trip to Florida when I was still in high school, in a restaurant called Dutch Pantry or something kindred. Its sweet-sour celery-seed dressing was a revelation to a teen-ager who usually ate iceberg lettuce with vinegar and oil, the way my dad liked it. Later, a similar dressing was marketed by a St. Paul company called Eggert's. And the St. Paul Hotel served such a dressing on its strawberry-spinach-brie salad.

One day, when I wanted that flavor for a salad I was taking to a party, I experimented until I came up with this satisfying formula.

A "dollop" of honey is about 2 tablespoons, or as much as glugs over the edge of the jar with a quick tilt.

Wild Salad is a Winner
March 13, 1988

I've found the formula for success: It's pepper cheese.

That revelation introduced my winning salad in another contest for food writers, one in which we were challenged to take small steps toward cutting fat.

Inspiration came from a refrigerator clean-out. I had pepper cheese, cooked ham and vegetables on hand. Add them to wild rice, toss it all with a low-fat curry dressing, and the salad showed potential. Further, as a frequent recipe contest judge myself, I knew that if I wanted seconds of something, it was going to win money. Salad on the Wild Side had that "give me more" quality. And it captured $1,000.

SWEET-SOUR CELERY SEED DRESSING
Makes 1 cup

Juice of 1 lemon
Cider vinegar
1/3 cup sugar
2 tablespoons celery seed
1 teaspoon Dijon mustard
Dollop of honey
1/2 cup oil
5 green onions, thinly sliced (optional)

Squeeze lemon. Place juice in measuring cup. Add enough cider vinegar to reach 1/2 cup mark. Place in mixing bowl. Whisk in sugar, celery seed, mustard and honey. Slowly whisk in oil until well blended. Stir in onions, if desired.

A reader says . . .

Although I have acknowledged your gift before, I feel I should let you know that we did, indeed, receive a check for $1,000 from your Paul Newman prize, apparently signed by Paul himself.

— Susan L. Larson,
Second Harvest St. Paul Food Bank

SALAD ON THE WILD SIDE
Makes 6 servings

Salad:
- 1 cup wild rice
- 2 tablespoons salt-free chicken flavor instant soup mix (or use 2 chicken bouillon cubes)
- 4 ounces nearly fat-free cooked ham or turkey ham, cut in julienne strips
- 3/4 cup hot pepper cheese, cut in julienne strips
- 3/4 cup broccoli florets, broken into small pieces
- 1 carrot, peeled and cut into thin rounds
- 3/4 cup red pepper strips
- 4 green onions, cut into thin rounds
- 3/4 cup walnut halves
- Freshly ground black pepper

Dressing:
- 1/2 cup canola oil
- 2 tablespoons lemon juice
- 2 tablespoons white-wine vinegar
- 1/2 teaspoon dry mustard
- 1/2 teaspoon curry powder (or more to taste)

To cook wild rice: Rinse wild rice with hot water. Drain. In saucepan, combine rice with 3 cups hot water and instant soup mix or bouillon. Simmer, covered, for 35 to 45 minutes, or until water is absorbed and rice is tender. Cool.

To mix salad: In large mixing bowl, toss rice with ham, pepper cheese, broccoli, carrot, red pepper, onions and walnuts. Add a few grinds of black pepper.

To make dressing: In small bowl, beat dressing ingredients until emulsified. Taste to see if more curry powder is needed. Pour over salad. Toss to mix well. Chill before serving.

Blue-Eyed Guys
October 20, 1985

Paul Newman was an occasional subject of the column over the years, and I wrote about him with hardly controlled gushes. The man in my house wondered why I made such a fuss when I was testing recipes made with the actor's newly introduced food products:

My husband was getting defensive. "What's so special about Paul Newman? He's no great cook," he growled.

"Ah, but those beautiful blue eyes," said I, the Newman fan in our family.

My husband took off his glasses and batted Nordic blue eyes at me, repeating, "What's so special about Paul Newman?"

Newman Film Festival

July 26, 1992

For his second recipe contest, Newman invited food writers to send entries. As I sent in three recipes for judging, I worked Newman's movie titles into the column:

DEVILISH SHRIMP BISQUE

Makes 4 servings

4 tablespoons butter
1/4 cup flour
2 cups milk
1/4 cup olive oil
1 pound peeled and deveined shrimp,
    cut in half lengthwise
4 green onions, chopped
1/2 jar (11-ounce size) Newman's Own
    All-Natural Salsa (your choice of
    medium or hot)
1/4 cup sherry
1 tablespoon Worcestershire sauce
Freshly grated parmesan cheese
    (optional)

In large saucepan over medium heat, melt butter. Add flour. Stir until thoroughly combined. Reduce heat. Add milk. Stir until smooth and creamy. In saute pan, heat olive oil. Add shrimp and chopped green onions. Saute until shrimp are opaque. To milk mixture, add shrimp mixture, salsa, sherry and Worcestershire sauce. Heat until bubbling. Serve immediately, with grating of cheese. Pass warm garlic toast.

Will my favorite dreamboat actor, Paul Newman, be a "Hustler" and rush to try these recipes? Might he do a "Sundance" over my Devilish Shrimp Bisque, my Chicken on the Wild Side, my Saucy and Slim Veg-A-Mac — or am I just "Kid"-ding myself?

Those are the dishes I've concocted for the food-writers' division of Paul Newman's salsa recipe contest, and I'll be a "Cat on a Hot Tin Roof" throughout "The Long Hot Summer" until "The Verdict" is announced. It's not "Winning" "The Prize" and getting "Pocket Money" that motivates me. I'll never get to see "The Color of Money," since all the awards are donated to the winners' designated charities.

I'd feel "The Sting" of losing only because it would mean that I'd get no chance to go to New York for the finals, where Newman himself judges the finished dishes. I'm hoping "Somebody Up There Likes Me," but there'll certainly be an "Absence of Malice" on my part should another of my food-writing colleagues get to gaze into those Newman blue eyes.

Somebody up there did like this Devilish Shrimp Bisque, declared $2,500 winner of the food writers' contest. I developed the recipe by altering a favorite shrimp bisque recipe, seasoning it with Newman's salsa. And the American Cancer Society, Second Harvest St. Paul Food Bank and a Macalester College scholarship fund benefited from my win.

Bombing Bombe

August 21, 1994

Paul Newman was calling again — for entries in his cooking contest. And I called on readers to help me when my Bombe-Bolina was bombing:

Last year, no inspiration hit me, but this year's competition, for which food writers must use Newman's just-introduced Bombolina Sauce for Spaghetti, got my inventive juices flowing via word association. Bombolina. Bombe. I would make a bombe or dome-shaped pasta dish and call it Bombe-Bolina.

Easier said than done.

Call this a work in progress. I'm still trying to get it to work perfectly, and if anyone wants to help tinker with the technique, I'd appreciate your advice.

The flavor of this vegetarian pasta dish is not debatable. Everyone loves the blend of vegetables, basil sauce and cheese.

Making it all hang together is the issue.

My vision is of a perfect pasta dome embedded with a starburst of red and green pepper strips, emulating Italian flag colors. In my image, the pasta behaves so beautifully that it can be sliced into wedges, revealing vegetables within.

Dream on.

Readers to the Rescue
September 11, 1994

I told readers that my original recipe tasted like a winner, but the pasta shell I packed around the bowl slid south when the bombe was unmolded. Here are some of their solutions:

"It sounds like you have an implosion bomb," chuckled one of my helpful callers, Catherine Litch of New Richmond, Wis. She suggested gluing it all together with a thick bechamel sauce.

Deborah Norrie of Rochester, Minn., thought the bombe might stay put if it were served at room temperature.

Dorothy Verstraete of Mendota Height, Minn., said, "Ten cups of moist vegetables really need a tablespoon of cornstarch to relieve some of the fluid pressure inside the mold."

I tried that classic trick, thickening the vegetables before adding the sauce, and it worked beautifully.

Other helpful readers suggested a polenta shell. Or rice would be nice. Or rosamarina, which is rice-shaped pasta. Unfortunately, that pasta is unknown in my favorite Grand Rapids market, but the place does stock acini de pepe, tiny rounds about the size of half-hearted sleet pellets. The pasta swells to the girth of immature peas during cooking, and I thought the pieces might glue themselves into a bombe shell around the vegetables. Almost. It might have worked if I'd had time to let this version cool in the pan, as Deb Norrie does, but the Lake Hungries were banging their knives and forks. Alas, another reject.

Also on my answering machine, Amy No-Last-Name thought elbow macaroni built up in a springform or angel food cake pan would do the trick. But the shape wasn't what I was after.

Angie Ibarra — a sister food writer (her columns formerly appeared in the Stillwater, Minn., Gazette) and author of one of the more memorable cookbooks ever discussed in this column: a gourmet treatise on liver — had a gourmet idea for this project as well. She suggested making pinwheels out of lasagna noodles and gluing them into the pan with cheese. Inspired, I bought sheets of fresh pasta; spread them with a mixture of cheeses, butter and egg; rolled them up; cut circles; and plastered them into my 10-cup aluminum bowl. In a couple of places, they were plastered too successfully and didn't slide out when the pan was inverted, but the recalcitrant pieces were easy to shove back into place. With a starburst of sauteed peppers on top, the bombe was a blast! I sent it to Newman, calling it Bombe-Bolina Elegant.

Marie Mickelson of Columbia Heights, who wrote, "I fell in love with Paul Newman about the same time

---

A reader says . . .

I was a new bride when I began trying your recipes, always feeling we had similar tastes. I have raised two girls and still delight in "from scratch" cooking.

— Carla Moody, St. Paul

BOMBE-BOLINA — EASY VERSION
Makes 6 to 8 servings

10 cups chopped vegetables (broccoli, cauliflower, peeled eggplant, bell pepper in various colors, zucchini, mushrooms, red onions, carrots, garlic, etc.)
2 tablespoons olive oil or canola oil
2 tablespoons butter
Seasoning to taste (freshly ground pepper, Italian seasoning, garlic salt)
1 jar (28 ounces) Newman's Own Bombolina sauce, divided

12 ounces angel-hair pasta, cooked al dente
1 egg, beaten
2 cups (8 ounces) freshly grated parmesan cheese, divided
About 15 strips of red and green bell pepper
Nonstick cooking spray
Parchment paper or foil

To cook vegetables: In Dutch oven, heat oil and butter. Saute vegetables until slightly softened. Season vegetables as they cook with freshly grated pepper, Italian seasoning and garlic salt. Stir in 1 cup Bombolina sauce. Set aside.

To prepare pasta: Cook pasta according to package directions. Drain. Rinse lightly with cold water (you want some starch to remain). Toss with beaten egg and 3/4 cup parmesan cheese.

To assemble: Thoroughly spray 10-cup aluminum bowl with nonstick spray. Cut parchment paper or foil circle to fit bottom of bowl. Spray with nonstick spray before fitting in bottom of bowl. When pasta is just slightly cooled, spoon enough into bowl to just cover bottom. Spoon about half of vegetables over pasta. Sprinkle with parmesan cheese. Repeat layers, finishing with a layer of pasta. Pack down with spatula. Cover bowl with double layer of foil (spray area that will touch pasta).

To bake: Place in 350-degree oven for 25 minutes, or until bombe is heated through. Remove foil. Allow bombe to cool slightly in bowl for 5 minutes.

To serve: Meanwhile, heat remaining Bombolina sauce (in its uncovered jar in microwave, if you wish). Saute pepper strips in a little oil. Run sharp knife around sides to loosen bombe. Invert bombe onto large serving plate. Pour ring of sauce around bombe. Make starburst of alternating red and green pepper strips on top of bombe. Cut into wedges to serve. At table, pass remaining sauce and remaining grated cheese.

I fell in love with Elvis," suggested that the bombe should be layered, alternating pasta and vegetables, with sauteed peppers, applied afterward, as the crown. It slid out of the pan perfectly that way. That version I sent under the title, Bombe-Bolina Easy.

"The Verdict:" Upshot of all this experimentation is that the easy version of Bombe-Bolina rocketed to second place in the contest. No lunch with Newman this time, but again, $2,500 for my favorite charities.

A Dreamy Dish

June 12, 1994

Blame it on jet lag. Mornings after homeward trans-Atlantic flights I'm usually awake pre-dawn and slightly groggy.

Just off the plane from Stockholm, however, I awoke at the usual too-early hour, but this time alert to the vivid dream dish I'd invented in my sleep.

Contest entrants have told me they keep pen and paper beside their bed to jot down nighttime recipe inspirations because they fear they'll forget by morning.

I didn't have to write down anything — my creation was clearly memorable. I dreamt about a dish I even named in my sleep: Shrimp on the Half Shell. Each supersize shrimp, half its shell cut away, was topped in my fantasy with a blend of butter, onion, garlic, lemon juice and fresh horseradish.

SHRIMP ON THE HALF SHELL

Makes 4 servings

1 pound extra-large (12 count) shrimp in
    shells
1 large lemon, halved
1/2 cup white wine or white vermouth
1 teaspoon lemon pepper

1/2 cup fresh horseradish root, peeled and
    finely grated
4 tablespoons (1/2 stick) butter
2 green onions, minced (white part only)
2 cloves garlic, peeled and minced

To steam shrimp: Rinse shrimp well. Place in large saucepan. Squeeze in juice of half lemon. Add white wine or white vermouth, lemon pepper and enough water to nearly cover shrimp. Cover pan. Place over medium-high heat. Steam shrimp just until pink (do not overcook). Remove from heat. Cool slightly.

To prepare sauce: Peel and grate horseradish. In small saute pan, melt butter. Add green onions and garlic, sauteeing over medium heat until onions and garlic soften. Add juice of remaining half lemon and about 1/2 cup grated horseradish. Cook, stirring, until horseradish is soft and has lost its "burn."

To broil shrimp: As soon as shrimp can be handled, use very sharp knife, preferably serrated, to

cut away half of shell from tail to top, removing vein from each shrimp in the process. Heat broiler. Place half-shelled shrimp in baking pan, shell side down. Spoon some horseradish mixture on top of each. Broil until mixture bubbles and browns slightly. Serve immediately, to be eaten with knife and fork, cutting flavored shrimp meat away from lower shell.

Optional garnish: Cook 1 cup additional finely grated horseradish in sprayed nonstick pan, stirring until strands brown lightly and sharp flavor softens. After topping on broiling shrimp starts to bubble, sprinkle each shrimp with browned horseradish strands and return pan to oven for 1 to 2 minutes, watching so horseradish strands don't burn.

Why fresh horseradish, when in all my recipe-testing career it has never appeared in this column as an ingredient? In my post-flight stupor, I must have been remembering fresh horseradish that kept appearing during our three weeks of Nordic travels, pretty amazing to those of us with the lifelong impression that Scandinavian food is bland.

T'aint so anymore. Ten years ago, I was startled to see a Mexican restaurant in Helsinki. Now, that city has the full range of spicy dining options, and Thai food is the current hot item.

Sometimes, the grated horseradish strands we kept experiencing in Scandinavia were briefly precooked, then used as a garnish on meats, such as those served at Helsinki's Savoy restaurant, lending characteristic flavor but diminished heat. Other times, the fresh root was simply grated as a fiery condiment.

The most memorable application was in a soup of pureed artichokes, Arctic shrimp and fresh horseradish daringly served at the gorgeous Royal Park Radisson, built in former military barracks overlooking Haga Park in suburban Solna, about five minutes from downtown Stockholm.

That incredible soup, savored the evening before we flew home, must have been in my dreams when I so clearly envisioned Shrimp on the Half Shell. But would my dream recipe work in the wide-awake reality of my kitchen? With a little experimentation, it did, and nicely.

A reader says . . .

Although I am an avid reader of the news and business sections, I turn to your column first. Thanks you for being part of my Sundays for so many years.

— Kathleen Lambrecht, St. Paul

The Day I Had Lunch With Paul Newman
October 25, 1992

How could I resist? Lunch with Paul Newman was too tempting.

But when I heard I'd won the food-writers' division of Newman annual contest with my recipe for Devilish Shrimp Bisque, I groaned about the date of the luncheon. It was smack-dab in the middle of a food trip I was leading to the Low Country of South Carolina and Georgia. I'd have to leave Hilton Head before dawn, fly via Charlotte to New York City, have lunch at the Rainbow Room atop Rockefeller Center, then take two flights to Savannah and a long cab ride to catch up with the group by dinner time.

Too much trouble?

Are you kidding?

About a half-hour into the commuter flight between Hilton Head and Charlotte, I realized that the pantyhose I'd pulled out of the suitcase that morning were a pair that bags at the ankle (but obstinately refuse to run, so I can't throw them away).

Lunch with Paul Newman wearing sagging socks? Never!

As soon as my cab from La Guardia deposited me at Rockefeller Center, I detoured into Saks Fifth Avenue, where I told the clerk I wanted pink pantyhose to match my dress. She climbed a ladder to reach the very top shelf, where she extracted a $15 pair, imported from Switzerland. Fifteen bucks for pantyhose? What the heck! When will I ever have lunch with Paul Newman again?

Toting my little Saks sack, I ducked into the Rainbow Room ladies lounge, where I learned that the Swiss don't sell much stretch for $15. As I yanked, pantyhose ripped. Fortunately, the resulting run stayed above hemline until the lunch ended.

My food-writer best friend, Janice Okun of the Buffalo (N.Y.) News, also a Newman devotee, had a spare frequent-flyer ticket, so without much urging on my part, she, too, arose before dawn and flew to New York just for the lunch.

Eleanor gazes into those famous blue eyes during lunch with Paul Newman.

"I know of no other actor I'd do this for," she swears.

We sipped cocktails made from Newman's Own Old-Fashioned Roadside Virgin Lemonade based on wife Joanne Woodward's recipe (she wasn't there), and chatted with the likes of Harry Smith of "CBS Morning News" (tall, friendly), until the low-key event got under way.

Good Housekeeping editor John Mack Carter, whose magazine co-sponsors what Newman calls "The Culinary Oscars," opened the ceremonies by

mentioning a few of the 6,000 entries that didn't become finalists. Among them, Pit Stop Pot Roast (evoking Newman's penchant for auto racing), which required a three-pound pot roast soaked in Newman's Own Italian dressing and a 200-mile car trip. The roast, directed the entrant, is to sizzle on the manifold; after 100 miles, you stop the car and turn the roast over.

Another, using Newman's Bandito salsa, was named Bandito Chicken, and began, "First, you steal a chicken."

Then came the afternoon's entertainment, which Carter described as "watching Paul Newman eat lunch" when the actor judged the several finalists in the open-to-the-public division of the contest. Tucking a napkin under his chin, Newman said, "At last year's finals, I dribbled sauce on my shirt. I'm not going to do that again."

Ever the observant reporter, my friend Janice opened her column about the contest with this tidbit: "Item for a lull in conversation: When Paul Newman eats, he does so in the Continental style— the fork remains in his left hand throughout."

Janice also noted for her readers that Newman tied a blue napkin neatly over his light blue shirt and navy

---

A reader says . . .

I am a devoted fan of yours. I do not like to cook, but I thoroughly enjoy your articles about food and your culinary trips.

— Caroline Hanna, Little Canada, Minn.

blue tie — "all the better to bring out the baby blues, my dears ..."

This year, he didn't dribble. The napkin remained pristine, although halfway through judging, realizing that every eye was on his face and fork, he asked, "Does anyone know how to do this gracefully?" Never mind. He managed, even when slurping stretchy mozzarella strings.

With no script, no director, but playing to cameras that recorded his every bite, Newman ad libbed. Tasting Bagelroonies, a broiled bacon and cheese concoction flavored with his Sockarooni sauce, he quipped, "Are these a relative of Mickey Rooney?"

Assessing food, he admits, is tough. "Isn't there anything in bathing suits I can judge?" he wondered. After he'd tasted all seven entries, Newman said, "I'm going to take another run at it." And he tasted them all again.

His Connecticut neighbors and partners in the Newman food venture, author A.E. Hotchner and his wife, Ursula, were invited by Newman to taste the finalists' recipes as well, but when the three huddled by a gilded statue to determine the winner, Newman overruled their opinions.

The top prize, he decided, should go to Janet Sutherland of Escondido, Calif., who blurted out after a grinning Newman had just kissed her, "Oh gosh, I knew he had good taste."

The Assistance League of Escondido Valley, which finds clothing for needy schoolchildren, will get a $50,000 donation from Newman, whose company — which was begun "as a joke," he told me — has donated all of its profits, about $50 million in the last decade, to an array of worthy causes.

As for my shrimp bisque recipe, it had already won the food-writers' division, judged by the Rainbow Room's executive chef Andrew Wilkinson, who told me it came down to a two-way contest between my soup and an alligator recipe sent by a Florida writer.

Since shrimp are easier to buy than alligator, my bisque triumphed, and the $2,500 it won will be donated to the Second Harvest St. Paul Food Bank, the American Cancer Society and the Ivan Burg journalism scholarship at Macalester. I get to keep a plaque.

Of course, everyone is salivating for details of the Newman lunch. I admitted to one of my co-workers that talking to the movie star didn't make me weak in the knees or the slightest bit fluttery. "Let me take your pulse," she offered.

So what is he really like? At age 67, he's a bit long of tooth and totally gray-haired, though his patented smile is still devastating.

"He's quite magnificent," Janice said, ogling when Newman arrived at the lunch.

But my husband's eyes are more true blue.

A napkin protecting his tie, Newman, assisted by a Rainbow Room chef, judges entries.

1990

*— Of brides, birthdays, broccoli and
potatoes – couch and otherwise —*

Spud Duds

January 7

In my "to be tested" stack for almost a year has been a squat volume called "The Official Couch Potato Cookbook." I'd decided the cookbook and couch-potato era were passe, but CBS "This Morning" just staged a fashion show of couch-potato clothes: soft, loose, zippered lounge wear from such big-buck designers as Norma Kamali and Calvin Klein. Does this mean my old pink-fleece robe will no longer do?

Cooking Under Pressure

February 4

Pressure cookers were returning to the cooking scene:

Many of us won't have to buy a new one, just dig deep into cabinets to find our Old Faithfuls shoved out of sight when microwave ovens became the preferred tool for time-saving cookery.

The rest of you probably never dared to own one, because all your relatives loved to kid Aunt Sadie about the time her pea soup erupted out of the pressure cooker to create a certain Jackson Pollock effect on her kitchen ceiling.

Here Come the Brides

July 1

My husband and I might have gone out for a quiet dinner on our 25th anniversary June 20 had it not been for a wild idea.

Among our friends are a half-dozen couples who also wed in 1965. Considering today's divorce statistics, remaining married for 25 years is quite an accomplishment, yet the Big Silver isn't celebrated today the way it was in small towns when I was growing up. My husband and I thought we'd make our date an occasion to be shared only with friends who would most appreciate this mutual anniversary year.

The evening turned out to be more silly than significant, rating highest on the laugh meter of any party we've ever given.

The Trudells take the cake — Jayne in her dress and George in formal wear over Bermudas.

We set the scene: Lohengrin and Purcell wedding marches on the tape player. White paper bells, silver streamers and "Happy Anniversary" banners decorating doorways. We rented a silk flower bridal bouquet dripping with white orchids and stephanotis, bought boutonnieres for the men and filled a brimming punch bowl for all.

I had my hair done as it was on my wedding day and pinned my veil in place. Lace stockings and a blue garter were the only other wedding attire that still fit. My husband wore a narrow black tie, white shirt and black suit, just as he had 25 years ago.

Most of us "brides" displayed our wedding dresses on hangers dangling from the banister as part of the decor. But Jayne Trudell marched in wearing full regalia, from bandeau veil to flowing train. Her "groom" George followed in his formal finery — including dove-gray vest, wing collar and matching gloves. Below his black tuxedo jacket he wore white

Bermuda shorts and tennis shoes. The Trudells definitely stole the show.

We giggled over each other's wedding pictures and took turns posing, bouquet in hand, for the traditional cutting-the-wedding-cake photos. And then we ate, probably much more than any of us did during the excitement of our original wedding days.

Each course, from beef tenderloin and gravlax appetizers to layered and frosted sandwich loaf to hot chicken salad to beef stroganoff to a watermelon boat, represented something from all of our wedding receptions. Even the cake was baked with several flavored layers.

I had told the chef preparing our wedding reception 25 years before at The Gaslight, a restaurant which used to be at Seven Corners in Minneapolis, that I wanted a nosegay of daises as the ornament on our cake. I still laugh at our wedding pictures showing my new husband and me cutting into a cake from which long-stemmed daisies sprouted in a rangy bouquet.

Each in Its Own Season
July 22

There are no fruit flies on me. This is fruit season — the season of my discontent.

Watermelon tastes more like water than melon. Cherries aren't cheap. Peaches aren't even remotely peachy. And the outlook for a crop in the northern blueberry bogs is bleak. We even let grass grow on a promising wild strawberry patch in our lake lawn, but got only a quarter cup of berries for our efforts. I suspect birds harvested the rest.

When I was a kid, peaches would be "in" for only a short time. We'd get a call from our family grocer that Colorado clings had arrived during that small window of opportunity, just a week or two, when the fruit was perfectly ripe for canning. Our kitchen became a cauldron, summer heat intensified by boiling water to loosen peach skins and the mini-geyser billowing atop mom's huge pressure canner crowded with quart jars.

My cousin's husband, Looch, has an opinion on any subject, and it's usually audacious enough to promote debate. But I don't argue with him about his theory on fruits and vegetables. Looch says, "Eat each one when it's in prime season. Eat so much that you're sick of it and don't want it again for a full year until it's in season again."

"We've gotten caught up in a system of shipping fruit earlier and earlier," said Ramsey County Extension Agent Don Olson, noting that the first fruit to reach market commands top price, even though it's not at its best. "The error is on both sides. The public takes food production for granted and wants everything all the time. Growers respond by picking and shipping products for longer periods."

Maybe It's Our Cold Winters
January 14

Is it to-MAY-to or to-MAH-to soup?

Does one eat it or drink it?

Which is better: milk or water to dilute tomato soup?

Whatever you do or say is correct, apparently, because none of the celebrities who came to Minneapolis last week for a whiz-bang promotion honoring the 20 billionth can of Campbell's Tomato Soup could agree.

"Lifestyles of the Rich and Famous" host Robin Leach, hired as emcee by Campbell's for what he termed with his usual hyperbole, "a production of epic proportions," toned it down a bit. "I'm still loud enough to be heard by people in Duluth listening in on a pair of soup cans joined by string," he said. Only when he read a proclamation from Mayor Donald Fraser did he go full-voice, announcing that Minneapolis was chosen for this hoopla because its citizens consume the most tomato soup in the country.

That should be Minneapolis and St. Paul, of course. We in St. Paul (and all surrounding suburbs) eat as much soup and make as many porcupine meatballs as folks west of the Mississippi. Campbell looked at metro statistics, but with typical coastal myopia, the soup company saw "Minneapolis-St. Paul" but said, "Minneapolis."

Wading Through Brunch
March 25, 1990

"Oh, I couldn't invite you for dinner. What if something went wrong?"

We food writers hear that all the time. So do cooking teachers, home economists and other food professionals. Take my advice: Invite us. No one will be more understanding if you trip en route to getting dinner on the table.

Case in point: I hosted a Saturday brunch and guests included three cooking teachers and a wine expert.

Testing recipes, I served them swamp water. Actually, the brunch punch — a blend of V8 juice, orange juice and basil — only looked like an environment friendly to frogs. It didn't taste that bad, but funniest thing, no one asked for a refill.

Fortunately, I'd prepared a hefty appetizer plate. It had to sustain brunchers long after the proposed time to eat. I was casual about getting started on the main course because no baking time was listed in the recipe. About a half-hour before I thought we should be brunching, I mixed up Sombrero Eggs. They were rather soupy, but I stuck them in the oven anyway. Thirty minutes later, the eggs were still a golden pond, not even starting to set around the shores. Another 40 minutes passed before the eggs were servable.

Defining Dining

November 18

From a column about the Minneapolis Woman's Club cookbook, "10,000 Tastes of Minnesota":

Someone, during the Bicentennial, challenged me to define American food. I could do little besides babble about its diversities.

More recently, someone else asked for a definition of Minnesota food, and beyond the obvious native ingredients — walleye, wild rice, wild berries — I was back to babbling.

Come on, how would you categorize what Minnesota eats? Lefse, lutefisk? Pasties, porketta? Kolaches, krumkaka? Wake up and smell the 21st century.

Read My Lips: No Broccoli

October 14

Food news came from a rather unexpected source, the White House, when George Bush announced that he has waged a lifelong campaign against broccoli:

To George (now saying "Read My Budget") Bush, broccoli must seem appetizing indeed, now that he's got a steaming fiscal mess on his plate.

During the broccoli wars, a California broccoli marketer shipped 10 tons of the green stuff to the White House. First Lady Barbara graciously accepted a broccoli bouquet and a sheaf of recipes that might soften ornery George's attitude. The rest was donated to a Washington, D.C., food bank supported by the United Fresh Fruit and Vegetable Association.

Steffanie Connors, media information specialist for that association, wished Bush would express his dislike of other vegetables. "The commodities we market are so healthy, but they don't always have news value," Connors said. When the broccoli uproar was at full boil, she was getting 100 calls a day from newshounds sniffing for a quote.

I bet every broccoli grower in California votes for Bush in '92, as long as he keeps bad-mouthing their produce.

Even the President might unzip those readable lips to allow Broccoli Strudel into the inner workings of government. The Democrat majority among our lake neighbors said they'd pass a law that everyone should try it. However, phyllo dough, that tissue-paper-thin Greek pastry, more fragile that cobwebs, makes the strudel more difficult to wrap up than the federal budget.

All the women at our cabin formed a caucus, huddled over the counter trying to make the delicate dough behave. One of our guests, Tui Flower, New Zealand's most renowned food writer, was best able to control the fragile sheets. But then, she later told our city neighbor's rambunctious dog to sit, and he did — a trick that even obedience school couldn't instill. Both phyllo and Fido react favorably to this no-nonsense New Zealander.

A reader says . . .

You and your good recipes! I've read your articles and clipped your recipes for years. You got me excited about making Chili Citrus Chicken. My son is a carry-out at Lunds in Highland, and he said they have pepper jelly because they'd received calls asking about it since your recipe came out. See the effect you have on us!

— Phyllis Hollihan, St. Paul

BROCCOLI STRUDEL
Makes 6 servings

1 package frozen chopped broccoli,
   thawed and drained
1/4 cup plain or seasoned bread
   crumbs
1 teaspoon dry mustard
1 tablespoon caraway seeds (optional)
2 tablespoons grated parmesan cheese
6 ounces skim-milk mozzarella, grated
2 green onions, finely chopped
1 tablespoon margarine, melted (or
   more as needed)
3 sheets phyllo dough (12-by-17-inch),
   from frozen package
Nonstick cooking spray

To prepare filling: In mixing bowl, combine broccoli, bread crumbs, dry mustard, caraway seeds, cheeses and green onion.

To prepare phyllo: Handling phyllo dough according to package directions, lay 1 phyllo sheet on large piece of plastic wrap. Sparingly brush margarine on dough, using light pastry brush. Repeat layering 2 more times.

To fill phyllo: Carefully mound broccoli mixture toward 1 end of dough, leaving about 2 inches on each end. Smooth mixture with hands. Using plastic wrap, lift phyllo and roll it, starting at full end of dough. Carefully roll dough around broccoli mixture, tucking bits in at ends if they fall out. Roll up, jellyroll fashion. Spray cookie sheet with nonstick spray. Place roll on cookie sheet, seam side down. Brush top with remaining margarine.

To bake: Bake in 375-degree oven for 35 minutes, or until browned. Allow to cool slightly before slicing.

Premier Cru Burger
April 1

The recipe came from, of all places, France, where American fast-food hamburgers were not-so-long-ago considered a threat to French cuisine. I looked at the directions and wondered how any hamburger so loaded with ingredients could call itself "perfect." It read more like the formula for meatloaf. But when tested, it proved its perfection.

Americans might guzzle Coke, but Barton and Guestier, better known as B&G wine exporters,

THE PERFECT HAMBURGER
Makes 16 burgers

2 eggs
1/2 cup celery, finely chopped
1/2 cup onion, finely chopped
1 teaspoon chili powder
1 tablespoon Worcestershire sauce
1 teaspoon Dijon mustard
Salt and pepper
1 peeled tomato, finely chopped
4 pounds ground round (extra-lean
   ground beef)

In large mixing bowl, combine eggs, vegetables and seasonings. Add meat. Blend. Mold into desired shapes. Grill, barbecue or saute.

suggested that the hamburger should be washed down with their 1988 bordeaux. I think the burgers are so good they're worthy of Lafite Rothschild.

They're juicy, and yet the eggs hold them together so they don't crumble through the grates on the barbecue. We offered them to company with a tray of "fixings" — lettuce, tomatoes, cheese. But a rerun the next night proved the burger was best on its own.

Golden Potato Salad
May 20

My 50th bashes — one in St. Paul and one at the lake — were cause to roast the birthday girl with over-the-hill hilarity. I drink a toast to all of you who've been there with this greeting-card sentiment:

WORLD'S GREATEST POTATO SALAD
Makes 12 to 15 servings

Marinade:
- 1/2 cup oil
- 1/4 cup white-wine vinegar
- 1 teaspoon dry mustard (or more)
- 1 tablespoon sugar
- 1 teaspoon paprika
- 1 teaspoon salt
- Generous grindings of black pepper

Salad:
- 5 pounds potatoes, boiled and peeled
- 6 green onions, sliced
- 1 large sweet onion, finely diced
- 3 cups salad dressing (Spin Blend preferred)
- 1/4 cup cream or half-and-half
- 1 to 2 tablespoons prepared mustard (Dijon preferred)
- 6 ribs celery, finely chopped
- 8 eggs, hard-cooked

To make marinade: Combine oil, vinegar, mustard, sugar, paprika, salt and freshly ground pepper. Beat with wire whisk until well blended.

To prepare potatoes: Boil potatoes until tender but not mushy. Drain. Peel as soon as possible, while still very warm. Slice potatoes into large bowl or 10-by-15-inch glass cake pan. As soon as a layer of potatoes covers pan, sprinkle with some green onion and sweet onion. Drizzle with some marinade. Repeat layers of potatoes, onions and marinade until all are used. Cover with plastic wrap. Refrigerate several hours, or until thoroughly chilled.

To make salad: When ready to mix salad, combine salad dressing, cream and prepared mustard. Taste and add more mustard, if desired. Add chopped celery and chopped eggs to potatoes (reserve some center slices of egg for garnish, if desired). Stir in dressing mixture until potatoes are coated. Adjust seasoning to taste. Spoon salad into lettuce-lined serving bowl. Garnish with egg slices. Sprinkle with paprika.

"On your 50th birthday, remember this: Like good wine, we grow more mellow with age. Or is it as we age, we grow more mellow with good wine?"

For the party at the lake, guests chowed (as Aric would say) on Perfect Hamburgers and what I immodestly call World's Greatest Potato Salad. My mother always marinated warm potatoes for salad so flavor penetrated them. Using her technique, I built a recipe, shared here. I make it by instinct, but this is close enough.

French Cuisine on a Fiver

August 5

In this year of a big birthday and significant anniversary, we also celebrated the 30th year since two college friends and I spent three months traveling abroad, an adventure we called "Europe '60:"

That perfectly marvelous summer provided more education than a year of college, and it changed my life, attuning me to European culture and food, turning me into an avid traveler who's returned to Europe 15 times and chased around the rest of the world.

Thirty years ago, it was a big deal to go. None of our parents had crossed the Atlantic, and we three sent lengthy letters home every few days to share our experiences with them. Recently rereading my letters from that era of "Europe on $5 a Day" (we often spent less), I laughed about how much I detailed money spent and food eaten.

A letter from Rodez, France, inspired our reunion menu. I'd written about checking into the nicest hotel in town ($4 for a room for three, a splurge after staying in youth hostels for 25 cents a night). "For dinner, we also decided on the best restaurant in Rodez, really fancy and modern. Now get this: We had a five-course meal — potato soup with very fine noodles; sliced sausage; baked salmon garnished with peas and potatoes, salad, lemons and tomatoes; lamb

chops with peas baked in a pastry shell, asparagus and shoestring french fries; and for dessert, rich vanilla custard ice cream with ladyfingers — all for $1.75 apiece including 12 percent service charge. We got clean plates and silver with each course, and had wine to boot. Can you imagine?"

Cost for re-creating that menu for my traveling companions, minus the sausage course, was more than $80 for ingredients alone. Thirty years later, I don't remember how those lamb chops were seasoned, but this Time-Life version flavored with onion juice, olive oil and fresh thyme would make any French restaurant proud.

LAMB CHOPS WITH THYME

Makes 4 servings

8 lamb loin chops, cut 1 1/2 inches thick and trimmed of fat
1 medium-sized onion
1 teaspoon salt
2 tablespoons olive oil
1 tablespoon chopped fresh thyme
Parsley

Grate onion. Sprinkle with salt. Let rest for 10 minutes. Squeeze onion between palms to extract juice. Add juice to olive oil. Lay chops on wax paper. Brush onion-oil on both sides of chops. Sprinkle thyme on both sides. Cover chops with wax paper. Let rest for 2 hours. Grill, preferably over hot coals, placing chops 3 inches from heat. Grill for 5 minutes on each side. Arrange chops on platter. Garnish with parsley. (Note: If you don't want your hands to reek, grate onion into glass pie plate and press with spatula or spoon, tilting plate so juice runs to collectible spot.)

1991

— Caesar becomes suspect, fat becomes phobic, cooking is pared to lowest common denominator —

Please Don't Pass the Gravy
February 24

I don't know what scares people more about food these days — the fear of fat or qualms about cooking?

Remember those simpler days when our main concerns were counting calories and making sure we acquired the daily alphabet of vitamins? Now, the Number One worry of most Americans is not just fat, but whether that fat is saturated or unsaturated, prefixed by poly- or mono-, is serum or dietary, or elevates HDLs or LDLs. Good gravy! (But don't put any on your potatoes.)

Dipping into KISS Cooking
Also February 24

Speed-scratch cooking, in which a cook invests some emotional involvement and a touch of homemade effort when enhancing basic convenience fare (such as gussying up a cake mix) was being promoted by Land O Lakes:

Some years ago, the motto of food writers was Keep It Simple, Stupid — KISS for short. Researchers told us people wanted recipes with no more than four ingredients.

Quick Fruit Dip is speed-scratch at its speediest: Mix 1/2 cup nonfat salad dressing, such as Miracle Whip Free, with an 8-ounce carton of lemon-flavored yogurt. That two-component dip drops to the lowest common denominator of what can be termed a recipe. The only other time in all these years of testing recipes that we've run a two-ingredient recipe was for another fruit dip, suggested by Audrey Ledding of White Bear Lake: Combine a 7-ounce jar of marshmallow creme and an 8-ounce package of cream cheese.

You'd have to be an absolute dip to be intimidated by either of these 15-second formulas, both so simple and speedy that they require no brain-strain at all.

Quick Fruit Dip is fit for the fat-phobic, too. Using no-fat dressing and similar yogurt drops the fat to a single gram, the cholesterol to zilch and calories to only 60 per serving. Just don't dip avocados into it.

Hail, Caesar,
But Hold the Eggs
April 21

From a column introducing Minnesota-made pasteurized eggs:

Poor Caesar. We have not been praising the salad lately, but burying it — to calm our fears of salmonella. I don't personally know anyone who has suffered salmonella poisoning from eating Caesar salad made with nearly raw eggs, but we're all nervous.

High-Test Wine
May 26

On a Sunday when I preached against food phobias:

Veal recipes have been scarce in the food column for the past couple of years, not from fear of eating veal, but because of my fears about inevitable allegations from anti-veal and animal-rights activists who claim publishing veal recipes is tantamount to endorsing cruelty to animals.

The latest jitters are metal based, about cooking in aluminum pans, for instance. "But if a person eats Rolaids, he's going to absorb scads more aluminum," maintains TV microwave chef Donovan Jon Fandre.

My relatives up north said they'd heard that storing liquor in crystal decanters, or even drinking alcoholic beverages out of crystal glasses, can leach lead. With all the wines we've sipped out of our Waterford, we must be as full of lead as '50s gasoline.

Maybe the Cleats Contain
a Daily Dose of Iron
June 2

That May 26 column about food phobias brought scads of letters from both the vocal anti-veal lobby and also from those who were fed up with food scares:

Among the "attagirl" comments was a letter from Sherman Shultz, my astronomy professor at Macalester College in St. Paul light-years ago, who professes irritation at "self-styled experts trying to save us all from some sort of imagined horrible death because of eggs, meat, butter, milk or whatever is in fashion to decry this season." He added, "Just remember the fate suffered by old man Rodale, the former editor of Prevention, who simply keeled over during a television interview and dropped dead, in spite of all his preaching on organic this and organic that."

I also remember, Sherm, that diet guru Nathan Pritikin didn't survive to collect Social Security.

WCCO radio voice Steve Cannon has his "Mrs. J.R. of Wayzata," the only person who writes him with any regularity (probably even after he retired in 1997). I have my own frequent source, a gravel-voiced guy who never says his name but always speaks his mind. His comment about last week's column: "The next thing you know, we'll all be eating sanitized cardboard."

Regular Caller also mentioned a mother who stopped sterilizing her baby's bottles the day she discovered the child chewing on his daddy's golf shoes.

The Dishwater Tasted Good

February 3

Let me define Kitchen Crisis. It is that instant when one reaches for the pan in which pear cooking liquid has been carefully reduced to syrup for flavoring the custard of an elaborate pear tart, only to see that pan just coming out of the dishwater in the hands of a helpful husband.

Yes, it's true, I did put that pear syrup pan close to the sink to cool. How was my husband to know what he thought a panful of "scum" was vital to the recipe?

This kind of crisis occurs only when guests are due in a half-hour and the usual pre-party hysteria is at its height.

Trendwatch: Food as Medicine

September 1

Here's a word to remember: "nutraceutical."

According to regulatory language, "nutraceutical" refers to "any substance that may be considered a food or part of a food and provides medical and health benefits, including the prevention and treatment of disease." Watch for debate about this new amalgamation of preventing and treating diseases, now blocked in this country because our standard federal regulations are set up to deal with food and with drugs, but not with food as drugs.

Purloined from the Porch

July 14

From a column about barbecued burgers:
Someone swiped our Weber from the back porch. It was nearly new, a Christmas gift to my husband, who'd fired it up only a few times before it disappeared. I can only hope that the crook cook now using it cremates every steak, and that all his barbecuing tastes like charcoal-lighter fluid.

Macaroni Madness

January 27

If you are beyond a certain age and anything other than Italian, you probably say "macaroni." Unless you are beyond a certain age, non-Italian and a native Minnesotan, in which case you say "Creamettes."

Macaroni or the ubiquitous Creamettes, in my childhood, were the basis of many a cheap meal. Pasta, in today's vernacular, refers to something more pricy, like eight bucks for an appetizer combining a dime's worth of noodles, a few flecks of dried tomatoes and herbs, and maybe an aggregate half-dollar in cream and cheese. Very elegant. Very expensive.

Cases of reverse chic abound, such as when the macaroni-and-cheese phenomenon hit Manhattan last year. Midwest comfort food was the craze, though how comforting it was to pay $15 for a plate of something one step above Kraft Dinner is debatable.

I heard of a fierce and feared executive, a high-octane woman in the New York advertising industry, who burst into tears when a costly plate of restaurant macaroni and cheese was placed before her. "This is just like my grandma used to make," she blubbered.

Grandma could have bought a week's worth of groceries for the price of that single serving of macaroni, which didn't even bother to masquerade as pasta.

Food writer James McNair, who was interviewed when the pasta book in his single-subject series was introduced, swears this bacon-tomato dish is one of Sophia Loren's favorites. If it would make us all look like Loren, pass the platter, please. I used smoky Wisconsin-processed thick-cut Nueske's bacon, but regular bacon would add a crispier quality.

This is the potato chip of pastas — you can't eat just one serving.

Cure You or Kill You
February 17

"Thai Penicillin" was what those at our table, top bidders for a Tested Recipes cook-your-own dinner at a United Way silent auction, dubbed Hot-and-Sour Shrimp Soup after it instantly cured one taster's sinus condition. I loved its intense character so much that I made another batch for a midweek dinner party, efficiently simmering the broth ahead of time and allowing it to stand, unstrained, for two hours. Big mistake. Bitterness leaching from lime skins overpowered even such pervasive flavors as cilantro and jalapeno.

BACON AND TOMATO PASTA
Makes 4 entree or 8 appetizer servings

1/2 pound smoked bacon, cut into
   1-inch lengths
1 cup finely chopped yellow onion
2 cups peeled, seeded and chopped fresh
   tomatoes or drained canned tomatoes
1 cup packed chopped fresh basil, divided
4 quarts water

1 tablespoon salt
1 pound dried pasta, such as penne or
   rigatoni
1/2 cup heavy cream
Fresh basil sprigs for garnish
Freshly grated parmesan cheese

To prepare sauce: In saute pan or skillet, saute bacon over medium-low heat until done but not crisp. Add onion. Cook, stirring frequently, for 5 minutes, or until onion is soft and lightly golden. In food processor or blender, combine tomatoes and 1/2 cup chopped basil. Puree to coarse consistency. Add to bacon-onion mixture. Increase heat to medium-high. Bring to a boil. Reduce heat to low. Simmer for 30 minutes.

To cook pasta: In large pot, bring water to a rapid boil. Stir in salt. Add pasta. Cook until tender, but still firm to the bite. Drain.

To serve: Drizzle heavy cream into simmering sauce. Add remaining 1/2 cup chopped basil. Heat through. Toss with drained pasta. Garnish with basil sprigs. Serve immediately. Pass cheese at table.

Memories of North Shore Sundays

June 30

On occasional summer Sundays of my childhood, Mom packed a picnic for our all-day excursion to the North Shore.

Freshly smoked ciscos snagged at a roadside fish shack were the only purchased grub we ate within sight of Lake Superior. Sometimes, we'd drive a dusty road just a bit inland and park in the yard of a tarpaper-covered house, where my parents and their friends (we were usually a two- or three-car caravan) would negotiate with a weathered fisherman who had a knack for smoking whitefish.

I don't remember restaurants along the Shore. All that was on my 10-year-old mind was finding a picnic table near Gooseberry Falls, where we'd unload the potato salad, ham sandwiches and fried chicken.

Some families probably still carry picnics, but today's typical Shore explorer more likely packs a

HOT-AND-SOUR SHRIMP SOUP

Makes 4 servings

1/2 pound medium-sized raw shrimp
1 tablespoon vegetable oil
5 cups chicken broth
2 stalks lemon grass, cut into 1-inch pieces
  and crushed
Peel from 1/2 lime
1 serrano or jalapeno chili, cut in half
1/2 cup canned straw mushrooms
2 1/2 tablespoons lime juice
1 tablespoon Thai or Vietnamese fish sauce

Garnish:
  2 green onions, including tops, thinly
    sliced
  2 tablespoons coarsely chopped cilantro
  1 1/2 tablespoons coarsely chopped
    mint leaves
  1 serrano or jalapeno chili, seeded and
    slivered

To prepare shrimp: Shell shrimp. Rinse shells. Pat dry. Cut shrimp in half horizontally. Rinse and devein.

To make broth: Place large pot over high heat until hot. Add oil, swirling to coat surface. Add shrimp shells. Cook for about 30 seconds. Add broth, lemon grass, lime peel and chili. Bring to a boil over high heat. Reduce heat to medium-low. Simmer, covered, for 20 minutes. Strain broth. Discard seasonings.

To cook shrimp: Return broth to pot. Heat to a simmer. Add shrimp and mushrooms. Cook for 2 minutes, or until shrimp turn pink. Stir in lime juice and fish sauce.

To serve: Ladle soup into individual bowls. Garnish with green onion, cilantro, mint leaves and slivered chili.

Note: Fish sauce, lemon grass and straw mushrooms are available in Asian markets.

wallet filled with money and looks for places to exchange it for good eating.

That column about recipes from a North Shore cookbook yielded this treat favored in a Two Harbors restaurant:

Cardamom Toast is a real northwoods dunker, served at Shari's Kitchen, a small cafe mingled with oldies and goodies at Carousel Antiques on Highway 61. Despite the "Swedish" name of these toasts, proprietor Sharon DeLeo said she got the recipe from a Finnish friend in Ely. My cousin Betty (all Finn, like me) has been making something similar for years, but she got her recipe, flavored with anise, from an Italian friend.

Built-in "Chaser"
August 11

These easy-to-measure margaritas have become a favorite of ours for summer parties. They're mellower and lower in alcohol than the usual margarita blend, and no one guesses they contain both tequila and a beer "chaser."

SHARI'S KITCHEN SWEDISH CARDAMOM TOAST
Makes about 30 slices

1 cup margarine
1 1/2 cups sugar
2 eggs
1 cup sour cream
3 3/4 cups flour
1 teaspoon baking soda
2 teaspoons crushed cardamom seed

Mix all ingredients in order listed. Spread on lightly greased 9-by-13-inch pan in 2 long strips. Bake in 350-degree oven for 30 minutes, or until golden brown. Cut each strip into 1-inch-wide pieces. (Note: You'll need 2 baking pans to hold all the pieces.) Place pans on top and bottom racks in oven. Bake for 20 minutes. Rotate pans, top rack to bottom and bottom rack to top. Continue baking until slices are golden brown. Remove toast from pans. Cool on racks.

BEER MARGARITAS
Makes 6 cups

1 can (6 ounces) frozen limeade
   concentrate, thawed and undiluted
1 limeade can beer
1 limeade can tequila
4 cups crushed ice
Lime wedges for garnish

In container of electric blender, pour limeade concentrate. Use limeade can to measure beer, then tequila. Add crushed ice. Process until smooth. Garnish margarita-filled glasses with lime wedges.

Readers to the Rescue

— The Column was Two-way Communication —

Most wonderful, through all the Tested Recipes years, has been my ongoing interchange with readers, who've called, written, commiserated, chided, laughed and cried along with each weekly installment.

And they've sent recipes. If I needed one, I only had to ask, and it arrived in the mail within days. Nearly every contribution was tested. These were the ones other readers told me they liked best.

Baking at its Most Basic
October 23, 1983

Recipes came in all flavors — and lengths. When I was speaking to the Woodbury Women's Club, member Barb McCarthy gave me the quickest muffin recipe I've ever tried: Combine 3 cups of self-rising flour with 3 cups of any-flavor ice cream. Bake as usual for muffins.

Investing my favorite butter pecan ice cream in it, I told readers that it does work, but melt the ice cream before measuring, because when frozen, its volume is greater than when it's liquid. The Office Hungries were challenged to guess the recipe, but they were stumped. When I told them ice cream was the secret ingredient, one murmured, "That's like tearing down a mansion to build a shack."

Philosophies Slathered With Sauce
June 5, 1977

Eunice Spence of River Falls, Wis., is a gal after my own heart.

In three pages, typed single-spaced, Eunice philosophized about kitchen perfection — of lack thereof:

"Were it not for those occasional mistakes you report — and dozens of the like I make myself — life would be boring, indeed.

"It's great fun to try nailing currant jelly to the wall just to enjoy the reaction of onlookers.

"It's surely a fact that hindsight is better than foresight, especially when it comes from those 'behind'.

"What a life that must be, always keeping up appearances. Appearances, mind you, from a single angle."

Spence wrote of her many cooking disasters, not among them her recipe for barbecue sauce, which she'd been making for years. I tried it without liquid smoke, which I didn't have on hand (besides, smoky flavor is not my favorite). MSG is also dispensable.

EUNICE'S BARBECUE SAUCE
Makes about 5 cups

1 envelope unflavored gelatin
1 1/2 cups water, divided
2 tablespoons cornstarch
1/2 cup vegetable oil
1/4 cup grated onion
1 can (about 10 ounces) tomato puree
1 1/2 cups ketchup
1 tablespoon prepared mustard
1/2 cup bottled lemon juice
1 scant cup brown sugar
1/4 cup white sugar
2 teaspoons or more liquid smoke (optional)
1/2 teaspoon each: sweet basil, garlic salt, ginger and monosodium glutamate (optional)
1/4 teaspoon ground cloves
2 tablespoons Worcestershire sauce

Soak gelatin in 1/2 cup water. Blend cornstarch with 1/2 cup water. Stir in oil. Grate onion into saucepan. Add 1/2 cup water, tomato puree, ketchup, mustard and lemon juice. Heat to a boil. Add sugars, seasonings, Worcestershire sauce and gelatin mixture. Cook for 10 minutes. Add cornstarch-oil mixture, stirring well. Cook until mixture thickens. Remove from heat. Use for barbecuing.

Anonymous Boursin
July 20, 1980

The recipe for Homemade Boursin arrived on a mimeographed sheet with only the name Betty Ramsey on top:

Wherever you are, whoever you are, Betty, thanks for the recipe; it's a goody. Boursin is a creamy French cheese flavored with herbs and garlic, and the real stuff is rather expensive.

My sister-in-law, Ilene Aune from Amherst, Mass., introduced me to Boursin a dozen years ago, so we tested this recipe while she was visiting last week. If ever there was one who could detect bogus Boursin, it's Ilene. She gives this version high marks, especially for its buttery texture.

In garlic, it's right up there, maybe too much. Perhaps use only one clove. Our baby Schnauzer, who thinks he's people, was sniffing about as we were sampling the homemade Boursin, so I gave him a crackerful. When he gave me a lick later, his breath was quite fragrant.

A reader says . . .

I travel for my work, and I always check out food columns in Chicago, Detroit, Atlanta, San Francisco, Milwaukee, Boston, Washington. Yours remains my very favorite. I can't tell you how many of your recipes are in my permanent collection. My daughter is a great cook, too, and she says at least 10 of her favorite recipes are from your column.

— Judy Leahy, St. Paul

HOMEMADE BOURSIN
Makes 1 1/2 cups

1 package (8 ounces) cream cheese
6 tablespoons butter
2 teaspoons green onion, finely chopped
2 teaspoons minced parsley
2 cloves garlic, crushed

Mash cream cheese with butter and green onion. Add parsley and garlic. Season to taste. Shape into flat ball or brick. Cover. Refrigerate. Age for a few days. Roll in parsley before serving. Serve with crusty French bread. (Note: If mixture is blended in food processor, it comes out thinner and can be used as a dip.)

A Quick Tumble Off the Wagon
January 13, 1980

"How you egg me on!" I chided readers. But I couldn't be distressed about more hits for my chocolate addiction when readers sent such divine recipes. We tried them during a "sick-and-tired-of-New Year's diets chocolate orgy."

Lorraine Schifsky of St. Paul sent Surprise Cupcakes, saying, "Fantastic for all you chocoholics. Mmmm, delicious, like candy." I agreed, promising to tattoo the recipe for Surprise Cupcakes on my beating arm. They're going into the Tested Recipes Hall of Fame, along with Everyday Cookies and Four-From-One Fruitcake.

The "surprise" is a fudge-like pecan-studded center in the cupcakes, which bake with a crackly top and brownie-like texture. Frosting is unnecessary. Correct: The recipe contains no baking soda or baking powder.

Later, I heard from some readers who said they were having trouble with the cupcakes sticking to paper cups. You might try forgetting the papers, greasing the pans heavily, and removing the cupcakes within minutes after they emerge from the oven. Or you could lightly spray the liners.

SURPRISE CUPCAKES
Makes 12 cupcakes

4 squares semisweet chocolate
2 sticks regular margarine
3/4 cup chopped pecans
4 eggs
1 cup flour
1 3/4 cups sugar
1 teaspoon vanilla

Melt chocolate with margarine. Add pecans. Set aside. Mix but do not beat eggs, flour, sugar and vanilla. Fold lightly into chocolate mixture. Spoon into cupcake liners placed in cupcake pans. Bake in 325-degree oven for 35 minutes.

End-All of Chocolate Recipes

January 13, 1980

On that same Sunday, we ran Elsa Clay's recipe for Pecan Fudge Pie. Clay, who lives in St. Paul, sent what she called "the chocolate recipe of all chocolate recipes, and that's the end of it."

Does that mean, Elsa, that you never, ever want us to test another chocolate recipe? Oh dear. Cold turkey.

"After one bite," Clay went on in praise of her recipe, "you'll be eternally grateful to me for finally cleaning my closets. This Pecan Fudge Pie clipping surfaced in the middle of ancient stuff I unearthed while tackling the hall closets. In the process, incidentally, I also discovered another of the Dead Sea Scrolls and the original manuscript for the Old Testament. Well, it has been awhile ... "

My testing results were enthusiastic: A chocolate whopper that has true chocoholics rolling their eyes in ecstasy. It's extremely rich — slice slimly.

I suggested that graham-cracker crust might be appropriate, but nobody else agreed. A 10-inch pie pan will hold it better than a 9-incher.

PECAN FUDGE PIE

Makes a 9-inch pie

9-inch unbaked pastry shell
**1 package (12 ounces) semisweet
   chocolate pieces**
1/4 cup half-and-half
4 eggs
1/2 teaspoon salt
2 teaspoons vanilla extract
1 cup light corn syrup
2 tablespoons butter, melted
About 5 ounces chopped pecans

In saucepan over low heat, melt chocolate. Add half-and-half, stirring constantly. Set aside. In medium bowl, beat together eggs, salt, vanilla, corn syrup and melted butter. Mix well. Slowly add chocolate. Fold in pecans. Pour into pie shell. Bake in 350-degree oven for 45 to 50 minutes, or until center is set. Cool. Serve topped with whipped cream.

Spaghetti Sauce Second to None

September 13, 1981

Audrey Ferrey of Shoreview wrote, "A year or so ago, you printed a recipe titled the Second Best Spaghetti Sauce in the World. (Note: Actually, it was in 1978, and the recipe appears in the chapter recounting that year.)

"I tried it, and because of its flavor and simplicity, it immediately replaced the spaghetti sauce I learned to make when I was first married — my standby for a good 20 years.

A reader says . . .

*I have saved many of your Tested Recipes
pages in a bag, and if I get desperate or
hungry, I can always go there and spend
some time with you.*

— Elaine Anderson, Roseville, Minn.

"This split my family into two factions. Half hailed the new sauce as a decided improvement, while the other half remained loyal to the old favorite. Now, when we're having spaghetti, the next question is, 'Which sauce — yours or Second Best?' So I humbly submit the Third Best Spaghetti Sauce in the World. It's mild, rather sweet, something like Ragu."

I tried Ferrey's version and found it second to none.

Entertaining
Shrimp Casserole
January 18, 1981

Gerrie Given, wife and mother to the men who run St. Paul's Prom Catering Co., contributed this recipe to

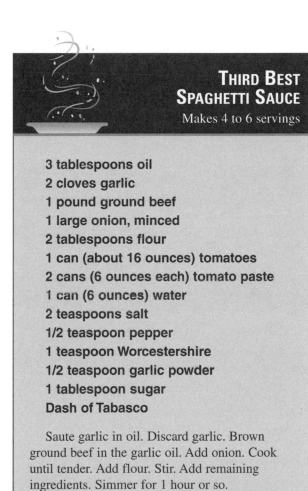

THIRD BEST SPAGHETTI SAUCE
Makes 4 to 6 servings

3 tablespoons oil
2 cloves garlic
1 pound ground beef
1 large onion, minced
2 tablespoons flour
1 can (about 16 ounces) tomatoes
2 cans (6 ounces each) tomato paste
1 can (6 ounces) water
2 teaspoons salt
1/2 teaspoon pepper
1 teaspoon Worcestershire
1/2 teaspoon garlic powder
1 tablespoon sugar
Dash of Tabasco

Saute garlic in oil. Discard garlic. Brown ground beef in the garlic oil. Add onion. Cook until tender. Add flour. Stir. Add remaining ingredients. Simmer for 1 hour or so.

Note: "This is thick and can be thinned with water, red wine, vermouth, what have you," Audrey Ferrey wrote. "It doesn't have to be thinned if you like a sauce that won't slide off your spaghetti," I told readers.

SHRIMP CASSEROLE
Makes 6 to 8 generous servings

1 cup thinly sliced green onion
1/2 cup butter, divided
5 tablespoons flour
2 1/2 cups chicken broth
1/2 cup clam juice
1/2 dry white wine
1/2 cup heavy cream
1/2 teaspoon oregano
1/2 cup parmesan cheese, divided
2 whole garlic cloves
1/2 pound mushrooms, sliced
8 ounces vermicelli (thin spaghetti)
4 cups cooked, shelled extra-large shrimp

Saute green onion in 1/4 cup butter. Mix in flour. Add broth, clam juice, white wine, cream and oregano. Simmer for 3 minutes. Stir in 1/4 cup parmesan cheese. Set aside. Melt remaining 1/4 cup butter. Add whole garlic cloves and mushrooms. Cook quickly. Discard garlic. Bring salted water to a boil. Cook vermicelli until just al dente (cooked but still firm). Combine vermicelli with sauce, mushrooms and shrimp. Pour into buttered 9-by-13-inch casserole. Top with remaining 1/4 cup parmesan cheese. Bake, uncovered, in 375-degree oven for 20 to 25 minutes, or until bubbly.

a holiday entertaining story, proclaiming it "probably the best tasting casserole — just yummy." I later tried it for the column and have made it many times since. Two hints. Barely cook the vermicelli so it doesn't get mushy (or you can use other less delicate forms of pasta). And to extend the shrimp, cut them in halves from top to bottom.

Contributor Unknown
April 26, 1981

Readers can also include in-house personnel. The name of the newspaper copy-desk person who contributed this recipe has been lost over time, but even unattributed, it's worth inclusion for its ultra-chocolate, ultra-easy results.

TRIPLE WHAMMY CAKE
Makes 1 bundt cake

1 package (2-layer size) regular chocolate
    cake mix (no pudding added)
1 package (4-serving size) instant
    chocolate pudding mix
2 eggs
1 3/4 cups milk
1 package (12 ounces) chocolate chips

Combine cake mix, pudding mix, eggs and milk. Beat by hand (or with a mixer) for 2 minutes. Stir in chocolate chips. Pour into greased bundt pan. Bake in 350-degree oven for 50 to 55 minutes. Cool for 15 minutes in pan before turning onto cake plate. Serve plain or dust with powdered sugar. Or top with chocolate frosting to make a quadruple whammy.

Pate for Liver Loathers
December 26, 1982

Marjorie Hartig Beer Nunn became a friend in the most intimate way — she was the doctor who delivered Aric. We've maintained a friendship, though we don't see each other very often now that she lives in Texas. But years ago, we often shared parties, and at one, she introduced me — a nonliver lover — to this simple but excellent pate. Of course, I had to pass it along to readers.

MARJORIE HARTIG'S LIVER SAUSAGE PATE
Makes 12 servings

1 bouillon cube
1 package unflavored gelatin
1 can (10 3/4 ounces) consomme
3/4 pound best-quality liver sausage
1 package (8 ounces) cream cheese
Grated onion to taste
Tabasco and Worcestershire sauces to
    taste

Dissolve bouillon cube and gelatin in consomme. Pour one-quarter of mixture into well-buttered mold. Chill. Put remaining consomme mixture into blender. Add liver sausage, cream cheese, grated onion, Tabasco and Worcestershire. Blend until smooth. Pour mixture into mold. Chill for 12 hours or more. Unmold. Serve with snack-size rye bread.

Eggy Answer to Crust Queasies

November 14, 1982

June Gerten of White Bear Lake volunteered her favorite pie-crust recipe after I'd mentioned, when testing pasty recipes, that the coward's answer to pastry is refrigerated crust from Pillsbury (a new product in 1982). "Tsk, tsk," said Gerten, who sent her recipe. It doesn't contain lard, which some of us die-hard pie bakers and pasty makers prefer, but she swore by it.

EGG PIE CRUST

Makes 4 pastry rounds

1 whole egg
2 tablespoons white vinegar
1/2 cup water
3 1/4 cups flour
1 tablespoon sugar
3/4 teaspoon salt
1/2 teaspoon baking powder
1 1/4 cups Crisco

To make pastry: Beat egg with vinegar and water. Set aside. In bowl, put flour, sugar, salt, baking powder and Crisco. With electric mixer on low, mix until it resembles coarse cornmeal. Make a little hole. Pour egg mixture into middle of dry ingredients. Using rubber spatula, toss flour mixture into liquid. Mix until dough clings together. Using hands, form into firm ball. If dough is sticky, dust with a little flour. Chill for 20 to 60 minutes, or longer if you wish, but let it warm up longer when ready to use.

To roll pastry: Cut dough into 4 equal parts. Form each quarter into a ball. As you roll dough, use light strokes, pushing it into circle with heel of hand. Turn over. Redust with small amount of flour on board and rolling pin so dough won't stick. Turn round several times during rolling until it is size of pan plus 1 or 2 inches.

Au Gratins to the Max

June 27, 1982

Chuck Jameson was catering director at the Radisson St. Paul Hotel when he gave me this recipe, so rich, but so easy.

CHUCK JAMESON'S AU GRATIN POTATOES

Makes 8 servings

8 medium red potatoes
10 ounces sharp cheddar cheese
1 teaspoon salt
1 pint whipping cream
1/4 cup bread crumbs
1 tablespoon butter

Boil potatoes. Cool. Peel. Shred on medium grater. Shred cheese. Alternate layers of potatoes and cheese in greased 9-by-13-inch baking pan. Sprinkle with salt. Pour unwhipped cream over all. Top with bread crumbs mixed with butter. Bake in 350-degree oven for 50 to 60 minutes.

Lefse Finally on the Grill

October 13, 1985

My cousin Betty Rostvold, married to a Norwegian, asked me if I had an easy lefse recipe. Just that day, I'd gotten an idea for lefse made with instant mashed potatoes sent by Barbara Blomker of Roberts, Wis. Betty immediately tried the recipe, and her husband gave it his Norsk endorsement. She suggested that the dough be rolled into golf-ball sizes, refrigerated, then taken from the cooler as each is rolled. Both Blomker

LEFSE

Makes about 2 dozen

3 cups instant potatoes (Potato Buds preferred)
1 cup powdered milk
1 1/2 teaspoons salt
1 tablespoon sugar
1/4 pound (1 stick) butter
3 cups water
1 1/2 cups flour

In large bowl, combine instant potatoes, powdered milk, salt and sugar. Melt butter in water. Bring mixture to a rolling boil. Pour butter mixture over dry ingredients. Mix well with large spoon. (Note: It will be the consistency of mashed potatoes.) Cover bowl with damp cloth. Refrigerate until cold. Add flour. Blend with pastry blender but finish mixing with hands until smooth. Cool well again. Form mixture into 2 or 3 rolls similar to making sliced refrigerator cookies. Slice off piece of dough about golf-ball sized. Roll thin. Fry on very hot lefse grill until lightly browned on both sides.

and Betty said a long, thin, wooden lefse stick will make turning the rounds much easier.

"What did you use for a lefse grill?" I asked my cousin. "A lefse grill," she answered. It had been given to her years ago as a hint that she might make the Scandinavian specialty. "We've been cooking pancakes on it until now."

What a Way to be Squashed

November 18, 1984

Daniel and Lola O'Brien, former St. Paulites who had retired to Henning (in Minnesota's northwestern lake country), sent this recipe they'd created to glorify autumnal squash. "If you don't have all the herbs and spices mentioned, use larger portions of the ones you have; the mixture can absorb a lot of seasoning," Lola told us. She also said that the recipe can be cut in half, or extra filled squash can be frozen.

A reader says . . .

Through Testing Results notations, your recipes are as treasured as if they'd been exchanged with a long-time friend. I appreciate the testing being done for me, allowing our table to have so many special foods. I'm one of your Reader Hungries.

— Edith Barnes, Arden Hills, Minn.

STUFFED BUTTERNUT SQUASH
Makes 6 to 8 servings

2 pounds pork sausage (unseasoned, or use ground pork)
1 pound hamburger
2 ribs celery (with green leaves)
1 green pepper
2 cups chopped zucchini
1 medium onion
1/3 cup salad oil
7 ounces seasoned croutons
1 cup raisins
3 to 4 tablespoons Worcestershire sauce
1/2 teaspoon sage
1/2 teaspoon poultry seasoning
1/2 teaspoon Italian seasoning
1/4 teaspoon rosemary
1 teaspoon seasoned salt (Lawry's Seasoning preferred)
1 cup water
3 to 4 butternut squash

To make filling: Lightly brown crumbled pork and hamburger. Do not drain. Dice celery, green pepper, zucchini and onion. Add oil and vegetables to meat. Cover. Steam for about 5 minutes. Put croutons and raisins in large bowl. Sprinkle with Worcestershire sauce. Add meat and vegetables to bowl. Sprinkle with sage, poultry seasoning, Italian seasoning, rosemary and seasoned salt. Toss gently but thoroughly. Add water. Toss again.

To fill squash: Cut squash in halves. Remove seeds. Place each half on large square of foil. Heap stuffing in cavities. Wrap completely in foil. Place in pan or on cookie sheet. Bake in 375-degree oven for 1 hour, or until cooking fork penetrates squash easily. Serve with extra butter, salt and pepper.

College-Bound Cookies
October 11, 1987

When I asked for packable cookies that could be sent to a son in college, Joan Tubbs of New Richmond, Wis., contributed these, which were air-expressed, with two other kinds, to Aric and his dorm buddies for assessment. When the cookies arrived, Aric's

BEST EVER COOKIES
Makes about 6 dozen

1 cup brown sugar
1 cup white sugar
1 cup margarine
2 eggs
2 1/4 cups flour
2 teaspoons baking powder
1 teaspoon baking soda
Pinch of salt
1 cup coconut
1 1/2 cups oatmeal
1 cup chocolate chips
1 cup raisins
1 cup chopped walnuts (optional)
White sugar for dipping

In mixing bowl, cream sugars and margarine. Add eggs. Mix well. Add dry ingredients, coconut, oatmeal, chocolate chips, raisins and nuts. (Note: Dough will be very stiff.) Form into walnut-sized balls. Dip tops in white sugar. Bake in 350-degree oven for 12 to 15 minutes.

popularity rating went up several notches. "Everyone chowed," he told me over the phone. His dorm mates voted the chocolate-chocolate-chip cookies best, but Best Ever Cookies were my favorites.

Tubbs said she mailed batches of these cookies to her son, John, a 1987 graduate of University of Wisconsin-Madison.

Super Bread
January 26, 1992

During the general hysteria of the 1992 Super Bowl, which proved to the world that Minnesota in midwinter can be bearable, I escaped the downtown

hubbub for a more down-to-earth situation: speaking to the White Bear Lake Welcome Wagon. That group had chosen an ecology theme for the year, and put together a booklet called "Earthly Delights," sharing recipes from their annual tasting party, including this earthy bread contributed by member Mary Hittner.

BULGUR BREAD
Makes 4 large loaves

1 1/2 cups water
1 1/2 cups bulgur wheat
4 packages dry yeast
3 cups warm water, divided
1 tablespoon salt
1/3 cup margarine
1/2 cup honey
2 cups whole-wheat flour
8 cups white flour, divided

To make dough: In large microwavable bowl, combine 1 1/2 cups water with bulgur. Warm at full power for 9 minutes, or until water is absorbed. Meanwhile, in small bowl, soften yeast in 1 cup warm water. Add salt, margarine, honey and 2 cups warm water to hot bulgur mixture. Stir to soften margarine and dissolve salt. Add whole-wheat flour and 1 cup white flour to bulgur mixture. Beat well. Mix in yeast mixture. Use enough of remaining 7 cups white flour to make a workable dough. Knead for 5 minutes. Let rise in warm place for 1 hour.

To finish bread: Punch dough down. Shape into 4 large or 8 small loaves. Let rise again. Bake in 375-degree oven for 30 minutes.

A reader says . . .

I dearly love your column, and it's the first thing I read. It has been great to follow your son's growing up, your disasters and successes, your husband's diets, your remodeling, and, yes, the dogs, dear souls. Your columns are like a visit with a dear friend.

I'm preparing for our Norwegian church bake sale coming up, and beside my Norwegian cookies, I am preparing the cardamom cookies and cardamom toast that I got from your column. Last year, the cardamom toast was the first to run out. Thank you for all the testing, eating, humor — and just you.

— Irene Small, Detroit Lakes, Minn.

1992

— Juicers and bread machines please the burgeoning vegetarian crowd —

Getting Juiced
May 24

We're drinking our lunch because Jay Kordich and his Juiceman II machine came to town:

The Juiceman is the fastest talker I've ever encountered. And juicing produces the fastest food. Kordich, who has been hawking juicers for 40 years, has finally hit the big time via TV infomercials and a fast-selling book. Now a millionaire after a lifetime of lean years, he spiels like an old-time carny, displaying incredible energy for a 69-year-old guy. Juicing, he says, is the secret to his vitality.

Likewise, his Juiceman II buzz-saws through vegetable pulp and fruit rinds in a flash, producing frothy food in liquid form. We've been juicing at our house for two weeks, grinding heaps of carrots, apples, cabbage, celery, parsley, even beets — enough to create a mountain of compost.

Bread Machines a Rising Phenomenon
December 27

Chances are, based on how fast they were selling before Christmas, a bread machine was under your tree this year.

The mechanical home bakers have been around for several years, but just in the last few months, sales rose faster than dough on a warm day. Not surprisingly, the crowd gathered around the demo table in Dayton's downtown St. Paul store just before Christmas was, except for me, all men.

Some were reaching for credit cards, thinking they'd found the solution to the what-to-get-for-the-wife problem. But a number of the men already owned machines and were asking the demonstrator questions.

Considering how men love kitchen gadgetry, as proved by the gender of that crowd, I did the logical thing and got a bread machine for my husband, who's always seeking breads made without oil or sugar.

The box was to have been wrapped and put under the tree, but he spotted it in the back seat of the car, and before I could screech, "Do Not Open Until Christmas," he had the machine unpacked and was measuring flour.

Bye-bye, Burgers
June 28

Vegetarianism was invading our eating habits, as my husband followed the McDougall Plan, the most stringent of vegan regimes, hoping it would get him off the handful of pills he took daily for his blood pressure and other afflictions:

No meat of any kind, no oils, no fats, no dairy, no caffeine. No food fun for 12 days. But that zealous change did wonders for my husband's various maladies, and he was able to toss away — instead of toss down — a daily dose of pills.

One of my co-workers, devoted to the cause of animal rights, has become such a fervent vegetarian that she won't eat soup if the broth ever said hello to a chicken. She's a radical-etarian.

What am I? How about an opportun-etarian? At home, I occasionally test recipes with meat (which my husband carefully removes from his portion and feeds to the dog), but day-to-day meat meals are a memory. However, if I'm at a luncheon or dinner where meat is served, I don't miss the opportunity to enjoy it.

Vegetarianism is a cloak that fits everyone, depending on how it's draped. Trend forecaster Faith Popcorn says the direction toward vegetarianism is inevitable.

Farewell to Fat
December 6

We used to live off the fat of the land. Where has it all gone?

I open my refrigerator and what do I see but no-fat cream cheese and two brands of low-fat mayonnaise and reduced-cholesterol eggs and fat-free sour cream, all cuddled next to the skim-milk carton.

Hello, Again, Sugar
August 30

Funny how we rattle different dietary worry beads. Not so long ago, sugar and calories were the culprits. Fretting about kids' cavities, we bad-mouthed sugary cereals.

Now, we fret over fat — and sugar may be a surprise beneficiary. We shamefully submit to cravings demanded by a raging "sweet tooth" when it should really be called a "fat tooth." Most of what we crave — ice cream, rich cakes and buttery cookies — get more of their calories from fat than from sugar. Nutritionists are suggesting that "satisfaction" calories usually supplied by fat can be significantly replaced (along with their attendant calories) by using a bit more sugar.

Grand Old Reunion
June 14

Mary Smail of the Macalester College Alumni Office had just finished assuring our Class of '62 reunion committee that "not too many show up for the 30th" when out of my mouth popped, with no forethought, the offer to host a Sunday brunch the morning after our class dinner.

About three months later, Mary mentioned that more were signed up for our 30th than came to our typically well-attended 25th. And just a month ago, she reminded us that reunion weekend would coincide with Grand Old Day.

Oy vey! Grand Old Day. How could I have forgotten that the first Sunday in June is utter chaos just a few steps from our house? I'll tell you how. We usually escape to the lake to avoid that annual madness.

Our back yard, where I intended to seat part of the brunch crowd, is a half-block from that raucous event's

THREE-CHEESE VEGETABLE BRUNCH BAKE
Makes 10 servings

1/2 pound fresh, trimmed asparagus
1/2 cup chopped red bell pepper
2 tablespoons butter
7 cups Vienna or French bread, cut in
   1-inch cubes
1 cup (4 ounces) shredded Swiss
   cheese
1 cup (4 ounces) shredded Monterey
   jack cheese
5 eggs, beaten
2 1/2 cups milk
1/4 cup sliced green onions
1 tablespoon Dijon-style mustard
1/4 teaspoon freshly ground pepper
2/3 cup sour cream
1/4 cup freshly grated parmesan cheese

To prepare vegetables: Cut asparagus into 1-inch pieces. In medium-sized skillet over medium heat, saute asparagus and red bell pepper in butter for 2 minutes, or just until crisp-tender. Set aside.

To make casserole: Lightly butter 13-by-9-by-2-inch baking dish. Place bread in dish. Top with vegetable mixture. Sprinkle with Swiss and Monterey jack cheeses. In small bowl, combine eggs, milk, onion, mustard and ground pepper. Carefully pour egg mixture over top. Cover dish with foil. Refrigerate overnight, or up to 24 hours.

To bake: Bake, covered, in 325-degree oven for 50 to 60 minutes, or just until set. Spread sour cream over top. Sprinkle with parmesan cheese. Bake, uncovered, for 10 minutes, or until crusty and lightly browned.

epicenter. Rock bands blast paint loose on all the houses near the intersection of Grand and Victoria.

Before the bands got too loud, we managed to serve brunch, including among the morning meal this vegetable-cheese bake, which I found in Richfield's Hope Presbyterian's cookbook, sent to my by another former Mac-ite and dorm friend, Donna Meigs Morgan.

Everybody Loved Wizzie
August 16

Life's most valued friends are the ones who make us laugh.

Remembering Elizabeth "Wizzie" Hurley Fiorito brings a smile at this time of sadness over her passing. Laughter is her legacy. She was an original, both intelligent and truly witty, tossing one quip after another into conversation, each punctuated with her irresistible throaty chuckle.

Wizzie had planned to be at our lake house last weekend when, instead, a raging form of lung cancer took this vivacious woman still in her 40s. The long-anticipated trip north was part of the goal-setting that made her last long enough to see her sons graduate. When the unexpected sad news came, I quickly gathered some of her favorite recipes for a column, and these calzones went on to become a community favorite. Dedicated food lover Wizzie, who had two kitchens in her Dellwood home, had been writing a cookbook right up to the end. Her co-author, Sharon Stumpf, supplied me with the text, in Wizzie's words, that would have accompanied this party appetizer:

"This was originally made by an Italian couple in Minneapolis who had a little restaurant. Mother and Dad always bought it for their New Year's open house. When the couple died, my mother had to re-create this wonderful recipe because it not only tasted great, but it could be made ahead and kept warm on a serving tray, eaten easily out of hand. Now, we've gone one better and made it — no kidding, Mom — with frozen bread dough."

Sharon Stumpf recommended the recipe because "every and anybody likes it." Sort of like Wizzie, I guess.

WIZZIE'S MOM'S CALZONE FOR A CROWD
Makes 15 servings

2 tablespoons olive oil
2 cloves garlic, minced
1 large onion, diced
3 eggs
1 cup shredded mozzarella cheese
1 cup grated parmesan cheese
2 cups ricotta cheese
3 tablespoons chopped parsley
3/4 teaspoon salt
Pepper to taste
3/4 pound hot Italian sausage, cooked, cooled and crumbled
2 loaves frozen bread dough, thawed
1 egg, beaten for glaze

To make filling: In skillet, heat olive oil. Saute garlic and onion until translucent. Remove from heat. Cool. In large bowl, combine eggs, cheeses and seasonings. Stir in cooked sausage and onion mixture.

To make calzone: Lightly oil 11-by-14-inch jellyroll pan. Roll dough into 2 rectangles. Fit 1 rectangle in pan with dough overlapping sides. Spread filling over dough. Cover with second piece of dough. Pinch to seal. Brush top with egg glaze. Slit top at 2-inch intervals to allow steam to escape. Let rest for 20 minutes.

To bake calzone: Bake in 375-degree oven for 40 to 45 minutes, or until top and bottom crust are golden. Cool slightly. Cut into squares.

Hostess-Friendly Enchiladas
December 6

Here's the answer to your holiday-entertaining prayers — a casserole that needs to be made ahead so the tortillas can soak up sauce. With fresh salsa decoration, the tortillas look Christmasy.

That was the assessment of this Mexican meal developed to showcase a new product from St. Paul's Old Home Foods.

CHICKEN ENCHILADAS
Makes 6 servings

3 cups cooked, cubed chicken
3 cans (10 3/4 ounces each) cream of chicken soup
1 carton (8 ounces) extra-thick plain yogurt
2 cans (4 ounces each) diced green chilies
Freshly ground black pepper
18 regular-size flour tortillas
2 cups shredded cheddar cheese
1/2 cup chopped green onions

To make filling: In saucepan, mix chicken, soup, yogurt and chilies. Cook over medium heat, stirring constantly, until boiling. Reduce heat. Simmer for about 5 minutes.

To make enchiladas: Place 2 heaping tablespoons of filling on each tortilla. Roll up. Place in large baking pan. Pour remaining filling mixture over tortillas. Sprinkle with cheese. Top with green onions. Bake in 350-degree oven, uncovered, for about 30 minutes. (Note: If using glass pan, reduce heat to 325 degrees.) If desired, serve enchiladas topped with salsa.

1993

— *We hit the quarter-century mark and meet skinny pizzas and wraps* —

25 Years, 3,000-Plus Recipes — and Counting
August 22

Excerpted from the 25th anniversary cover story:

Twenty-five years of tenacious testing. This Sunday madness is, to my knowledge, the longest lived personal food column in the country.

When the idea popped into mind one summer day in 1968, I surely didn't think that, 25 years and more than 3,000 recipes later, the column would still be a weekly feature. I didn't think that each of those years would add another couple of pounds, either. If I had, I would have started writing a diet column.

Technology has evolved relentlessly in these 25 years of cooking. In the early 1970s, we were the first on our block to own a microwave oven, and when I tested recipes in it, only a few readers could re-create them. In those days, I had to give conventional cooking times as well. Now, about 90 percent of all households own a microwave.

Who would have thought that cookbooks would be on computer disks, or that famous chefs could give us private lessons on our kitchen VCRs? When Prodigy was first introduced in this area, I put out a request for chocolate sauce over that "electronic back fence" and, within hours, pioneer Internet users sent sauce recipes from the four corners of America.

Perhaps this column should be written from Jurassic Park. I'm one of those dinosaurs who still cooks from scratch even in these take-out times. At first, the testing task was daunting, since my degree is in journalism, not home economics. Twenty-five Augusts ago, I wrote about juggling two pie recipes at once, in what the headline called "a formidable task." Now, such a challenge wouldn't muss a hair.

Mechanical Bread
January 17

Everywhere I go, people want to talk about bread machines. While I was doing a stint in the Pioneer Press booth at the Women's Expo in Minneapolis, Diane Castellano of Eagan told me about her newfangled addiction to bread baking. "I didn't even know where to buy yeast before I got my machine," she laughed.

I was talking with my friend June Gosule Zieff of Marblehead, Mass., who produces exotic breads in her Dak machine to feed her husband's racing-yacht crew. June had a sensational idea to share: When making raisin bread or even raisin-studded muffins, use chocolate-covered raisins. What an irresistible inspiration.

Falling Into
Recipe Success
April 4

The monumental task of opening a month's accumulation of mail (after a trip to Australia and New Zealand) has its bright spots, such as a letter from Alice Marks of Roseville, who wrote about her Saturday-morning coffeecake adventure:

She arose early to surprise her family with a treat, intending to try a recipe that required a white cake mix, three eggs and a can of strawberry pie filling (she substituted blueberry), all blended and baked in a greased and floured bundt pan at 350 degrees for 40 to 45 minutes.

"What could be simpler? I dumped everything into a big bowl and let my upright mixer do the work while I read my morning Pioneer Press," wrote our loyal subscriber. "Somehow, the vibrations from the mixer caused the cabinet door above to fly open, and a large bag of chocolate chips was deposited into the batter."

Can't you just see it? This is better than an "I Love Lucy" episode.

Marks managed to pull the batter-laden bag from the bowl, but it was ripped open by the beaters "and the chips had to stay."

Disaster? Not at all. "Except for being the color of dust bunnies that have been under the bed for a long time, the cake was a hit. The blend of blueberries and chocolate is surprisingly good."

Wrap It Up
May 23

From a column about Nicole Routhier's book, "Cooking Under Wraps," a forerunner of the "wraps" trend in American fast food:

Challenge: Name a culture's cuisine that doesn't include some wrapped food. I can't think of one.

Everybody, regardless of ethnic background, has grown up eating something wrapped in dough, crust, tortillas, crepes, eggroll wrappers, even leaves.

Pizza on a
Starvation Diet
June 20

Our favorite foods are under fat attack, noted in a column about a book called "Skinny Pizzas":

Now that fat is where it's at, it's inevitable that pizza, America's favorite food, is being put on a diet. Certainly author Barbara Grunes has skimmed and trimmed, and in the process, she's invented new toppings (bok choy, mango salsa) and styles (crab-cake pizza and cheesecake pizza) that folks in Naples couldn't have imagined when they first spread herbed tomato sauce on bread dough.

But I have one major problem with the book — and, in fact, with a lot of diet foods: serving size. Who would consider 1/12th of a 12-inch pizza a serving? OK, maybe it's a serving, but it certainly isn't a meal. Nutritional data for such a skinny slice looks good on paper, but who'll stop at just one?

A reader says . . .

Really enjoy your recipes, your comments and your ability to admit that even an expert can have failures.

— Veda Stone, Eau Claire, Wis.

No Waffling on this Issue

August 8

From a column about waffles:

I worry about the next generations. They may believe waffles only come out of toasters, the same way brownies are born in microwave ovens. The luxury of eating homemade waffles became endangered about the time that Eggo produced its first push-button breakfast. Not that we ever had the toaster variety in our household, but then, I'm a scratch cook, another endangered species.

Throw That Doughnut Overboard

September 26

My food writer friend, Janice Okun, told her readers in Buffalo, N.Y., about cleaning her cupboards in preparation for a move from a large house with big kitchen to a condo, where the advantage is a pretty view and lots of sunlight. Her new kitchen, as she put it politely, is "compact," but then she's also her newspaper's restaurant critic, and she and her husband eat out a lot.

Said Janice, "This is a desert island column — in reverse. I'm not asking what kitchen gadgets or appliances you'd need if you were marooned after a terrible shipwreck. I'm asking what gadgets or appliances you'd pitch overboard."

During her own packing, Janice "was utterly ruthless, performing feats of triage not to be believed. Out with the 15 dishes shaped like seashells. Out with the 3-foot corkscrew that looked like a souvenir from the Inquisition. Out with anything that couldn't be washed in a dishwasher. It was a terrific catharsis."

So I asked readers what they'd keep or cast away:

Many responded, extolling their favorite utensils, but my favorite message was from an unknown caller who said, "Age and lifestyle determine kitchen gadgets. I'm 63, and I haven't used my doughnut cutter for 25 years. That would be the first to go." Amen

I'd Die Before I'd Tell You

November 7

It's about time we had a new pepper steak recipe at our house. I'm still using one that's practically antique, typed on a gravy-stained recipe card during my earliest days at this newspaper when I was Betty Service, writing the Forum and Exchange columns. Betty Service met her demise long ago, but that pepper steak recipe lives on as a family favorite.

While reading the latest issue of Electricity and People from the Northern Electric Cooperative Association in Virginia, Minn., which I still get as a legacy from my parents, I was intrigued to find a pepper steak recipe flavored with grape jelly.

"This has a secret ingredient," I told the Lake Hungries who were busy sopping up pepper steak sauce with chunks of bread. When no one offered any guesses, I told them about the grape jelly and how compatible and color-matched it was in a wine-flavored sauce.

My cousin Betty laughed. Just that afternoon, she'd been reading an article about a fellow who claimed to have a secret ingredient in his spaghetti sauce, but refused to reveal it, even on his deathbed. His survivors deduced his mysterious addition was grape jelly by all the empty jars they found in his house.

BEEF PEPPER STEAK IN WINE
Makes 6 to 8 servings

2 pounds beef round steak

1/4 to 1/2 cup all-purpose flour

1/4 teaspoon pepper

1/4 teaspoon oregano

1/4 teaspoon paprika

2 tablespoons shortening or vegetable oil

1 to 1 1/2 cups water

1 can (16 ounces) stewed tomatoes, coarsely chopped

1 cup ketchup

1/2 cup burgundy wine (or other red wine)

1/4 cup grape jelly

2 large green peppers, cut into 2-inch strips

1 medium onion, sliced

Trim meat. Cut into 1 1/2-by-1/4-inch strips. Combine flour, pepper, oregano and paprika. Add meat strips. Toss to coat evenly. In 3-quart saucepot or Dutch oven, brown flour-coated meat in shortening or oil. Add water. Bring to a boil. Reduce heat. Cover. Simmer for 1 to 1 1/2 hours, or until tender, adding water if needed. Combine tomatoes, ketchup, wine and jelly. Add to meat. Return to a boil. Add green peppers and onion. Reduce heat. Simmer for 5 minutes. Serve atop hot buttered egg noodles or rice.

Senator, Do You Make a Peachy Pie?
August 15

Braham, Minn., site of an annual pie festival, got tangled in politics when Minnesota Senator Dave Durenberger's "peachless" peach pie was declared a winner. But was it really his recipe? Could it have originated in a General Foods ad printed in 1977, as a St. Paul attorney told me after the first story appeared.

We had Piegate right here in Minnesota:

Does General Foods (now Kraft General Foods) still legally own a 16-year-old recipe concocted to promote its Jell-O and CoolWhip products? If the senator "borrowed" that particular recipe, "we have no legal issue," is General Foods' position, "though we would be happy to get credit," said a company spokesperson.

The senator's recipe varied from the original by using a pint instead of a cup of peach ice cream; I tried it and it works, though it may be softer than first intended.

I've judged enough recipe contests to know that people think they are entering a recipe they consider "original" because it's been in the family for years and no one remembers the source.

A reader says...

Sure enjoyed your column about waffles in the Sunday paper. My neighbor and I discussed this, and we, too, worry about young people not knowing about food from scratch. Also, they will never know how to sharpen a knife on the bottom of an earthenware bowl.

— Ruth Campbell, Cedar Lake, Wis.

I wanted to know if Creamy Peach Pie actually had come out of the senator's own family recipe box, or if a helpful staff member had submitted it under his name.

Granted, Durenberger and his staff have had a lot on their plates lately. I started inquiring about the pie recipe a day after a paternity suit against the senator had been in the news and just before the Senate voted on the budget. There was never any hope of speaking to Durenberger directly, so I talked to his press people in Minneapolis and Washington, D.C.

Folks in the senator's Minneapolis office were a bit testy. Spokesman Bill Fritts spoke: "Who the hell cares? Now, we'll probably be in court because someone is suing him over a pie recipe." Probably not, I assured him, but this inquiring mind still wanted to know if the senator ever actually made the pie.

"I don't think this is a pie Dave cooked up himself. But this is actually something he enjoys because he loves ice cream," Fritts said. "Maybe his mom made it for him, but someone on staff may have sent it to Braham."

Ed Belkin, senior director of communications in the Washington, D.C., office, a more jovial soul, had heard about the pie. The day news broke of the senator's first prize, Jay Leno on "The Tonight Show" joked about peach pie with no peaches in it. "Maybe Durenberger took a cue from the Clinton tax cuts that have no cuts in them," Leno quipped.

Several conversations later, Belkin finally related that the pie "is one that's served for office birthday parties," and the recipe is routinely sent out, "if someone requests a recipe from the senator."

The folks in Braham say they made no such request.

For a peach pie with peaches actually in it, we tried the Braham Pie Contest's third-prize winner in the fruit and berry pie category, entered by Marian Milbridge of North St. Paul. If you don't have allspice, omit it, or substitute a touch of nutmeg.

PEACH LOVER'S SOUR CREAM PIE
Makes a 9-inch pie

1 unbaked 9-inch pie shell
Filling:
   3 cups peaches (fresh, frozen or canned)
   3/4 cup sugar (less if using presweetened peaches)
   2 tablespoons flour
   1 cup sour cream
   2 eggs
   1/2 teaspoon vanilla
   Dash of salt
Topping:
   1/3 cup sugar
   1 teaspoon cinnamon
   1/2 teaspoon allspice
   1/3 cup flour
   1/4 cup butter, softened

To make filling: Place peaches in 9-inch unbaked pie shell. Mix sugar, flour, sour cream, eggs, vanilla and salt. Pour over peaches. Bake in 450-degree oven for 15 minutes. Reduce oven temperature to 350 degrees. Bake for 30 minutes.

To make topping: Mix sugar, cinnamon, allspice, flour and butter. Sprinkle over pie. Reduce oven temperature to 325 degrees. Bake for 20 minutes. (Note: This makes a somewhat dense streusel; if you want just a sprinkle, cut topping ingredients in half.)

A Dog's Life

— And Death —

Ever the most eager recipe tasters in our household have been our dogs: a silver Schnauzer named Brandy and Scotties Tigger, Shadow, and lately, a new puppy. They adored everything I cooked, and since they were such a precious part of the family, I must include segments about their comings and goings.

Tigger, Foe of Toes
March 21, 1976

We have a new member in our family, a Scottie pup whom Aric named Tigger because he bounces when he walks, just like Winnie the Pooh's pal. He's regally pedigreed, fathered by a 10-times Best of Show champion, making the rest of our family feel like plebeians. But we don't think about that much, dealing as we are with puppy antics. For instance, when I was testing a potato omelet:

The omelet-making went something like this: Peel and saute potatoes while enduring needle-sharp Scottie nips. Ditto, the onion, while feeding this new gourmet in our household bits of filet from the previous night's dinner out, hoping to divert him from my slippered feet. When the meat was finished, he turned his attention to dessert — my big toe.

Later, when my feet were safely encased in shoes, that game was over but he was still hungry. He chose the morning paper over a yummy dish of Puppy Chow, making confetti of the newsprint. How you gonna keep 'em downing dry food after they've seen filet?

Two months later, on May 23:
Let me tell you about our dog Tigger, who's been eating rather well lately. We've noticed green leaves in the kitchen and back hall for several days, and finally discovered that they were from flower cuttings my husband was rooting on our front porch. To get them, Tigger had to cross our living room — forbidden territory, so we were doubly perturbed.

"That darn dog has been having a green salad every day," fumed his outraged master. Are we raising a canine epicure?

Sad Farewell to Tigger
October 29, 1978

I have lost my most devoted recipe taster. To him, everything I cooked was delicious. Nothing was a disaster. Just last Sunday, I wrote how he licked his chops over Veal Scallops in Champagne Sauce.

By the time you read that, our dog Tigger was dead, killed instantly as he raced to catch up with Aric near my parents' home, dashing into the path of a gravel truck.

The tragedy happened right in front of our 9-year-old, his first experience with grief. Yet he seems better able to accept Tigger's death than my husband and I, who had just left to work on our lake place and didn't know what had happened until after my dad had buried the dog. I guess that's why humans have funerals: to realize the finality of it all. We're all still feeling blue, and I'm re-experiencing the sadness of losing a half dozen childhood dogs, all hit by cars.

Tigger was a character, and we adored him during his short but exuberant life. A coal-black Scottie, he was impossible to photograph because his only touches of color were pink tongue and white teeth. It's tough to make a dog smile for a picture; he came out looking like a black dust mop with pointy ears.

His registered name was Timber Lane's Macalester Lad, but Aric named him Tigger after the "Winnie the Pooh" character because when he was chosen from the litter of bitty puppies, his legs were so short that he bounced rather than ran. My brother-in-law called him "the mechanical dog" because he did look rather like a wind-up toy as he romped.

His pedigree was regal: Scottie fanciers will know his father, Ch. Firebrand's Bookmaker, frequently judged Best of Show. We didn't exhibit Tigger; we hardly trained him to do anything more than sit up when offered a handout. He was expected only to be an affectionate pet, which he accomplished brilliantly in the 2 1/2 years he enlivened our home.

If a dog can have a sense of humor, Tigger was a Scottie Bill Cosby. He made us laugh. He and Baron, the German Shepherd next door, were best buddies, separated only by a fence along which they raced daily, barking with mock ferociousness. Baron had longer legs, but Tigger used strategy. Off they'd go like a shot, Baron ahead. But halfway down the fence, Tigger would reverse course and beat the Shepherd back to the starting point. Baron fell for the ploy every time.

Like many intelligent dogs, Tigger cocked his head to listen and seemed to understand what we said. The two words that delighted him most were "walk" and "ride," the latter because it meant we were going to northern Minnesota, to my parents' home and our nearby lake place, usually stopping to buy him a dish of Dairy Queen en route.

A city dog confined to our back yard, Tigger was happiest when he could run free, exploring the northern woods. He was the scourge of chipmunks (though he never actually caught any), once shredding

BEEF JERKY

Makes 3 dozen pieces

1 beef flank steak, approximately
    1 pound
1/2 teaspoon garlic salt
1 1/2 teaspoons salt
1/4 teaspoon freshly ground black
    pepper

To prepare meat: Freeze steak partially for easy slicing. Trim off all visible fat. Using a sharp knife, cut flank steak lengthwise (with grain) into strips approximately 3/16-inch thick. Combine garlic salt, salt and ground pepper. Sprinkle mixture over sliced meat. Mix well to distribute evenly.

To cook meat: Arrange strips of meat, flat and close together, on wire rack or racks, in shallow baking pan. Bake in 175-degree oven for 8 to 10 hours, or until dry and almost crisp. Cool on absorbent paper. Store in covered container.

Note: There are countless variations of this recipe; my mother's neighbor, Milly Sorenson, adds soy sauce, Worcestershire sauce, liquid smoke and lots of pepper to her jerky seasoning mix.

a metal drain pipe with his powerful terrier teeth because he thought a chipmunk was hiding within.

Running free — and that unexpected truck as he raced from the path to the road — did him in.

It's silly to be so sentimental over a dog, but we miss him every day, everywhere we look. If there's a Pooch Paradise, I hope it's well stock with veal in champagne sauce and Dairy Queen treats.

Tiger could hear the refrigerator door opening from two rooms away. On the last morning of his life, he pounced on a plastic bag of beef jerky, made by my mother's neighbor, when it fell out as the refrigerator door was opened. He really thought he had a prize. Although he didn't get it all, he sat up his straightest for a morsel.

Aric loves beef jerky, too; it was the treat he chose when we were consoling him last weekend. So I tested a simple bake-while-we-slept recipe, and Aric, our perky jerky connoisseur, pronounced it good.

Many letters of consolation arrived after that farewell-to-Tigger column, my favorite from Sharon Nechville of Eagan, who owned a "squatty Scottie named Snuff, the same age as was Tigger."

Sharon wrote, "Shortly after I got Snuff, you told about trying to function in the kitchen with Tigger chewing your bare toes. That was the same day Snuff managed to unzip the cover of one of my sofa cushions and shredded foam all over the living room. He was so happy; I was so disgusted. But it was nice to know that crosstown, someone else was living with a terrier terror."

Aric and his buddy, Brandy.

"Baby" Announcement
May 25, 1980

We have a new use for old newspapers at our house. Aric named the newcomer Brandy, and he's an adorable 8-week-old miniature silver Schnauzer.

I'll tell you how much this bouncing pound of fur has taken over our lives. A recent morning, I reached for a box of Bran Chex and poured for myself, after grabbing the wrong carton, a breakfast bowl of Puppy Chow.

One night was an example of the new animal-oriented lifestyle at our house. My husband tossed the sheet over my head at 4 a.m. and told me there was a bat in our bedroom. He dispatched that critter, but the commotion woke up the dog who needed to be "watered" outside in the pitch dark. Once that business was done, Brandy wanted to play and was loudly resentful at being put back into his cage for more sleep.

I settled back into bed and when the dog finally quieted, I could hear a mouse cavorting in the corner of our bedroom. I decided to ignore that for the moment, but then birds started their pre-dawn chirping right outside the bedroom window. It was a short night.

Homemade Doggie Chewies
February 15, 1981

Dog Biscuits were among my most frequently requested recipes. They first appeared when Brandy was a pup in the Culinary Cues column, which I wrote and which often appeared adjacent to Tested Recipes.

After interviewing a pair of Kansas City guys who market fancy doggie treats, that recipe was officially tested in December 1976, when I tried it, much to our Shadow's tail-wagging delight. I bit into one, too, to find it tasted like very firm whole-wheat bread. The recipe was given to me by Mrs. Lloyd Hesse of St. Paul, who cut them with a bone-shaped cookie cutter. Shop at a co-op for the grains so you can get just as much as you need.

DOG BISCUITS
Makes 7 to 8 dozen large bones

1 pint chicken stock or other liquid (use more for softer dough)
1 package dry yeast
1/4 cup warm water
3 1/2 cups all-purpose flour
2 cups whole-wheat flour
1 cup rye flour
1 cup corn meal
2 cups cracked wheat
1/2 cup nonfat dry milk
4 teaspoons salt
1 egg mixed with 1 tablespoon milk for brushing

Warm stock or other liquid to lukewarm. Meanwhile, dissolve yeast in 1/4 cup warm water. Add stock. Add all dry ingredients. Knead for about 3 minutes, working it into a stiff dough (or one that you find workable if using more liquid). Roll dough into 1/4-inch-thick sheet. Cut with any type cookie cutter. Place on baking sheet. Beat egg and milk. Brush over biscuits. Bake in 300-degree oven for 45 minutes. Turn off heat. Leave in oven overnight. (Note: There is no sugar or shortening in this recipe.)

Pooch in the Soup
October 24, 1982

Cat fanciers, tune out. This column is going to the dogs. Today's treatise is based on a book called "Feeding Fido" by Joan Cone, written for those who put more effort into nourishing their dogs than just keeping their can openers in working condition.

Our chief taster for the book's recipes was our Schnauzer, Brandy — but first, we had to find him.

Has Brandy grown tired of Alpo day after day? Is he seeking other gourmet experiences any chance he gets to sneak out of the back yard? On a recent Friday, he disappeared when my husband was readying the car for a trip to our lake place. For hours, my husband scoured the neighborhood, getting hoarse from calling the dog's name, using up half a tank of gas plus muscle power when he tried searching via cycle.

For days, we called the pound, the police, the University of Minnesota, and the Food and Drug Administration to make certain our pooch wasn't in some research lab puffing cigarettes. I placed a newspaper ad, wondering who would take our calls if we were at the lake.

Several days later, my husband was giving me a ride home from work after we'd just about decided the dog was gone forever. Almost home, who should we see, sitting on the corner of Grand and Dale, but Brandy, looking streetwise.

He didn't seem awfully concerned about his plight, and he, too, was probably on his way home, just four blocks to go. His adventure must have been tiring. He snored all the way on our postponed trip to the lake.

Some of the recipes from "Feeding Fido," such as Dandy Doggie Kidney Loaf, might have made Brandy happy, but I wanted to try something we could taste, too. When my husband inquired about dinner, I told him we were having dog food that's people food.

"Can't we have people food that the dog can eat?" he moaned.

We found this soup to be rather bland, though we all ate it for dinner with no howls of protest.

Brandy liked it best straight. When I mixed it with dry dog food as the book suggests, he carefully nosed aside the nuggets and ate only the goulash. He's a discriminating diner.

DOGGIE MAIN DISH SOUP
Makes 2 quarts

1/2 pound beef chuck, round steak, beef or deer heart
1 tablespoon corn oil
4 cups water
2 cups V-8 juice
1 cup diced raw carrots
1 envelope (1 3/4 ounces) American-style spaghetti sauce mix
2 cups chopped cabbage
1/2 cup shell or elbow macaroni

Cut meat into small cubes. Brown meat in oil in large heavy pan. Add water, V-8 juice, carrots and spaghetti sauce mix. Cover. Simmer for 40 minutes to 1 hour, or until meat is tender. Add cabbage and macaroni. Simmer for 10 to 15 minutes, until tender.

Chicken Wings Don't Buffalo Brandy
February 20, 1983

None of our dogs ever turned up a nose at Tested Recipes, even when I tried the new hot, really hot item, Buffalo chicken wings:

Our Schnauzer, Brandy, was very interested in all this wing nibbling. Let's face it, he's interested in whatever we eat. He's a great fan of chicken skin, but I am not, so I gave him skin from every wing I ate.

He seemed just a bit hesitant before taking each morsel, but didn't refuse. Then I realized that I had dredged each wing through hot-sauce-laden butter before pulling off the skin. Brandy was getting much more fiery flavor than I was. Boy, did he drink a lot of water that night.

Brandy Goes Bump in the Night
July 15, 1990

That old Scottish prayer about "things that go bump in the night" used to amuse me. Nevermore.

The saddest "bump" I ever heard was in the early-morning hours last Sunday at our lake place.

Nothing much bothered our feisty Schnauzer, Brandy, but he wasn't fond of thunderstorms. He must have heard the rain begin, crept up the stairs to our loft bedroom and misstepped into eternity.

The bump woke us. Brandy didn't even whimper. His neck was broken. And so were our hearts.

During the 10 years that dear little dog has been part of our family, I've often mentioned him here. No one was happier than Brandy to see me in the kitchen, testing recipes. As far as he was concerned, everything I cooked was delicious. He was ever hopeful for tidbits, never turning anything down, not even skin from Buffalo chicken wings drenched in hot sauce.

He learned early on that doggie bags were meant for him, and he'd sit up his straightest when he saw one dangling from my hand after an evening out.

Among our most-told stories is one about a lunch during which my husband and I gnawed dry tasteless rice cakes, then just arriving on the food scene. Meanwhile, from a doggie bag brought home the night before from Tulips restaurant in St. Paul, Brandy savored leftover entrecote of beef with Bordelaise sauce.

His two favorite words were "Alpo" and "ride," and his preferred destination was our lake place. He would snooze the entire three highway hours, but the instant the wheels touched the gravel road into our cabin, he'd leap to the window, quivering in anticipation.

Brandy loved the lake, where he could run free. There he remains. Evermore.

Sound the Bagpipes!
December 30, 1990

Two weeks ago, I asked for help naming our new dog, and you readers really responded. Winning suggestions in our Name the Scottie contest are:

Connoisseur: Connie, for short, because she's a food writer's dog.

Glenna: Nicknamed Glennie, after the glens of Scotland.

Angel the Holy Terrier: When our Christmas puppy is good, she's very, very good. When she's bad, she's just being a terrier.

Smidgen: A cooking measurement impossible to define.

McLassie: To be known as Classy, which Scotties certainly are.

Of the more than 80 suggestions you sent, Scottish names led the pack, among them Lorna Doone, Annie Laurie, Miss Duffy, Thistle, Piper, Heather and McTavish.

McFoodie was suggested. "That's a McMouthful," said one of my workmates.

Several picked up on Bonnie, one suggesting she could be called Bonbon. Several thought she should be named Bon Appetit.

Gala was suggested. So was Fala in memory of President Roosevelt's Scottie. That brings to my mind Fala Lala, in honor of the holiday season.

Food names aplenty filled my mail. Gourmet was suggested by one of our Christmas guests, who then made it The Frugal Gourmet, since Scots are known to be thrifty.

I leaned toward McLassie Connoisseur. A food writer friend of mine suggested Potlikker, since the dog was sure to lick pots. As I recall, it was easier to choose a name for our son.

My husband had the final say. Trying to come up with a name regal enough to go on American Kennel Club papers, he thought up Princess Ebony Shadow. I wanted to tack on "of Macalester" in honor of my alma mater, but there weren't enough spaces on the AKC form.

Shadow she is.

Christmas, Dog Style
December 22, 1996

So, what pooch presents are under your Christmas tree?

Shadow, our Scottie, gets into the present frenzy every year, ripping wrappings to get to the latest squeaky trinket.

Last year, friends brought her a Christmas stocking filled with such nummies as pigs ears for her chewing pleasure. The sock was inadvertently left propped against the fireplace in the living room, where she is not allowed to go.

A couple of days after Christmas, frustration overcame discipline. My husband saw Shadow dragging the sock into the entry hall with an "After all, it's mine" look on her face.

This year's Shadow shopping was left within dog's reach. She immediately investigated, and when the items she thought should be hers were snatched away and put on a shelf until Christmas, she planted herself where she could stare longingly at the toys, hoping we'd relent. We haven't.

I've always been a dog person, even though I owe my very existence to a cat. During the terrible influenza epidemic of 1918, when the child who would become my mother was 4 years old and on the brink of death, my grandmother brought a barn cat into her bedroom. The little girl loved kittens so much that having one to snuggle revived her enough to survive the flu.

Shadow, left, and Princess, the new pup and our consolation.

A Royal "Baby"

September 7, 1997

Our dog Shadow has a shadow following her everywhere.

During August at the lake, we spotted an ad for Scottie puppies, just 8 weeks old, available in Marcell, north of Grand Rapids. So we went to look. I cuddled the sweetest-faced female out of the litter of four. She licked me on the chin, and that did it.

Shadow, now nearly 7 years old, is a patient baby-sitter for this new bouncing black bundle, who for its first week with us remained nameless. You helped with a similar quandary when Shadow was a puppy, so I dug out the 1990 columns recounting our Name the Scottie Contest. You suggested a slew of ideas, but after reviewing those monikers, we just couldn't decide. Then we awoke last Sunday to the sad news from Paris and London about the tragic death of Diana.

In her honor, we're calling this new pup Princess.

Shadow's Tragic Demise

November 23, 1997

She was the sweetest, gentlest, dearest, most ladylike dog. Princess adored her. So did we during the seven years she graced our home.

We had never before come to the lake this late in the season, but this year, we are spending Thanksgiving week here, and all our northern relatives have been invited for the big dinner.

On this Sunday morning, the two dogs went out for their sunrise constitutional. Princess came back. Shadow didn't. We searched and called. Hours later, it was Princess who led us to the lake shore. There, in a hole cut near the shoreline so deer hunters staying next door could get sauna water, Shadow met her fate. She fell in and couldn't pull herself out, drowning in that freezing hell.

She, like all of our dogs, loved being at the lake. So do we. But this Sunday morning, that feeling is sadly tarnished by losing, here, again, another cherished member of the family.

1994

— Cookbooks, coffee and cookies,
Charlie the Tuna —

Lasso That Lobster
January 9

After two years of celebrating elsewhere, we revived our almost-annual Dream Entree New Year's Eve party for a group of friends not offended by being asked to bring the item they might order if they were dining out elegantly.

On some New Year's Eves, we've chased live lobsters around the kitchen. "Only if you put it on a leash," I warned my lobster-loving friend, fearing she might bring an entree that was still breathing.

"Obedience training," she promised. But she brought more sedate salmon steak instead.

Stonehead Finns
January 16

From a column about a northern Michigan Scandinavian cookbook:

We in Minnesota believe, myopically, that we are the haven for most Scandinavian ex-patriots, but northern Michigan also has an enclave. For hordes of immigrants, including my own maternal grandparents, Michigan was their first stopping place in America, before they packed up and headed west to Minnesota.

But many didn't move on to homestead the unfriendly soil of this state's northern reaches, where Finns are still referred to as "rock farmers" — "Hey, Toivo, nice crop of boulders you got there. You gonna cook up some stone mojakka?"

Charlie, the Champ
June 19

From a column featuring tuna recipes:

During the past decade, Americans have righteously been claiming they're hooked on more fish and seafood meals. If you ask what varieties they've eaten most, hardly anyone mentions tuna. Yet, that's the seafood we've always depended upon — at least, since cans were invented — and it occupies the largest category of fish consumed.

Because it has remained the most inexpensive meat alternative, because it's always on the shelf, and because we turn to it when we run out of imagination or energy for anything else, tuna is the most underappreciated but overutilized species. It's the peanut butter of the fish industry.

Why Cookbooks Are So Often Our Subject
November 13

Cookbook authors have been trooping through my office so frequently that, one morning, four in a row were interviewed. The chair they all sat in didn't reach room temperature for nearly three hours. A co-worker said every time she walked past the conference room, she'd see me taking notes, but the person talking was always different.

From September to early November, we witness the annual cookbook deluge as publishers hustle titles in time for holiday buying. So many books have arrived this fall that when the heaps on my desk reached wobble-height, I started stacking a cookbook fortress around my feet. Then, I got a rather pointed message from the bosses, warning me that the fire marshal was coming for his annual inspection, and I'd better find somewhere else to stash the stuff. No easy task.

Awash in Coffee
November 27

We live in a part of St. Paul where insomniacs must abound, based on the amount of coffee that's being poured. In the short stretch of Grand Avenue, from Lexington to just beyond Dale, my latest count is five coffeehouses (another recently closed) — and that's not counting Cafe Latte.

At work, I'm deluged with data about coffee innovations, including a Kahlua coffee with a different kind of buzz.

What must Mrs. Olson be thinking? Her Swedish-style coffee is quickly becoming passe. That old classic Hills Brothers now comes in French vanilla, Irish creme and hazelnut, inspired by a national survey that suggested 68 percent of coffee drinkers are interested in trying new flavors. Not me. I'll take tea.

Using Your Noodle
February 20

Writing about a College of St. Benedict community nutrition class in which students created easy-to-make dinners using "challenge foods":

Isn't this just human nature? The gambling dens near St. Cloud, Minn., offer a free bingo card in exchange for a nonperishable donation to area food shelves. What do most people give? A packet of Ramen noodles, which frequently sell five for a buck. Gamblers get cheap bingo cards. Foods shelves get heaps of Ramen. And their clients wonder what to do with oodles of wavy noodles once they tire of soup.

Other abundances attractively priced to givers, but not so appealing to hungry people trying to create a meal, are pumpkin and cranberries (usually donated after the holidays by people cleaning cupboards), Rice-a-Roni, cream soups, macaroni and cheese, dry soup mixes and bottom-price-rung vegetables, such as kidney beans. Food stores and meat processors donate ground beef and turkey as they confront their freshness dates.

Nothing is wrong with any of those foods. But think about it — what kinds of meals could you plan with such limited ingredients, especially if your cupboard was bare of seasonings and short on cooking utensils?

This casserole is one that accomplished the class mission. Another that worked was Spaghetti Casserole made with a half-pound of ground beef, onion soup mix, tomato sauce, pumpkin, mushrooms and Ramen noodles, minus seasoning.

FOOD SHELF ZESTY CRANBERRY CASSEROLE

Makes 4 to 6 servings

1 pound ground beef
1 package onion soup mix
1 box Rice-a-Roni
2 tablespoons margarine
2 cans (6 ounces each) tomato paste
1 can cranberries, jellied or whole berry
1/2 cup water
1 can whole-kernel corn, drained

Brown ground beef with onion soup mix. Cook Rice-a-Roni according to package directions, using margarine. Combine all remaining ingredients in separate bowl. (Note: Sauce will be thick.) Combine sauce, beef and rice mixtures. Place in 9-by-13-inch baking pan. Bake in 350-degree oven for 40 minutes.

Lemonade Cookies on Trial

July 1

When life hands you lemons, you can make lots more than lemonade.

Perhaps its the season, but lemon recipes have been as abundant and as irresistible as a tall glass of lemonade on a 90-degree day.

Lemons are Fourth of July sparklers to our meals. They radiate liveliness on what we eat, but add virtually no calories or sodium. Lemons can be ours any time of year, but in summertime, they lift us out of dining doldrums.

CALIFORNIA LEMONADE COOKIES

Makes 3 dozen cookies

1 1/4 cups granulated sugar
3/4 cup butter-flavored shortening (or 1/2 cup regular shortening and 1/4 cup butter)
2 tablespoons fresh lemon juice
1 tablespoon grated lemon peel
1 teaspoon vanilla
1 teaspoon lemon extract
1 egg
1 3/4 cups flour
1 teaspoon salt
3/4 teaspoon baking soda
1/2 cup sweetened flaked coconut (optional)

To make cookie dough: In large bowl, combine sugar, shortening, lemon juice, lemon peel, vanilla and lemon extract. Beat at medium speed of electric mixer until well-blended. Beat egg into creamed mixture. Combine flour, salt and baking soda. Mix into creamed mixture just until blended.

To bake cookies: Drop rounded tablespoons of dough 2 inches apart onto ungreased baking sheet. Sprinkle with coconut. Bake 1 sheet at a time in 375-degree oven for 8 to 10 minutes, or until cookies are set and edges are golden brown. (Note: Watch closely so coconut doesn't burn.) Cool for 2 minutes on baking sheet. Remove cookies to foil-covered counter. Cool completely.

In a week when almost everyone was drinking up O.J., I was thinking of lemonade. Lemonade Cookies to be exact. The only thing they have in common with O.J. Simpson is that both come from California. A few Lemonade Cookies were eaten, I must admit, while watching the televised O.J. murder hearings, but the best evidence of their appeal was from the jury of my lake peers. They gave the cookies a speedy trial and voted unanimously in their favor.

Jammin' on Jambalaya
October 16

So why, my first question to Barbara Davis probed, would you introduce a new line of barbecue-style marinades in mid-October, at the end of the Minnesota cookout season?

Davis thinks her timing is impeccable. When snow starts flying, tastes of summer are even more seductive. And there's nothing more warming than a spicy meal when the Fahrenheit heads south. This off-season approach to product marketing was intended from the start. "We gave this project the code name Winter Smoke," she said.

Barbara, widow of barbecue sauce master Ken Davis (she now runs the Minneapolis company he founded), is a home economist who worked for General Mills, so developing recipes to go with the selection of sauces was her delight. Of the ones we tried, I was most thrilled about this quicker-than-average Minnesota-style jambalaya. A double batch is recommended because everyone will surely want seconds.

MINNESOTA JAMBALAYA
Makes 6 servings

- 1 jar (8 ounces) Ken Davis Jazz It Up Southwestern Marinade Sauce (or medium-hot salsa)
- 1 pound raw shrimp, shelled and deveined (no need to thaw if frozen)
- 2 spicy smoked sausage (1 pound total), sliced into 1/2-inch pieces
- 2 tablespoons butter or margarine
- 1 large onion, chopped
- 1 large green bell pepper, seeded and chopped
- 1 large red bell pepper, seeded and chopped
- 2 large tomatoes, chopped
- 1 cup uncooked long-grain rice
- 1 cup coarsely chopped smoked ham
- 1 can (14 1/2 ounces) chicken broth

Reserve 2 tablespoons marinade. Marinate shrimp in remaining sauce for 30 minutes or more. In Dutch oven, brown sausage over medium heat. Remove sausage. Melt butter in same pan. Add onion and peppers. Cook for 3 to 4 minutes, or until onion is translucent and tender. Add reserved marinade to tomatoes. Add tomatoes to pan. Cover. Cook for 15 minutes. Add sausages, rice, ham and chicken broth. Heat to a boil. Reduce heat. Cover. Simmer for 20 minutes. Stir in shrimp and marinade. Cook, stirring, for 3 to 5 minutes, or until shrimp are pink. Serve immediately.

1995

— Garlic, gooey desserts, lovelorn guys —

So What's New?

January 8

Trend trackers are doing their annual new-year dance, tippy-toeing through predictions of what's to be on our plates for the coming year. They all agree that pasta is at the top of the heap. A prediction almost as universal is that we'll be seeing more slimmed-down versions of old favorite foods.

Marcella, the Garlic Guru

June 25

How, a woman in the audience inquired during a speech I gave last winter, could she avoid garlic. She didn't like it. It didn't like her, "but it's everywhere," she wailed.

Experiencing Rocky Mountain-high cuisine in Aspen, Colo., during a food-and-wine festival there earlier this month and remembering that plaintive query about garlic, I focused, during her master class, on how Italian cooking teacher and author Marcella Hazan told us she handles it. Precision is the key.

"Garlic is the most misunderstood, misused food in the States," says Hazan, who divides her time between Venice, Italy, where she runs a school, and Long Island, N.Y., base for her American appearances.

"If you smell it, you've probably burned it," she said. "Let me show you how to use it without taste, smell or the discomfort of 'repeat.' Burned garlic is what prompts stomach acidity."

Before a single clove is peeled of its papery husk, ponder the food it is to flavor. Hazan used parboiled spinach and precooked broccoli as examples. "Spinach has a light taste, so you need less garlic, perhaps only garlic-flavored olive oil. Broccoli, cauliflower and savoy cabbage are stronger, so they can accept more garlic."

A reader says . . .

Your column always interests me. Tonight, I cooked Pad Thai, and though I had never tasted it before, I was able to create it easily with your directions.

— Faye Duvall, White Bear Lake, Minn.

Herman He-men Can Cook

July 2

On this Fourth of July weekend, we turn attention to a certain group of young men who, unlike those young rebels of 1776, are seeking less — not more— independence.

They're the bachelors of Herman, Minn. Last summer, they gained international fame as they attempted to lure female companionship to their small farming community, which doesn't have a bumper crop of eligible women.

Now, a new cookbook from Herman suggests that these rural Romeos can get along just fine without wives — at least when it comes to cooking. I called six bachelors about their recipes in the book, and in four cases, reached only their answering machines, probably installed so as not to miss any messages from adoring females. When this inquiring female left a message to please call back, they were too shy to reply.

Lettuce Entertains Us

July 16

Opening a column on salad dressings:

Like leaves of butter lettuce pushing up through warm garden soil, salads have become a layered experience.

Have you noticed, on restaurant menus, how much verbiage describes a bowl of vegetables and its explicit dressing? Such detail! Sometimes, it takes longer to read about a salad than it does to eat it.

In simpler times, the waitress would rattle off three or four options — French, Italian, blue cheese — perhaps Thousand Island in more worldly establishments. Underneath the chosen slather was the inevitable chopped iceberg garnished with granite wedges of tomato. Maybe an equally rocklike scattering of croutons. Ho hum.

Salad as Experience began to sneak up on us in the '80s, maybe the latter '70s, when a blend of greens and meats was as likely in the entree column as on the salad list. Vinegars were no longer limited to white cider, but might be red from raspberries or the deep mahogany of balsamic. Oils were more likely pressed from olives and walnuts than from corn.

To all this, I said, "Great. Keep this rarefied rabbit food coming."

Madison County Madness

October 8

Loved the book. Haven't seen the movie yet. But now "The Bridges of Madison County," that tale of fervent Iowa romance, has crossed over into a cookbook, "The Recipes of Madison County."

As proof of "Bridges" continuing appeal, publisher Oxmoor House gambled with a phenomenal press run of 160,000 copies for a first cookbook by two unknown Des Moines authors.

What's next in the romantic best-seller's span of longevity? The Furniture of Madison County fashioned from old bridge beams?

Perhaps Iowa Pea Salad of Madison County will become America's next comfort food, served for $20 per pea-sized portion at gourmet restaurants.

Top of the Heap Burritos

September 17

I have stacks of good intentions. I am surrounded by piles of recipes that I intend to test someday, which is often later than sooner, as newer ones accumulate atop the heap.

For instance, I received a sheaf of wonderful-sounding quick entrees from Christine Cobb, the new consumer-product marketing director for the Minnesota Pork Producers Association, but only Thai Pork Burritos made it to the top of my stockpile. After testing the burritos, I advise you to stop whatever you're doing and try them, too — immediately. Don't let this recipe with its pleasurable blend of flavors get buried in your "someday" stack.

On the Bean Scene
August 20

From a column on the Les Dames d'Escoffier barbecue potluck supper:

Future archaeologists unearthing latter 20th century flotsam will likely find that we've buried ourselves in recipes. They're everywhere. I flipped through the latest Dayton's Today catalog and was startled to find an entire feature on chef's recipes, new coverage for that publication, I later learned.

THAI PORK BURRITOS
Makes 4 servings

1 pound lean ground pork
2 tablespoons grated fresh ginger root
1 garlic clove, peeled and crushed
1 small onion, thinly sliced
2 cups coleslaw mix with carrots
1 teaspoon Asian sesame oil
3 tablespoons soy sauce
2 tablespoons lime juice
1 tablespoon honey
2 teaspoons ground coriander
1/2 teaspoon crushed red pepper
4 large (10-inch) flour tortillas, warmed
Fresh cilantro, chopped, for garnish

Heat large nonstick skillet over high heat. Add pork. Cook, crumble and stir for 3 to 4 minutes, or until pork is no longer pink. Add ginger, garlic, onion and coleslaw mix. Stir-fry with pork for 2 minutes, or until vegetables are wilted. In small bowl, combine all remaining ingredients, except tortillas and cilantro. Add to skillet. Cook, stirring constantly to blend all ingredients well, for 1 minute. Spoon equal portions of mixture onto warm flour tortillas. Garnish with cilantro. Roll up to encase filling.

BLACK-BEAN SALAD
Makes 4 to 6 servings

1 can (15 ounces) black beans, drained and rinsed
1 1/2 cups cooked corn kernels
2 tomatoes, diced
1 red pepper, diced
1 green pepper, diced
1/2 cup chopped red onion
1 to 2 fresh jalapeno peppers, minced
1/3 cup fresh lime juice
1/3 cup olive oil
1/3 cup chopped fresh cilantro
1 teaspoon salt, or to taste
1/2 teaspoon cumin
1/2 teaspoon ground red chilies (not powdered), or cayenne to taste

Combine all ingredients. Cover. Chill. (Note: Can be make a day ahead of serving.)

But we haven't reached the plateau of one recipe too many because someone always needs a new idea. For a women-in-food club event, I contributed a couscous salad I found in that Dayton's article. Another member of the newly organized Twin Cities Les Dames chapter brought a trendy black-bean salad. She's Nancy Cooper, diabetes nutrition specialist for the International Diabetes Center, Minneapolis, who credited a friend "who's a really, really good cook" with the recipe.

Earthshaking Cake

October 1

No matter how many attempts at healthful eating were presented in this column over the years, lost recipes most frequently requested by readers were almost always the gooiest desserts, such as altogether bad, but oh so good Earthquake Cake.

Just after that recipe ran in the column on September 10, I wrote about a visit with Art Ginsburg:

His fame name is Mr. Food, not Mr. Freud, but unlike the original Viennese couch potato, Mr. Food knows what women want: easy solutions to their deepest problem, daily dinner drudgery.

"From the requests I get (from his nationally syndicated television show audience) I know what people really want. Desserts. Put my Death by Chocolate bars next to a fruit platter at a party and

EARTHQUAKE CAKE

Makes 9-by-13-inch cake

1 cup coconut
1 cup chopped nuts
1 chocolate cake mix
1 package (8 ounces) cream cheese
1/2 cup softened butter
1 teaspoon vanilla
2 cups powdered sugar
3/4 cup chocolate chips

Grease 9-by-13-inch pan. Sprinkle coconut and nuts on bottom of pan. Mix cake according to directions on box. Pour over coconut and nuts. Mix cream cheese, butter, vanilla and powdered sugar. Drop by spoonfuls over cake mix. Sprinkle with chocolate chips. Bake in 350-degree oven for 50 minutes.

guess what disappears first? People want gooey and gratifying."

Believe me, Mr. Food, after 28 years of food writing, this does not surprise me.

Here's an earthshaking example. Andrea Navara contributed this cake to the Home of the Good Shepherd cookbook, "Sharing Our Best," which I wrote about in that September column:

When you take this cake from the oven, you'll understand the name. All the underlying riches create craters in the crust, cracking like an L.A. freeway after a tremor. It's as bad as a cake can be, considering coconut, nuts, cream cheese, butter and chocolate chips, but so good that the Lake Hungries fought over the last crumbs. I used a devil's food cake mix in keeping with the other sinful ingredients.

A reader says . . .

Anyone can write recipes, but you give it your personal touch. You've got fans across the country.

— Mary Grace Rae, St. Paul

Holidays

— A Reason for Recipes Year 'Round —

A Christmas to Remember
Christmas Day 1988

Christmas memories: How we treasure them. Like fingerprints, each person's lifetime recollection is unique. Some years, some gifts, some foods, some circumstances stand out in the annual accumulation.

I remember Childhood Christmas Age Six as the best. World War II had been over for a year, and consumer goods were available again. Best of all, the country home my parents had built in 1942, finally, after wartime materials restrictions, was wired for electricity.

On Christmas morning, a Silvertone radio-phonograph, which was taller than I was, had the place of honor in our living room. A huge red bow was draped around its streamlined corners and across the apron of brown frieze stretched over its speakers. Just at my eye level was the radio's dial, and at tummy height was the drawer turntable, where I stacked my Christmas present album of "Let's Pretend" fairy tales. That's when my folks weren't playing Bing Crosby's "White Christmas." Dolls and toys from that Christmas are long gone, and I wore out those 78 rpm records, but the "Let's Pretend" music still plays in my mind.

The phonograph, after years of neglect in an unheated building, was dusted off last summer. Once again, its tubes, massive compared to today's transistors, slowly glowed and the radio sounded as clear as that Christmas morning four decades past. If we tuned the dial today, we'd probably hear Bing Crosby's rendition of "White Christmas."

The All-Time Best Fruitcake
Nov. 25, 1973

For three decades, I said "Happy Holidays" to readers by trying recipes that might become their own Christmas classics.

Over the years, readers got the message: This food writer adores fruitcake. During the early years, I tried new ones almost annually, but none was as good as Four-From-One Fruitcake.

"Four-From-One Fruitcake is a keeper," I wrote, not fully realizing how prophetic that comment was. This elegant fruitcake, nearly all fruit and nuts, hardly any cake, is the all-time most requested Tested Recipe. Baked in a 9-by-13-inch pan, it is cut into four strips,

FOUR-FROM-ONE FRUITCAKE

Makes 4 fruitcake logs

4 cups walnut halves and large pieces
1 1/2 cups halved pitted dates
1 1/2 cups whole candied cherries
1 1/2 cups candied pineapple chunks
3/4 cup diced candied orange peel
1 cup plus 2 tablespoons sifted flour
1 cup plus 2 tablespoons granulated
   sugar
3/4 teaspoon baking powder
1 teaspoon salt
4 eggs
1 tablespoon vanilla
1 teaspoon rum flavoring
1/4 cup rum, brandy or dry sherry,
   optional

Combine walnuts, dates, cherries, pineapple and orange peel. Resift flour with sugar, baking powder and salt over fruit. Mix well. Beat eggs with vanilla and rum flavoring. Pour over fruit mixture. Stir until well blended. Turn into paper-lined and greased 9-by-13-inch baking pan and spread evenly. Bake below oven center at 275 degrees for 1 1/2 hours, or until fruitcake tests done. Remove from oven. Cool in pan for 30 minutes. Remove from pan. Lift off paper. Sprinkle with rum or other liquor of choice. Sprinkle again later in cooling process. When thoroughly cooled, cut fruitcake crosswise into 4 even strips. Wrap each in wax paper, then in foil. Store in cool place.

some to be enjoyed at home, some to be given as gifts. So many in our circle want it that I bake a triple recipe every year.

From that very first testing, and every year until it closed in the mid-1990s, I used the extra-size, wonderfully juicy bulk candied fruit sold at Gleason's Specialty Shoppe downtown St. Paul. I recommended its holiday supplies so frequently that the Gleason's staff kept a supply of Four-From-One recipes on hand. It was a blow to all of us when Gleason's closed, and I haven't found anything to match what was sold there. We do our best with grocery store candied fruit, and I now candy my own orange peel.

"I've never made a cake in which the flour and eggs were incorporated independently," I told readers. Dry ingredients are mixed with the fruit first, then the flavored eggs are stirred in. It works well, but use your largest bowl.

Line the baking pan with parchment paper, use more rum flavoring, if you wish, and don't be scotch with the brandy or rum (the latter my preference for soaking the cake).

The beauty of these fruitcake bars is in the glistening, supersized chunks of fruit in each slice. So leave the cherries whole, cut the pineapple rings into no more than six wedges and let their stained-glass color shine through each morsel.

Over the years, the recipe was reprinted many times in the column because readers kept asking for it. For the November 27, 1983, redux:

I don't have to look at a calendar, listen to a weather forecast, or check to see if department stores have their Christmas decorations up to know that the holiday season approaches. I just answer my telephone and hear people asking for Four-From-One Fruitcake. They've lost the directions and usually they don't remember the name, but they describe it as a fruit-packed cake that's cut into strips. And they invariably add, "It's the best fruitcake I've ever made."

Bourbon Cake Without the Booze

November 28, 1971

At a newspaper food-editors' conference, one of the Southern writers extolled Kentucky Bourbon Cake. By coincidence, the Bourbon Institute sent its recipe for Original Kentucky Bourbon Cake about a month later. But when I read the recipe, no bourbon was listed. The institute's director became quite flustered when I phoned him about the omission. He thought the cake needed about 1 cup.

A week later, a corrected recipe arrived, and the bourbon was boosted to 2 cups. "This is getting better by the minute," I thought, tucking the recipe in my to-be-tested file. And now I have.

Male readers are probably nudging their wives, "Hey, Mabel. Here's a fruitcake for you to try."

Well, Mabel, go ahead and bake the dickens out of these cakes. And be prepared to invest a little money in them, too, what with a pint of bourbon, top-grade pecans and candied cherries, plus a half-dozen eggs.

The photo that accompanied the cakes showed them baked in star shapes. I tried several stores seeking 5-inch star pans without success. I cut the hunt short

because I was shopping with our 2-year-old, who was more interested in riding escalators than browsing in housewares departments.

ORIGINAL KENTUCKY BOURBON CAKE

Makes 2 star cakes or 3 loaf cakes

- 2 cups red candied cherries (about 1 pound), chopped
- 1 1/2 cups light seedless raisins (about 8 ounces)
- 2 cups bourbon
- 1 1/2 cups butter or margarine
- 2 1/3 cups firmly packed brown sugar
- 2 1/3 cups granulated sugar
- 6 eggs, separated
- 5 cups sifted cake flour, divided
- 4 cups pecans (about 1 pound)
- 2 teaspoons nutmeg
- 1 teaspoon baking powder

To soak fruit: Combine cherries, raisins and bourbon. Cover. Let stand overnight. Drain fruit. Reserve bourbon.

To make cake: Cream butter and sugars together until light. Add egg yolks. Beat well. Combine 1/2 cup flour and pecans. Sift together remaining 4 1/2 cups flour, nutmeg and baking powder. Add flour mixture and reserved bourbon alternately to butter mixture, beating well after each addition. Beat egg whites until stiff but not dry. Fold whites, soaked fruit and pecan-flour mixture into batter. Turn into 2 greased 5-inch star-shaped molds, or 3 medium bread pans lined with greased wax paper. Bake in a 275-degree oven for 3 1/2 hours. Cool. Remove from pans. When ready to serve, frost, if desired, with powdered-sugar icing.

Scott, standing, joined our family, including 4-year-old Aric, in time for Christmas 1973.

Snowballs Fly During Hard Winter

December 2, 1973

With energy shortages increasing daily, it's going to be a make-do-or-do-without winter. A friend commented on how many women he sees knitting these days; warm sweaters are going to be the height of fashion this winter.

CINNAMON SNOWBALLS

Makes 6 dozen or more

1 cup butter or margarine
1 1/4 cups sifted powdered sugar, divided
1 1/2 cups sifted flour
1/4 teaspoon salt
1/2 teaspoon cinnamon
1/2 teaspoon nutmeg
3/4 cup quick or old-fashioned oats, uncooked
1 tablespoon vanilla
3/4 cup ground walnuts
3/4 cup ground pecans

Beat butter until creamy. Sift together 3/4 cup powdered sugar, flour, salt, cinnamon and nutmeg. Gradually add to butter. Blend well. Stir in oats. Blend in vanilla and nuts. Mix well, about 5 minutes. Shape to form small balls. Place on ungreased cookie sheets. Bake in 300-degree oven for 25 minutes. Remove cookies from cookie sheet. While hot, sprinkle with half of remaining powdered sugar. Cool. Sprinkle again.

Recipes crossing my desk lately are tending toward practical, old standards using common and inexpensive ingredients. These cookies, though not exactly cheap to make, are a classic Christmas treat. You know Cinnamon Snowballs by several other names: Russian Tea Cakes, Mexican Wedding Cakes, Pfeffernusse. This version, with the addition of cinnamon and nutmeg, is just as good as its cousins. But I wonder why they weren't named Cinnamon and Nutmeg Snowballs, since equal measures of both spices are used?

Torte of a Thousand Possibilities

December 9, 1973

Anticipating holiday partying, we tried this Tree Trimmer's Torte:

It's a delightful recipe, but I strongly disagree with directions to only grease the pans. I recommend that they be greased, then lined with wax paper or parchment. I had a terrible time getting the layers out of the pans, finally resorting to prying them with a spatula, which carved numerous crevices in the meringue.

Variations would be feasible: How about replacing cherries with creme de menthe in the whipped cream, and shaving chocolate over the torte's top? Or adding strawberries to the whipped cream? Or chocolate? Or rum? Or brandy? My mouth is not only watering, it's about to flood.

A reader says . . .

I have clipped your recipes column many times. I'm right now baking muffins from your column.

— Alice Cederberg, Maplewood, Minn.

TREE TRIMMERS' CHERRY MERINGUE TORTE

Makes 8 to 10 servings

3/4 cup unsifted flour
1 teaspoon baking powder
1/4 teaspoon salt
1/2 cup (1 stick) butter or margarine, softened
1 1/2 cups sugar, divided
4 eggs, separated
1 teaspoon vanilla
3 tablespoons milk
1/4 cup chopped pecans
1/4 cup chopped maraschino cherries
1 1/2 cups heavy cream, whipped

To make batter: Sift together flour, baking powder and salt. Set aside. Cream butter and 1/2 cup sugar until very light. Add egg yolks, 1 at a time, beating well after each addition. Beat in vanilla. Set aside.

To make meringue: Beat egg whites until frothy. Gradually beat in remaining 1 cup sugar. Continue beating until soft peaks form. Set aside.

To assemble cake: Alternately blend sifted dry ingredients and milk into creamed butter mixture, beginning and ending with dry ingredients. Spread into 2 greased 9-inch round cake pans. Spread meringue mixture evenly over batter in both pans to within 1/2 inch of pan edge. Sprinkle 1 layer with pecans.

To bake: Bake in 350-degree oven for 25 to 30 minutes, or until done. Cool in pans on wire racks. Gently loosen edges with spatula before removing from pans.

To make filling: Fold cherries into whipped cream to use as filling and frosting. Start with plain meringue layer, top side up. Spread with filling. Top with second layer, pecan side up. Spread remaining cherry cream around sides of layers. Chill. Cut into wedges to serve.

Bread Burns While Seamstress Fiddles

April 7, 1974

I love to sew. When I start communing with material and machine, time has no meaning. So that's why Brazilian Easter Bread burned.

Also, the timer on my oven has a buzzer that is timid — when it works at all. More often it makes no more than a little hiccup when the zero mark is reached. I was busy sewing when I smelled these loaves baking. "I'll go down and check them as soon as I finish this collar," I told myself. Meanwhile, deep brown smells were wafting up to my sewing room. When the collar was done, the bread was done in.

The loaves weren't so burned that the office crew didn't demolish them. The bread was rich and chunky with fruit and nuts, resembling giant hot cross buns.

This was the first recipe in the column printed with both familiar and metric measurements. In 1974, we thought we'd soon be cooking with grams and liters. That was one food prediction that has yet to come true, so metric has been deleted here. Scalding milk isn't necessary; just heat it to lukewarm in microwave oven before adding yeast.

A reader says . . .

That was a lovely eulogy to Wizzie Fiorito. I was on a trip that she and her husband, Stan, took to Italy. I came to know the scope of Wizzie's life and the pleasure she took in food. What a funny and beautiful lady. Your tribute touched me deeply because it was right on.

— Marguerite Baglio, Shoreview, Minn.

BRAZILIAN EASTER BREAD
Makes 2 large loaves

1 can (20 ounces) crushed pineapple
1 cup milk
2 packages active dry yeast
4 eggs
7 to 8 cups flour, divided
1/2 teaspoon salt
1/2 cup sugar

1/2 cup butter, melted
1/2 cup chopped Brazil nuts
2 tablespoons candied orange peel, minced
1 tablespoon grated lemon peel
1 teaspoon cinnamon
2 tablespoons butter

To make bread: Drain pineapple very well, pressing out liquid. Scald milk. Cool to lukewarm. Dissolve yeast in cooled milk. Stir in eggs, 3 cups flour, salt, sugar and melted butter. Combine well-drained pineapple, Brazil nuts, candied orange peel, grated lemon peel, cinnamon and 1 cup flour. Stir into dough. Add enough additional flour to make a stiff dough. Turn out onto well-floured board. Knead dough until smooth and elastic, adding more flour as needed. Place in greased bowl. Cover. Let rise in warm (85-degree) place until doubled in bulk. Turn out onto floured board. Knead slightly. Divide dough in half.

To shape loaves: Cut off about a handful of dough from each half. Shape large sections into 2 round loaves. Place on greased baking sheet. Divide small pieces of dough in half. Roll each piece into a rope the length of round loaves. Lightly place 2 ropes on each loaf in shape of a cross. Cover. Let rise until doubled again.

To bake bread: Bake in 375-degree oven for 40 to 45 minutes, or until well browned. Brush hot loaves with butter. Slice to serve.

The Dough Arose
April 13, 1980

Here comes Peter Cottontail, hopping down the Tested trail ... Easter Bunny Bread appeared a week after the 1983 holiday:

He's either a week late or a year early, depending on your optimism or pessimism. I'm optimistic about the honey-oatmeal dough out of which Bunny Bread was swirled. It's a slightly sweet, lightly colored, perfectly textured bread that, until next Easter, could be formed into a May flower or a Memorial Day flag — or simply as coiled or regular loaves.

Bunny Bread starred at an Easter brunch set for 11 a.m. last Sunday. Timing was critical because church isn't over until about 10:30, and on Easter, we had to be there at least a half-hour early to wedge ourselves into the sanctuary.

The bread was mixed and put in the bowl at 8:45. Our dough arose — and arose — while we were in church singing "Christ Arose." We got home to a brimming bowlful.

After twirling it into a bunny shape, the bread got short shrift on second rising because time before brunch was disappearing faster than Aric's chocolate Easter eggs. His Easter basket was also my brunch centerpiece, and he worried that guests would raid his candy cache. He tried to eat as much before brunch as he could without getting his fingers slapped too often.

EASTER BUNNY BREAD
Makes 1 bread bunny

Bread:
- 3/4 cup milk
- 1/4 cup butter or margarine
- 1 package active dry yeast
- 1/4 cup warm water
- 3 1/4 to 3 1/2 cups all-purpose flour
- 1 cup quick or old-fashioned oats, uncooked
- 1/3 cup honey
- 1 egg
- 1 1/4 teaspoons salt
- 1 teaspoon cinnamon

Icing:
- 1 1/2 cups powdered sugar
- 2 tablespoons milk

To make bread: In a small saucepan, heat milk and butter over medium heat, stirring occasionally until butter is melted. Cool to lukewarm. Dissolve yeast in warm water. In large bowl, combine butter mixture, dissolved yeast, 1 cup flour, oats, honey, egg, salt and cinnamon. Mix well. Add enough additional flour to make a soft dough. Knead on lightly floured surface for 8 to 10 minutes, or until smooth and elastic. Shape to form a ball. Place in greased large bowl, turning to coat surface of dough. Cover. Let rise in warm place for 1 hour, or until doubled in size. Punch dough down. Cover. Let rest 10 minutes. Divide dough in half.

To shape bunny body: Form half of dough into 36-inch rope. Loosely roll up dough, spiral fashion, pinching dough to seal end tightly. Place spiral 3 inches from bottom of large greased cookie sheet.

Press down lightly. Divide remaining dough in half. For bunny head, shape half into 25-inch rope. Loosely roll up spiral fashion. Seal end tightly. Attach to top of body on cookie sheet by pinching dough together. Divide remaining dough into thirds. For tail, shape one into 15-inch rope. Roll into a spiral. Attach to one side of body. Shape remaining dough into two 3-1/2-inch long ears. Attach to top of head.

To bake bread: Let rise for 1 hour, or until nearly doubled in size. Bake in 350-degree oven for 30 to 35 minutes, or until golden brown. Cool on wire rack.

To make icing: Combine powdered sugar and 2 tablespoons milk. Mix until smooth. Drizzle over cooled bread.

PUMPKIN PECAN PARTY PIE

Makes 8 to 10 servings

1 1/2 quarts butter pecan ice cream
1 cup sugar
1 cup canned pumpkin
1 teaspoon cinnamon
1/4 teaspoon ginger
1/4 teaspoon nutmeg
1/4 teaspoon salt
1 cup whipping cream, whipped
1/4 cup packed light brown sugar
2 tablespoons butter
1 tablespoon water
1/2 cup chopped pecans

To make ice-cream crust: Thirty minutes before preparing crust, put deep, 9-inch pie pan in freezer. When ready to make crust, working quickly, line bottom and sides of cold pan with ice cream. Build up crust 1/2 inch above edge of pan by overlapping tablespoons of ice cream. Freeze for at least 2 hours.

To make filling: In saucepan, combine sugar, pumpkin, spices and salt. Cook over low heat for 3 minutes. Cool. Reserve 1/4 cup whipped cream for garnish. Fold remaining whipped cream into pumpkin mixture. Spoon into frozen ice-cream crust, swirling top. Freeze for at least 2 hours.

To make topping: In small saucepan over medium heat, combine brown sugar, butter and water. Bring just to a boil. Cook for 1 1/2 minutes. Remove from heat. Stir in pecans. Cool. Spoon mixture around edge of pie between filling and crust. Mound or pipe 1/4 cup reserved whipped cream in center. Freeze until just before serving. Let mellow for 10 minutes in refrigerator before cutting into wedges.

Pumpkin Pie Over a la Mode

November 24, 1974

"Killer diller" alternative for Thanksgiving pumpkin pie, this tradition-bending pie was built around my favorite ice cream. Testing Results advised:

Don't let the praline topping cool too much as I did; it got solid in the refrigerator in just a short time. Just cool it enough so it won't melt the ice-cream crust and filling. To make sure the ice cream won't crystallize, cover the pie with plastic wrap when it's in the freezer.

"Enough is enough," I decided, so I didn't slather additional calories of whipped cream atop the pie. Raves greeted the dessert when it was served to friends late one evening. Small slices proved sufficient. To keep the servings from skating around the plates, put a small paper doily under each serving.

It's In the Cards

December 21, 1975

Readers often asked where recipes originate. This festive pudding came from our Christmas cards. Last January, when cards were half-price, this thrifty soul found a stack of greetings with a sketch of Christmas pudding on the cover and the recipe inside. Their appeal might have been limited to others, but not to a food writer.

Savings were wiped out because the recipe had to be tested. Suppose we hadn't tried it, and it was awful. Some of our friends might have made it and gotten so mad they'd strike our names from their Christmas-card lists forever. Didn't dare chance that.

Apparently, the card company had the good sense to try the recipe first, because the pudding is lovely, especially when wrapped in brandied hard sauce. Our cards could go out on schedule.

The card artist took liberties, studding the pudding with colorful bits of candied fruit. I advised readers to follow that sugarplum vision by adding a 1/2 cup of chopped color. You don't need a covered pudding mold. Any heatproof ring mold or deep bundt pan will do, sealed with several layers of foil tied tightly with string.

Battle of the Butter
November 30, 1975

White fruit cake had never been attempted for the column, so as the 1975 fruitcake season started, I told readers about making a double batch:

CHRISTMAS PUDDING
Makes 8 to 10 servings

Pudding:
- 1/2 cup all-purpose flour
- 1/2 teaspoon baking soda
- 1/4 teaspoon salt
- 1 teaspoon ground cinnamon
- 1/2 teaspoon ground cloves
- 1/2 teaspoon nutmeg
- 3/4 cup fine dry bread crumbs
- 1/2 cup butter
- 3/4 cup firmly packed brown sugar
- 3 eggs
- 1 package (8 ounces) pitted prunes, cut up
- 1 package (8 ounces) pitted dates, cut up
- 1 cup seedless raisins
- 1 tablespoon grated orange rind
- 1 cup chopped pecans or walnuts
- 1/4 cup brandy or dark rum

Hard sauce (optional):
- 1/2 cup butter
- 1 1/2 cups sifted powdered sugar
- 1 pasteurized egg
- Brandy or rum

To make pudding: Grease 8-cup mold very well. Sift together flour, soda, salt and spices. Stir in bread crumbs. Cream butter and brown sugar until light and fluffy. Beat in eggs, 1 at a time. Blend in flour mixture. Fold in prunes, dates, raisins, orange rind, nuts and brandy or rum. Pour into mold. Cover tightly.

To steam pudding: Place in large kettle of boiling water (water should be two-thirds the depth of mold). Keep water boiling gently at all times. Steam pudding for 3 1/2 hours, or until pudding is firm. Unmold. Serve while still warm.

To make hard sauce: Beat together butter and powdered sugar. Beat in egg. Add brandy or rum to taste. Serve over slices of warm Christmas pudding.

In retrospect, that was foolhardy. Not only was I risking about $15 worth of ingredients on an unknown recipe, but I found out the hard way that a home-size mixer cannot cope with two pounds of butter.

Not that I didn't try. The butter was hard; soft butter would have behaved better. Most of the solid butter wrapped itself around the beater and refused to budge. The rest was pelted around the kitchen, sending me chasing flying butter missiles. Maybe if the sugar was added, the butter would settle down, I reasoned. So in went 4 1/2 cups sugar — which only made the flying missiles sugar-coated. The beater was groaning with its load, threatening to add either smoke or sparks to the chaos.

I backed down, took half the butter and sugar out of the bowl, and continued as for a single recipe. All went well until the cakes came out of the oven. At that midnight hour, I soaked the two large cakes with rum, put them in plastic bags and tried that old trick of sucking out the air to create a vacuum. The air in those bags was rife with rum, and I nearly passed out from the fumes. Don't try it unless you want a quick drunk.

The cake (or cakes) definitely need aging, a minimum of 10 days. If you don't want one huge, heavy cake, try baking it in a 10-by-15-inch pan and cutting it in strips, a la Four-From-One Fruitcake. In this case, you would get five from one.

Mincemeat-Pumpkin Truce

November 21, 1976

It's amazing how battle lines are drawn between mincemeat partisans and those who prefer pumpkin. This recipe proved an excellent compromise for "I can't decide" pie eaters. At the office, when I brought this dessert for tasting, two distinct groups emerged among the mincement vs. pumpkin opinionated. But my co-workers agreed to a truce over this peacemaker pie. Maybe Secretary of State Henry Kissinger could bake a few of these and take them to the Middle East.

WHITE FRUITCAKE
Makes hefty tube cake

4 cups flour
1 pound (4 cups) pecan halves
1/2 pound (1 1/2 cups) golden raisins
1/2 pound candied red cherries
1/2 pound candied green cherries
1/2 pound candied pineapple, chopped
3/4 pound combination of diced candied lemon peel, orange peel and citron
2 cups butter
2 1/4 cups sugar
6 eggs, separated
1/4 cup lemon extract (2 1-ounce bottles)

To make fruitcake: Using 1 cup flour, dust pecans and fruit in extra-large mixing bowl, beginning with smaller pieces. In another bowl, cream butter until it is smooth. Add sugar. Beat until light and fluffy. Beat in egg yolks until mixture is thick and lemon-colored. Beat in flavoring and 1 cup flour. Add remaining flour. Beat until smooth. Gently fold batter into fruit-nut mixture. Beat egg whites until stiff but not dry. Fold into batter.

To bake fruitcake: Spoon into greased and parchment paper-lined 10-inch tube pan. Bake in 275-degree oven for 4 1/2 hours. Age at least 2 weeks.

Note: If necessary, soften raisins by placing in boiling water for 10 minutes. Cool. Drain on clean towel. If some of the fruit is not available, mixed candied fruit may be substituted.

The only sour note is the sweetness (to some people, obviously of the pumpkin persuasion) of prepared mincemeat. Those who make homemade mincemeat can modulate the sugar. Or how about soaking the commercial stuff in brandy before spreading it (drained, of course) in the pie. Now we're talkin'!

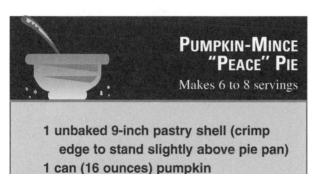

PUMPKIN-MINCE "PEACE" PIE

Makes 6 to 8 servings

- **1 unbaked 9-inch pastry shell (crimp edge to stand slightly above pie pan)**
- **1 can (16 ounces) pumpkin**
- **1 can (14 ounces) sweetened condensed milk**
- **2 eggs**
- **1 teaspoon cinnamon**
- **1/2 teaspoon salt**
- **1/2 teaspoon nutmeg**
- **1/2 teaspoon ginger**
- **1 1/3 cups mincemeat, bottled or homemade**
- **Whipped cream and nuts for garnish (optional)**

In large mixer bowl, combine pumpkin, sweetened condensed milk, eggs and spices. Mix well. Spread mincemeat on bottom of pie shell. Top with pumpkin mixture. Bake in 425-degree oven for 15 minutes. Reduce oven temperature to 350 degrees. Bake for 30 to 35 minutes, or until knife inserted 1 inch from edge comes out clean. Cool thoroughly before cutting. Garnish as desired. Refrigerate any leftovers.

Lime for Christmas Time

December 18, 1977

Even if your cookie cache is already full, you have to stuff in a batch of Lime Bars, I urged near the end of the 1977 Christmas baking season:

The shortcake crust is tender and buttery-good. The topping has a delicate lime essence that is much more refined than lemon bars. You might ease up on the sugar a little, and a drop of green coloring in the lime layer would identify the bars. Everyone at a holiday party thought they were lemon bars. Make these at the last minute, because the topping gets tacky if it stands too long.

LIME BARS

Makes about 4 1/2 dozen

- **2 cups flour**
- **1/2 cup powdered sugar**
- **1 cup butter or margarine**
- **4 eggs**
- **2 cups sugar**
- **Dash of salt**
- **1/3 cup fresh lime juice**
- **Powdered sugar**

In bowl, combine flour and powdered sugar. Cut in butter. Press mixture into 13-by-9-inch baking pan. Bake in 350-degree oven for 20 to 25 minutes, or until golden. Meanwhile, beat eggs at high speed with electric mixer until light and pale yellow in color. Gradually add sugar and salt. Add lime juice. Continue to beat at high speed. Pour over hot crust. Return to oven for 20 to 25 minutes longer, or until golden. Sprinkle at once with powdered sugar. Cut into bars.

Eat "Dessert" First
March 27, 1983

"Aha! Fooled 'em" opened a pre-April Fool's Day bit about reversing the usual order of things. This meatloaf was "dessert." "Sandwiches" of poundcake slices filled with strawberries and cream were the entree. Neither husband nor son raised an eyebrow, but they're accustomed to eating sometimes-odd tested fare. I kept prodding to see if they'd guess the trick. Aric's assessment: "You must have finally figured out that there's never any room for dessert so we're having it first."

Dinner progressed quietly for a few minutes until Aric said, "Mom, can I have another sandwich?"

"Eat your cake," his father said sternly.

Independence Day Legends
July 10, 1977

Our first Fourth of July party has become legend. The barbecued turkey was basted with champagne left over from our wedding. The barbecuers got basted as well, and when we were finally eating after sunset, my new husband gave me such a big bear hug that we went, heels over head, backward off the picnic bench.

The next year, in a rousing game of badminton, he plowed into a backyard jungle gym. His forehead still bears the semi-circular scar.

Those were the years when the annual celebrations with two neighbor families were definitely kid oriented on behalf of their large broods — rented ponies for rides, a helium tank for blowing up balloons. Our Aric didn't come on the scene until the fifth annual event. He's part of the legend, too, for the time, at age 2, when he broke into a chorus of "Happy Birthday" upon seeing his first sparkler.

These Little Legs soused in tempura batter were among our contributions — it was our year to bring

APRIL FOOL'S MEATLOAF CAKE
Makes 8 servings

Cake:
    2 eggs, slightly beaten
    1/2 cup milk
    1/2 cup ketchup
    1/4 cup Worcestershire sauce
    2 cups soft bread crumbs
    2 pounds ground beef
    Parsley flakes for garnish
Potato frosting:
    1 envelope (5-serving size) instant
        mashed-potato granules
    1/2 cup shredded cheddar or
        American cheese

To make cake: In large mixing bowl, combine eggs, milk, ketchup and Worcestershire sauce. Add bread crumbs and ground beef. Mix well. Spoon into 2 well-greased 8-inch layer cake pans. Bake in 350-degree oven for 40 to 45 minutes.

To make potato frosting: Prepare instant mashed potatoes as directed on package. Stir in shredded cheese.

To frost cake: Carefully turn 1 meatloaf layer out of pan onto serving plate. Spread with half the frosting. Top with remaining meat layer. Cover with remaining frosting. Sprinkle with parsley flakes, if desired.

appetizers. But do you know what "recipe" everyone at the party wanted? The sweet-sour sauce my husband stirred together to use as a dipping sauce. Don't ask. He knows what he used (plum jelly, mustard, vinegar and soy sauce), but he doesn't remember how much of each.

"LITTLE LEGS" TEMPURA

Makes 16 to 20 appetizers

8 to 10 chicken wings
1/2 cup ginger ale
1/2 cup flour
1 egg, well beaten
1 teaspoon soy sauce
1 teaspoon salt
1 cup vegetable oil

Remove tip from each chicken wing. Cut remainder of wing into 2 parts. Mix ginger ale, flour, well-beaten egg, soy sauce and salt very quickly and with as few strokes as possible. Heat oil in large skillet to 350 degrees. Dip each wing piece into batter. Fry "little legs" in hot oil for 8 to 10 minutes, turning often to brown evenly. Serve hot with sweet-sour sauce, Oriental mustard or chutney.

Sweet Holiday Traditions

January 2, 1983

Very few Tested Recipes have had such frequent reprises at our house as these two, first published in 1983. We make them every Christmas. I stir caramels; peanut brittle is my husband's project. Be patient with the caramels; they will eventually reach perfection. For both recipes, trust your candy thermometer. And don't try to double the brittle recipe; my husband did one year, creating an overflowing mess. The caramels were originally in a Land O Lakes holiday pamphlet, and I liked the muzzled bite of chocolate gluing down a pecan half.

Another Christmas candy we always make is Velvet Chocolate Fudge, included in the 1982 chapter.

BUTTERY PECAN CARAMELS

Makes 64 caramels

2 cups sugar
2 cups half-and-half, divided
3/4 cup light corn syrup
1/2 cup butter
1/2 cup chocolate chips, melted
64 pecan halves

In heavy 4-quart saucepan, combine sugar, 1 cup half-and-half, corn syrup and butter. Cook over medium heat, stirring occasionally, for 7 to 8 minutes, or until mixture comes to a full boil. Add remaining 1 cup half-and-half. Continue cooking, stirring often, for 35 to 40 minutes, or until a small amount of mixture dropped into ice water forms a firm ball, or candy thermometer reaches 245 degrees. Pour mixture into greased 8-inch square pan. Cover. Refrigerate for 1 to 1 1/2 hours to cool. Cut into 64 pieces (warm slightly first if they're too firm). Drop 1/4 teaspoon melted chocolate on top of each caramel. Press pecan half onto chocolate. Cover. Store refrigerated.

DIXIE PEANUT BRITTLE
Makes about 3 pounds

2 cups granulated sugar

1 cup light corn syrup

1/2 cup water

1/2 teaspoon salt

4 cups raw shelled Virginia-type
   peanuts, skin-on

2 tablespoons butter

2 tablespoons baking soda

In heavy saucepan, heat sugar, syrup, water and salt to a rolling boil. Add peanuts. Reduce heat to medium. Stir constantly. Cook until syrup spins a thread, or until candy thermometer reaches 293 degrees. Add butter, then baking soda. Beat rapidly. Pour onto buttered surface, spreading to 1/4-inch thickness. When cool, break into pieces.

Don't Jiggle This Jingle Bowl
December 25, 1983

A stunning starter for Christmas dinner, this chilled cranberry soup and the decorating technique were shared by chef Pierre Checchi when food writers visited the kitchen of the 95th Restaurant atop the John Hancock tower in Chicago. On Christmas Day 1983, I told readers all about it:

If all goes well this morning, if I can mix sour cream to the same consistency as the soup so it doesn't sink or blur, if my hand is steady when making the webs, if we don't jiggle the plates as they're carried

CHILLED CRANBERRY SOUP
Makes 6 servings

2 oranges

1 lemon

1 pound fresh or frozen cranberries

1 cup sugar

1 quart cranberry juice

2 cups red wine

Cinnamon stick

Cornstarch (2 or more tablespoons)

Sour cream

Half-and-half

To make soup: Grate orange and lemon rinds. Juice oranges and lemon. In large saucepan, combine rinds, juices, cranberries, sugar, cranberry juice, wine and cinnamon stick. Bring to a boil. Simmer for 5 minutes, or until cranberries are tender. Remove cinnamon stick. Soften cornstarch in a little water. Stir into soup until it is desired thickness. Pour soup into blender. Mix until smooth. Chill in covered container.

To serve soup: Ladle soup into chilled soup plates. Combine sour cream and half-and-half so it is the same consistency as soup. Make a cone from a triangle of parchment paper. Fill cone about half full with sour-cream mixture. Gently squeeze thin line of mixture, starting in center of bowl, in spiral of about four circles. Using toothpick, from center, make 4 lines through spiral at right angles. From outside, make lines between each of the previous four lines to make a pattern similar to that used to decorate Napoleon pastries.

into the dining room, this prelude to turkey should be spectacular.

All went very well, and our guests clustered in the kitchen to watch me decorate the Christmas-red soup. For understated decor, you can make a tiny spiderweb or snowflake on just one side of the bowl.

PEA PODS WITH SWEET RED PEPPERS
Makes 4 servings

2 tablespoons sesame seeds
2 teaspoons cooking oil
2 packages (6 ounces each) frozen Chinese pea pods, thawed and drained (or use fresh, trimmed pea pods)
1 large red bell pepper, thinly sliced and blanched
1 teaspoon sesame oil

To brown sesame seeds: Place sesame seeds in small skillet over moderate heat. Cook, stirring constantly, until seeds have begun to brown. Remove to small dish. Set aside.

To stir-fry vegetables: In large skillet, heat cooking oil over medium-high heat. When oil is hot, add pea pods and peppers. Cook, stirring constantly, for 1 minute. Remove from heat. Stir in sesame oil (the pungent-flavored Chinese kind). Place in serving bowl. Sprinkle with toasted sesame seeds. Serve immediately.

In Honor of the Ox
February 24, 1985

Chinese New Year is a movable holiday, always cause for feasting. Over the years, tested Chinese dishes have honored the weeklong celebration, among them these pea pods, a quick, colorful idea that appeared in 1985, the Year of the Ox.

Passing the Lutefisk Test
December 21, 1986

Eighteen years I've been writing this column, and I've managed to avoid the ultimate test — cooking lutefisk. Heck, I just tasted it for the first time last year.

Not that I didn't grow up smelling the stuff at Christmas. My mother bought dried slabs of lye-treated cod that looked like legs of long johns left on the clothesline to freeze solid in winter. She soaked it herself, and then cooked it for my grandfather's holiday treat. Paint practically peeled off the kitchen walls during the smelly and selfless process. I just now figured out the reason my aunt always had Thanksgiving dinner — she escaped having to cook Grandpa's Christmas lutefisk.

I broke down and tried lutefisk as served by Twin Cities restaurateur Tor Aasheim, as he learned to make it when he apprenticed at the Bristol Hotel in Oslo. (At one time, more lutefisk was consumed by Minnesota Norwegians than by Norwegians in all of Norway.) Since I'd steeled myself to eat it, it wasn't so bad. Mustard cream sauce, crumbled bacon, maybe a dribble of bacon fat are Tor's keys to palatability. Also, icy aquavit with a beer chaser are requisites, to anesthetize the taste buds and the taster.

Cooking it in the microwave oven, covered with plastic wrap, helps keep the aroma contained.

TOR'S LUTEFISK
Makes 4 to 6 servings

2 pounds lutefisk
3 tablespoons butter
3 tablespoons flour
1 cup milk
1/2 cup cream
Salt and pepper
1 1/2 tablespoons prepared mustard
4 slices bacon, cooked crisp and crumbled

To cook lutefisk: Boil in salted water, steam or microwave. Drain, skin and remove all bones. Meanwhile, cook and crumble bacon.

To make sauce: Melt butter. Stir in flour. Cook for 2 minutes, stirring constantly. Pour in milk and cream. Season to taste with salt and pepper. Stir until thickened. Add mustard (use more if desired).

To serve: Spoon sauce over hot lutefisk. Sprinkle with crumbled bacon. If desired, serve with boiled potatoes.

EASTER NESTS
Makes about 24

1 pound milk or semisweet chocolate (use chocolate chips and you won't have to temper the chocolate)
1/4 to 1/2 pound long-strand coconut
4 ounces jellybeans (marbleized ones are attractive)

Heat chocolate slowly over hot water until it's melted. Stir in coconut until it has a nest-like texture. Drop spoonfuls of mixture onto cookie sheets covered with wax paper, spreading them into "nests" about 2 inches in diameter, higher on sides than middle. Position 3 jellybeans in center of each nest. Chill briefly. Wrap each nest in plastic wrap (the tinted kind would be nice). Use them to fill Easter baskets or as Easter dinner favors.

Foxy Caramels
December 16, 1990

Seven years ago, for a food section cover story, Kathy Fox of Minneapolis, famous for her caramels, gave me detailed instructions for perfect results. Each year around this time, I get frantic calls from readers who have lost Fox's recipe, and they all tell me her caramels are the best they've ever made.

Fox has this advice, based on years of experience as she's made hundreds of pounds of these delectable candies: Use an accurate thermometer, pre-measure ingredients, don't quit stirring even to answer the phone, and wear an oven mitt on your stirring hand.

Nesting Urge, Chocolate Style
April 12, 1987

Every Easter, for Aric's basket, I bought jellybean-filled chocolate "nests" at Maud Borup candy shop in downtown St. Paul. Aric was almost 18 years old by the time I tried this recipe. Wish I'd gotten it much sooner.

KATHY FOX'S CARAMELS
Makes 2 1/2 pounds

1 cup butter
2 1/4 cups brown sugar
1/4 teaspoon salt
1 cup light corn syrup
1 can (15 ounces) sweetened
  condensed milk
1 teaspoon vanilla

In heavy 3-quart saucepan, melt butter. Add brown sugar and salt. Stir in corn syrup. Mix well. Stirring constantly, gradually add milk. Stirring over medium heat, cook for 12 to 15 minutes, until candy reaches firm-ball stage, or 242 degrees on a candy thermometer. Remove from heat. Add vanilla. Pour into well-buttered 9-by-9-inch pan. Cool for 4 to 6 hours. Cut and wrap caramels.

Note: Fox makes a double batch using the "dump" method of measuring: One pound butter, a 2-pound bag of brown sugar, a 16-ounce bottle of corn syrup and 2 cans of Eagle Brand milk. Expect to stir a double batch for 25 minutes.

WHITE FUDGE
Makes about 1 1/2 pounds

2 cups sugar
1/2 cup sour cream
1/3 cup white corn syrup
2 tablespoons butter
1/4 teaspoon salt
2 teaspoons vanilla
1/4 cup candied cherries, quartered
1 cup coarsely chopped nuts (slivered
  almonds are nice)

In saucepan, combine sugar, sour cream, corn syrup, butter and salt. Bring slowly to a boil, stirring until sugar dissolves. Without stirring, boil over medium heat to soft-ball stage, or 236 degrees on a candy thermometer. Remove from heat. Let stand for 15 minutes or longer. Add vanilla. Stir until mixture begins to lose its gloss. Add cherries and nuts. Put in buttered shallow pan. Cool completely.

Snowy Fudge for Winter Partying
December 20, 1992

Sour cream tempers the sweetness in this snowy fudge sent by reader Mary Raiter of St. Paul Park, Minn., who got it from her mother-in-law, also Mary Raiter of Breckenridge, Minn. The fudge reaches soft-ball stage quickly, but takes awhile to cool enough to be beaten into substance.

Santa Ron plays Christmas dinner sommelier.

1996

— A wedding in the family, and
Miss Piggy says fat's where it's at —

As Low as It Can Go
March 10

Penned on a recently received unsigned postcard was this plea: "How about some good down-to-earth recipes with only five to six ingredients?"

We aim to please, and then some.

How about two-ingredient recipes?

Beyond that, it's dry toast or frozen pizza, and the end of cooking as we know it.

Among the two-ingredient recipes wrung from a cookbook by that name was Insanely Delicious Couldn't-Be-Easier Hors d'Oeuvres, which involved stuffing wonton wrappers into miniature muffins tins, dropping in sugar-cube-size squares of hot pepper cheese, and baking in a 350-degree oven for 6 to 8 minutes, or until the cheese melts. Aric, who never found a food too spicy, added a dab of salsa to his share of the cheesy morsels.

Excedrin isn't Romantic
February 11

A romantic Valentine's Day dinner could cause that migraine-induced turn-down, "Not tonight, honey, I've got a headache." Red wine, chocolate, aged cheese, cakes, sour cream, even passion fruit can douse the fires of love. Rather than a juicy steak accompanied by cabernet, a Valentine menu for the migraine-disposed should be salmon with couscous and steamed vegetables (no MSG), tossed salad with vinaigrette, and a meringue heart filled with berries and fresh fruit.

King Tut Ate 'Em
February 11

Beans are such an ancient food that they were discovered in Egyptian tombs. "Those were probably the same ones most of us have at the back of our cupboards," quipped Michele Nolden, chef at that center for serenity and good health, The Marsh in Minnetonka, Minn.

Cooking with dried beans, which have climbed to the peak of the new nutritional pyramid, is nothing new, yet it's totally up to date. Nolden urged her spa cooking-class student to dust off those legumes. Or better yet, buy some new ones because oldies can become mummified.

Good Chicken, Better Eggs
March 31

From a column about methods to reduce cholesterol in eggs through breeding and feeding chickens:

Here's my answer to that amusing conundrum.

The chicken came first. Then, came the egg. Then, came the effort to make them both low, low, lower in fat.

Chicken has been the good actor in the anti-fat drama for which we're all the audience. Eggs have been cast as the villain.

Miss Piggy Ties on an Apron
April 21

It had to happen — backlash against anti-fat militants. Who better to campaign on behalf of more butter and cream than America's favorite porker femme fatale:

Glam ham Miss Piggy has been hogging the spotlight this week, appearing on the "Today Show" and on "Regis & Kathie Lee," rooting for her new book, "In the Kitchen With Miss Piggy."

The Moi Madame and her Henson henchmen have penned a book that made me squeal with giggles. "When I was approached to write this cookbook, moi thought: Why not, if Oprah can do it," the inde-fat-igable Miss Piggy states.

Testing recipes is OK by our favorite curlytail as long as they're chocolate (this moi can identify with that) blended with her favorite pantry ingredients — ice cream, whipped cream, heavy cream, Creamsicles, marshmallow creme, cream puffs, etc.

Leaning on her friends in the celebrity world for recipes, Miss Piggy critiques each dish's dish. Elizabeth Taylor's Spicy Chicken coated with curry, cumin, ginger, turmeric, garlic, onion and fresh ginger — but no oil or other marinade — was rather dry, the author thought. However, the spicy mixture, says Miss P. "also makes a tingly and tasty facial mask. Simply smooth on, wait 10 minutes, rinse, and follow with a chocolate mud pack. Voila! Vous are ready for a night of dinner and dancing!"

Acquired, Not Inherited
April 28

Observations in a column testing recipes from a 1930s Pillsbury cookbook, encased in an aluminum cover, purchased at the Minnesota State Fairgrounds antiques sale:

My ancestors weren't into antiques. According to family lore, my grandmother stripped ornate carvings from gilded picture frames and tossed them into a bonfire. To her, the plain inner molding was more "modern."

I grew up in a house furnished with ever-changing new things, so inheriting accoutrements "with their own ghosts," as a friend describes antiques, was not my lot.

So where did my passion for antiques originate? Why can't I stay away from Rose Galleries (in Roseville, Minn.) on Wednesday auction nights? Why do we trudge past every booth filled with vintage collectibles at Gold Rush Days in southern Minnesota's Oronoco and Rochester?

One motivator was the house we bought 30 years ago. It was old, large and needed to be filled with furniture of appropriate scale and age. And then we built a lake house, which gave me even more space to embellish.

The St. Paul house was adequately stuffed years ago, but accumulation is ongoing. Some people do drugs. I do rugs. And china. And Victorian furniture. Somewhere, surely, there's an AA group for the likes of us Antiques Addicts.

Deadly Dinner Partners
October 6

Today's recipe for a best-selling cookbook involves a few recipes and a lot of murder and mayhem. From a column about author Diane Mott Davidson who stirs up mystery plots with caterer Goldy as the main ingredient:

Inviting "Murder She Wrote" character Jessica Fletcher to your party is as hazardous as hiring Goldy Bear Schulz as your caterer.

With those women around, someone's destined to die.

But Can Gloria Cook?
September 15

I remember when the Women's Movement was very serious business. Marches, boycotts, group hand-wringing that finally led to a grip on corporate rungs were big news during my first decade at this newspaper.

Eventually, humor trickled into the solemn cause. Jokes about women weren't considered funny, but women themselves began seeing amusing aspects of the ongoing battle.

What's funny about the newly published "Wild Women in the Kitchen" is not only its droll

storytelling, but that is puts women leaders through history just where the Women's Movement didn't want them — in the kitchen.

Gloria Steiman and Bella Abzug probably wouldn't consider "Wild Women" amusing, especially its cover portraying 1960s housewives wearing white sunglasses and serving pigs-in-a-blanket. That neither of those wild women of the Women's Movement is mentioned in the book is not a put-down of their political efforts. It's just that the book's collaborators probably couldn't make any connections between those two and food.

Aric and Jennifer Make It Official
January 14

An engagement announcement was the first item I wrote as a 22-year-old new hire at the Pioneer Press.

I'm a little rusty now at social announcements, and this may not be the usual format, but it is with pleasure that we announce that our son, Aric Aune, and Jennifer Rowan are engaged. She is the daughter of Mike Rowan of Hastings, Minn. (Steamboat Inn customers will recognize him as the longtime manager of that St. Croix River landmark) and Kathleen Cognetta of Cottage Grove.

Jennifer grew up in Hastings, graduated from Hamline University and is now a legal assistant. She met Aric three years ago when she pinch-hit as a banquet waitress at the St. Paul Radisson Hotel, where he was a manager.

Aric proposed on Christmas Eve, hiding the ring in a huge carton weighted with barbells — that old trick. A summer wedding is planned.

According to etiquette, the bridegroom's parents invite the bride's side for dinner. Mike Rowan and his wife, Roberta, and Kathy Cognetta and her husband, Jim, joined us and the soon-to-be-newlyweds, who had just finished a whirlwind afternoon of touring potential reception sites and seeing a jeweler about wedding bands.

We parents listened enraptured as Jennifer described the seed pearls and removable train of her current favorite in the wedding-dress search. Dinner-table conversation centered on the number of guests at the reception and who will be in the bridal party.

Ah, the excitement of it all.

Aric created this recipe, inspired by a similar salmon fantasy served by Chef Ron Bohnert at the Radisson. For the engagement party, the bridegroom-to-be prepared the salmon all by himself, except for asking his dad to blanch spinach in the microwave. "Zap it in the nuker," Aric instructed.

ARIC'S SALMON WELLINGTON
Makes 4 servings

Poaching liquid:
- 2 cups white wine
- 4 thin lemon slices
- 4 scallions, chopped
- 1 garlic clove, halved
- 1/4 teaspoon seasoned pepper medley
- 1/2 teaspoon seasoned salt
- Dash of olive oil

Wellingtons:
- 4 pieces of salmon fillet, 6 ounces each
- 1 bunch spinach, blanched in the microwave
- 8 slices dilled Havarti cheese
- Phyllo dough or puff pastry
- Melted butter

Sauce:
- 1/2 cup half-and-half or cream
- 1 cup grated dilled Havarti cheese
- Dill to taste, fresh or dried
- 1 teaspoon finely chopped scallions
- 1/4 cup white wine or dry sherry
- Dash of Worcestershire sauce

To poach salmon: In large saute pan, combine white wine, lemon slices, scallions, garlic, pepper medley, seasoned salt and olive oil. Bring to a slow boil. Add salmon pieces, flesh side down. Cook until salmon just starts to become opaque. Turn over. Poach until fish is cooked medium, but still slightly rare. Drain salmon. Using small sharp knife, lift off skin.

To assemble Wellingtons: While salmon is poaching, blanch cleaned spinach leaves, covered, in small amount of water in microwave until just barely softened. Cut 8 lengthwise slices, 1/4-inch thick, from piece of Havarti cheese. Spread out 4 sheets of phyllo dough or puff pastry. In center of each, place about 5 medium spinach leaves, 1 slice of Havarti, 1 piece of salmon and another slice of Havarti. Cover with spinach. Wrap up dough. Brush lightly with melted butter. Place on greased baking sheet. Bake in 375-degree oven for 15 minutes, or until pastry is browned and cheese is melted.

To make sauce: In saucepan, heat half-and-half. Add 1 cup grated Havarti, dill, chopped scallions, white wine and Worcestershire sauce.

To serve: Spoon a little sauce over each portion of Wellington. Serve immediately.

Jennifer and Aric toast their future together.

Salmon fillets were enfolded in phyllo sheets, but Aric prefers puff pastry "because you can wrap it tighter." He restrained himself when cooking for his future in-laws, but he sometimes adds a touch of cayenne pepper to the sauce. (Note from Mom: These salmon packages are quite spectacular, and the fish remains wonderfully moist.)

If his intent was to impress his future in-laws, Aric made points. He certainly impressed his own mother.

Summer Showers

July 14

Three weekends to the wedding, and we're sloshing through a band of showers. Also, as the bridegroom's parents, we're immersed in an ocean of rehearsal-dinner plans.

PARTY FOCACCIA SANDWICHES
Makes about 25 portions

1 purchased bakery-style focaccia bread (about 8 inches in diameter, 1 1/2 inches thick)
8 ounces Neufchatel or cream cheese, softened
2 to 3 tablespoons low-fat milk
1/4 cup sun-dried tomatoes in oil, patted dry, chopped
4 teaspoons chopped fresh basil leaves, or 1 1/4 teaspoons dried basil
4 teaspoons chopped fresh thyme leaves or 1 1/4 teaspoons dried thyme
1 small garlic clove, minced
8 ounces thinly sliced deli smoked turkey breast
1 1/2 cups packed fresh spinach leaves, stems removed

To make sandwich: Using long, sharp serrated knife, split focaccia bread horizontally in half. Place halves, cut side up, on cutting board. Set aside. In small bowl, combine Neufchatel cheese and milk, stirring until smooth. Add tomatoes, basil, thyme and garlic. Mix well. Divide cream-cheese mixture in half. Set half aside. Spread remaining mixture evenly on both focaccia rounds, spreading to edges. Arrange spinach over cheese mixture on one half. Arrange turkey evenly over spinach. Spread remaining cream cheese mixture over turkey. Top with other bread round. Wrap focaccia round securely in plastic wrap. Refrigerate for at least 1 hour or overnight.

To serve: Using long, sharp serrated knife, cut focaccia round into 5 lengthwise strips. Cut each strip crosswise into 1 1/2-inch pieces. Use toothpicks topped with cellophane frills to hold sandwich squares together, if necessary.

All this pre-wedding entertaining is so much fun, I'd like to do it all over again. But since Aric is my only offspring, and he's anticipating married bliss, I expect this will be my last time to be a nuptial mom.

My contribution to one shower was an appetizer everyone thought quite appetizing, a low-fat (so we'll fit in our wedding dresses) stuffed focaccia round enriched with basil, spinach and sliced turkey. You don't have to be celebrating a wedding to try it.

Flaming Vegetables
December 8

Those whom I told that my new daughter-in-law, Jennifer, offered to do Thanksgiving dinner commended her bravery.

"Imagine, having you for a mother-in-law and having to cook for you," one friend marveled.

"I'm easy," I assured her. And grateful. Happy to pass the mantle (translation: happy to let someone else cook), though Thanksgiving is seldom our duty.

Last year, we feasted at the Steamboat Inn in Prescott, Wis., with Jennifer's family.

Two years ago, we were in Massachusetts for Thanksgiving. A couple of years before that, we were on a cruise ship traversing the Panama Canal. Those who reached the dining room before we did reported that the ship's interpretation of an American turkey dinner was not exactly accurate. I ordered lobster.

As on that shipboard Thanksgiving, we mostly float on this holiday. Christmas is when we stay put and cook.

As for Jennifer's courage at tackling the turkey, she managed her first Thanksgiving with aplomb. I was the one burning everything in sight when preparing vegetables that were our contribution to dinner.

On Thanksgiving morning, I rummaged through all the Christmas gifts purchased during the last year during our travels, at sales, even at the auction, and spent six hours getting a head start on the wrapping.

All of a sudden, it was past time to start fixing the vegetables.

Four burners were flaming at once. I put carrots, apple juice and dried cranberries to cook while tending the other vegetable combos.

Suddenly, I smelled something burning. A rubber scraper had gotten too close to the fire and was in flames. I tossed that into the sink to douse it.

A moment later, the plastic handle of one of my better knives was melting, also too close to the fire.

What demons were at work?

Aromas of burning rubber and plastic were so acrid that I didn't smell what was really burning — the carrots. The 1/2 cup of apple juice required for the recipe I was testing barely covered the bottom of a saute pan. Put it over medium-high heat, also as directed, and you'll have a charred pan requiring a couple of Brillo pads.

We salvaged the top unburned layer of carrots and served them at Thanksgiving dinner, along with the story of how they'd inadvertently flambeed.

A reader says . . .

It was always a moment of relief, distraction, time away from the real world when I read your culinary adventures. I always clipped one or two recipes to try "in a quiet moment." Now that I, too, have only two to cook for, there's less reason to clip, but I continue. I always bring some Eleanor recipe cards when I visit our kids in Missouri, Wisconsin and Florida.

— District Court Judge Mary Louise Klas, St. Paul.

1997

— Tested Recipes column breathes its last —

And So We Said Farewell ...

September 14

In the long-gone hot-type era of journalism when Tested Recipes first appeared, we pecked -30- on our old upright Remingtons to indicate the end of a story.

Now into its 30th year, this food column, which began July 21, 1968, has had a remarkably long run, unmatched in the nation.

But it is time, on my computer, to write -30- on it and, using another bit of journalese, to "put it to bed."

In so many ways, this column has been a partnership, as you readers have sent me family favorites, given me suggestions to keep my Paul Newman contest pasta mold from sliding off the plate, and constantly shared your opinions by mail or phone. You have been a great joy and resource for me.

This has been a very personal column. I've told you about my family, introduced you to friends in food, taken you on travels. I had the idea to start the column nine months before my son, Aric, was born, in effect, a double conception. You lived through his childhood "yucks" as he bluntly assessed my testing efforts, through his grade-school birthday slumber parties, and we all sent him off to college with cookies. I told you about celebrations when he married lovely Jennifer Rowan.

Aric has just begun an MBA program at the University of Minnesota's Carlson School of Management, as he, too, enters another phase of his career. He's lived his entire life with a mother always trying new recipes on him. Now, perhaps, I can finally go back and repeat some of the ones he really liked.

For three decades, I've talked about "my husband," St. Paul's best known anonymous man. He's been my unsalaried co-cook for all these years, the one who's boned the chickens and made the crepes. He's sometimes even tackled recipes when necessary, once volunteering to assemble a soup I'd intended to try, but couldn't when I was sidetracked into the maternity ward. He thought he turned the pot off, but it was on simmer the whole time he was out seeing his baby son and celebrating fatherhood. When I told readers how the new dad burned the soup, he took that teasing with good grace, as he has through all our tell-all mishaps over the years. It's only fitting that he is now finally recognized. Ron Aune, my dear, I couldn't have done this column without you.

It tickles me when a caller or someone I meet in public can quote verbatim incidents from this column, even those printed years ago. I'm pleased it has meant as much to you as it has to me.

I'm delighted when I see Tested Recipes repeated in area church cookbooks because that means they have become others' favorites, and are further woven into the fabric of community cooking.

This column has been for "scratch" cooks, perhaps a vanishing species. And so this column vanishes, too. Goodbye, Tested Recipes.

-30-

Before the column disappeared, we shared a few last recipes and food tales:

Bathroom Duties
January 19

It was my turn to hop on the hot plate.

I'm usually lounging comfortably in the audience at a cooking demonstrations, but at the Women's Expo, I had to talk and cook at the same time.

I'd forgotten the pain of schlepping food and equipment. It's not so bad to teach a class in my own kitchen, where all those little essentials — hot pads and measuring spoons — are only a drawer away. But hauling everything I needed to the Minneapolis Convention Center on a Sunday, when the temperature was below zero and parking spaces were as rare as white truffles in risotto, made me wonder why I can never remember the word "no" when such requests arise.

My load of groceries wobbled on its luggage-cart wheels, splashing milk. A trail of white dribbles marked my route through the crowd to the Northstar Services Cooking Stage. I thought weather and the football play-off games would thin the crowd. Wrong. Thousands of football widows showed up, and they got into any food-giveaway line, including mine.

The cooking area was the best — and worst — of all worlds. Radiating warmth was a green behemoth AGA cooker, the always-ready European epitome of appliances. Its top hot plates are perpetually at boiling or simmering heat, and several ovens are always preheated for long slow baking or hot fast searing.

Contrasted to the wonders of that $10,000 range were a sink with no water and a vacuum-cleaner booth just behind my back. Its great sucking sounds made it impossible for me to hear audience questions.

To overcome that racket, I wore a microphone clamped over my head, which did a great job of wrecking my hairdo. When I bent over to get an ingredient out of a bag, the battery pack fell out of my Ritz Cooking School apron pocket, pulling the microphone with it. As I grabbed for it, I somehow managed to get food in my hair. Or so an audience member gently told me.

The lowest moment came between demonstrations, when I hauled my dirty cookware to a distant ladies' room. While I hunched over a sink, wearing my white apron, swabbing pots, a woman came out of one of the stalls and told in urgent tones, "Ma'am, would you put some toilet paper in there?"

CREAM OF BELGIAN ENDIVE SOUP
Makes 4 servings

2 Belgian endives, cored
1 white onion, diced
1 garlic clove, minced
2 tablespoons butter
2 large potatoes, peeled and diced
2 cups chicken broth
1 cup milk or cream
Salt and pepper, to taste
Chopped chives

Mince Belgian endives, reserving a few small whole leaves for garnish. Saute minced endive, onion and garlic in butter for 3 minutes. Add potatoes and chicken broth. Simmer for 15 minutes, or until potatoes are soft. Put endive mixture in blender or food processor. Process until smooth. Add milk, salt and pepper. Blend. Serve hot or cold. Garnish with small Belgian endive leaves and chives.

Back on stage, I made recipes reflective of recent travels. For the first session, in the AGA's ovens, I baked South African Bobotie, that nation's flavorful version of hamburger hot dish. Later, I stirred stovetop Cream of Belgian Endive Soup, tasted during a visit to the endive-growing region of that Benelux nation.

WALNUT SPINACH STRAWBERRY SALAD

Makes 8 servings

Salad:
- 1 1/2 pounds fresh spinach, thoroughly cleaned
- 3 cups fresh strawberries, washed and hulled
- 1 large red onion, sliced thin
- 1 cup walnuts

Dressing:
- 3/4 cup sugar
- 1 teaspoon dry mustard
- 1 teaspoon salt
- 1/3 cup cider vinegar
- 2 teaspoons chopped scallions
- 1 cup vegetable oil
- 1 1/2 tablespoons poppy seeds

To make salad: In serving bowl, arrange spinach, strawberries, onion and walnuts. Refrigerate until needed.

To make dressing: In blender, combine sugar, mustard, salt and vinegar. Blend until smooth. Add scallions. Continue to blend. Slowly add vegetable oil while blender is running. Blend until dressing is thick. Stir in poppy seeds. Pour over salad mixture. Toss. Serve.

Picking While Swatting
July 6

The strawberry farm near our lake house wasn't quite ready for pickers, so with recipes to try, I waded into the wild.

Berry bowl in hand, off I went, saturated with Off. My ankles and arms were sprayed, my neck was misted, but I didn't bug-proof my backside. When one bends to pick low-to-the-ground wild strawberries, guess what's the biggest target for flying biters?

Dainty, delectable native strawberries beckoned in ripe profusion, flourishing as recent hot, moist weather compensating for an inclement spring. Strawberries were everywhere — and so were mosquitoes. I couldn't have made enough strawberry-spinach salad for Thumbelina with the berries I picked before retreating indoors.

So I picked strawberries in the store for Walnut Spinach Strawberry Salad, my blending of elements from two recipes in a book compiled by members of the North American Strawberry Growers Association. Make it even more like a restaurant-style experience by topping portions with a wedge of molten brie.

Foiled Again
July 13

Poor Pat Schweitzer. She doesn't line her ham baking pan and spends the entire holiday party scrubbing implacable burned residue.

Her barbecued food falls through the rack.

Her meat gets freezer burn.

She's become a walking, talking commercial for the hazards of not using foil since her employer, Reynolds Aluminum, made her the somewhat hapless star in its television commercials.

Home economist Schweitzer was originally a Minnesota farm girl, and for the column about her serendipitous TV stardom, she shared this three-ingredient recipe, nearly instant gratification for those craving chocolate. Toffee Crunch Brownies were reduced to crumbs in no time, and unlike Schweitzer in the ham commercials, I didn't waste any time scrubbing the pan.

TOFFEE CRUNCH BROWNIES
Makes 24 squares

1 package (1 pound, 5.2 ounces) fudge brownie mix
1 cup crisp rice cereal
1/2 cup English toffee bits (Heath Bits)

Line 9-by-13-inch baking pan with aluminum foil. Spray with nonstick cooking spray. Set aside. Follow package directions to prepare brownie mix. Spread batter evenly in pan. Sprinkle cereal evenly over batter. Press lightly. Sprinkle toffee bits evenly over cereal. Bake in 350-degree oven for 30 to 35 minutes, or until brownies are set. Cool in pan on wire rack. Lift foil to remove brownies from pan to cutting board. Fold foil back to cut brownies

Muffins That Didn't Make It
July 20

An unexpected dictum from an editor that I could no longer write about contests I judged scuttled the July 20 column, so this intriguing muffin recipe never saw print. It was the winner in the Pequot Lakes Bean Hole recipe contest, entered by Norma Weinzierl of that northern Minnesota lake-country community. Nobody could guess the starring ingredient when the muffins were brought to the office. Beans add a rosy hue and a dose of fiber, though fat is in full force.

When I was in Pequot Lakes to view the doings, 2,280 showed up to eat their fill of free beans from five huge kettles of beans buried overnight to cook. The pots were so heavy, they had to be lifted from the cooking pits with a backhoe.

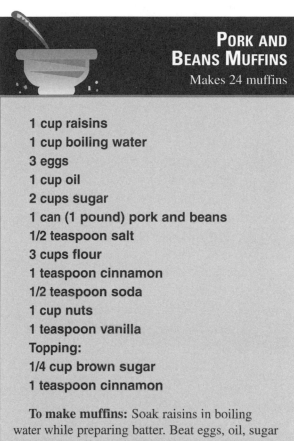

PORK AND BEANS MUFFINS
Makes 24 muffins

1 cup raisins
1 cup boiling water
3 eggs
1 cup oil
2 cups sugar
1 can (1 pound) pork and beans
1/2 teaspoon salt
3 cups flour
1 teaspoon cinnamon
1/2 teaspoon soda
1 cup nuts
1 teaspoon vanilla
Topping:
1/4 cup brown sugar
1 teaspoon cinnamon

To make muffins: Soak raisins in boiling water while preparing batter. Beat eggs, oil, sugar and beans until beans are broken up. Add dry ingredients, nuts and vanilla. Add drained raisins.

To bake muffins: Spoon batter into well-greased or sprayed muffin tins. Combine brown sugar and remaining teaspoon of cinnamon. Sprinkle on top of each muffin. Bake muffins in 350-degree oven for 30 to 35 minutes. (Note: Or spread batter into 3 greased loaf pans and bake at 350 degrees for 1 hour.)

Leftovers

— *Everything that Wouldn't Fit Elsewhere —*

You've likely noted, paging through this cookbook, that it's not arranged in the classic manner, with chapters devoted to meats, vegetables, breads, pies, etc.

Instead, divisions center on people, places and events. Or years.

"Year" chapters are limited to three or four recipes. And other categories don't always jive with intriguing recipes rediscovered in this 30-year retrospective.

So here is a collection of all those favorites that didn't fit anywhere else, but were too good to exclude. These are leftovers you won't want to toss.

Mess Becomes Marvelous
May 17, 1970

Addictive is a good way to describe Oatmeal-Dill Bread. Amazing is another.

Amazing because I couldn't believe that the gosh-awful mess of cottage cheese, oatmeal and dill seed, reeking of onion, would ever turn into an edible bread. But it did, and I dared readers to try it.

In 1970, dill seed wasn't easy to find in stores, but today, that should be no problem. We tend not to use dried minced onion much anymore; don't hesitate to substitute 2 tablespoons or more of finely chopped fresh onion. "This is a heavy-textured bread which would be even heavier if the flour weren't sifted, so take an extra minute to do it," I wrote. Today, flour is supposedly presifted, but still, take that extra minute.

Now, who's going to accept that dare?

A reader says . . .

I've really enjoyed your delectable columns since I've become a resident of Mahtomedi. Just a few weeks ago, I was actually thinking about what a feat you've accomplished. Then came the article on Tested Recipes' 25th anniversary!

— Candia Lea Cole, Mahtomedi, Minn.

OATMEAL-DILL BREAD
Makes 2 casserole loaves

2 teaspoons instant minced onion, or 2 tablespoons finely chopped onion
1/2 cup water
2 cups large-curd creamed cottage cheese, warmed
3 tablespoons butter or margarine
1/4 cup sugar
2 teaspoons salt
1/2 teaspoon soda
3 1/2 cups sifted all-purpose flour, divided
2 eggs
2 packages dry yeast
1 cup quick or old-fashioned oats
2 tablespoons dill seed

To make batter: Combine onion and water. In large bowl, combine cottage cheese, butter, sugar, salt, soda and onion-water mixture. Add 2 cups flour, eggs and yeast. Beat 2 minutes. Stir in oats, dill seed and remaining flour. Cover. Let rise in warm place for 1 hour, or until double in size.

To bake bread: Stir batter down. Place batter in 2 greased deep casserole or souffle dishes. Brush tops with melted butter. Let rise, uncovered, in warm place for 45 minutes, or until nearly double in size. Bake in 350-degree oven for 35 minutes. Remove from casserole. Brush tops with melted butter. Sprinkle with salt.

Good Puppies!
September 6, 1970

At State Fair time in 1970, I tried this recipe in honor of a co-worker who was crazy about corn dogs, a.k.a. Pronto Pups:

SUN DOGS
Makes 20

Lard or oil
2 packages (1 pound each) wieners
20 wooden skewers
1 cup flour
3/4 cup cornmeal
2 tablespoons sugar
1 tablespoon dry mustard
2 teaspoons baking powder
1 teaspoon salt
2 tablespoons shortening
1 cup milk
1 egg

To prepare wieners: In pan suitable for deep-frying, heat at least 2 inches of lard to 375 degrees. Remove wieners from package. Insert 1 skewer lengthwise into each.

To make batter: Combine dry ingredients in mixing bowl. Cut in shortening. Add milk and egg. Stir to remove most of lumps. Dip wieners into batter, turning to coat evenly. Fry in fat for 2 minutes, or until golden brown. Drain. Serve with mustard, if desired.

"She did pretty well by these corny dogs, eating three after they were cooked, and one raw wiener in anticipation," the column reported.

We still work together, and I go to lunch with her frequently. Believe me, she doesn't allow herself such excesses these days.

The thick batter adheres better when the wieners are dried with paper towels. "It's easier to dip the wieners if the batter is poured into a tall drinking glass," was suggested in the testing notes. However, the thick batter coated just over a dozen wieners, so I told readers, if they wanted to fry 20 Sun Dogs, they'd have to increase the batter by 50 percent.

There wasn't a dissenting vote from my officemates on this recipe (I actually tested it at the newspaper). Fried in fresh fat, these dogs turn golden brown instead of the chocolate tone of those at the Fairgrounds.

'Fess up time: I used lard — two pounds — to make this recipe. But then, we didn't know much about our triglycerides in 1970.

Chew on These

December 6, 1970

"Bits of cherries give these bars an appropriate holiday look," I wrote about these treats tested in time for Christmas baking. When I brought them to the office, there was one small debate. I pronounced maraschino as "ma-ras-she-no," which caused longtime columnist and resident office grammarian Betty Roney, devouring one of the bars, to give me a disapproving look. "Ma-ras-ski-no" she managed to say with her mouth full. But she was so mellowed by the Chew-Chews that she agreed, no matter the pronunciation, the bars were still good.

CHEW-CHEWS
Makes 24 bars

Crust:
- 1 cup unsifted all-purpose flour
- 1/2 cup butter, softened
- 3 tablespoons sugar

Topping:
- 2 eggs, slightly beaten
- 3/4 cup sugar
- 1/4 cup unsifted all-purpose flour
- 1/2 teaspoon baking powder
- 1/2 teaspoon salt
- 1 teaspoon vanilla
- 1 1/3 cups (about) flaked coconut
- 1/2 cup chopped maraschino cherries
- 1/4 cup chopped walnuts

To make crust: Combine flour, butter and 3 tablespoons sugar. Blend well. Press mixture firmly in bottom of 9-inch square pan. Bake in 350-degree oven for 25 minutes.

To make topping: Combine all topping ingredients. Spread mixture over baked crust in pan. Bake in 350-degree oven for 35 minutes. Cut into bars while still warm.

A reader says . . .

I do enjoy reading your "chatty" columns, and the recipes, of course.

— Ailene Niemi, North Branch, Minn.

Taste of Paradise

June 7, 1970

"Polynesian and Chinese restaurants, watch out! It's possible, with today's recipe, to make sweet-sour pork as well or even better than that found in such eateries," the column enthused. Some might like an extra tablespoon of vinegar, we suggested then, though we liked the sauce because it wasn't cloying. Try simmering the pork in the sauce for a minute before serving.

ORIENTAL SWEET-SOUR PORK

Makes 4 servings

Fried pork:
- 1 egg, slightly beaten
- 1/4 cup cornstarch
- 1/4 cup all-purpose flour
- 1/4 cup chicken stock
- 1 teaspoon salt
- 1 pound boneless pork, trimmed and cut into 1-inch cubes
- 2 cups vegetable oil

Sauce:
- 1 tablespoon vegetable oil
- 1 clove garlic, minced
- 1 large green pepper, cut into 1-inch squares
- 1 can (about 13 ounces) pineapple chunks, drained
- 1/2 cup chicken stock
- 1/2 cup maple syrup
- 4 tablespoons red-wine vinegar
- 1 teaspoon soy sauce
- 1 tablespoon cornstarch dissolved in 2 tablespoons cold water

To prepare pork: Combine egg, cornstarch, flour, chicken stock and salt. Dip pork cubes in egg-flour mixture, coating each piece well. Pour oil into large frying pan. Heat until hot. Drop half of coated pork cubes, 1 at a time, into oil. Fry for 5 to 6 minutes, or until done, turning occasionally. Remove with slotted spoon. Place pork on wire rack in shallow pan. Keep warm in 250-degree oven. Fry remaining pork. Keep warm.

To make sauce: Drain off and discard oil from large frying pan. Set frying pan over high heat for 30 seconds. Add 1 tablespoon oil. Heat for 30 seconds. (Note: If oil smokes, turn heat down to medium.) Add garlic, green pepper and pineapple. Stir-fry for 2 to 3 minutes, until pepper and pineapple take on some color. Add chicken stock, syrup, vinegar and soy sauce. Bring to a boil. Boil rapidly for 1 minute. Add cornstarch mixture. Cook until sauce is thick and clear, stirring constantly.

To serve: Arrange fried pork on platter. Pour sauce over pork. Serve immediately with hot rice.

Hold the "Garbage"
February 6, 1972

Changria was a surprise favorite. It's a variation on the Spanish fruit and wine drink sangria, this one flavored with cranberry juice in addition to red wine (we used an inexpensive burgundy, but Mogen David would fit the "sweet red wine" descriptor). After tasting, we decided not to add extra sugar. Changria is pretty in the pitcher, but with all that "garbage" (my husband's term) in it, pouring takes some dexterity. Have a spoon on hand to hold back the fruit slices.

CHANGRIA
Makes 2 quarts

2 canned or fresh peach halves
1 orange, sliced
1 lemon, sliced
1 lime, sliced
1 quart cranberry juice cocktail, chilled
1 quart sweet red wine, chilled
Sugar to taste

Place fruit in pitcher. Crush with back of long-handled spoon. Add cranberry juice and wine. Add sugar to taste. Stir to dissolve sugar. Garnish with additional fruit slices. If desired, add plain or cranberry juice ice cubes.

Oyster Gumbo, Then and Again
July 30, 1972

"Sadly, I predict that not many of you will try this recipe because it calls for an unusual spice and because many of you might be leery of oysters," was the comment when this gumbo first appeared. "Please reconsider," I begged, telling readers that gumbo file powder was available in St. Paul. "It's a powder made from young sassafras leaves and thyme leaves. Story has it that the Indian word for sassafras is kombo, translating to 'gumbo' in Creole talk," I said in 1972. (I've learned since that the word has African roots.) I loved this Opelousas Oyster Gumbo (named for a city in Louisiana) when I first tested it, and it's one of the rare recipes that's been repeated at our house.

Oyster Gumbo Update
January 1, 1995

Planning Christmas dinner was a chance to be culinarily sentimental and dig backward. Besides, I couldn't serve that Paul Newman shrimp soup yet again, even if Christmas is all about tradition.

Opelousas Oyster Gumbo first appeared in this column on July 30, 1972, and we made it one other time for a midwinter party in the mid-'70s. Since then, it's been mouldering in the archives. We thought it was a shade spicy then. My, how our taste buds have toughened in 20 years.

I made this recipe right to the letter on Christmas morning, and its flavor effect produced a dull thud. So my husband and I went to work on it. I added more gumbo file, then did a number with cayenne. Still, our double batch was at half flavor-strength. So, my husband doused it with Worcestershire sauce.

Still not enough.

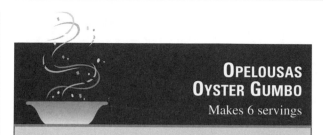

OPELOUSAS OYSTER GUMBO
Makes 6 servings

1/4 cup flour

1/4 cup bacon drippings, butter or margarine

1 cup chopped green peppers

1 cup chopped onions

1 clove garlic, crushed

2 cups water

2 tablespoons chopped parsley

1 1/2 teaspoons salt

1/4 teaspoon pepper

1/4 teaspoon thyme

Dash of cayenne powder

1 bay leaf

1/2 pound peeled deveined raw shrimp

1 pint oysters with liquid

Gumbo file

Tabasco sauce (optional)

3 cups hot cooked rice

Brown flour in drippings until it is deep red-brown, stirring constantly to prevent burning. Add green peppers, onion and garlic. Cook until vegetables are tender. Stir in water, parsley, salt, pepper, thyme, cayenne powder and bay leaf. Cook slowly for 30 minutes. Add shrimp and oysters with their liquid. Bring to a boil. Cook 5 minutes, or until shrimp are pink and oysters begin to curl. Remove from heat. Add gumbo file to taste (at least 2 teaspoons). Add hot-pepper sauce if you like gumbo with more pep. Serve in shallow bowls over beds of hot cooked rice.

What put it over the top was a jolt of Jamaican jerk sauce. Then, the gumbo grabbed us. Not too hot, but definitely kin to Creole. If you decide to make this antique recipe, don't hesitate to renovate it to your taste.

Vichyssoise of a New Hue
July 30, 1972

Inspired by a July hot spell, we tried a chilled carrot vichyssoise, so good that a renowned finicky eater among our guests asked for a supply to take home. It's the prettiest orange hue, which we topped with chopped chives for color and flavor contrast. I warned readers that the entire recipe won't fit into a blender container so they'd have to puree it in batches. I'd tested it because it sounded so unusual, but a short while later I got a sheaf of recipes for watercress, almond, turnip, sweet potatoes and apple vichyssoises, so apparently, anything goes.

Betty Roney, word expert in the Family Life department, has been crusading for years for the proper pronunciation of vichyssoise. It has a "z" sound at the end: "vichyswaaz." Can you say that with a mouthful of soup?

P.S. Writing in another column about potato-based vichyssoise, I told the story of my husband's brother, invited to a fancy dinner while he was in college, who couldn't wait to taste vichyssoise listed on the menu because it sounded so elegant. One spoonful, and he realized that it tasted the same as the potato soup his mother made frequently in an effort to economically feed five kids. He immediately gained new respect for her cooking.

CARROT VICHYSSOISE
Makes 6 servings

3 cups pared sliced potatoes

2 cups pared sliced carrots

2 leeks, thinly sliced (white part only)

3 cups boiling water

4 chicken bouillon cubes

1 teaspoon salt

2 tablespoons butter

1 cup heavy or light cream

1 cup milk

1/4 teaspoon Tabasco sauce

In large heavy saucepan, combine potatoes, carrots, leeks, boiling water, bouillon cubes and salt. Cover. Cook for 40 to 45 minutes, or until vegetables are very tender. Put mixture through strainer, sieve, food mill or blender. Add butter, cream, milk and hot-pepper sauce. Mix well. Chill. Serve cold. Or reheat in double boiler over hot water. Top with grated carrot, parsley or chives.

GRAPES FLORENTINE
Makes 6 servings

1 1/2 pounds (3 to 4 cups) seedless
    green grapes

3 egg yolks

2/3 cup sugar

2/3 cup Marsala wine or sherry

1 cup whipping cream

1 square semisweet chocolate

Rinse and drain grapes. Remove stems. Chill. Beat egg yolks in top of double boiler until thick and pale yellow. Gradually add sugar, beating constantly. Stir in Marsala or sherry. Place pan over simmering water. Cook, stirring occasionally, for 30 minutes, or until mixture thickens. Remove from heat. Chill thoroughly. Whip cream. Fold into cooled mixture. Pour half of grapes into 6 stemmed glasses. Spoon cream mixture onto grapes. Top with remaining grapes. Make chocolate curls using potato peeler. Garnish desserts with curls.

Gussied Grapes
October 7, 1973

Green grapes remain among the most affordable, available fruits. They're pleasing plain, but sometimes it's fun to gussy them up. This easy company dessert appeared, with the advice that "sherry flavored whipped cream custard is a rich reward for our efforts," and the recipe can be made ahead "with little fear of disaster" (unlike the burned-crust chicken I made for that same Sunday).

This Chicken Likes to Party
May 27, 1973

If I were served Chicken a la Cheddar at a restaurant or a party, the cook would be praised all the way home. A cheesy variation of chicken Kiev, it's a delicious and elegant dinner item that deserves to be invited to your next party.

My resident meat cutter (also paper hanger, carpenter, light bulb changer, etc.) skinned and boned the chicken, giving me an extra strip of meat from

CHICKEN A LA CHEDDAR
Makes 8 servings

Chicken:
- 1 stick (10 ounces) sharp natural cheddar cheese
- 4 whole chicken breasts (2 1/2 pounds), boned and skinned
- 2 eggs, beaten
- 3/4 cup dry bread crumbs
- Butter or margarine for browning
- 1/2 cup chopped onion
- 1/2 cup chopped green pepper
- 1/4 cup butter or margarine
- 2 tablespoons flour
- 1 teaspoon salt
- 1/4 teaspoon pepper
- 3/4 cup water
- 2 cups cooked white rice
- 1 cup cooked wild rice

Sauce:
- 1 1/2 cups sliced fresh mushrooms
- 1/4 cup butter
- 3 tablespoons flour
- 1 chicken bouillon cube
- 1/2 cup boiling water
- 1/2 cup milk
- 1/3 cup dry white wine

To prepare chicken: Cut cheese into 8 equal sticks. Cut each chicken breast in half. Flatten each to 1/4-inch thickness. Roll each piece around 1 stick of cheese. Secure with toothpicks. Dip chicken in egg. Dip in bread crumbs. Brown in butter or margarine.

To bake chicken: Saute onion and green pepper in 1/4 cup butter or margarine. Blend in flour, salt and pepper. Gradually add water. Cook, stirring constantly, until thickened. Stir in white and wild rice. Pour mixture into buttered 7-by-11-inch baking dish. Top with chicken. Bake in 400-degree oven for 20 minutes.

To make sauce: Saute mushrooms in butter. Blend in flour. Dissolve bouillon cube in water. Gradually add to mushroom mixture. Stir in milk. Cook, stirring constantly, until thickened. Add wine. Heat fully. Serve over chicken and rice.

each breast, which he called the "tenderloin." I was wondering how to cook those extra bits of meat when necessity became invention's mother. The chicken strip isn't large enough to cover the ends of the cheese sticks, but if it is wrapped around the long way and fastened with toothpicks, it keeps the melting cheese from escaping.

Smooth Spiked Soup
October 28, 1973

"The soup hardly needs sieving," was the comment about this beer-flavored pea soup. These days, if we made it, we'd be more likely to smooth it in a food processor, an appliance unknown in 1973.

SPIKED SPLIT PEA SOUP

Makes 8 servings

1 pound split peas
2 cans or bottles (12 ounces each) beer
5 cups water
2 to 2 1/2 pounds ham hocks or bones
1 medium onion, chopped
3 or 4 ribs celery, with green tops, chopped
1 teaspoon garlic powder
1 teaspoon salt
1/8 teaspoon pepper

Combine all ingredients. Simmer for 1 hour and 20 minutes, or until peas are soft. Cut off any bits of ham from bones. Push soup through sieve. Return ham pieces to soup. Reheat.

Deja Vu Vegetables

Undated, probably from 1974

Rereading these 30 years of recipes, I came across this vegetable medley, and thought, gee, that seems familiar. I dug through files and found a hand-written recipe, nearly the same, titled Betty Levin's Vegetable Casserole. Betty was the first woman photographer at the old St. Paul Dispatch-Pioneer Press in the World War II era, and then she became one of the Twin Cities' premiere wedding photographers. I wrote down her recipe after I'd been at a party where Betty brought her colorful melange.

According to the column accompanying this Vegetable Medley (undated, but I think from about 1974), I got the original recipe from Elsa Clay of St. Paul, who said in a chatty letter, "Five of us polished off the whole flamin' pan, which is supposed to serve 8 to 10." I complimented it "for the riotous color it puts on a plate" and for its glistening tapioca glaze.

It was several years later that Betty Levin gave me her recipe embellished with butter and sugar. I had forgotten that I'd tested a similar recipe years before, and now I wonder if maybe Betty got hers from the Tested Recipes column.

SUPER GOOD-O BAKED VEGETABLE MEDLEY

Makes 8 to 10 servings

1 1/2 cups thinly sliced onions
1 1/2 cups thinly sliced carrots
3/4 cup green pepper, cut in chunks
2 cups sliced celery
2 cups green beans (canned or frozen)
2 cups undrained canned or stewed tomatoes, broken up
1 to 2 teaspoons salt
Pepper to taste
3 tablespoons tapioca

Combine ingredients in flat baking dish (not aluminum). Cover tightly with foil. Bake in 350-degree oven for 70 minutes. (Note: Betty Levin's version, which I have made more recently, adds 2 tablespoons sugar and 4 tablespoons butter, cut in chunks, to the casserole before baking.)

Consoling Corn Fritters

August 18, 1974

My only pleasurable memory of the summer of 1959 is corn fritters. That was the vacation after my freshman year in college, and I was elated at having found a job as a children's recreation director at a resort near Cable, Wis.

The owner said he hired me over several older applicants, mostly teachers. I was to get $2.50 a day for each child I shepherded that summer. The owner, who had just purchased the resort and was hiring his first recreation director, was certain I'd make a fortune.

I didn't. Most families who stayed at the resort entertained their own kids. It slowly dawned on my naive mind that I had been hired because I was the only one who hadn't demanded a guaranteed salary. It was a devastating experience during which I exchanged three months of vacation for $40 and a suntan.

Corn fritters were a bright spot that summer, a cheap lunch to feed the help, made by a Cable-area farm woman who was the resort's cook. She had the most work-gnarled hands I'd ever seen, huge from milking cows, but she certainly could make superb fritters.

Until this recipe crossed my desk and unlocked all those memories, I hadn't thought of those fritters for years. Testing the recipe revealed how simple they are.

CORN FRITTERS
Makes 10 to 12 fritters

1 package (10 ounces) frozen whole-kernel corn
1/2 cup all-purpose flour
3/4 teaspoon baking powder
1 teaspoon salt
1/8 teaspoon pepper
3 tablespoons milk
2 tablespoons shortening, melted
2 eggs, well beaten
Oil or fat for frying
Maple syrup

Thaw corn. Drain well. Mix flour with baking powder, salt and pepper. Add milk and melted shortening to eggs. Add to dry ingredients. Blend well. Stir in corn. Drop batter from a tablespoon into 1/2 inch of hot oil or fat in skillet. Fry fritters for 5 minutes, or until golden brown on all sides. Drain on absorbent paper. Serve with syrup.

Hot Time Had By All

August 17, 1975

We laughed in the face of adversity. My husband wanted a big party for his 40th birthday. All the plans were in place when, just 72 hours before his birthday, his Minneapolis business was destroyed by the most spectacular fire I have ever seen and never hope to see again. Nothing was left but charred timbers crumpled in the basement. Firemen, called for the 4 a.m. four-alarmer, were still dumping water on the ruins at midafternoon. Overnight, more than 40 people were out of work.

But the birthday bash wasn't doused. My husband is an optimist. Invitations were out. The party was on. After all, life begins (again, in his case) at 40.

These mushrooms were eaten as fast as they could be brought to the food table. As one of my husband's former employees explained on his fifth trip to fill his plate, "This has to last me until next week. I don't have a job, you know."

We knew.

HAPPY HOUR MUSHROOMS
Makes 36 portions

36 medium-size fresh mushrooms
3 tablespoons butter, melted
1 stick butter, softened
1 clove garlic, minced or mashed
2/3 cup grated Monterey jack cheese
2 tablespoons red wine
2 tablespoons soy sauce
1 package toasted onion dip mix
1/3 cup crushed corn chips

Remove stems from mushrooms. Wash caps. Brush with melted butter. Combine softened butter, garlic and grated cheese. Mix well. Add wine, soy sauce, dip mix and corn chips to make a paste. Fill mushroom caps with mixture. Place on baking sheet. Broil for 3 minutes, or until bubbly and lightly browned.

Conference Encounter
October 19, 1975

Back in the days when the newspaper sent me to food-editors' meetings and conferences (in more recent years, I've spent my own dough to go), I would return with an array of recipes to share with readers. One

night, after a huge conference dinner, we wandered into a late-night wine party where Dessert Cheese was an enticement. I couldn't stay away from that bowl, no matter how my waistband was straining.

This so-simple blend can be served as a dessert or appetizer dip. Today's cooks can cut calories by using Neufchatel or another reduced-fat cream cheese brands.

DESSERT CHEESE
Makes 2 1/2 cups

2 packages (8 ounces each) cream cheese
1/4 cup unsalted butter, softened
1 cup sifted powdered sugar
2 tablespoons orange juice
1 tablespoon grated orange peel
1/2 teaspoon vanilla
Orange slices

To make cheese: In small mixer bowl, combine all ingredients, except orange slices. Beat on low speed until mixture is smooth. Chill for 1 hour.

To serve: Mound into dish or smooth on serving tray. Garnish with orange slices. Serve with sliced apples or pears, unsalted walnuts or pecans, or toast rounds.

Double Treat Doughnuts
April 20, 1975

Stunned at the price — $1.50 for a dozen plain bakery doughnuts — I turned to this recipe that had been in the recipe stack for months. "I'm tempting, test me," it called every time I flipped past it. Raised doughnuts aren't challenging to make, but they take patience to wait through two risings, especially when promise of goodies is imminent. These aren't a treat to stir up before breakfast, unless you're an insomniac.

The bonus is the half-dozen caramel pecan rolls made from the holes. "I can't say which is better — the doughnuts or their glorified holes — but do try both," I urged readers. If you don't have leftover mashed potatoes, make a single serving of instant ones.

OLD-FASHIONED DOUGHNUTS WITH A BONUS
Makes up to 30 doughnuts and 6 pecan rolls

Dough:
- 1 cup warm water (110 degrees)
- 2 packages active dry yeast
- 2/3 cup sugar
- 1 teaspoon salt
- 1/2 cup mashed potatoes, at room temperature
- 1/4 cup margarine, at room temperature
- 1 egg, at room temperature
- 4 to 5 cups unsifted flour, divided

Syrup for pecan rolls:
- 1/4 cup light brown sugar
- 2 tablespoons light corn syrup
- 2 tablespoons margarine, at room temperature
- 18 pecan halves
- Vegetable shortening or oil for frying

To make dough: Measure water into large, warm mixing bowl. Sprinkle in yeast. Stir until dissolved. Stir in sugar, salt, potatoes and margarine. Add egg and 2 cups flour. Beat until smooth. Stir in enough additional flour to make a soft dough. Turn out onto lightly floured board. Knead for 8 to 10 minutes, or until smooth and elastic. Place in greased bowl. Turn to grease top. Cover. Let rise in warm place, free from draft, for 1 hour, or until doubled in bulk.

To make syrup for pecan rolls: While dough rises, in saucepan mix brown sugar, corn syrup and margarine. Heat, stirring, until margarine melts. Divide syrup mixture evenly among 6 greased muffin pan cups, 2 1/2 inches in diameter. Arrange 3 pecans halves in bottom of each cup. Set aside.

To shape dough: Punch dough down. Turn onto lightly floured board. Roll dough to 1/2-inch thickness. Cut with 2 1/2 inch doughnut cutter. Place doughnuts on greased baking sheets. Arrange 5 doughnut holes in each muffin cup. Reroll dough as needed to complete cutting. Cover doughnuts and rolls. Let rise in warm place, free from draft, for 1 hour, or until doubled.

To fry doughnuts: Fill deep skillet or pan with 2 inches of shortening or oil. Heat to 375 degrees. Add doughnuts, several at a time. Fry 1 minute on each side. Drain on paper towels. If desired, shake in bag with powdered sugar or a mixture of granulated sugar and cinnamon.

To bake rolls: Bake in 350-degree oven for 20 minutes, or until firm and browned. Immediately invert rolls onto plate to cool.

Have Recipes, Will Travel
August 1, 1976

No matter where we traveled, I gathered recipes and sometimes tested them in borrowed kitchens. Visiting Amherst, Mass., I tried this summer buffet idea, buying fruit in one of the world's great roadside stands, Atkins. Everything for the salad was purchased there, except rum imported from Minnesota in a jelly jar. (Why buy a full bottle in Massachusetts when the recipe calls for only a half-cup?) I wished afterward I'd packed dark rum to intensify the flavor diluted by all the watermelon juice.

A reader says . . .

Your fans look forward to your writings, your ideas and your recipes.

— Nancy Skadron, Mendota Heights, Minn.

ALFRESCO PEACHES IN MELON BOWL
Makes 8 servings

Fruit mixture:
1 small watermelon
1 cantaloupe
1 small honeydew melon
4 small peaches, peeled, sliced and
    sprinkled with lemon juice
Lime-rum marinade:
2/3 cup sugar
1/3 cup water
1/3 cup lime juice
1/2 cup rum (dark rum preferred)
Orange cream dressing:
1/3 cup mayonnaise
1/4 cup light corn syrup
1 tablespoon orange peel
1 tablespoon orange juice
1/4 teaspoon nutmeg
1/2 cup whipping cream, whipped

To prepare fruit: Cut "lid" off 1 end of watermelon. Cut small slice off bottom so melon will stand upright. Using ice-cream scoop, make large watermelon balls. Using melon baller, make smaller cantaloupe and honeydew balls. Gently toss melon balls and peaches. Put fruit into watermelon shell.

To make marinade: In saucepan, combine sugar and water. Bring to a boil. Reduce heat. Simmer for 5 minutes. Remove from heat. Add lime juice and rum. Cool to room temperature. Pour over fruit in watermelon. Replace watermelon "lid." Chill for at least 2 hours.

To make dressing: Combine mayonnaise and corn syrup. Blend until smooth. Add orange peel, orange juice and nutmeg. Mix well. Fold in whipped cream. Refrigerate until needed.

To serve: Spoon out portions of marinated fruit. Top with dollop of dressing. (Note: The dressing may curdle slightly if placed directly on fruit; spoon it alongside and dip pieces of fruit into it.)

Cannelloni for All Comers
December 12, 1976

When we realized we couldn't possibly consume all these chicken-filled crepes ourselves, we called in reinforcements for an impromptu dinner. One of the diners commented that the finely chopped filling would be appreciated by someone with false teeth.

Aha, a recipe for the Efferdent crowd.

It was also appreciated by another of our guests who had only a few teeth, an 11-month-old baby who happily munched tidbits, washing them down with slugs from her bottle. Her slightly older brother and sister, for whom I had made macaroni and cheese, thinking they would disdain crepes, also gobbled the mock cannelloni.

Aha, a recipe that appeals to all ages.

Partial credit for testing the cannelloni, I told readers in that 1976 column, goes to my Equal Half. (I don't say Better Half in these days of female liberation.)

We Didn't Forget the Flour
June 19, 1977

"I felt like I ate the United Nations," I said, recounting a multiethnic, many-course dinner at Milwaukee's International Institute during the first conference organized for the fledgling Newspaper Food Editors and Writers Association, which occurred during my presidency.

During my term, I bounced to other food events in 1977 and 1978, from New York to Honolulu, packing in far too many meals. I'd go, gain four pounds, come home and lose two. The next week, I'd jump on plane to eat more, gain four pounds, come home to lose two.

CHICKEN WALNUT CANNELLONI
Makes 6 servings

- 12 crepes (homemade or purchased)
- 2/3 cup walnuts, toasted, divided
- 1/3 cup finely chopped onion
- 1 tablespoon butter
- 1/2 teaspoon Italian herb seasoning
- 1 cup ricotta cheese (or sieved dry cottage cheese)
- 2 cups diced cooked chicken
- 2 tablespoons chopped parsley
- 1 1/2 tablespoons chopped capers (optional)
- 5 tablespoons grated romano cheese, divided
- 1/2 teaspoon salt
- 3/4 cup milk
- 1 can (10 3/4 ounces) cream of chicken soup

To assemble cannelloni: Bake crepes, if making homemade ones. (Note: See His, Hers and Ours chapter for recipe.) Set aside. Chop toasted walnuts into medium-fine pieces. Set aside. Saute onion in butter with herbs until soft. Mix with 1/2 cup walnuts, ricotta cheese, chicken, parsley, capers, 3 tablespoons romano cheese and salt. Stir milk into soup. Add 1/2 cup diluted soup to chicken mixture. Roll chicken mixture, evenly divided, in crepes.

To bake: Place cannelloni in shallow buttered or sprayed baking pan. Spoon remaining soup mixture over crepes. Sprinkle with 2 tablespoons romano cheese. Bake in 350-degree oven for 20 minutes, or until thoroughly heated. Sprinkle with remaining walnuts just before serving.

It doesn't take much of a mathematician to compute how that adds up to a round figure.

At the Milwaukee meeting, I became enamored with this Ukrainian Chocolate Nut Torte, which became the first testing experiment with flourless chocolate cake. Readers were assured we hadn't forgotten the flour, and I admonished them to bake the cake very well done, until it draws away from the sides of the pan. Placing wax paper under the batter and crumbs might help getting the layer out of the pan, Testing Results suggested.

UKRAINIAN CHOCOLATE NUT TORTE
Makes 12 servings

Torte:
- 1/4 pound (1 stick) unsalted butter, at room temperature
- 1 cup sugar
- 7 egg yolks and 1 whole egg
- 1 can (5 ounces) chocolate syrup
- 1 cup walnuts, finely ground
- 7 egg whites
- 2 tablespoons bread crumbs
- Additional bread crumbs to line cake pans

Butter cream icing:
- 1 package (3 ounces) chocolate pudding mix (not instant)
- 1 cup milk
- 1 1/2 sticks unsalted butter
- 3/4 cup sugar
- 2 pasteurized egg yolks (optional)
- 1 tablespoon rum flavoring

To make torte: In large mixing bowl, cream butter at medium speed of electric mixer until light and fluffy. Add sugar. Add egg yolks, 1 at a time. Continue beating at low or medium speed after each addition. Add whole egg, still beating. Add chocolate syrup and ground walnuts, still beating. Continue beating until mixture looks well blended. In separate bowl, beat egg whites at high speed until fluffy. Fold in bread crumbs. Using wooden spoon, gently mix egg whites into chocolate batter.

To bake: Grease 2 round 8-inch cake pans with butter. Sprinkle sides of pans with bread crumbs. Pour batter into pans. Bake in 350-degree oven for 45 minutes to 1 hour.

To make icing: Cook pudding according to instructions on package, using 1 cup milk instead of 2 cups. Cool completely. In large mixing bowl, cream butter and sugar until fluffy. Add egg yolks, 1 at a time. Beat at low speed, adding cold pudding, 1 tablespoon at a time, until all pudding is used. Add rum flavoring. Beat until mixture is well blended.

To fill and frost: When cake is completely cooled, remove from pans. Split layers in half horizontally. Cover each layer with icing. Place on top of previous layer. Decorate top and side as desired. (Note: After layers are cooled, centers may sink; this is normal.)

Donn's Is a Delight
November 26, 1978

A food writer is supposed to have an eclectic palate that willingly samples anything. I'd grown up with little appreciation for blue cheese, but, fortunately, I'd overcome that childhood aversion when, early in my food-writing career, I was given a round of Maytag Blue made in Newton, Iowa, where the washers and refrigerators also originate. With the cheese came a small recipe booklet, and Donn's Delight was among the suggested ways to use this sudden cheese oversupply.

Blue-cheese dressing was a gauge whe[...] a restaurant. And I'd tested several Roquef[...] dressing recipes by the time I met Maytag [...] none was as good as the simple dressing cre[...] by Donn, a Maytag Dairy executive. After the recipe appeared in the Sunday column, it became an everyday favorite of my readers, who I told, "If I ever have the audacity to open a restaurant, this is the dressing on which my salad reputation will be risked."

DONN'S DELIGHT
Makes about 1 cup

2 ounces blue cheese
1/2 cup mayonnaise
3 tablespoons light cream
1 teaspoon sugar
1 teaspoon parsley flakes
2 teaspoons lemon juice
2 teaspoons vinegar
1 teaspoon grated onion
1/2 teaspoon Worcestershire sauce
1/2 teaspoon prepared horseradish
1/4 teaspoon garlic salt
Freshly ground pepper

Warm blue cheese to room temperature. Add mayonnaise. Blend thoroughly until smooth. Add remaining ingredients. Mix well. Cover. Chill.

WILD RICE BAKED CHICKEN
Makes 4 servings

2/3 cup uncooked wild rice
4 ribs of celery, sliced (2 cups)
1 medium green pepper, diced (1 cup)
1 1/4 cups water
2 teaspoons chicken bouillon granules
    or 2 bouillon cubes
1 teaspoon salt, optional
2 whole chicken breasts, halved and
    skinned
Soy sauce

In bowl, thoroughly wash wild rice in warm tap water. Drain in strainer. In buttered 2-quart casserole or baking dish, mix wild rice, celery, green pepper, water, chicken bouillon and salt. Place chicken on top of rice mixture. Brush with soy sauce. Cover dish. Bake in 350-degree oven for 1 1/2 hours, or until rice is tender. Garnish with celery leaves, if desired.

A Double Homecoming
October 7, 1979

For re-entry into Western fare after my first trip to China in 1979, I tried this easy, good-enough-for-company chicken and wild rice bake and told readers it was "simply superb." For today's tastes, especially if using a salty bouillon, you may wish to reduce or eliminate the salt.

I also made this dish to celebrate my husband's homecoming after he'd had surgery to remove a pituitary tumor. "Do I cook better than they do at the hospital?" I asked him. "Just to be home eating with you would make mud pie taste like French Silk," he said.

Isn't he sweet?

Fudge Nudges Temptation's Limits
February 13, 1983

If you adore milk chocolate and are as nuts about German chocolate cake frosting as I am, I almost hesitate to recommend this recipe. A pre-Valentine column enthused, "It's so irresistible that you'll be eating it nonstop." Faced with such temptation, cutting the recipe in half might be wise. Use very low heat, or the topping will surely scorch.

Eleanors in Abundance
January 8, 1984

Have you noticed that most baby girls now seem to be named Jennifer or Kristin, Lisa or Julie? How long has it been since anyone named a newborn Ethel or Edith or Esther. Or Eleanor?

GERMAN CHOCOLATE FUDGE
Makes about 4 pounds

Fudge:
- 3 cups sugar
- 3/4 cup margarine
- 1 can (5 1/3 ounces) evaporated milk
- 3 packages (4 ounces each) German's sweet chocolate, broken into pieces
- 1 jar (7 ounces) marshmallow creme
- 1 teaspoon vanilla

Frosting:
- 1 can (5 1/3 ounces) evaporated milk
- 2/3 cup sugar
- 1/4 cup margarine
- 1 egg
- 1 teaspoon vanilla
- 1 1/3 cups flaked coconut
- 1 cup chopped pecans

To make fudge layer: In heavy 2 1/2- to 3-quart saucepan, combine sugar, margarine and evaporated milk. Bring to a full rolling boil, stirring constantly. Boil for 5 minutes over medium heat, stirring constantly to prevent scorching. Remove from heat. Stir in chocolate until melted. Add marshmallow creme and vanilla. Beat until well blended. Pour into greased 9-by-13-inch baking pan. Chill for several hours.

To make frosting: Combine evaporated milk, sugar, margarine, egg and vanilla. Cook, stirring constantly, for 8 to 12 minutes over medium heat, or until thickened. Remove from heat. Stir in coconut and nuts. Cool, beating occasionally. Spread over fudge. Chill until firm.

MEATBALLS IN GINGER SAUCE
Makes 6 to 8 servings

Meatballs:
- 5 slices bread
- 1/4 to 1/2 cup milk
- 2 pounds ground beef
- 2 eggs
- 1 medium onion, minced
- 1 teaspoon salt
- 1/8 teaspoon pepper

Sauce:
- 10 to 12 gingersnap cookies
- 2 cups tomatoes
- 1/2 medium onion, minced
- 1/2 cup brown sugar
- 1/4 cup vinegar
- 1 teaspoon salt

To make meatballs: Break bread into pieces. Soak in milk. Squeeze out excess liquid. Mix soaked bread thoroughly with remaining meatball ingredients. Roll into walnut-sized balls. Bake on 11-by-17-inch pan in 425-degree oven for 15 to 20 minutes. Remove from oven. Let stand for 15 minutes. Pour off fat. Place meatballs in large casserole. Cover with sauce. Bake in 350-degree oven for 45 minutes, stirring occasionally.

To make sauce: Crush cookies (blender works well). Set aside. Combine remaining ingredients. Simmer for 20 minutes. Add cookie crumbs, a little at a time, until sauce is thickened and glossy.

I was the only Eleanor in all three grades at Hibbing High, and I don't recall any others when I was at college, except for an older woman who came back to school after her children were grown. That's strange because I was born the year FDR won his third term. I've heard of boys named Franklin Delano after the President, but as much as she was admired, Eleanor Roosevelt wasn't a namesake for girls in my generation. They were all Mary Anns and Carols, Jeans and Shirleys.

Most people think my name honored Mrs. Roosevelt. My Democrat dad would have been in favor of it, but my Republican mother wouldn't. Actually, my name was suggested by my mother's two young nieces, who concocted a combination of my mother's name, Ellen, and my father's name, Ero. For that, they gave up naming me Laurel. Sigh.

That treatise opened a column about a luncheon at which all the guests were named Eleanor or spelling variations thereof. Hostess Martha Oviatt, who ran a tour service called Daytripping, noticed that her mailing list contained an inordinant number of Eleanors, so she gave a lunch where they could all meet one another. I was invited to join the same-name event. These meatballs were on Martha's menu.

Corny's Nutty Idea
December 16, 1984

For many years, Cornelius O'Donnell, "Cornelius From Corning," was the person who developed recipes to use in Corning cookware. He gave me this nibble idea when we shared judging duties at a March of Dimes Gourmet Gala in Minneapolis. It became a Tested Recipe for a holiday party for which the participants had bid, during the St. Paul Chamber Orchestra's silent auction, on a chance to cook and eat in our home. Some even got to wash dishes for their money.

POSH PECANS
Makes 2 1/2 cups

3 packages (6 ounces each) pecan
   halves
1/2 cup butter
1/2 cup sugar
2 tablespoons dark rum
1 teaspoon freshly ground nutmeg
1 1/2 teaspoons salt (or to taste)

Place pecans in shallow Pyrex or other baking or roasting pan. Heat in 300-degree oven for 15 to 20 minutes, shaking pan occasionally to stir pecans. In small pan on rangetop or in microwave oven, heat remaining ingredients, except salt. Pour over roasted pecans. Stir well to coat. Bake for 10 to 12 minutes. Remove from oven. Allow pecans to dry on wax paper. Salt to taste. Store in covered container.

Walleye Most Wonderful
September 1, 1985

Almost every summer, I traveled around Minnesota and Wisconsin to see what was cooking at resorts. One of my favorite stops has been Kavanaugh's Sylvan Lake Lodge near Brainerd, where the food is so good that it's been collected in two cookbooks. This, with pecan butter, is a classic Kavanaugh menu staple, glorifying Minnesota's official fish.

WALLEYE WITH PECAN BUTTER SAUCE
Makes 2 servings

Walleye:
   2 walleye fillets (6 ounces each)
   1 egg
   1/2 cup milk
   1/3 cup flour
   1/2 teaspoon salt
   1/2 teaspoon paprika
   1/8 teaspoon white pepper
   1/8 teaspoon garlic powder
   Vegetable oil
Pecan butter sauce:
   4 tablespoons butter, melted
   1 teaspoon lemon juice
   Dash of garlic salt
   1/2 cup chopped pecans

To cook fish: Beat egg and milk together. Mix flour and spices. Dip fish fillets in egg mixture, then in flour mixture. Fry in hot oil for 2 to 3 minutes per side, or until golden. Serve with sauce on top of fish.

To make sauce: Beat butter, lemon juice and salt together. Stir in pecans.

Exclusively Izatys Walleye
September 7, 1986

"You're getting a scoop, an exclusive," Steve Dubbs told me as his mother, Dorothy Dubbs, was about to reveal recipes from their family's Izatys Lodge on Lake Mille Lacs, grandest of Minnesota's 10,000 lakes. "We've never given them out before, though we've had plenty of requests from newspapers and magazines," he said.

Here is their secret (until my column appeared) recipe for crunchy fried walleye.

WALLEYE PIKE IZATYS STYLE

Makes 4 servings

2 cups flour
1/4 cup cornmeal
1 teaspoon paprika
Dash of salt
2 eggs
1/2 cup milk
4 (8-ounce) walleye fillets
Vegetable shortening

Divide flour into 2 pans. Set 1 pan aside. Into other pan of flour, mix cornmeal, paprika and salt. In third pan, whip eggs. Add milk. Using fresh walleye fillets, dip them first into plain flour, then in egg wash, again in flour, then in flour-cornmeal mixture. Fry in hot shortening (with a touch of butter, if desired) until golden brown.

New Age Sausages

January 6, 1985

Michelle Schmidt created this brunch idea for her book, "New Almond Cookery," built on emerging California Cuisine. We loved the glazed sausages when they were tested, and my comments about the book were so enthusiastic that a blurb was excerpted to use in national ads promoting the almond recipe collection.

SHERRIED SAUSAGES

Makes 6 to 8 servings

3/4 cup cream (sweet) sherry, divided
1 pound pork sausage links, cut into thirds
1/2 cup blanched, slivered almonds, toasted
1/2 cup sliced green onions
1/4 cup fresh orange juice

Pour 1/2 cup sherry over sausages. Cover. Simmer for 10 minutes. Drain off excess fat. Continue to cook sausages, uncovered, turning frequently, until brown and glazed. Add almonds and green onions. Saute, stirring frequently, for 1 minute. Add remaining 1/4 cup sherry and orange juice. Cook until liquid is reduced by half, or until it reaches a syrupy consistency. Serve hot.

A reader says . . .

In the two weeks since your article appeared, orders have come in for more than 150 copies of our cookbook. The Scandinavian Society has never been so rich!

— Arnold Nelson, Ludington, Mich.

Cornsticks were Minnesotan-made
November 17, 1985

Lunch at Campton Place, near Union Square, was our first destination when we arrived in San Francisco. I didn't know at the time that the crispy cornsticks and the marvelous blueberry nectarine buckle that I'd raved about during that lunch were the work of St. Paul native Steve Froman, graduate of Central High, who'd become pastry chef at the top-rated San Francisco restaurant. We met for the first time several days later at a Napa Valley food event. He's just one of many Minnesotans who've added their influence to California Cuisine.

Froman escaped academia at the University of Minnesota to study pastry-making in Europe. He returned to the Twin Cities to bake at The Restoration on St. Paul's Grand Avenue and 510 Haute Cuisine in Minneapolis. Marriage took him to Europe for a year and then to New York. Eventually, he flew right over Minnesota to California, where he found, he says, his true home "and certainly one of the better jobs in San Francisco."

He crafts 180,000 of these feathery cornsticks a year, and when he shared the recipe, he broke it down from 500 units to make a formula for 12. That's why you'll notice some odd fractions. Never mind; it works just fine.

CAMPTON PLACE CORNSTICKS
Makes 12

1/2 cup yellow cornmeal
1/2 cup flour
2 tablespoons granulated sugar
1 1/4 teaspoons baking powder
1 teaspoon salt
Optional: 1/2 cup fresh corn, chopped
    pepper or crisp bacon crumbles
7/8 cup heavy cream
1 egg yolk
2 1/4 ounces melted unsalted butter
1 egg white

Place empty cornstick molds in 425-degree oven. In large bowl, mix dry ingredients, adding optional ingredients at this time. In separate bowl, mix cream, egg yolk and melted butter. Stir cream mixture into dry ingredients until well-mixed. Beat egg white until stiff. Fold into other ingredients. Remove hot cornstick molds from oven. Grease lightly. Spoon or pipe batter into molds. Bake in 425-degree oven for 15 to 20, or minutes until golden.

Fajitas for an Adventurer
August 31, 1986

Clipping his loosely tied apron strings, our 17-year-old adventurer spent a month and wore out a pair of boots hiking and mountain climbing in the Olympic Peninsula of Washington state. When Aric told me about clinging to the faces of sheer cliffs, I tuned out. There's only so much a mother wants to know.

Before he left on his Widjiwagan Explorer trip, Aric made one request. For his first meal back home, he wanted fajitas. This family favorite, clipped from a magazine recipe, is the one we made when he returned, and every summer thereafter when he came home from college.

We embellish our fajitas with chopped tomatoes, green onion, grated cheddar and sour cream, in addition to the guacamole the recipe includes. We should call them Fajita Tacos.

Fajitas

Makes 6 servings

1 1/2 pounds beef skirt steak (or flank steak or top round steak cut 1/2- to 3/4-inch thick; pork or chicken may also be used)
1 cup picante sauce
1/4 cup vegetable oil
1 teaspoon lemon juice
Dash of pepper
Dash of garlic powder
Chunky guacamole (avocados mashed with diced tomato and sliced green onion, moistened with picante sauce and lemon juice, and seasoned with salt)
12 flour tortillas, 8- to 10-inch size, heated

To marinate meat: Pound meat with meat mallet to tenderize. Place in plastic bag. Combine picante sauce, oil, lemon juice, pepper and garlic powder. Pour into bag. Fasten securely. Refrigerate for 3 to 24 hours, turning several times. Drain meat, reserving marinade.

To cook: Place meat on grill over hot coals or on rack of broiler pan. Cook for 5 to 6 minutes on each side, or until done, basting frequently with reserved marinade. Remove from grill.

To make fajitas: Slice meat across grain into thin strips. Place meat on tortillas. Top with guacamole and additional picante sauce. Roll up. (Note: Add cheese and chopped vegetables, if desired.)

Mama D Keeps Dancing

March 26, 1989

On this Easter morning, heavenly light is likely gleaming on silver-haired Mama D as she sits in church. God must love her. Lord knows, everyone else does.

Love and ladlefuls of her own outspoken philosophies are the high-octane that keep restaurateur Giovanna D'Agostino speeding through life on overdrive. In her mid-70s, she can still dance a lively tarantella, as she demonstrated during a party last fall celebrating the 60th business anniversary of the Twin

Mama D's Cheesecake

Makes 6 to 8 servings

3 cups ricotta cheese
1 1/4 cups sugar, divided
Grated rind of 1 orange
Grated rind of 1 lemon
1 tablespoon vanilla
4 eggs, beaten
1/2 cup all-purpose flour
1 carton (8 ounces) sour cream

Mix cheese, 1 cup sugar, orange and lemon rinds, vanilla and eggs. Blend until smooth. Add flour. Mix again. Pour batter into greased 8-inch-square baking dish. Bake in 375-degree oven for 70 minutes. Mix sour cream and 1/4 cup sugar. Spread over cheesecake as topping. Bake 10 minutes. Cool.

Cities' other famous mama: Congie Vitale of the Venetian Inn (who died in 1997, bless her soul).

"While I'm living, I'm moving," Mama D says. "I tell senior citizens groups, 'Don't just sit and watch that booby tube. Call someone over for coffee.' "

When Mama D puts on the coffeepot, she might serve this rustic-textured cheesecake. You can use low-fat ricotta and sour cream to trim calories.

House Calls
May 13, 1990

Those of us who were little kids pre-TV and VCRs remember when visiting the neighbors was an evening's entertainment. Nothing fancy or dress-up. Just go over, talk for a while, sip something, have a few cookies, then go home wearing the unspoken pleasure of friendship like a warm coat against the Minnesota chill. Even winter's deep snowdrifts didn't make us hibernate.

Neighbors seldom bothered to call first. A knock on the door and a cheery, "Anybody home?" announced the visit. And if nobody was home, the visitor would walk down the road and knock on another door. I always thought my mother was constantly baking to please my dad, but now I realize she never wanted to be without something to serve with coffee when the neighbors knocked.

Big-city life just doesn't work that way, especially in this era of two-career families, when the biggest thrill of the day is coming home and shutting the door behind us.

In a story about our neighborhood's progressive dinner, the citified way to circulate, this colorful and fragrant entree was served at our house. "This little piggy has gone high class," I told readers.

PORK TENDERLOIN WITH RASPBERRY MINT SAUCE
Makes 8 to 10 servings

1 1/2 pounds pork tenderloin (about 2 whole tenderloins)
2/3 cup water
1/4 cup raspberry vinegar
1/3 cup sugar
1 cup fresh mint leaves
2 tablespoons snipped fresh chives
1 tablespoon cornstarch
1 tablespoon water
1 1/2 cups fresh or frozen raspberries, thawed

Place pork tenderloin in shallow baking pan. Roast in 350-degree oven for 30 minutes. Meanwhile, in medium saucepan, combine 2/3 cup water, vinegar and sugar. Bring to a boil. Add mint leaves and chives. Cover. Simmer for 15 minutes. Strain. Reserve liquid. Bring liquid to a boil. Gradually stir in cornstarch combined with 1 tablespoon water. Cook, stirring, until thickened. Remove from heat. Fold in raspberries. Serve sauce with pork tenderloin slices.

Milky Way of M&M's
March 10, 1991

These otherworldly cookies were the favorite at a food-writers' meeting in Dallas, when M&M's in a box for baking purposes were introduced. If the box isn't available, just buy an 11-ounce bag and eat the extras. We decided these cookies would survive mailing to Desert Storm troops stationed in Saudi Arabia, everyone's focus when the recipe appeared.

OUT-OF-THIS-WORLD CHOCOLATE COOKIES

Makes 5 dozen

2 cups all-purpose flour
1 box (3 1/2 ounces) chocolate-flavored
   instant pudding mix
1/2 teaspoon baking soda
1 cup (2 sticks) butter, softened
1 cup firmly packed light brown sugar
2 eggs
1 box (10 ounces) plain M&M chocolate
   candies
1 cup chopped nuts

In small bowl, combine flour, pudding mix and baking soda. Set aside. In large bowl, combine butter and brown sugar. Beat until creamy and smooth. Beat in eggs. Gradually beat in flour mixture. Stir in candies and nuts. Drop slightly rounded tablespoonfuls of dough onto ungreased baking sheets. Bake in 350-degree oven for 10 to 12 minutes.

A Fresh Bite

November 10, 1991

Fresh Veggie Pie hawked at the Minnesota State Fair was such a delight that when I noticed a similar recipe in a newspaper food ad, I had to try it for the column. Experimenting to make the recipe even more healthful, I used one package of crescent rolls and one of the new Hearty Grains bread sticks dough (which I liked better

as a crust). At the Fair, grated cheddar cheese was sprinkled over all. To reduce the fat, that cheese is expendable, and you can substitute lighter versions of cream cheese and mayonnaise.

CONFETTI BITES

Makes 15 pieces

2 packages (8 ounces each) refrigerated
   crescent rolls
2 packages (8 ounces each) cream
   cheese
3 tablespoons mayonnaise
1/2 teaspoon dried basil leaves
1/4 teaspoon garlic powder
Chopped fresh vegetables, such as red,
   yellow and green peppers; broccoli;
   carrots; green onion; cauliflower; and
   mushrooms
Salad Supreme seasoning

Press crescent roll dough into 10-by-15-inch baking sheet to form crust. Bake in 350-degree oven for 12 to 15 minutes. In small bowl, combine cream cheese, mayonnaise, basil leaves and garlic powder. Spread thinly over cooled crust. Top with chopped vegetables. Sprinkle generously with Salad Supreme seasoning blend (or herbs and seasonings of your choice).

Utterly Buttery
March 15, 1992

Many a recipe for English toffee has been tested in our kitchen, but this, found in Minnesota's Northern Electric Cooperative Association's newsletter, is the all-time easiest. It practically drips butter when it's warm. Put it in the freezer to help the chocolate set up, and you won't notice the butter so much — at least not enough to impede uncontrollable nibbling.

ENGLISH TOFFEE BARS
Makes 36 pieces

1 cup pecans, chopped
3/4 cup brown sugar
1/2 cup butter
3/4 cup chocolate chips

Sprinkle pecans evenly in 9-by-9-inch pan. In saucepan, combine brown sugar and butter. Bring to a boil, stirring constantly. Boil for 7 minutes. Pour hot mixture over nuts. Sprinkle with chocolate chips. Cover so chocolate chips melt. Spread chocolate evenly. Slice when warm. Or refrigerate, then break into pieces.

A reader says . . .

Love following your columns and your adventures.

— Pat Burbank, South St. Paul

Feeling Crabby
April 10, 1994

Seafood, like real estate, is a matter of location, location, location. We were on the North Carolina coast last month, buying fresh-caught crabs by the bushel. They're not exactly a bargain anymore — $40 for that big basket — but what fun to have the opportunity for such feasting.

Our Korean daughter-in-law, Kyong, and her friend, Patty, also Korean and also married to a Marine, were in charge of the crab cooking. It is not an aspect of the project I care to contemplate, especially when the critters scratch to get out of the steaming pot.

After we'd eaten more than half of the pile of cooked crabs, Kyong, Patty and I started "picking" for recipes I wanted to try the next day. That's a task! It

CRAB CAKES
Makes 4 servings

1 pound crab meat
2 eggs, slightly beaten
1/2 green pepper, chopped fine
1/2 medium onion, chopped fine
1/4 cup celery, chopped fine
1 teaspoon garlic powder
1 teaspoon celery salt
2 teaspoons lemon juice
1/2 teaspoon Tabasco sauce (or to taste)
1/4 cup cracker meal

Mix all ingredients thoroughly. Form into 3-inch cakes. Fry in small amount of hot oil (part butter, if you wish) until golden brown.

Recipe Index

Recipe Index

Recipe Index

Recipe Index

Recipe Index

Additional copies of

"Always on Sunday"

may by ordered directly from the publisher

Enclose $19.95 per book
— *plus* —
$3.95 for shipping of 1-3 books
$7.95 for shipping of 4-7 books

In Minnesota please add 6.5% sales tax.
In St. Paul/Minneapolis please add 7% sales tax.

For quantity orders, call about specific pricing.

Forward your order including name, address, phone number and request for special autograph dedication.

Remit with check or money order in U.S. funds to:

SUNDAY PRESS
853 Lincoln Avenue
St. Paul, Minnesota 55105
612-227-2277

Credits for Photos and Illustrations